Before Writing

'In this exciting and thought-provoking book, Gunther Kress contributes to our understanding of how children learn to read and write . . . This is a clearly written and accessible book and Gunther Kress is a keen observer of children and of society, combining close observation with insightful interpretation. Overall, this book is a basic rethinking of the field of children's emergent literacy. It provides ideas, possibilities, frameworks and challenges to researchers, trainers and teachers.'

David Barton, *Lancaster University*

Gunther Kress argues for a radical reappraisal of the phenomenon of literacy, and hence for a profound shift in educational practice. Through close attention to the multitude of objects which children constantly produce (drawings, cuttings-out, 'writings', collages), Kress suggests a set of principles that reveal the underlying coherence of children's actions in making meanings and allow us to see them in relation to their own moves into writing.

This book provides a fundamental challenge to commonly held assumptions about language and literacy, thought and action. It places that challenge in the context of speculation about the abilities and dispositions which will become essential for children as young adults in the decades ahead, and calls for the radical decentering of language in educational theory and practice.

Before Writing will be of special interest to professionals in all areas of education, scholars of linguistics, cultural studies and psychology, and to anyone with a vested interest in how children learn.

Gunther Kress is Professor of English and Education at the Institute of Education, University of London. His publications include *Language as Ideology* (1993), *Learning to Write* (1994) and he co-authored *Reading Images* (1996) with Theo van Leeuwen.

Before Writing

Rethinking the paths to literacy

Gunther Kress

NATIONAL UNIVERSITY
LIBRARY   SAN DIEGO

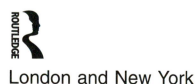

London and New York

First published 1997
by Routledge
11 New Fetter Lane, London EC4P 4EE

Simultaneously published in the USA and Canada
by Routledge
29 West 35th Street, New York, NY 10001

© 1997 Gunther Kress

The author has asserted his moral rights in accordance
with the Copyright, Designs and Patent Act 1988.

Typeset in Baskerville by Keystroke,
Jacaranda Lodge, Wolverhampton
Printed and bound in Great Britain by
TJ Press (Padstow) Ltd, Padstow, Cornwall

All rights reserved. No part of this book may be reprinted
or reproduced or utilized in any form or by any electronic,
mechanical, or other means, now known or hereafter
invented, including photocopying and recording, or in any
information storage or retrieval system, without permission
in writing from the publishers.

British Library Cataloguing in Publication Data
A catalogue record for this book is available from the British Library

Library of Congress Cataloguing in Publication Data
Kress, Gunther R.
   Before writing: rethinking the paths to literacy/Gunther Kress.
   1. Language arts (Elementary) 2. Reading (Elementary) 3. English
language—Composition and exercises—Study and teaching
(Elementary) 4. Literacy. 5. Children—Language. I. Title.
LB1576.K67 1996
372.6—dc20   96–16358

ISBN 0–415–13804–3 (hbk)
ISBN 0–415–13805–1 (pbk)

For Michael and Emily
two great makers

Contents

Colour plates

The author's thanks go to Andrew Lambirth for his permission to reproduce Plate 6, and to Olayinka, the young artist.

Figures

The author's thanks go to Christina Tsai, and Sarah, for permission
to reproduce the pictographic writing in Figure 3.5.

Preface

Next to the emotional relations which children form with people in the broad ambit of their family, in its network of carers, parents, siblings, aunts, uncles, grandparents, neighbours and friends, the school provides the most significant experiences for children through the years of childhood and teenage. It is so important that we often name the period *before* children enter school as the pre-school years. At present the school is still consolidating its position; the period of schooling is becoming longer, both by eating away at the 'pre-school' years, and by extending its reach in the later years of schooling. More children stay longer at school than ever before.

The causes are complex, both culturally and economically. The so-called developed economies of the world need a highly educated (or perhaps it is now 'trained') workforce; but paradoxically those economies have jobs of the kind that demand higher and higher levels of skills for fewer and fewer young people. So high levels of education are in fact not required for a large number of the school population, or so it seems. This leads to deep dissatisfaction and disillusion on the part of these young people, and rightly so. It also leads to accusations made by politicians against institutionalized education, in particular the charge that the school system is not 'delivering' the right education or training to provide the economy with the right kind of workforce and young people with jobs.

The education system has a duty to ask constantly about its values, practices and assumptions, in relation to society generally, and to the economy in particular. This is beyond dispute. The education system cannot, however, produce jobs in the economy at large. That is not its function. Where it does interact crucially with the economy is in asking fundamental questions on the one hand about its curricula in relation to the short-term needs of the economy; and more significantly, on the other hand about the medium term, the next two or three decades: what kind of future is that likely to be? What kind of dispositions will be needed by children now starting school, who will be entering their adult lives in fifteen, twenty years' time?

As far as I can see – and I have no insight other than what is available on every business-page of any newspaper; what is evident by looking at communication anywhere, by watching what people are doing, buying, enjoying – that future will be different in far-reaching ways. Twenty years ago, in 1975, I knew no one who owned their own computer (I bought the first computer, a Sinclair Spectrum I think, in 1982, for my then 14-year-old son). Now most people of my acquaintance – not to speak of work – own one or more and upgrade to newer, faster, more 'powerful' models every two years or so. I still write by hand, which is becoming a severe problem for me. But these are relatively superficial indicators. Twenty years ago most people expected to be in work, to stay in one job – or at least in the same profession – for a lifetime; they knew that their industry, their profession would always be needed, and with them their skills. They knew that the state would provide a pension for them, look after them if they were ill; and do the same for their children.

These certainties are gone. But these certainties had fostered and developed, and had themselves depended on certain kinds of dispositions. An economy that rested on stable industries with unquestioned long-term futures, needed a stable workforce with developed and specific skills; regulated training (apprenticeships); clear career-structures; and patterns of hierarchy and recognition. These structures have also gone, and with them the need for the dispositions which previously were not just valued, but essential. It is not clear to me that the education system has yet realized the magnitude of this shift, let alone begun to ask what changes in practices, values, theories and assumptions will need to follow from this shift. One way of thinking about the current system, somewhat provocatively, is to see it as still providing the kind of education which was necessary for and suited to a nineteenth-century economy, founded on industrial mass production. In many ways this is what it still delivers. Young people can see the lack of fit between the implicit (which increasingly become less explicit) promises of gaining school knowledge and the prospect of a job, let alone the guarantee of a career.

These uncertainties have begun to produce an unease about education which makes it possible for certain governments to contemplate large-scale restructuring of institutionalized education, and even to contemplate what is effectively a withdrawal of state support for education. This already occurs in a variety of seemingly unconnected ways. In Britain it takes the form of handing certain kinds of authority to individual schools, including authority over (declining) budgets. This move has gone hand in hand with the elimination of mediating layers of structure – in England the local education authorities; and the privatization of inspection, and advisorial services. Coupled with this is the introduction of a voucher system, which will enable parents to cash in 'their' voucher as part-payment for pre-school education.

Whatever else is unclear, it is increasingly apparent that many areas in Education need to be reconsidered. And this is where this book aims to make its contribution. Let me explain. In the complex mesh of social systems, economic organization, and education, the school has to date either seen it as its task to understand the 'needs' of society, or it has acted broadly within generally unquestioned assumptions. But the task of the school has changed, and is changing. It cannot simply 'follow the lead' of society, because society in the shape of its political and intellectual leaders has lost its sense of direction – as is amply demonstrated by the increasingly shrill pronouncements of politicians, and certain other 'opinion-makers'. For instance, a call for the return to the moral and cultural certainties of a bygone age may stand as one example, as does a call for the forms and contents of teaching to be designed for the needs of an economy which no longer exists.

The first and real question for education, and for schools, concerns human dispositions: what are the qualities, habits, skills, attitudes, naturalized and habituated practices which will be required by young people for productive engagement with the world of two, three or four decades hence: that is, a period that looks forward to the time when they will be fully active in their societies; and about the same span of time which many readers of this book will have as their own working (and certainly schooling) lifetime? Here the education system not only can but needs to *act*, not merely follow. It can and must actively intervene in proposing new aims, new goals, new tasks, *new visions* in relation to what it will do for and with young people. This task must begin with a searching examination of the relation between the present practices of schools, and the theories which underpin them. Theories of language and literacy, and theories of meaning-making more widely, are fundamental in this respect. Not only does language provide the means through which we make sense of a very large part of our environment, but it also provides us with the means to express our sense of that environment for others. Writing allows us to externalize our relation with that environment, *and* to communicate it to a potentially large, disparate and distant audience. Language gives us the means to put our conceptions to others; to imagine other ways of being; and to make these public, and the subject of debate.

The significance of *theories* of language for education is different. We can continue to assume, as we have throughout this century, that language is a stable system, beyond the effect of individual influence, either for social reasons ('the force of convention') or for psychological reasons ('the nature of the brain, or mind'). The social perspective legitimates teaching language as a system of rules which must be 'acquired' in their proper form, for example, as standard forms of the language. It encourages 'correctness', adherence to authoritative systems, and does not raise the question of individual freedom of action other than within the constraints of this system. Psychological considerations make it possible to see the purpose of teaching to be to aid learners in developing their innate, inherent potential 'properly' or 'fully'. Neither of the two approaches envisages the possibility of productive, transformative action by an individual, child or adult, in relation to language or literacy. But in the new social, economic and communicational environment, this is precisely what is needed. This new environment is one which will demand habits of innovation, as entirely usual, unremarkable, unexceptional. To produce those dispositions we need a different theory of language, one which treats language as a phenomenon in continuous, dynamic change, due to the action of individuals – whether children or adults – in everyday life. *Such a theory will treat individual speakers or writers not as language users but as language makers.* It will regard the actions of individuals as expressive of their interest and it will regard that interest as a complex of social, cultural factors that make up the history of all of us, of present circumstances, and of affective states, all at one time.

In such a theory, each instance of language interaction is seen as producing a change in language. Language is considered as being remade constantly by those who 'use' it: every time a word is used it is changed; every time a grammatical structure is used that is changed. Such a theory has two outcomes, pedagogically: it forces us to look quite differently, and much more seriously, at children's writing (and speech); and it forces our attention away from seeing competent adherence to rules as sufficient, and to focus on a concern with the competent development and enactment of *design*. I will develop this matter at some length in the chapters that follow.

There are several factors which call for such a change in theory. New technologies of communication, for instance, cannot be properly understood using our present theories; cultural and social change, such as increasing multiculturalism, similarly demands new thinking. Above all there are changes in the landscape of communication which are having far-reaching effects on the use, valuation and place of language. Modes of communication, other than language, are becoming increasingly prominent and even dominant in many areas of public communication in which language was formerly used exclusively or dominantly. This is true of visual images in particular. We are, it seems, entering a new age of the image, a new age of hieroglyphics; and our school system is not prepared for this in any way at all. Children live in this new world of communication, and on the whole seem to find little problem with it.

For children the problem remains, largely, that of the learning of writing and reading. It is here that one main emphasis of this book lies. However, I should say at once that this is *not* a book about the development of writing, gradually step by step, although this is commented on in passing, tangentially. The main points of this book are (a) we cannot understand how children find their way into print unless we understand the principles of their meaning-making. (b) Children make meaning in an absolute plethora of ways, with an absolute plethora of means, in two, three and four dimensions. (c) Different ways of making meaning involve different kinds of bodily engagement with the world – that is, not just sight as with writing, or hearing as with speech, but touch, smell, taste, feel. (d) If we concede that speech and writing give rise to particular forms of thinking, then we should at least ask whether touch, taste, smell, feel, also give rise to their specific forms of thinking. (e) In our thinking, subconsciously or consciously, in our feelings, we constantly translate from one medium to another. This ability, and this fact of **synaesthesia** is essential for humans to understand the world. It is the basis of all metaphor, and of much of our most significant innovation. We may want to foster rather than suppress this activity. (f) In the new communicational and economic world, it may well be that all of these will be essential requirements for culturally, socially, economically, *humanly* productive and fulfilling lives.

So it is my aim to rethink children's paths into writing in this context. I believe we will need a much more generous understanding of 'cognition' than the sparse understanding we have now – and one that does not sever pleasure from thought, and thought from emotion, feeling, affect. This sounds unrigorous, 'soft'. I am firmly of the view that it is essential. Just at the point when electronic technologies are promising or threatening (or both) to take us further from our bodies, it may be essential to insist on all the potentials which we have as bodily humans and which, for most of us, we are not encouraged to develop and use. Many issues are not fully explored in this book, and some are hardly touched on at all. For example, I say next to nothing about issues of culture; and nothing significant about gender – even though one or two of my examples cry out for a full exploration. These I will leave for another time; and if my omissions spark an energetic response in someone, then that has been a good effect.

Although I locate myself in the current debate, I am aware that this is a dangerous thing to do, because my interest in these ideas is actually quite outside the confines of the present lamentably narrow range of views – ungenerous, deeply unimaginative as many facets of that debate are. I expect that my argument will be misread, from both extremes. So I will say clearly: my intention is for a much more serious engagement with form – but form as meaning, not with form as formalism. I am interested in opening reading to the fullest degree, drawing in whatever can be drawn in – but showing to readers precisely what they are engaged in in that complex activity of reading. I am firmly convinced that the best teaching has come from teachers who have acted clearly and strongly in the authority of their knowledge. My argument is absolutely not that teachers should abandon their authority – they know that learning is action and work. Hence I am clear that we need to understand reading as active, as making meaning – however unfashionable that phrase may be. But it is not meaning-making in a vacuum, as in too many versions of cultural studies, which imagine that texts can be read in any way, pleasing the will of the reader alone. That view strikes me as deeply irresponsible – socially, politically, and pedagogically. Texts have structure, the structure given to them by the interests of their makers. It is with texts as structures that readers engage, in active transformative work.

Above all, this book tries to look freshly at children's engagement with print by treating this as just one of a plethora of ways in which they make meaning before they come to school. Unless we understand the principles of making meaning in *all* of the ways in which children do, we won't – so I argue – really understand the ways in which they try to make sense of print. In a time when the landscape of communication is changing so decisively, we cannot in any case continue to ignore their making of *signs* and *messages* in such a vast variety of modes, in two or in three dimensions, spatially or temporally constructed. All of these will have an entirely new importance in the communicational world of the day after tomorrow, economically, culturally and personally. All of these offer different ways for us as humans with our physical, sensory bodies, to engage with the world; and all of them offer different ways not just of *feeling*, but of knowing; all offer different forms of cognition.

It is commonplace to say that school is the place which asks children to focus on the world through writing. One can also say that school is the place which insists, slowly but inexorably, that the world cannot be known *other* than through the abstractions of written language (and to a lesser extent those of mathematics). But this imposes a willed limitation on the possibilities of kinds of thinking and of forms of representing. One consequence of the proposals made in this book is that we can get away from talking about non-verbal communication, about extra-linguistic or para-linguistic forms of representation: both treat language as central and other modes as peripheral. Perhaps we should try new forms, such as the para-gestural, or the non-visual, to refer to language – as in 'Apart from images, humans use a whole host of non-visual or para-visual means, such as spoken and written language for instance.'

I have attempted to write this book accessibly for anyone with an interest in these issues; I hope that in doing so there has been no loss of seriousness, or loss of precision. But I feel that if I can't write clearly enough for teachers, parents, carers, as well as teacher-trainers, students, and education professionals generally then I have lost the point of this exercise. As I read through the draft of this book I can see myself slipping back far too often into old modes, into writing as an academic. Still I hope that this has not happened too frequently for the book to remain accessible, and perhaps enjoyable, for the readers whom I have in mind.

The ideas put forward here are likely to be ill-received in some quarters; they are out of the official spirit of the times. But then it is not the purpose of academic work to lend support to notions which are unsupportable. Current official notions of literacy are so ungenerous, so unreflecting about the real needs of young people in the societies of the next decades, that it is essential to advance alternative conceptions, even if they find no official favour. I am convinced that it is the duty of academics to become involved in the design of alternative conceptions of the future, alternative to the bleak visions now painted in official common sense – the visions of the so-called 30–40–30 societies, in which 70 per cent of the population are consigned to lives of despair and misery.

The book is based on two distinct footings. On the one hand, I have tried to observe what young humans – between the ages of 6 months and 8 years – actually do do, with less focus on their spoken or written language, though not neglecting this by any manner of means. On the other hand, I have been involved in years of conversations and of co-operative work with colleagues, friends and researchers through which many of the ideas that appear here were formed.

My interest in the issue goes back some twenty years. In the preface to *Learning to Write*, which I wrote in October 1979, I said:

> there are several omissions in the book, which I regret. I have not included pictures in my discussion, although nearly every text that I discuss had a picture with it, and it is quite clear to me that the picture forms a part of the whole text for the child; it seemed to show the same conception expressed in non-verbal form. Perhaps a book on writing need not concern itself with

pictures, though a more comprehensive notion of 'text' will have to include both the verbal and the pictorial elements of the one text.

I am glad to have had this chance at long last to say something on this issue. For that I owe thanks to many people. First and foremost to Michael Kress and Emily Kress, and to their friends, particularly to Lola, Carmen and Iona. Without their ceaselessly exuberant making of images, objects, constructions, games there would be nothing to talk about. And, nearly as important, a deeply felt 'Thank-you' to the teachers and the headteacher at Yerbury School here in Tufnell Park. Something is going very right there. After four years or so, our children still come home from school every afternoon full of enthusiasm, and they leave that way in the morning. I am certain that that is due to the commitment, imagination and professionalism of their teachers.

I have been lucky in the many colleagues, friends, and researchers with whom I have been able to learn over a long period, in Australia, and now here in London. Theo van Leeuwen and I have been working on visual communication and ideas about texts for some ten years now, and I would like to give particular thanks to him. Many of the ideas in this book are the outcome of our constantly pleasurable collaboration. When you step into new territory it is essential that there are those around you who are interested in what you are doing and who take it seriously. Jon Ogborn's and Joan Bliss' interest has been invaluable for me in this respect. Their view of cognition as action, of meaning as work, is one I have adopted and adapted, I hope productively.

I cannot mention all those from whose ideas and support I have benefited in quite different ways but I must mention some: Ben Bachmair, Ingrid Gogolin, Jean-Jacques Boutaud, Anne Piroëlle, Jill Bourne, Euan Reid, Mary Kalantzis, Bill Cope, David Barton, Paul Mercer, Sonia Pimenta, Maria-Alice Descardeci, Kate Pahl, Adrien Abbott and Mary Wolfe.

There are others, whose help is every bit as crucial as that of academic friends and colleagues. When I first mentioned the idea of this book to Julia Hall, then at Routledge, she expressed immediate enthusiasm; this proved invaluable in making me feel confident about the project, and in giving me the platform for these ideas. I wish to thank her for that essential support. Judy

Benstead assisted, as the German idiom has it, *mit Rat und Tat* –
with advice and in deed. She made my impossible timetable
possible. I would like to acknowledge her professionalism and her
great kindness.

Jill Brewster has been there on every bit of this journey. She is
everywhere in this book; without her it literally would not exist.

London, February 1996

Chapter 1

Literacy, identity and futures

LITERACY IN THE CONTEMPORARY CONTEXT

Every generation produces amongst its wider agenda of concerns one or two issues which define its fundamental anxieties. Literacy is fast becoming a favoured candidate for one of these. The reasons aren't all that hard to find. The technologically developed societies of the world – no longer just of the West – are moving from an era defined by industrial production into a new era, defined by 'information'. It is the new raw material and the new commodity. It has its own new technologies, which at times seem to be producing the vast changes in which we are all caught up, and yet are also no more than a part of a complex web of factors which are interlocked in a dynamic of their own making; or so it seems.

Information comes dressed in many clothes: in numbers, in images, in the binary code of current electronic technologies, and, still, in language. Language is the medium we all understand. Even those of us who are frightened by numbers and wouldn't even bother with binary codes – even though they are on every item we buy from the supermarket – understand language. Language itself comes in two still deeply distinct forms: as speech and as writing; and not all of us have full command of language in the written mode. Language is the medium which all of us know intimately; and despite the constant voices of most politicians and nearly all the media, most of us now actually know writing well enough to read it. It is no surprise that worries about this new age find their focus in information, and in that medium of information which most of us know and all of us use – language in its written form: literacy.

By a further turn of this screw, literacy itself is highly susceptible to the effects of the web of factors I hinted at above. Multiculturalism is a deeply unsettling force; as is electronic communication. The globalization of finance, production, economics, have all made English into the possession of the educated and affluent groups around the world. Electronic communications have globalized and internationalized the mass media, and with them, culture. Travel is cheap enough to be available to vast numbers, and essential for nearly as many. So the medium which is, perhaps wrongly, the focus of our anxieties, is undergoing quite rapid changes. Just when we seem most in need of stability, literacy is turning out to be highly unstable.

So who is to blame? Teachers? Schools? Children? Parents? The education establishment? Not the government, for it is in charge of distributing blame. Perhaps we can only blame each other. In the meantime children are left to get on with finding their own paths into literacy. As there are now no longer any certainties, we have to make do with *conviction* instead. And so one group pursues its conviction against those of others. It is not a satisfactory position.

Not only is literacy unstable, dynamic, fluid, with the seemingly stable boundaries between more speech-like and more writing-like forms of the language undergoing rapid unravelling due to social and technological factors, other forms of communication are making increasing and massive inroads into the domains of communication formerly securely settled by written language. A look at the front page of any tabloid newspaper in the United States, in the United Kingdom or in Australia – as nearly anywhere in western Europe – will show the retreat of language. Print is, literally, being pushed off the page. But the changes go much further. A momentary pause outside a fun parlour in any town shows young people engaged in furious concentration with pseudo-interactive electronic games. These are no longer linguistic at all. Muscular, cognitive, and affective dispositions are being formed here which have little or nothing to do with the habits which people of my generation – I am in my mid-fifties – associated with writing and reading: quiet, concentrated, reflective analytic activity. Outside the fun parlours not only teenagers but people in their thirties glide past on roller-blades, encased in a cocoon of music transmitted as directly as technology can do that at the moment into the ears of the self-absorbed, individuated, maybe alienated, and no longer social individual.

These are just some of the indicators of changes which, *pace* our regrets or nostalgias, are remaking the landscape of communication. The changes which characterize workplaces are no less startling, nor less far-reaching. The old skills are no longer enough; not now, and certainly not in the future. In the face of these changes I do not think that we can stay with our old inherited contradictory common sense about communication, representation, meaning-making, in the private or in the public domain.

This is also the world which is utterly normal for my children. None of these things is strange or perturbing to them. To them what is strange is my puzzlement, dislike, disdain, incomprehension. It is clear to me that the present literacy curricula – whether in the theories which are implicit and active in them, or whether in the scope of things they include – are not adequate to prepare children for the demands of the new world of communication. They do have to be rethought. As with all rethinking, we need a starting point and for me that starting point is the attempt to understand newly and freshly, if that is possible, how children themselves seem to tackle the task of making sense of the world around them, and how they make their meanings in that world. In other words, children live in this multifaceted communicational world from the moment they are born; and they do seem to be able to make sense of it. They seem neither overwhelmed by the multitude of the most diverse messages coming to them, nor unable to absorb and transform them into what seems like a coherent, integrated sense. At least that is what I judge from their play, from their actions, and from the representations which they constantly make.

In other words, my strategy is, as it has been for many others before me and now, to trust children; and to try to see by a close look at their actions what I might come to learn. At the same time I do think that I have a real contribution to make. I do not think for one moment that the modes of thinking, the forms of action, the practices, the value systems which characterize, still, the world of my communicational and representational environment, are now useless. Although they were founded on a partial myth, namely the single focus on language, printed, written language, as the central, most valuable form of communication, many of its practices and assumptions will remain essential. For instance, we will not be able to do without reflection in the future; without habits of careful, relatively distanced analytic, reflective engagement with the world, in the forms of rationality which writing and print made into valued habits. We will not be able to do without the possibility of producing new insight, new understanding, new knowledge about our world, even though the modes which seem to be emerging as dominant in the world of popular culture, of the media, but also in education, in educational thinking, and in the rhetoric of politicians about all that suggest that that world has no further relevance for them.

In relation to the former, the world of popular culture, I think of the 'pace' of currently available children's programmes on television: rapid fire, succession of events, succession of images; rapid editorial cutting from one shot to another, from one segment to another; rapid speech, rapid music. No time here at all for reflection. The image of children and of entertainment implicit in the *form* of such programmes is that of young humans who need to be constantly distracted; who have the attention span of a flea; who will zap to the next channel should the pace slacken for a moment. The pace of music videos now is the same: rapid cutting; total absence of narrative; dominance of a fast rhythmic beat; and so on. Compare either with their counterparts of thirty years ago: *Blue Peter* in Britain; film clips of those well-groomed young men, the Beatles, in concert; and you see the difference.

The notion of what children are which is implicit here is more than just a notion of children (misguided or not): it acts as a constant suggestion to children to make themselves in the image of that notion. This pace may come, perhaps has already come to constitute entertainment for them; it is the pace of life, in at least one domain, entertainment on television. But my intention is not to launch into the usual pessimistic diatribe, yet another jeremiad, because I happen to think that a world founded on 'information' as its central commodity and product may well demand exactly that pace, the ability to deal with events at this pace, as one fundamental and necessary disposition, in many of its tasks: in work and in other public domains; perhaps in many domains of the private as well.

I also happen to think that the world caught in the 'information explosion' – so called – may need the move to the visual as its new and more effective medium of communication. A graph or a bar chart can display vast quantities of information, and complexities of relations between them at one glance, which it would take pages of written language to transmit and explain; probably less effectively, and certainly differently. I suspect that the information explosion, and 'information overload', are effects of and are produced by the potentials of the written medium, which is, however, no longer capable of serving as an efficient or sufficient mode of analysis, display and integration. The 'training' which children receive in front of their fast-paced programmes, or in the electronic fun parlour, or, in the case of the more affluent child, at home with video and computer games, may turn out to be among the most useful and essential that they receive.

The contribution which I and those of us who have responsibility for thinking about young people's lives in that future might be able to make, is not to saddle them with our nostalgias, with our histories, not to try to anchor them in our pasts. Rather, it is to assess, on the one hand, what of that past may be essential for them in their future, and how that might be integrated into means of learning, into curricula, together with the contents of the likely new demands, on the other hand. The task is to think about the shape of the curriculum, and about modes of learning which will allow them to lead productive, fulfilling lives when they are adults, in the societies of the near future.

SOME NECESSARY TOOLS FOR RETHINKING

A rethinking is in any case long overdue. It isn't just the needs of the day after tomorrow which make that essential; the needs of today demand it as well. The communicational landscapes of today, their relation to current forms of work and to current forms of pleasure, demand a recasting of our thinking about representation in the most far-reaching form. The world, now, is no longer a world in which written language is dominant. A distanced look at many public documents – not all it is true, but many – will reveal that the visual has reached a position of equality in many, and a position of dominance in some. The government speaks to its citizens in the equivalent of children's television, and with quite the same assumptions about the analytical capacities, attention span, and memories which Saturday-morning television makes about children. Armed with the advice of the research comm-issioned by advertisers, media consultants, audience researchers, public relations strategists, it is also training us into becoming differently constituted adult human beings.

In some domains of public communication this is done by a

proper appeal to being accessible, reader-friendly, by appeals to democratic notions of equity. Documents, questionnaires, information leaflets *are* set out more clearly, with better, clearer, simpler language, more inviting typefaces, good layout. They do require less effort; they are less impenetrable. But in requiring less effort, in becoming easier, they also, of course, have the effect of weaning us away from effort. The landscapes of communication are changing, are being changed in the most fundamental ways; and it is happening now.

A rethinking and new modes of thinking will have to be aware of these changes, speculate about the continuing changes, and their likely effects over the coming decades. If the landscape of public communication is now less dominated by written language, and coming to be more dominated by visual forms (though other modes of communication are also becoming increasingly important – music, sound, but also the body in its many potentials) then our former reliance on the study of language – linguistics – will no longer be sufficient to account for this new domain. In order to understand, analyse and describe the new social landscape of communication we will have to move to an enterprise which has the aim of understanding meaning in all its many manifestations in society – semiotics.

I am somewhat reluctant to introduce a range of technical terms, because these can seem to be merely a barrier to understanding. But some new terms can actually aid debate, by mapping out a new field, labelling some of its distinctively important features and allowing some security in the discussion. I will attempt to keep terminology to that level: using it where it is helpful, and certainly using it where it is essential; and keeping a close watch on myself so as not to let technical language proliferate, for its own sake.

We *do* not need, absolutely, a term for the study of all meaning-making, in any form, or in any mode. Semiotics comes from a Greek origin – the word *semeion*, meaning sign. Semiotics is the study of the meaning of systems of signs. Language is a system of signs; images are organized as a system of signs; clothing is a system of signs. This brings me to the second technical term, *sign*. A *sign* is a combination of meaning and form. Consider, for instance, the road sign 'Roadworks ahead'. Its form is that it is made of metal, it is triangular; on the front it has, inside a red border, an image of a worker pushing a shovel into a heap of dirt. Its *meaning* is 'there are roadworks going on'; and it uses the image of someone working

– inside the red warning border – as the form which conveys that meaning. The form is chosen because it is as close to being transparently obvious (in the cultures in which it was made!) to conveying the meaning which it is meant to convey. The fact that it is at times read as 'Man resting on a shovel' shows that, however jokingly, signs can be and are read according to a reader's interest in relation to a sign. To give another example. I do not habitually wear a tie; and do so only when in my view some occasion warrants it; it is therefore, for me, a meaningful act. When I do wear a tie I think about the nature of the occasion and how I should signal my assessment of it. As I have a very small stock of ties to select from, my possibilities of making a finely nuanced sign are severely limited. So I choose another medium in addition, namely the shirt that I will wear with the tie. For instance, a denim shirt with a Thai silk tie allows me to signal – or so I think – a nicely ambivalent set of messages. The sign that I make is, like the 'Roadworks ahead' sign, a quite complex one, despite my limited resources for making it. My colleagues, not used to seeing me with a tie, read it as a sign, and speculate, jokingly serious, about the meaning and the occasion.

So far I have also used another term which I use in a technical sense: *mode*. I want to use *mode* to indicate that we make signs from lots of different 'stuff', from quite different materials: sounds are variations of pressure in the air, and we use the physiology of our bodies to turn that physical, material stuff into signs: as speech, as music, as background noise in film, and so on. At times I use the term *media*, in order to focus more on the manner of dissemination: a *letter* as a medium of communication, and *writing* – the graphic material – as the *mode*; a *traffic sign* as the medium of communication, and the red border and the image inside it as the *mode*.

This may be the point to say something about my approach to children's (and adults') meaning-making. On the one hand I proceed on the assumption that when we make our signs we make them as (relatively) new combinations of form and meaning. This goes right against the common sense of most theorists as much as of the man and woman in the street, who assume that we *use* language, not that we *make* it. By complete constrast I wish to insist that we always make new signs – often imperceptibly different, even to the maker, and rarely conscious, even to the maker. In my view we make our always new signs in the environment of our constant interactions; but we make them out of the old, available stuff. One consequence of this is that all the outwardly produced signs are full of meaning. It is a view which seems to allow for degrees of meaning; not for errors, mistakes, 'just saying something without meaning it', and so on As a colleague put it to me, 'Some things are just "tentatives"' – exploration, trying something out; while some things are said with conscious full seriousness. This seems a perfectly good objection – but it still leaves all signs as meaningful. At the moment it seems safer to attribute meaning than to say 'this is meaningful; this not so much, this less so; this one hardly at all; this one not at all'. That approach makes it impossible to enquire into meaning in full seriousness.

LITERACY

Questions of literacy can be dealt with in many ways: for instance, they can be thought about from a linguistic point of view by focusing on the form of language; from a historical point of view by tracing change in forms and uses of literacy; or anthropologically, by comparing literacy uses in different cultures. In educational approaches, the essential context is that of meaning-making in a social and cultural environment, together with an attempt to understand what principles children themselves use in their representation of the world. That provides the possibility of a useful understanding of the actions of children, whether as writers or readers, in their early and steadily increasing engagement with the system of writing. At the same time, it offers a possibility of understanding the characteristics of the challenges which they face in doing so. These are prerequisites for the development of new curricula of literacy, and of the teaching strategies and methods best suited for their implementation. The theoretical approach that I adopt treats meaning-making as work, as *action*, which is itself best explained in terms of the social structures and cultural systems in which children and adults act in communication.

Several points are crucial; and two are of fundamental importance. First, in learning to read and write, children come as thoroughly experienced makers of meaning, as experienced makers of signs in any medium that is to hand. The wide range of media which they employ as a matter of course – toys and constructions of various kinds; Lego blocks; cardboard boxes; blankets; chairs; corners of rooms; pens and paper; scissors, paste and paper; and so on, are not taken up in schooling in a serious fashion. In school there is instead a focus on the single medium of lettered representation: literacy. Of course, there is some attention to other forms, such as painting, drawing, building, and play of various kinds. In many classrooms there is strong encouragement of these forms. But they tend to be treated, with entirely good intentions, as *expression* of the children's feelings, desires, emotions, rather than as forms of *communication*. In any case, as children move through the years of schooling, less and less emphasis tends to be given to these forms due to the demands of the present school curriculum.

Second, in the meanings which children make, meaning and form are indistinguishable wholes. That is, the form and the material of the signs made by children are for them expressive of the meanings which they intend to make. They are, literally, full of meaning. Let me give two examples. Say children want to play 'camping' in a room in their house, and they need a 'tent'. Blankets and bedcovers draped over chairs and table provide the material and the form which sufficiently express their meaning of 'tent', at that point. Or they want to play 'pirates' and therefore need a 'pirate ship'. A cardboard box provides a container, in which they can sit, it serves as the 'vessel', and the carpet as the ocean. The material of the box and its form, suit the meaning-needs of the children at this point. In their world, form and meaning are identical. With that disposition they come to the learning of writing, a system which has all the appearances of a system of signs in which form and meaning have no intrinsic connection: the letters *s h i p*, for instance, do not reveal the meaning that is attached to them in this sequence unless it is pointed out.

Not surprisingly this presents some child learners with a huge barrier. I will deal with some aspects of that complex problem, focusing on the characteristics of the signs which they make, and on their disposition to signs. The question of the assumed arbitrariness of signs in writing is therefore one central issue. A second issue is that of the distinctively different grammar of speech and writing, and its effects on the learning of writing. Because my emphasis in this book is on the years *before* writing, this is less of a concern for me here, though I will mention it because it does have decisive effects on the paths into literacy, even at a very early stage. This difference is now much better understood by linguists than it was some ten to fifteen years ago, but it has not yet passed into educational common sense either in the form of pedagogies or in curricula.

My approach is to treat the children by the time they come to school as competent and practised makers of signs in many semiotic modes. The task is to attempt to understand, from that point of view, the problems they encounter in learning to write. In particular I wish to reflect on the social, cultural and cognitive implications of the transition from the rich world of meanings made in countless ways, in countless forms, in the early years of children's lives, to the much more unidimensional world of written language.

The social semiotic theory which underpins my approach insists that all signs and messages are always multimodal. That is, no sign or message ever exists in just one single mode (for instance in 'language', 'writing'). An essay written at a university is written on a particular kind of paper – hastily torn from a notebook or carefully chosen for its look or feel; it is carelessly handwritten or neatly word-processed; it is either well laid out or it is inattentive to aspects of display. It has complex grammar, or not. All of these add meaning and are inevitably a part of writing, and impinge integrally on writing.

This is especially important because we are in a period of a fundamental shift in the relative uses and valuations of writing *vis-à-vis* other forms of communication, in particular the visual. This shift has the most far-reaching effects socially, culturally and cognitively.

A SOCIAL SEMIOTIC THEORY OF REPRESENTATION AND COMMUNICATION

Figure 1.1 was made by a 3-year-old boy. Sitting on his father's lap he talked about the drawing as he was doing it. 'Do you want to watch me? I'll make a car . . . got two wheels . . . and two wheels at the back . . . and two wheels here . . . that's a funny wheel.' When he had finished, he said 'This is a car.'

This was the first time that the 3-year-old had named a drawing, and it was this which initially proved both interesting and puzzling to me. How was this a car? Of course he had provided me with the key to an understanding of this drawing, through his commentary – 'I'll make a car . . . got two wheels . . .' For him a car, clearly, was

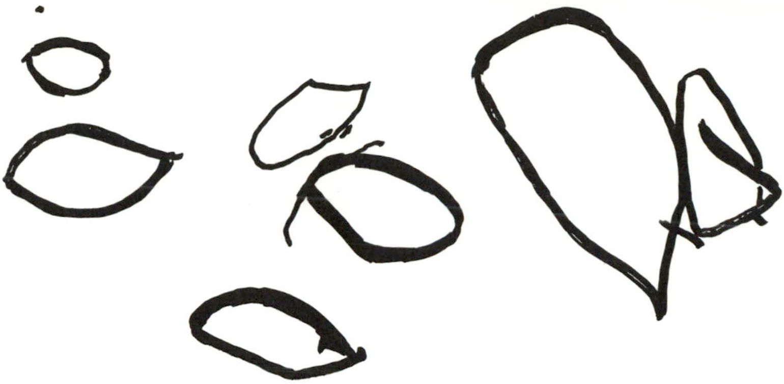

Figure 1.1 'This is a car'

first and foremost defined by the criterial characteristic of having wheels. His representation of the car focused on that aspect of the object to be represented, and he had the means available to him, for representing these features of *car*, namely wheels, or 'wheelness'.

Wheels may in any case be plausible as a defining feature of cars for many 3-year-old children. From a physical point of view their gaze is likely to fall on wheels as they walk up to a car; and the wheel's action – on a toy car as on a real car – is perhaps the most prominent feature; and so on. So a 3-year-old's *interest* in cars may plausibly be condensed into and expressed as an interest in wheels. They in turn are plausibly represented by circles, both by their physical visual appearance, and by a mimetic, gestural representation – the circular motion of the hand in making the circle gesturally repeating the action of the wheel in going 'round and round'.

I assume that all of us act precisely in this fashion in making signs. Signs arise out of our *interest* at a given moment, when we represent those features of the object which we regard as defining of that object at that moment (that is, *wheels* as defining of *car*). This interest is always complex and has physiological, psychological, emotional, cultural and social origins. It gets its focus from factors in the environment in which the sign is being made. We never represent 'the whole object' but only ever certain criterial aspects. Even in highly realistic adult representations only certain selected aspects are represented – never 'the whole thing'.

Signs are metaphors in many ways. In the car example there are two steps: (a) 'a car is (most like) wheels'; and (b) 'wheels are (most like) circles'. These structures are established by analogy. Hence the result is a (double) metaphor: circles are ((like) wheels; wheels are (defining of)) a car. Signs are the result of metaphoric processes in which analogy is the principle by which they are formed. Analogy is a process of comparison, or classification: *x* is like *y* (in criterial ways). Metaphors are classificatory statements, whether as 'My love is like the ocean' or as 'Selling tobacco is like drug-peddling'; as such they are crucial in cultural, social and cognitive ways. My metaphor about tobacco defines me as belonging to a certain social group; my metaphor about love gives you insight into my ways of thinking in my emotional life. Relations of power between makers of metaphors determine which metaphors will carry the day and pass into culture as 'natural', neutral expressions. Children are, on the one hand, less constricted by culture and by its already existing metaphoric arrangements, but on the other hand, they are usually in a position of lesser power, so that their metaphors are less likely to carry the day.

In this conception, signs are motivated relations of form and meaning, or to use semiotic terminology, of signifiers and signifieds. Makers of signs use those forms for the expression of their meaning which best suggest or carry the meaning, and they do so in any medium in which they make signs. When a child treats a cardboard box as a pirate ship that is the making of a sign, in which the material form (the box) is an apt medium for the expression of the meaning 'pirate ship', because what the child regards as the defining aspects of 'pirate ship' *at that moment* – its vessel-like qualities, 'containment', 'mobility', and so on, are sufficiently well expressed in the form (and the material) of the box.

Language is no exception to this; linguistic forms are also used in a motivated manner in the representation and communication of meaning. For a child in the pre-school years, there is both more and less freedom of expression. More, because they have not yet learned to confine their meaning-making to the culturally and socially facilitated materials, forms and media. And to the extent that they are unaware of conventions surrounding the making of signs, they are freer in that respect. They have less freedom because they do not have the rich cultural semiotic (meaning-making) resources available for their making of signs. So for instance, when a child, labouring to climb a steep slope, said 'This is a heavy hill', he is constrained by not having the word *steep* as an available semiotic resource. The same is the case with the semiotic resources of syntax, and of textual form. But using *heavy* to express 'this takes a lot of effort, it is hard work' is a motivated conjunction of an existing form (the word *heavy*) and meaning ('this is hard work').

As children are drawn into culture, 'what is to hand', becomes more and more that which the culture values and therefore makes readily available. The child's active, transformative practice remains, but it is more and more applied to materials which are already culturally formed. In this way children become the agents of their own cultural and social making.

The child's transformative, productive stance towards the making of signs is at the same time a transformation of the sign-maker's identity, their subjectivity. Certain of the child's sign-making practices are noticed by adults around them; and some of these (i.e. language, drawing, building) are valued, at least for a while. Many are not noticed, and not valued, or are relegated to the category of 'play', for instance. Those which are valued become subject to the regulatory intervention of culture and of society. Of these, the child's encounter with language and literacy receive most attention from adults, and these are therefore most subjected to regulation, in the process of the child's being drawn into culture. The adult's own overwhelming focus on language and literacy makes it difficult for us to see children's meaning-making principles. Those of their practices which we call 'play' we do not consider as a part of communication, and therefore not worthy of *real* investigation. And for those of their practices that we do focus on, and in relation to their learning of language and literacy in particular, we already have our fully developed even if inappropriate or even quite incorrect theories. No wonder that the child's own semiotic disposition is not recognized in most institutional settings. Worse, the folk-theoretical notions which most adults (including teachers, academics, and professionals in the health and welfare field) bring to these questions are positively at odds with the child's disposition. Notions of language as a relatively stable system, of signs as arbitrary and stable conjunctions of meaning and form, can lead to pedagogies and to curricula which are fundamentally mismatched with the potential, ability and dispositions of the child learners.

SOME CHARACTERISTICS OF SPEECH AND OF WRITING

One of the insights of social theories of language which is now taken for granted is that language varies as the social context varies. A social semiotic approach goes further; it takes the stronger position that it is social factors which lead people to *remake* language.

The reasoning is something as follows. There is an important distinction between representation on the one hand – 'What I want to say, show, mean' – and communication on the other – 'How I can get across to you what it is that I want to say, show, mean.' Each has, its own, special requirement. The requirements of *communication* are that the participants in an act of communication should make their messages as understandable for a particular person in a particular situation as it is possible to do. This makes it necessary that each participant chooses forms of expression which are at least in principle as transparent as is possible for the other participants. I can illustrate this by a brief anecdote. On a study leave from Australia some years ago, we lived in a town in the north of England. The children from the surrounding area came into our house to play with our children; this was unusual – children played in the street, and did not go into anyone else's home. When lunchtime came my partner would say things like 'Do you think it's time to go home now?' Our young visitors would say 'No.' My partner was not being transparent. She had to learn to say 'Go home now!' which was transparent, and to her, rude. Communication is a social action. It takes place in social structures which are inevitably marked by power difference. This power difference affects how each participant understands what 'as transparent as possible' means. Participants who have greater power are able to force other participants into greater efforts of interpretation. They have a different notion of 'transparency' than participants who have less power and have to make every effort to produce messages which truly require minimal efforts of interpretation. My partner had greater power than her young visitors; she tried to disguise this by 'being polite' – not revealing power; in doing that she forced the children to interpret her utterance. As it turned out, they didn't, or couldn't; and she had to assert her power directly.

The requirements of *representation* are that I, as the maker of a representation/sign, choose the best, most plausible form for the expression of the meaning that I intend to represent. The example of the car, above, is an instance of that: *circles* to stand for wheels, and *wheels* to stand for car. The *interest* of makers of the representation/sign leads them to choose one aspect of the thing they want to represent as being criterial at that moment for the representation of an object; they then choose the most plausible form which is available to them for its representation.

These two aspects of a message, the *communicational* (focused on the audience) and the *representational* (focused on the maker), are central to any understanding of the form and meaning of messages, written, drawn or otherwise. They are central in any attempt to understand the signs made by children, right through their years of schooling. They provide insights into their actions, and into the difficulties which they face in their engagement with writing. They are central also in understanding the complex processes of learning.

The social contexts of speech and writing differ in fundamental ways, and so do their psychological, cognitive contexts. The materiality of sound (the physical material nature of sound) and of the visual graphic medium of letters are further factors. I will mention only briefly some of those which have the most significant effects on the organization of speech and writing.

For speech, the demands of planning provide one limitation to the length of the normal unit. So do the demands of processing in reception in hearing, through the limitations of memory. These coincide to some extent with the limitations of the physiological production of speech. That is, the length of the unit which forms the basis of the spoken utterance is determined by the length of time it takes to expel air from our lungs in a normal breath. Informationally, elements of greater prominence are made distinct from those of lesser prominence through pitch variation. The materiality of sound means that sequence, saying one thing after another, is the fundamental semiotic factor of language in this mode; it forms the organizational logic of speech: one thing has to follow another. Whatever it is that speakers have in mind, in speaking they are bound by the logic of sequence in time.

These factors together produce a characteristic formal organization of spoken language namely, of *a single clause*; which is joined by various means (intonation, and, often through conjunctions of various kinds) to the next clause. Characteristically, these tend to be formed into often quite long 'chains', which have an overarching conceptual structuring – namely that of speech-paragraphs. Consequently, development takes place sequentially, by elaboration, restatement, repetition; usually nuanced by a complex system of means of conjunctions, of which intonation may be the most elaborate.

Here is a very brief example of speech-structure. The double slash / / marks the boundaries between clauses (or elements treated as clauses). Sometimes the link is made with a conjunction word; sometimes by intonation alone.

> See / / we went through this in '81 / / and / / I was one of the officials that were involved / / er once we'd worked out the severance side of things / / we were gonna have to deal with the people who wanted to relocate / / and they said to management / / we had hardship / / . . .

Language always occurs as text; never as just (a heap of) utterances. Children therefore always meet language as text. A fundamental question for a literacy curriculum is therefore that about the typical kinds of texts, speech-genres, which a particular child, or a group of children, or a community of children, bring as their linguistic resources to the learning of writing. For instance, a child who typically participates freely in interaction through dialogic forms of speech at home or in their peer group, may be disadvantaged in relation to the child who has experience of forms of communication of a more monologic, written kind, in a society which values writing above speech, and therefore values broadly monologic forms above dialogic ones.

For writing, the limitations of sequence (as well as the other limitations that I mentioned) are far less significant, and in many forms of writing they are replaced by processes of complex syntactic design, such as the subordination of one clause to another, embedding, for instance. These are often developed through careful and extensive editing. The limitations which exists for the size of the unit in speech is more or less absent for writing. I say 'more or less', because it is to some significant extent within a writer's discretion as to where, on a hypothetical continuum between more speech-like and more writing-like structures, she or he wishes to locate their writing (or their speech, with highly literate speakers).

Writing is a visual medium; and so time and temporality are

replaced by space and spatiality. Consequently the logic of temporal sequence is replaced by the logic of (an abstract) spatial arrangement, namely by hierarchy. In writing, development of a conceptual kind takes place by complex hierarchical interrelations of clauses, in which embedding of one clause in another is the characteristic mode. This produces the unit which we all know as the sentence.

Writing is the medium of overt forms of communication, of monologic genres. In speech the needs of the interlocutor are of primary concern; this is not the case in writing to the same extent. There those needs are replaced by the development of what the writer thinks is the appropriate conceptual or other structure of the text.

The learning of writing proceeds in exactly the same fashion as the development of other sign systems: employing the strategy of using the best, most apt available form for the expression of a particular meaning. Children use such representational means as they have available for making that meaning. The child's written signs are the effect of their meaning-making actions, arising out of their interest, using what they have available as representational means. Much of the rest of this book is an exploration of precisely these questions, and of children's strategies of dealing with these difficult issues. The signs which children make are, despite their differences from adult form, fully meaningful in every sense. The child's actions have to be understood as productive and trans-formative of their own representational resources, as well as of those of the community around them.

Chapter 2

'My Gawd, I made it like Australia'
Making meaning in many media

REPRESENTING THE WORLD

Our view of the world is in many ways pre-established for all of us. These habituated ways of seeing and of acting are nearly invisible to us; they have become second nature, obvious and beyond the need or the possibility of inspection. This naturalization has its foundation in the myriad of social and cultural experiences which make up our own personal histories. Nevertheless it may be useful to focus on two relatively different kinds of influences in this shaping of common sense: overt instruction, and our own practical experience. Overt instruction comes in many ways, from the parent or teacher's direct instruction: 'No, not this way, that way'; 'No, that's not the reason, this is'; 'No, that's not what you do, this is what you do.' In an example that sticks in my mind, a friend's friend, in teaching her 3-year-old to cook scones, says: 'No, James, you don't spit on the spoon' – when he had just done so.

'Practical experience' hardly needs elaborating, except perhaps to say that it might or does provide an often countervailing common sense to that produced by overt instruction, so that James may find that it is, after all, useful to spit on the spoon in order to get off some particularly sticky bit of doughy mixture.

It is this composite common sense which I would like to unsettle, in relation to our views of children's meaning-making. To do so, I will consider several quite ordinary and everyday kinds of activities which children of, say, up to 8 years of age happily, readily and constantly engage in, without particular prompting. Some of these examples I have to reconstruct here by telling alone. In one case in particular I have lost the object in question – let me call it the 'Panadol-man'; in other cases the 'objects' never really existed as objects – they were temporary arrangements of building blocks, pillows, blankets, chairs, dolls and so on, usually on a floor in the corner of a room, sometimes taking over and transforming the whole room. And not only were they temporary, swept away by the next order to 'tidy your room', 'tidy up the mess you've made in the living room', they were also constantly being transformed: a tent turning into a spaceship, turning into a house for aliens, turning into an ordinary family setting, and so on, and so on. Sequences of play have a relative stability, which, I imagine, appear to the children engaged in them as coherent, stable and persistent, because the changes, the transformations – each quite minute in itself yet adding up to significant change quite rapidly – are each of them well motivated by the substance of the play.

To start with two points central to an exploration of meaning begun in the first chapter: (c) the sign-maker's *interest*; and (b), arising out of that, the motivated nature of the sign. In all the examples which I will discuss here, as in all examples in all instances, my assumption is that at a particular moment we, all of us, act out of a certain interest in the environment in which we are, and that in our making of signs, that interest is reflected in the sign in the best possible way, in the most plausible fashion, in the most apt form. So the environment for two children may be: playing at home, in a room, playing at 'families', in which at this point in the play, the family wants to go out in the car. A 'car' is needed, so a car is made – a car which satisfies the purposes of the play (being capable of being sat 'in' for instance), and it is made out of materials which are to hand, and which can adequately represent the meanings which need to be made concrete.

As all signs are complex, then the further assumption on which I proceed is that all aspects of these complex signs are equally formed in that way. Reading of signs, whether made by child or adult, is therefore an attempt to uncover the complexity of that initial interest as it is represented in the sign. That is what I wish to show here: that all signs show rationality, logic, human desire and affect.

Consider the cars in Figure 2.1 and Plate 1. They are drawn at around the same time, together with many others, at a period of great interest by the drawer in this kind of car. Let me describe some of the differences and similarities. The car in Figure 2.1 shows a plethora of detail, all of it to do with power. This is expressed through drawing and through writing: the visual

Figure 2.1 Car in its environment

emphasis on the 'power units' (the rocket exhausts at the back, with red flames emerging from them; the rocket-launcher behind the driver which has just fired a rocket that is now above the driver's cabin; the streams of sparks and flames coming from the wheels, an effect of the enormous speed at which the car is moving; the dart-shape of the car itself; the streamlining over the driver's seat; and the energetically drawn lines of colouring-in, and of those indicating the ground, all suggesting movement, speed. Apart from the name of the car, the written labelling is about power too, indicating strength, or potential violence.

Other signs which express this same interest are colour and lettering; for instance the strong black lettering of *Power engin*; the colour-harmony of driver's dress, wheels and the car's name.

It is not difficult to read this 8½-year-old's interests in this sign; and all aspects of this complex sign are motivated expressions of his meanings. The child decided to cut around this picture, though he did not cut out the car, as he did do, by contrast, in Plate 1. Difference in cutting-out is therefore part of the complex sign too. His cutting-out tells us that what he has chosen to represent in Figure 2.1 is not the car just by itself, as 'object', but the car in a context, in an environment: on a road where sparks can fly, and dust can be thrown up by the wheels; where the exhaust flames and fumes are visible; as is the rocket which the driver/pilot has just fired. So this sign, Figure 2.1, is not just a sign of a super technologically advanced car, but a sign of that car in action.

The interest in speed and power is also there in the drawing of the car in Plate 1, but here it is an interest in a much more abstracted and intensified notion of speed, expressed through 'line', and through the coding of notions of aerodynamics. The detail of Figure 2.1 has been replaced by an intense concentration on the dart-shape; the aerodynamic line; the exterior design features; the paintwork – now in the reduced colour scheme (compared to the seven colours of Figure 2.1) of red and black. The surface of this object has been worked to a shiny finish, by intense rubbing with the red and the black pencils. When asked why he had made it shiny, the child said: 'Oh because I like it like that, it has to be like that.' Clearly, special effort has gone into producing the effect of glossy paintwork. The only technological gadgetry that remains are the two 'legs' below the car which, it appears from the sign-maker's spoken description, can be lowered in order to lift the car above obstacles on the road ahead, such as trucks for instance. The car's black logo, *M*, is on a tailfin, which lends a jet-like appearance to this car. Streamlining is emphasized by the style of the paintwork.

Above all, perhaps, the difference of interest between Figure 2.1 and Plate 1 is that of focus on the *elaboration* of technical/technological detail of power in one, as against its *concentrated, abstracted* expression in the other; and the emphasis on the car's performance in (relevant aspects of) its environment included in the cut-out representation of Figure 2.1, as against the car as object and its potential in Plate 1. As much effort has gone into the precision of cutting around the shape of the car in Plate 1 as into anything else.

Clearly the two images share an overarching interest. Yet there are also distinct and fundamental differences. Within the broad similarity of interest in power, speed, the differences point to importantly distinct conceptual and cognitive orientations: the relevant details of one object versus an intensification and abstraction of criterial features – how it works, what it is, as against 'its potential'; an object acting in its environment as against an object *per se*: 'action' as against 'being'; 'what it does' as against 'what it is'.

The resources available to this child for making these objects were the same in each case. First, there is a history of previous reading and seeing – whether of *Thunderbirds* as a television series, as comic-strip, as detailed technical information; or of James Bond films seen on television. Then the resources for actually making these two representations (and others at the same time – many not completed or ending up on the floor): paper, pencils, scissors, sticking tape (the car of Plate 1 is actually made from two bits of paper stuck together to give the elongated 'nose' of the car). But sameness of resources gives rise to importantly different design, to different representational, aesthetic, affective and cognitive purposes.

A third example of this 'car series' is shown in Figure 2.2. It was also made at this time. This object is three-dimensional: a craft (perhaps now a space-craft) with the same triangular, dart-shape, made from Lego blocks. As with Figure 2.1, the plethora of detail is pronounced; there are similarities of overall 'design'; and the same interest in speed and power. At this point the potentials – and limitations – of the representational resources become most noticeable. Lego blocks offer possibilities which paper does not; although paper, designed, painted and cut out, also offers possibilities which Lego does not – for instance, the possibilities of abstraction/intensification of Plate 1. But in Figure 2.2 issues of design arise even more insistently, as questions of symmetry, of balance, of 'making it work', as well as actual constructional possi-bilities and challenges. The cognitive potentials of the three objects are distinct; each offers possibilities and imposes limitations.

It is important to focus on the strong dynamic interrelation of the resources available for making – the representational resources – with the maker's shifting interest. In part it is suggested by and determined by the possibilities of the material; in part the maker of the sign shapes the material in accordance with his interests. But the possibilities of shaping differ for Lego blocks and paper. In the process of the making of these objects the child has explored, shaped, designed and remade for himself significant notions of a technical, aesthetic and cognitive kind. Cognitively – and conceptually – this exploration ranges from the still relatively two-dimensional representation of Figure 2.1 with its variety of con-cerns; to the bare three-dimensionality of the cut-out car of Plate 1, with the expression of its concerns; to the fully three-dimensional Figure 2.2 with its conceptual and cognitive challenges.

Figure 2.2 Lego car

The concepts explored in the making of each of these three objects are every bit as demanding, rewarding and significant as any concept expressed and explored in the medium of either spoken or written language. So are the cognitive challenges. Affectively each of the three offers totally different possibilities. An attempt to translate any of these into language reveals the real difficulty, in fact the impossibility of that task. These are ideas, concepts, notions, feelings, relations, affective states which are properly expressed in the way they are expressed here, and translation into language produces at best an impoverished account. Nevertheless, of the three it is perhaps Figure 2.1 which is most nearly translatable, perhaps in terms of 'has-relations': 'the car has a turbine engine, and it has secret weapons, and it has . . .', and of 'can-relations': 'it can fire rockets, and it can speed along on any surface, . . .' The two-dimensionality of that representation, its classificatory characteristics, are most writing-like. The cut-out car of Plate 1, a three-dimensional object, is already much more difficult to 'translate'; and the Lego construction could only be given in full translation, in '*précis*' form.

This translatability or the lack of it, can give us an important clue both about criterial aspects of writing and of two-dimensional representation, namely their relative flatness, and the cognitive and affective 'distance' from the maker. I can pick up, feel, handle, the cut-out car. It is a tangible object; it gives me the possibility of a real tactile relation. I can feel how heavy or light it is, how smooth its surface, feel its shape, its dynamic quality. This is obviously so with the Lego car also. It fulfils all the criteria and meets all the requirements of the detail of Figure 2.1, but in addition I can physically explore it; I can feel it. Above all, I can move it about and place it in entirely new environments, with other objects, to form new structures in new imagined and real worlds. Its affective qualities and potentials are entirely different from those of the flat, two-dimensional object. With the latter, any attempts to insert it into an imaginary new context do have to remain imaginary and distanced. The cut-out car and the Lego 'craft' actually can and do become real objects in this real world.

HOW REAL IS REAL? OR, IMAGINING IN DIFFERENT MODES

In my discussion of the three cars there are one or two points which have puzzled me, and which it may be worth pausing on for a moment. We see that children tell and write stories; we see them drawing and painting; less often between the ages of 4 and 7, when 'story' is important but writing is not yet controlled, we see them making stories, narratives which tend to be hybrid things with language used to indicate action and narrative sequence, and drawing used to represent, to display, the people and objects in the story. We see them making things, such as the Lego car, or the blanket tent, or the chair-and-pillow house, and so on. These are activities we notice and we think we understand: representing on paper, or playing on the floor, each at its own seemingly proper moment.

However, the activity which intrigues me is 'cutting-out', as in the car in Plate 1. Here the child has drawn a car, very competently, coloured it in, worked to produce a glossy surface; and then he cuts around it, with great care and precision. What has led him to do that? Why not leave the finished drawing as it is?

The cutting-out 'phenomenon' is common: in my 'collection' I have – produced by our children and by their friends, either by themselves, singly, or around a table where many share in the activity: tulips; a camel; a spider; a stag beetle; an elephant; a map of Australia; trees; table and chairs; a tent; butterflies; snowflakes; a circle; a heart (with carefully drawn red-line edging the inside); a hand; a dog; an accordion; scissors; a figure of a girl; flags; cars; rockets; various objects not now recognizable or recognized by their makers; a wristwatch, cut out and then glued; and lots of instances of cutting out with bits then glued on top. In fact, if we add *objects made from paper*, the list gets much longer, and includes things such as a recorder; necklaces; bracelets; puppets; kites (miniature, not 'real'); badges; 'presents' in envelopes, or folded, and stuck; and so on, and so on. Nearly all of these, though not all, were first drawn, quite carefully, as the camel in Figure 2.3, for instance, and the figure of the girl in Figure 2.4. In some instances, cutting-out acts as a kind of framing, as in the case of the car in Figure 2.1. Here the young maker, in talking (some weeks later) about his reasons for cutting around the drawings of Figure 2.1 and Plate 1 said that he wanted to have the detail of the surrounding environment in Figure 2.1, the detail of the rocket-launcher, of the road and so on. So here the criterion does seem to be 'framing'; as with many children's drawings, they are often on bits of paper together with other things, reused, remade, a spare bit of clean paper in one half of the page; so that the unwanted bits are cut off, and the wanted bits retained.

In the case of Plate 1 the reason given was different: 'Oh because I like it like that, it has to be like that.' Framing is obviously a reason here too, but framing in a much tighter sense, of precise focus, of rigorously excluding what is extraneous – and what is extraneous here is everything which is not strictly and centrally part of the object: 'it has to be like that'. It is of course notoriously difficult to extract from anyone their reasons for doing things which were done below the level of consciousness, whether with adults or children. So the 'I like it like that' is quite likely to include much greater complexity than that phrase suggests on the surface. The two parts of his utterance combine affect 'I like it like that', and representational necessity 'It has to be like that.' Each contains a complex of reasons, and desires.

One possibility which I hinted at earlier is that when the representation 'comes off the page', it enters another world. It shifts from the world of contemplation into the world of action, into the world of my practical here and now; from a world of mental action

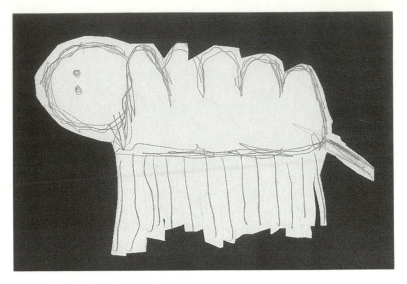

Figure 2.3 Camel (cut out)

Figure 2.4 Girl (cut out)

to a world of tactile, physical, objective action. While it is on the page I can do 'mental things' with it. It is a mental object, distanced from me, accessible by sight and imagination if *I* move into the (world of the) page. When it is off the page, I can do physical things with it. It has become a real object, accessible by feel and touch as well as by sight. It has become accessible to my imagination in a different manner, and it can enter, physically, into a world of imagination constructed with other objects of whatever kind.

Some clue to this may be given by observing what children do – though in my experience not all that frequently – with these newly made objects. They appear in games, as when the camel is made to march in puppet-theatre fashion across a table, to scare another player, or simply to be placed somewhere else. A clue is also given by further transformations wrought on some of these objects, so for instance in the stick puppet in Figure 2.5. It formed part of a cast of several such characters from a genre of fairy-tale. This representation can now act – in imagination – by being manipulated. Of course, in that action it then enters into a quite new mode, that of theatre; though for children that mode is frequently entirely contiguous with many other forms of play.

Cutting-out may offer the child one means of bridging a gap between two kinds of imaginative worlds, one in which the child 'enters the page' so to speak, and imaginatively enters into the life of objects in or on the page; and another in which represented objects come off the page and are brought into the world of physical objects here and now, which are then reanimated in the imaginative effort of the child. There is then a continuum for the child, between things on the page – one kind of distanced intangible reality; and things here and now, another kind of reality, not distanced but tangible. The two kinds of realism are linked through the actions of the child.

Both worlds engage the imagination of a child, or, are the effects of the imaginative action of the child; though the efforts are different, and I assume the effects are also. Presented in the way I have here, they represent alternatives, between practical engagement in and with a present three-dimensional world involving imagination; and mental engagement with a distanced world also involving imagination. In one case the movement is towards me and my present practical world; in the other case it is towards the distanced world, where I make the move *into* that world.

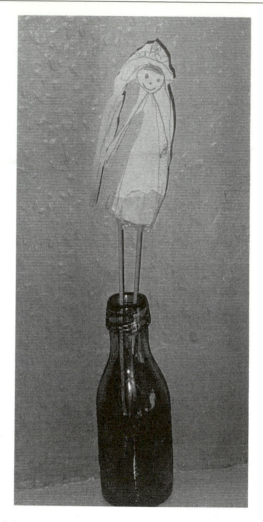

Figure 2.5 Stick puppet

Both involve imagination; and I do not wish to make value judgements of any kind on either of these two worlds. They correspond, perhaps too neatly, to stereotypes which already exist in entrenched form in western cultures, of 'the dreamer', 'the distanced person'; and 'the practical person', the engaged human being. My own interest at this point is rather different, not focused on evaluation, but on emphasizing that both involve efforts of imagination though differently so; that we need to ask whether both are crucial, important, essential; asking what each includes and excludes; and which of these – given my own context of work in institutionalized education – is more likely to bring benefits in a future world; or, turning that around, which of the two has what kinds of corollaries for practical and social action.

If I were to allow myself three value judgements they would be these. First, the successive transitions from one mode of representation to another – from drawing; to coloured-in, labelled drawing; to cut-out object; to the object integrated into a system of other objects, changing its potential of action; from one kind of realism to another; from one form of imaginative effort to another – these seem to me what humans do and need to do, and need to be encouraged to do as an entirely ordinary and necessary part of human development, whether in institutional settings or at home. Each of them engages the child differently in cognitive and affective action. The move, the transduction across modes, encourages the synaesthetic potentials of the child in their transformative, creative actions.

Second, it may be, and my discussion so far tends in that direction, that all modes and forms of representation present both potentials and limitations to meaningful action and to imagination. If the limits of imagination imposed by one mode of representation are reached it seems a decidedly positive situation to be able to move into another mode, which extends these limits in certain ways, or offers a different potential. This offers an enormous potential enrichment, cognitively, conceptually, aesthetically and affectively. It also represents, as far as I can judge, an essential skill for the social and economic futures of the post-industrial western world.

My third value judgement is this: if the limitation to one mode of representation *is* a limitation, then we should do everything we can to overcome that limitation. If it is a limitation on the totality of human potential, if it favours one aspect only, to the detriment of others, then we have, I believe, no justifiable reason for sustaining it.

'WHAT IS TO HAND'

If it is the case that each of the modes, forms and possibilities of representation offers possibilities *and* limitations, the choice of modes of representation clearly becomes highly significant. Hence too the anxiety of many parents, often fed by popularizing psychologists, about depriving children of 'stimulation', or of the means of 'growth'. Whole industries have grown up around these anxieties – from toys and their manufacture and distribution; to educational aids of very many kinds; apparatus for physical expression; and so on, and so on. A walk around any toyshop reveals the anxieties of the people in a particular neighbourhood, of any one era, of any one culture. Toyshops in Germany are and feel different from those in England; and the influence of class is readily seen by travelling from one type of suburb to another. The historical aspects of this issue can be seen vividly in visits to toy museums. Practices of child-rearing do not just fit in, more or less easily, with these fashions, nostrums and tendencies, they are shaped by them; as they are by all other social dynamics, which themselves exercise their effects.

Watching children in their making of objects, of representations, in their play, is somewhat inconclusive in this respect. On the one hand, they are of course influenced by the cultural, semiotic, social world around them: the shape of the three cars speaks clearly to that. But the cut-out shapes of girl and camel, and of the stick puppet, also speak of quite other dynamics, relatively uninfluenced by technology, current fashion or fad (such as the periodically produced fads of television characters and their accompanying merchandise). In point of fact in the production of the children whose objects I have gathered up more or less sporadically, and whom I observed with greater or lesser intensity, more or less engaged or tired – about six children in all, under my relatively interested gaze – in their production there is not that much direct evidence of fashion or fad. Yes, there are cars such as those here, or rockets, whose ancestry can be traced, not directly though perceptibly, to Thunderbirds and James Bond. But there are no Ninja Turtles, and only one example of Power Rangers, even though all were avid watchers of these at various stages. Fad and fashion are subject to the severe transformative work of children, mediated by informal networks of communication. Our then 2½-year-old son was very interested in a character called 'Lean Tomato' *before* he had seen the Ninja Turtles on television, and then later met this character Leonardo for himself. He had however been integrated fully into the transformative action on this series by other children at the crèche.

The manner in which fads appear is generally in a (heavily) transformed version: robots appear, so do spaceships and so do dinosaurs; but they tend not to bear the traces of their immediate origin. They do provide the stuff of the conceptual 'what is to hand', mingled in with older, deeper, narrative forms, which readily assimilate new types. Nevertheless, this conceptual 'what is to hand' is significant, because it in itself sets limits to and provides possibilities for imagination, opens up categories such as time and space, history and prehistory, and cultural differences of various kinds. It provides materials to choose from, and therefore materials for the differentiation of gender, for instance.

However, not everything can be to hand, and not everything can be made available, whether this is the conceptual stuff or the material stuff with which children make the signs that express their meanings. In any case children actively make their choices from what there is around them. Figure 2.6 shows a car, made on the bedroom floor by a 6-year-old and her friend. It is made from two wire-mesh drawers, a pillow, a red toolbox, and an assortment of other bits and bobs, passengers included. The toolbox serves as a bonnet, the two flanking drawers are the car doors, the central pillow is the/are the car's seats, on which – for a while anyway – the two 6-year-olds were happy to sit. A very short time after I had taken this photo, the car had already been changed beyond its shape in the photo. By the next morning the pillow and the upturned drawers were still on the floor, but there was no suggestion at all of them being a car.

The point, and it is a crucial point, is that these objects, or structures, or configurations, are temporary only, and are subject to constant transformation. And in this respect 'what is to hand' in this instance is ideal for the purposes of representation, because it lends itself so easily to change, modification, transformation. However, it is equally important to point out that these representations are not arbitrary: the logic of their makers' meanings is coded in their form. In Figure 2.6 the two flanking drawers are, quite clearly, the side doors – which all cars have. Here, as in all signs made by anyone, the children focused on what at that moment *they* considered to be criterial about 'car': that it should have seats to sit on, doors to get into it, and, less significantly perhaps, for after all, this car is *a car for playing in*, a small bonnet at the front. As this is not a car for driving – as it might have become had one of the children's brother made it or played with her or her friend – it

Figure 2.6 Pillow-car

also has no steering wheel, no gear lever. These simply aren't significant in this car; not because this car's makers do not know about them, but because they are not relevant for the purposes of this car's users and makers.

These forms of complex sign encourage and make possible a direct acting on and in the environment, and that is one of their most significant aspects. The car in the example above is just one element in a much more complex meaning-structure – the game as a whole – and it is the control, development, building, transformation of such complex meaning-structures, *co-operatively* very often though not necessarily so, which has deep cognitive and social effects. The physically produced sign is of course accompanied by the signs of speech, of gesture, of facial expression, by signs of engagement or disengagement. The children are in charge, they choose the materials which best serve their sign-making purposes, they construct the signs as plausible, apt expressions of *their* interest, and act transformatively on them. In this process they also produce their own materials of representations, which often depend only very indirectly or not at all on the adults' systems. Comments have been made from time to time on the private spoken languages developed by children: the material communications systems used and developed by them all the time go without comment.

Consider the instance of 'playing shops'. The range of signs developed, typically, in this game is enormous: A whole space has to be turned into this sign, the shop, with all its subsidiary signs – counters, advertising, checkout; 'goods' have to be produced; lists of goods for sale; money; and so on. In my collection there are a large number of purchases from several such shopping excursions: whistles; necklaces; bracelets; sealed little packages, still unopened; badges; musical instruments; pictures; puppets; and so on. Children see the complexity of the meaningful cultural world with absolute clarity; and in their making of meaning they construct elaborate, complex representations of that world – out of the materials which are to hand: bits of paper, glued, stuck, cut, folded, painted, cut out; bits of tinsel; old birthday cards; coloured string; and so on. In this process they construct complex alternative systems of representations, never arbitrarily, never simply copying, always producing forms which reveal and bear the logic and interest of their sign-makers' cognitive actions, and affective interests.

DESIGN AND INTENTION

The transformative action of childish meaning-making works relentlessly on their world. Their ravenous appetite for meaning-making leaves no object, no material untouched. All are drawn into structures which are both stable and novel. The voraciously analytical eyes of child sign-makers assess the semiotic possibilities of the world around them: 'reading', in the sense of detailed analytical scrutiny of all aspects of their world for their potential use in representation. What may at times seem like preposterous collages are no less deliberate than the modernist collages and constructions of a Picasso and a Duchamps: and as deliberate, usually, in their design.

The 4-year-old, sitting and kneeling on chairs with her two friends around the kitchen table, cutting out shapes from large sheets of blue paper was clear – even if somewhat surprised – about her creative activity when she uttered 'My Gawd, I made it like Australia' when she unfolded the piece of paper she had just cut out (Figure 2.7). Both her 'I made it', which is clear about authorship and agency, and her instant disposition to read meaning in(to) the object she had just 'made', show deliberation, planning, design, as a quite normal, expected, and unexceptional state of mind: even if, as here, the result was perhaps accidental more than deliberate.

There are however very many instances when *design* is absolutely clear. The most stunning example that I can recall concerns the Panadol-man, a figure which I have unfortunately lost. Sitting with her parents at the breakfast table on a summer weekend morning, the 4-year-old saw an empty packet of Panadol (an analgesic common in the United Kingdom). The package is blue with blue and white printing; inside are one or two white plastic sheets with pressed indentations in which the individual elongated tablets are sealed. She got up from the table, got a small pair of scissors from the kitchen drawer, and started cutting out the individual bubble-like indentations of the plastic sheet. This seemed like mere idle snipping. She then cut around the sides of the blue packet, so that it could be folded out, producing a flat piece of cardboard, twice the length of the initial packet. She cut around one end of the square unfolded cardboard, producing a blob at one end of the whole square. Next she went upstairs and returned with a roll of sticky tape. She now proceeded to tape the cut out bubbles onto the whole square, clearly now for us at last, as buttons. She proceeded in this fashion until she had a human figure, policeman-like in a blue uniform with white buttons. The whole sequence unfolded without fuss, without hitch, without talk, without any attention to the parents, one of whom was utterly astonished by the degree of planning, the precision of the staging, by the very fact of *design*.

I have another figure, the genesis of which I did not witness, but which also uses the Panadol-'bubbles', and which, on asking, I was

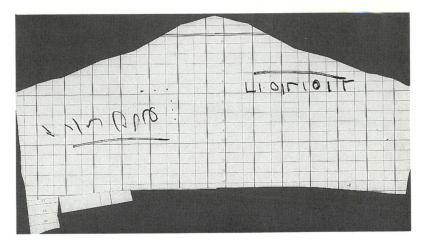

Figure 2.7 'My Gawd, I made it like Australia'

told was 'an alien'. It is a complex figure in its own right, made
again from what was to hand, but showing that the empty Panadol
sheets had achieved a kind of established place in the range of
materials for representation.

Attributing intention to children as young as 4 – or, as I would
want to do, even much younger than that – both accords with
common sense, and offends it. We know that children are clever,
even wise, at an early age; yet we may shrink from attributing full
intentionality to the things they do and make, so effortlessly, and
which look so unlike our adult conceptions of what things are and
should be. The incredulous response to attribution of intention is
also quite common in relation to things that adults do 'naturally',
automatically, unreflectingly. This is very much the case with
language. For instance someone says something to me to which
I take exception, and I tell them so. They may say 'But I didn't
really mean that', to which I'm likely to respond, overtly or silently:
'Yes you did, otherwise why did you say it?' Or, in my professional
role, I might analyse a bit of language, drawing out a particular
meaning, to which someone else might say: 'But how do you know
they really meant that?', 'How do you know they did that deliberately?' To which I would say that all I really know is that they did
it; and if what they did happens quite regularly, I feel justified in
attributing intention, *design*, even if that design was not overtly
there in the speaker's consciousness.

The problem is compounded when we look at images, because in popular understanding (aided by the absence of strong theoretical descriptions and explanations), pictures, images, are not usually subjected to the same analysis for meaning, not seen as being as much a part of *communication* as language is for instance. Images of most kinds are thought of as being about *expression*, not *information, communication*. We acknowledge of course that a political cartoonist working for a newspaper is intending to communicate, has meanings that he or she wants to convey; and we may acknowledge similar intentionality for certain kinds of photography, and some other forms of visual art. In general however, popular common sense says otherwise. And if the makers of the pictures, images, objects, are children, as I said above, the question of intentionality and design becomes contentious.

We have a choice to make: either we accept that makers of signs do so with intent – even if that is not fully overt and articulated by them, and that signs express their interests, complex and difficult to recover fully; or we assume that we live in a world of constant accidents. The choice may be particularly difficult to make with respect to children. However, the examples that I have so far cited in this and in the first chapter, seem to me harder to explain as accidents than as the result of design, deliberation, under-standing, intent. In fact, I find it entirely implausible not to accept that as my working assumption. And all my other examples, which can be multiplied endlessly by observing children everywhere, point in that same direction.

Of course, the corollary of this assumption is that we have to look at these childish productions with entirely new eyes, and with at least the same seriousness which we accord, say, to adults' use of language. Similarly, we will need to revalue the young makers of these objects. But that is my intention in this book.

As a final point here, we need to consider the question of whether we can aid this design, assist it, foster it, direct and channel it, or whether we should leave it unaided, undirected. This goes to the heart of educational politics. The preceding discussion in part provides my answer. In so far as I do think that there is a difference between the physically present object as sign, and the more dis-tantly represented object as sign (a drawing of a car on a sheet of paper, compared to the cut-out car, or the Lego car), and in so far as I think that different forms of cognition and affect are involved in either, my strong preference is for enabling the possibility of each, the availability of the means of producing both kinds of sign (and their many intermediary versions). To that extent at least my preference is for intervention, for aiding and abetting, for making sure that children have to hand what will make that possible.

'MERE COPYING'

Many objects given to children 'for their amusement', toys and games, seem to suggest mere use, rather than transformative action; mere copying, imitation rather than new making. For instance, our children have at different times been given stencils – the outline shape of animals and other objects of assumed interest to them. Or children are given objects which suggest one kind of use only – whether this is a battery-operated toy, or a box with shapes cut in it through which children stick matching shapes.

In my experience, the stencils are not much used by our children. When they *have* been, it is easy to see that mere copying holds only brief attraction. The shapes are traced to be coloured in, in various ways; or the traced shapes are arranged in tableaux where the interest clearly lies in the *arrangement* rather than in its elements. I have some instances of such shapes arranged along a real or imaginary line, possibly suggesting a narrative of some kind: of 'the horse is chasing the car' kind; although I have not tested this.

In the games which children play it is easy to see that all objects, all toys, no matter how seemingly predetermined and limited their assumed mode of use, are immediately integrated into patterns in which they might never have been imagined by their makers. Action-man can appear in an idyllic pastoral scene; teddy bears sit on spaceships – real or imagined. At the moment, there is a felt mat on the floor of our living room, which comes from a particular farmyard setting given to our children about two Christmases ago. Printed on it are roads, fields, fences, a pond, woodlands, grazing animals, farm buildings, and some other things. It is covered with none of the original model animals, vehicles and buildings that it originally had. Instead it has toy cars and trucks of a quite different kind; a plastic tree from somewhere else; the roof sections from another, quite separate farmhouse, assembled here without the walls, as a shed; two soup bowls full of water as watering holes for imported farm animals; two pencils; some sheets of paper; and so on.

The manner in which children assemble materials of all kinds – whether unshaped; shaped for entirely different purposes, such as the Panadol-bubbles; or specifically intended for particular kinds of uses, such as a certain toy – and then integrate them into schemes of their making, transforms all objects, no matter how static, stable, or resistant they may seem. What gets chosen, what gets integrated into what, and how, are subject to the transformative action of child meaning-makers.

As always pressures from outside can and do affect this transformative energy, into the directions of greater conformity. That clearly is another instance where the politics of child-rearing and of education enter into the picture. In my own observation I have no instances of mere copying; and I cannot imagine what they would be.

EXPRESSION IN MANY MODES: SYNAESTHESIA

The force of my argument is to suggest that there are 'best ways' of representing meanings: in some circumstances language may be the best medium; in some a drawing may be; in others colour may be the most apt medium for expression. In all signs which appear as messages in actual situations of communication – as against internal signs, the signs formed in the brain in reading, seeing, feeling or 'just' thinking – many modes of representation are always in use at the same time. Some may, however, be dominant or foregrounded. In a legal document, language seems so obviously the most significant medium that we hardly ever or never attend to typographic features, or to aspects of layout, or to the quality of paper.

But consider the images in Plates 2 and 3. The former was made by a 6-year-old girl, the latter by her 8-year-old brother. Both are 'jokes', the kinds of jokes children love, certain that it is a joke and a tiny bit worried about the reality depicted. The two images are largely means of displaying the iconography of Halloween. It seems clear that colour is one, perhaps *the* major representational factor here: the heavy black of the 8-year-old's image, 'alleviated' only here and there by small splashes of other colour; while the much lighter, brighter oranges, blues, reds, greens, yellows of the 6-year-old's picture signal a totally different 'mood'. Here too interest is coded in a motivated sign – through colour in this case, predominantly. A further point is that the dominant meaning is here expressed certainly not in language, not so much in the drawing, nor in the iconographical elements which are not so dissimilar, but in the medium of colour. This could be translated into language: 'For me Halloween means first and foremost bright colours, candles in bright orange pumpkins, and so on', or 'Halloween, for me, signals a gloomy, a bleak period of the year, and so on.' The joke – which depends on several other aspects of these images – would of course be lost; as would the overall impact.

This is one aspect of a communicational environment in which many media or modes are used simultaneously, with relatively little or no restraint, or constraint to use one rather than another. In that situation the child is able to foreground the medium or the modes which 'feel right', which seem best suited for the purpose. School by contrast encourages the use of language, written language, and more and more so as children get older. But even where a particular medium is favoured, there is constant transition, translation, transduction between different modes – in the brain, even if not necessarily visibly on paper or with other media or modes. It is important to insist on this constant work of translation, transduction, which takes place at a level in the brain beyond easy inspection – although we may 'catch ourselves' at times translating a sound into words, a string of words into colours, a smell into a tactile feeling, and so on. This synaesthetic activity is, it seems, an entirely common human characteristic, much more strongly present for some humans – even as adults – than for others, and seemingly more strongly present for children than for adults. It seems that growing into culture, at least in writing-centred western cultures, is at the same time a process of suppressing these synaesthetic qualities. It seems that we have to learn to forget this ability; it may be that we will now need to relearn it as a socially and economically essential attribute.

What is suppressed is not absent, of course; and in any case for younger children the ability is still more openly available than it is for adults. Figures 2.8 and 2.9 together are an illustration of what I regard this process to be. Figure 2.8 shows, in about half-size, six drawings made by Michael, at the age of 5, each on one page of a small-size notepad taken from the telephone table. The six drawings were therefore on separate bits of paper. They were made without anyone's particular notice; he was then found on the floor in the hallway sorting them into pairs, as in Figure 2.8.

'Me and the dog are in life, so they're in the correct order'

'The flying bomb is in the air and the plane is in the air, so they're in the correct order'

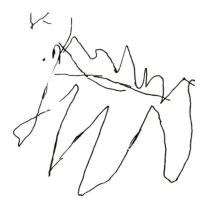

'The patterns are in the correct order'

Figure 2.8 Visual classification

MIC HAEI

Draw a line to join the things which are the same.

Figure 2.9 Physical classification

When asked by his father what he was doing he gave the answers which are the captions to the three pairs of images.

His activity here, once the drawings had been made was, quite clearly, that of classification: sorting the images into appropriate pairs. My assumption is that the drawings were done without the intervention of language; that is, I assume he did not think or say 'I'll make something with such and such subject-matter', nor do I think that language was involved in his classificatory actions, even though a more conventional account might assume this. The cognitive activity of classification proceeded, I assume, in the visual mode alone – until his father came along demanding an explanation, which he gave in language.

Some three weeks later school finished and he brought home some of his school books. It was then that I saw Figure 2.9, done, judging by the date, some three weeks before the drawing at home. Clearly the activity here is also classification: joining like with like. There exists between these two images a long and quite complex chain involving different modes of communication and representation. First, the teacher *speaks*, instructing the class to get out their books; she then tells them what they are to do; the children carry out this physical/cognitive task, tracing the lines connecting the like objects; the teacher then makes further comments; and the books are put aside. That has resulted in Figure 2.9. There follows a period in which there seems a communicational/cognitive silence: nothing seems to be taking place. But then some weeks later, the child makes the drawings of Figure 2.8, and now engages in a much more complex task of classification, taking place at a much greater level of abstraction than in the initial exercise.

What seemed like silence was in fact a period of cognitive activity; and what was at first an action explained in language – though carried out physically – has become an action taking place in a visual/spatial mode, though then explained in language. For me the most crucial point is that cognition has here happened in the visual mode, not in language. Language came in, in this case, only when an explanation was asked for. At that stage, language, acting as a universal communicational solvent, serves to describe, *after the event*, what has taken place.

It is essential to insist on uncoupling the link, in existing common sense, of cognition and language, in which the former is thought to depend on the latter, and not be fully possible without it. The position put forward here is different: all modes enable cognition, or, cognition is possible, takes place in all modes – but differently so. That is the central point: written language enables one form of cognition; drawing another; colour as a medium another; the production of physical objects and their interactive use yet others.

As a last example of this, consider Plate 4. The heading proclaims part of the story: it was drawn three days before the sixth birthday of the maker of this image. An approach which focuses on language alone would need to make reference to the caption alone: 'My birthday is in three days.' The impact of this image comes, however, not from this sparse bit of language, but from the drawing, from the joyful precision of the bow on the wrapped present, and I feel above all, from the exuberant strokes of colour, and this colour-palette itself. This is where the real meaning resides, for the child, in the joy and energy of the splashes of colour, and in the kinds of colour used.

How would *that* meaning be translated?

Chapter 3

Making sense of the world
'The seagulls are reading the newspaper'

SOME CURRENT IDEAS AND DEBATES ABOUT READING

In the kitchen of our house in London we have a print, given to us by friends on our departure from Australia, which shows some crumpled-up newspaper (the *Sydney Morning Herald* in fact) on a green background, with a broad band of yellow colour behind it, and dark blue with dashes of thinnish white lines behind that, to the top of the frame. Several seagulls are hovering above the newspaper, and one has landed on it. The print is titled *Fish and Chips Seagulls.* The title makes perfect sense to us; it codes a (now nostalgic) memory of going in the early evening to Bondi Beach, buying fish and chips wrapped in newspaper, and eating them on the lawn sloping down to the beach, with the overly insistent presence of flocks of seagulls in attendance on any bits of batter, chip, or fish that might be thrown to them. At breakfast one morning our then 3-year-old daughter looked up at the print and said 'The seagulls are reading the newspaper.'

It was a perfectly good reading of the print. Her sudden un-provoked, spontaneous announcement seemed to come for her as a full stop to a period of reflection, puzzlement perhaps. It had the tone of 'I've come to a decision about this.' It seemed that the print had posed a question for her that she needed to resolve – a bit of an otherwise familiar world which needed to be accounted for. The gap between her analysis and our own settled account of the picture points up the issue which has caused much debate: what precisely *is* reading, and how can we make sense of it. Let me then briefly draw out some of the implications of both readings – these are my readings of the readings – and then move on to a slower exploration of this issue.

The child's reading seems to rest on a complex logic something like this: 'The picture means something, it represents something, it communicates something. There is, in the (lower) foreground a bundle of half scrunched up newspaper – that must be the focal element, judging from its placing, here, right in the central foreground. Newspapers are "read", usually by people, but there are no people present, only seagulls, who seem very interested in this newspaper, so much so that one is standing on the paper, and has its head stuck right into the paper: it must be reading it. That's pretty funny, but there we are: the world is a funny place.'

The child's reading – if I have caught some of its elements correctly – is legitimate, in all its complexity: it is based on elements which are actually there in the image. She interprets the placing of the newspaper in the foreground; she infers accurately what newspapers are and what they are used for; and she interprets the indicated action of the only animate, sentient thing there. Animals, she knows from fairy-tales, do act intelligently, often in human-like manner. Just to restate a crucial point: the child's making sense, her reading of the world, is based on elements which are actually there in the image-text. She is entirely justified in her reading. Her reading is fully justified; it is a fully *motivated* reading.

By contrast here is my reading of the picture. It is formed powerfully by visual and other sensory memories of events, which are activated by the picture. I see the newspaper *not* first and foremost as newspaper, but as discarded wrapping for a meal of fish and chips. My memories include the sound of seagulls, the sound of the surf, of distant traffic, of human voices. The foregrounded element for me is a composite one, consisting of the flock of eight seagulls plus the newspaper. My reading – and I am no longer clear whether this forms or formed an initial part of my reading – includes the title *Fish and Chips   Seagulls*. My reading also includes – and this is now at a second level – noticing one of the smaller headlines on the front page, 'Rainforest battle'. The story is not legible, but I take the heading to refer to attempts by people then dismissively described as 'Greenies' to save remaining areas of the Australian rainforest, threatened by the wood-chipping industry, which exports the chipped-up forest trees to Japan for pulping in the paper-making industry. This makes me look again – and reread the tossed away, scrunched up newspaper, and makes me reflect on the ironies of the contemporary world: the thrown-away newspaper reminding me of the ecological problems produced by those who throw away the newspaper needing more paper . . .

The child and I have both produced a complex sign from the initial sign: the signs differ, though both make use of what is *there*, in the picture; and both make use of what is available in memory, in the brain, as cognitive resource, as knowledge, as stored culture – or however one wishes to describe it. It is decidedly not the case that 'we can read anything into a picture' (or a text); quite the opposite: even though the task is dauntingly complex, we can recover quite precisely what has led these two readers to their readings. There is nothing anarchic, wilful or terribly unpredictable about it.

It is also the case that the child's act of reading proceeds in much the same way as mine: the processes are the same. What differs lies in what we each bring to the reading, in the structures which already exist in our brains and in our lives to integrate an event or object and its meaning into. The principles are the same, for all readers: the readings differ. Not, as one kind of current common sense still has it, because we're all individuals and can read anything we want into anything, but rather because we are all individuals with distinct life-histories, which give us different means to bring to our readings. The processes and principles of the act of reading itself are the same.

One question raised by *my* reading, more than by the child's, is that of the limits of reading. Am I still reading this picture when I talk about hearing the sound of the surf, the cry of the seagulls? Neither are there in the picture. And certainly my musings on eco-politics are mine, though I think prompted by the deliberate action of the print-maker. If I think about the warm breezes coming off the ocean, have I gone well beyond the limits of reading this particular image? I'm not sure that there is any satisfactory answer to this, or any real point in searching for one. There are two principles however. One is that reading is sign-making, in which the object which is being read forms the substance of the new sign-making by the reader. In the technical terms introduced in Chapter 1, the text (or other object) which is read provides the 'stuff', the materials, the signifiers, around which the reader makes new signs. The scrunched-up foregrounded newspaper tells both the child-reader and me that this is an element to which particular meaning attaches: what meaning we then each attach to it depends precisely on the factors I have just mentioned. The child's experiences, knowledge *and* interest are different from mine; and so, from the same signifier we make differing signs. That is the first principle.

The second principle is that the boundaries of this sign-making are set by the reader. If from the conjunction of caption, newspaper, sand, ocean I have made a complex sign for myself – internally, silently – I am then able to let that sign act as the prompt for the making of another sign, and so on. This 'chain of signification' has an end when the *reader* decides to end it. The reasons for ending it are of interest in themselves, and as I will point out later in this chapter, have to do with our training as readers. If, for instance, we have been habitually encouraged to end the process of sign-making at a very early stage, we may come to think that it is not legitimate 'to read things into' a text; and that the boundaries of signs are established by the initial maker of the sign, and not to be tampered with by us. So in adult life I may feel uncomfortable about reading a story on the pages of a newspaper in conjunction with another story – or an image – on the same page. These are, however, socially established rules with social/ideological meanings: they can be rethought, and remade.

In current debates these are, broadly speaking, the positions between which the debate moves. They have different kinds of articulation: encoding–decoding for instance, as one view of the writer–reader–text relation, is one which severely limits the freedom of the reader (and in fact, implicitly, that of the writer); or 'interpretation' as another, in which the reader is set free to do as she or he wishes to do with the text.

My own position is as I have set it out above: reading is the making of new signs, by the reader, internally, silently. These signs are, like those made outwardly, *motivated* conjunctions of forms and meanings, and it is this which in fact provides a guiding principle for the reader in attempting to establish the meaning of the text. This search, as with outwardly made signs also, is guided by the reader's interest. Reading is a contested activity socially, and inevitably theories of different kinds develop around it, theories which are themselves social and cultural metaphors, which lead to prohibition, circumscription, concession, around the processes of reading. As always, there are choices to be made here. My guiding principle is: what kind of reader do we want to produce, and for what and whose ends?

HOW CAN WE GET EVIDENCE FOR READING?

Reading seems particularly prone to calling forth the bizarre in the field of theorization. I recall my first encounter with this when I took a job in what had been a teacher-training college in the late 1970s, and one of my new colleagues introduced me to a theory (?) called 'direct accessing'. This involved – and I know it only from his demonstration – sitting next to child-readers and shouting the words they were reading into their ear – I don't remember whether the left or the right, though I do remember it had to be the correct one in order to access, directly, the appropriate hemisphere in the brain.

The problem with reading more than with writing seems to be that something really important is going on, and we can't see any part of it. And so there are countless videos in which an attempt is made to see what readers are doing when they read. Of course there are as many videos looking over the shoulders of children to see what is happening in writing. Recordings track the extent of vocalization or subvocalization during reading, as means of showing the relation between spoken and written language: 'Are readers treating written language as speech written down?', 'Do they need a vocal implementation to aid their comprehension?', and so on.

Evidence for the processes and effects of reading remains indirect. Given that direct inspection is impossible, all we can obtain is better indirect evidence on which to base our speculations. My own attempts to get evidence are based on the assumptions which I outlined in the previous section: if reading is sign-making, which itself leads to new sign-making, then if we look at these newly made signs we might get an insight into what the reader did in making the initial signs in readings. Most or much of that sign-making is silent: the 'daydreaming' that leads me from looking at the scrunched-up newspaper to imagining the warm breezes coming off the sea at Bondi Beach is an example. But quite often the chain of sign-making quickly becomes external. I might get a note, at work; I need to respond quickly, and I do. That response is close to my initial reading, and so is more likely to capture 'what sense I made' of that note initially, than if my response had been delayed by a day or so, giving me time to travel along the chain of signification, or, to put it in ordinary parlance, giving me more time for reflection.

And so the evidence for reading which I have begun to attend to is this: the outwardly visible signs made by readers as soon as possible following their reading. Of course, this is using 'reading' as a metaphor – at this point anyway – for 'making sense of the world'. So for instance, when at breakfast our 3-year-old, looking at a small piece of toast I'm holding between thumb and forefinger says 'You made it like a crocodile', I feel justified in assuming that she had just 'taken in' the shape of that piece of toast; assumed that I had wanted to make it into a meaningful object (leaving aside for the moment that she is probably having a little joke with me); and has made her interpretation, her new – externalized – sign. This seems very good evidence for 'reading'. In the next section there is a more detailed look at a few examples, largely to give some substance to this idea, and to suggest how it may be used as a means for thinking about, describing, and documenting the processes of sign-making which reading is.

My interest at this point is in reading in an extended, metaphoric sense, as 'making sense of the world', both because it is an essential issue, and because it is necessary in order for us to understand 'reading' in the stricter sense of reading language in its written form. So the evidence will be somewhat wider than 'print'. But we cannot hope to understand the reading of 'print' by looking at that alone. At the same time, I will confine myself at this point to two-dimensionally expressed representations, acknowledging that that is a significant limitation. Two mistakes should be avoided. One is the assumption that in reading we deal with units all of one kind, of one size, at one level alone (that is, with letters, or with words, or with sentences, or with 'stories'). The other is the assumption that reading is bounded by the prior decisions of the maker of the initial sign – whether the novelist, the sub-editor in charge of the layout of a newspaper page, or whoever. Reading is the action of a reader: the actions of writers in their prior writing are significant but not decisive.

WHAT IS READING? SOME PRINCIPLES

Figure 3.1 shows the early writing of a 4-year-old girl. It is possible to discern attempts at writing LOVE, and, given that I know the context, I am fairly certain that there is an attempt to write LOLA, the name of her friend. The sign that interests me is the sign in the bottom left-hand corner. The child had asked me to write

Figure 3.1 'Thank you'

thank you for her, so that she could write it herself on a card for her friend. My hastily – and as it turns out, thoughtlessly written, *thank you* is produced here. The child took that away, and then returned excitedly, saying 'Look, I've done it.'

What is it that she had done? She had looked at the parent's sign, and had attempted to analyse it, to make sense of it: clearly there were a number of elements here, so one task was to identify these elements. How do you identify elements? It seems that you work, first, on the assumption that there is a logic in the making of signs, and that that logic broadly is that of the motivated relation between meaning and form. The 'meaning' in this case is 'integral element', and the formal means of expression of that meaning is, she assumed, that things which are closely connected are part of one integral element. Hence her elation at producing the novel letter/unit that she produced. The second assumption, therefore, is that formal organization (in this case, the connected-ness of lines) mirrors the organization of meaning (in this case the coherence of the elements).

Both these principles are, I believe, correct, and are correctly applied by this child. The problem in this case was the parent's lack of attention to this reader's situation. That is, the parent did not consider the child-reader's position in making this sign: for instance, the fact that she did not at that stage know letter-shapes, and could not know the principles of 'joined-up writing'. I would certainly complain if I had asked someone to teach me Arabic script and that person proceeded as I had done here. Having once undertaken that task I am aware how one attributes meaning to every squiggle, every line, many of which may be entirely marginal for the practised writer. This sort of inattention is a mistake which is entirely common, but one for which the child is of course not to be held responsible.

The parent's attention was focused on a unit of a different kind, a different size: the phrase *thank you*, and not on the units which the child was focused on, the elements/letters which make up that phrase. For the parent *thank you* exists as a single unit, or at least does so unless some good reason exists for that not to be the case. In other words, for both parent and child, writer and reader, the logic and the principles were right; but each was applying the right logic and principles to different types of units, to differently sized units, and to units of a different kind. The child was applying the principles to the unit 'letters', and the adult was applying them to the unit 'phrase'. That of course is an entirely usual situation in writing and reading, at least in part captured by exhortations such as: 'Keep the needs of your audience in mind.'

Nevertheless, even in this slight example, we can see the large theoretical conflicts in reading theory: between proponents of a view of reading as establishing correspondence between letter and sound (in this instance, that is close to the child's position), and those who see reading as making sense of larger level units, 'whole units of language'. My example illustrates that both are right, both are needed, though at different times, and for different purposes. Parent and child, as much as the two distinct theories, are focused on objects of quite different kind.

Before I restate the principles so far established, let me draw attention to a further issue brought up clearly by this example. Whatever it is that the child did in reading (and then reproducing) the letters in the parent's model, it was not mere copying. That would have led to a reproduction of all the joined elements in that initial sequence, the capital T and H joined together; nor is her new 'letter' an exact copy even of that part of the model which it

draws on most – the cross-bar on the T in the model is not copied
in the child's letter. The activity is not one of 'copying' in any sense
(for instance, 'acquiring', as in 'language acquisition'). The action
is one of perception, and then of transformation – the making of
a new sign. I will return to this point in more detail in the next
chapter; though even here we can see 'experimentation', transformation, with the letter *E*, for instance. The fact that the child's
new letter *TH* will not survive for long (though the various forms
of *E* persist for quite some time) is, from this point of view, beside
the point.

The principles for reading established so far are these:

1 Things which are closely connected in form (and/or materially)
  are connected in meaning: formal/material connectedness
  'means' coherence in meaning.
2 Formal/material organization mirrors the organization of meaning – that is, form is a good guide, the best guide to meaning
  available. Both of these exist within the overarching principle of
  (1).
3 Signs are produced out of the sign-maker's interest, as an
  expression of that interest. What the child reads and then
  expresses as a new sign is not, therefore, some abstractly or
  generally inherent characteristic of a text or of some object, but
  of those features which *the child-reader* considers as criterial at
  that moment.

In considering the next few examples I will focus on this aspect:
what is it that the child reader seems to have seen as the criterial
aspects or features of the text or object that was read?

To start with a relatively simple example (Figure 3.2). The child
(3 years and 3 months old) said, when he had drawn the picture
on the right of Figure 3.2: 'That's a ghost.' As we had quite
recently looked at and read him the book *Scary Story Night*, the
figure on the left (a traced version of the ghost-figure early in
the story) may have served as the model – though as a clichéd
version of ghost drawings it is pretty well ubiquitous in drawings
for children. The replicated figure suggests that the features which
the child regarded as criterial were the overall shape of the figure
of the ghost, and a reproduction of the protruding eyes. Whether
the pointed bottom of the child's ghost figure was a deliberate or
an accidental feature is impossible to establish; though intent has
to be kept as a possibility here; as perhaps it does in the case of

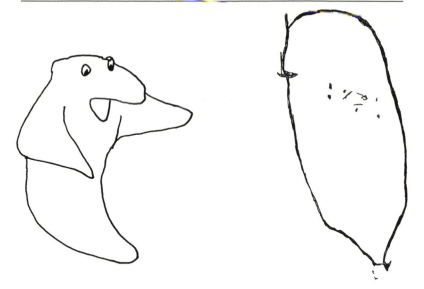

Figure 3.2 Ghosts
Source: Rob Lewis, *Scary Story Night*, Hemel Hempstead: Simon & Schuster, 1990, p. 8.

the backward-leaning angle of the figure, which is also a feature of the original. The 'eyes', if that is what they are, have become more central in the child's drawing, so that their visual salience through blackness in the original may here be being signalled by *centrality* as an indicator of salience.

These are the features which can give an indication of the child's interest in his reading of this (part of the) text: this is what seems most prominent about ghostness – or, at any rate, that is how he has transformed the idea of 'ghost' for himself. In this example, a relatively early instance in this child's figurative/representative drawing, there is of course the question of his representational abilities: he is able to do certain kinds of things – for instance to produce circular shapes (witness the example of the 'car' in Chapter 1, Figure 1.1) with certain additional features. There are no doubt real limitations on what he can do; though it needs to be said that that applies to all makers of all representations – adult or child, amateur or professional.

In the next example, Figure 3.3, the interest is different – it arises from the children's own concerns, and as a response to the kind of text being read. Here the children are reproducing an

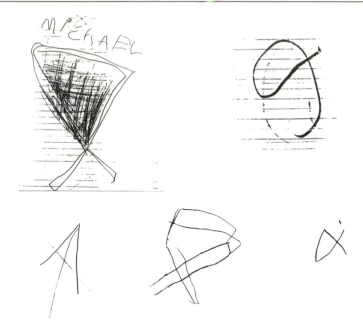

Figure 3.3 Tubular Bells

icon from the cover of a CD of Mike Oldfield's *Tubular Bells*. The three representations on the left are made by a 6½-year-old; the one on the right by his sister, then 4 years and 3 months old. The 6-year-old produced a whole series of these designs, all of them documenting his interest in this shape; as does his sister's reproduction. However, while her interest seems to be with the basic shape, his goes beyond that to wider aspects of 'design' – how to represent the three-dimensional appearance of the original, how to represent the twisting tube effect of the model; and how to use shading to produce effect. His interests are wider, and perhaps more intense: she may have produced her representation in a relatively casual fashion, doing it only because it interested her brother.

In Figure 3.4 there is also a contrast of interest. Figure 3.4a is drawn by a 6½-year-old, about a month before *Tubular Bells*. Figure 3.4b is drawn by his sister, at the age of 3 years and 10 months, but this time, on quite separate occasions, with no influence by one child on the other. Over two days the 6-year-old drew a series of hedgehogs, and in each case it seemed to be the basic shape which

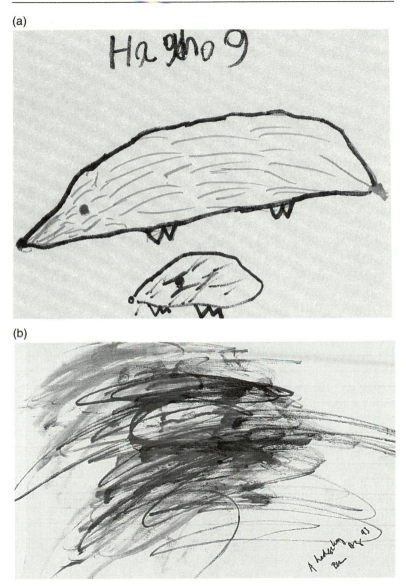

Figure 3.4 Hedgehog (a) and Bad Hedgehog (b)

was of most interest to him. He drew the shape first; in some cases, as here, he then filled it in with spikes; in others he drew the shape, indicated a snout and eyes; indicated legs and a tail in some cases, not in others; and left the drawings at that. Clearly the shape as such interested him most, though the spikes were clearly of interest too. Some of the shapes are more elongated, others more rounded and dumpy. As far as the spikes are concerned, the drawing gives the impression (and the evidence here is length of stroke; directionality, from left to right, slightly curved) of interest in the technical aspects of doing them. They seem executed, in all the instances I have, with great exuberance.

His sister's hedgehogs (she did two: a 'good hedgehog' and a 'bad hedgehog', the latter is shown here) made when she was 3 years and 10 months old, focus not so much on shape, but on the furry, spikey, spiney characteristics of this ball-animal. Shape is discernible – a kind of slightly distorted semicircular blob, like half an orange squashed out of shape; but that shape is established as an effect of the drawing of the spikeyness and furryness of this creature. Both children are *aware* of shape. For the 5-year-old, shape as an abstracted notion is prior, the centre of his interest; spikes are then indicated, in forceful, energetic, yet also intensely abstracted, strokes. What is represented is an abstracted, indicated spikeyness. For the 3-year-old the tactile characteristics of the hedgehog are prior, the centre of her interest; shape emerges as an effect of the concentration on representing these tactile characteristics, it is immanent in the object as a whole. The difference between bad and good hedgehog seems to be indicated mainly by the colour scheme: deep blues, pinks, yellow, green, orange for the bad hedgehog; and a light orangey-brown with a very little green for the good hedgehog. The bad hedgehog is drawn with larger, bolder, more energetic strokes than the good one.

It seems clear to me that there are distinctly different interests at work here: the tendency towards the abstraction of shape as against the interest in (the representation of) tactile characteristics; the exploration of aspects of design in the case of Figure 3.2, as against a relatively marginal interest (on this occasion) in basic shapes. The questions raised by this involve issues such as 'development', and gendered interests, among others, and I will discuss these later. However, while I draw attention to the possible limitations of 'ability' in the case of the 'ghost' (Figure 3.2) I am most reluctant to make too much of that factor; for one thing it is too readily used as a means of dismissing, ignoring, overlooking the real representational abilities of children at all ages. The child who drew the bad hedgehog at 3 years and 3 months is the child who drew the model of the skeleton of the *Tyrannosaurus rex* (Figure 4.7) some three months earlier. The powers of concentration, the control, the attention displayed in that drawing are such as to make me unwilling to talk too much about lack of ability.

Although I promised to confine myself in this chapter to the reading of two-dimensional objects and texts, I do wish, briefly, to stray into the readings of films and videos. Among the drawings and paintings in 'my collection' there are some made as a response to the watching of a film or of a video at home. There is, for instance, a fine drawing done in coloured pens of the 'King's servant', a bird from the film *Lion King*. It was done when the child came back in the afternoon from watching the film. It is magnificently coloured and though I haven't seen the film myself, I imagine that it must be an impressive character in the film. I am interested in two things in particular: how can one, or how does a child-viewer, condense the meaning of a whole film into an image? Second, I am interested in the fact that the signs produced as a result of reading a film tend to be poster-like displays. Whether the child is here reproducing either the genre of 'cover' on the video tape, or the advertising poster of the film, I am not sure. In any case, what is produced tends to lead the child to *design* a display which covers all the space available, that is, a whole page.

The image reproduced in Plate 5 was made after seeing the film *Jurassic Park*. The then 6-year-old designer produced the 'poster' without prompting. It shows a diplodocus poking its head up from the bottom of the frame, a stegosaurus walking across the middle background, somewhat higher up, in front of a rainbow and some tropical plants. The task here facing the child is to condense the meaning of the film, to produce his sign of the film (his sister who saw the film at the same time and who was less scared by the variously frightening scenes did not produce any images as a result of seeing the film) from the point of view of his interest. But the task is also, it seems, to produce a design which fully and satisfactorily uses the space which the page makes available.

To me this seems particularly interesting, in relation to the learning of writing, as indeed in a much more general way. Writing demands a range of skills to do with display, spatial design, spatial orientation, and so on, nearly all of which go unrecognized in discussions of the learning of writing. The significance of the page as a (visual) unit in written texts as much as in overtly visual texts is hardly discussed, but it is of fundamental importance for full control of writing. Consequently, the knowledge gained in the making of images of this kind cannot be overestimated. This is so for writing in its conventional sense, but it is vastly more important as visual forms of communication are becoming a central feature of the communicational landscape, where written language is already playing a far less central role than it did even twenty years ago. As texts draw more and more overtly on visual means of communication, the skills and knowledges of visual design and display will need to be fostered as a central part of any literacy curriculum.

To summarize briefly at this point: reading is the making of signs, 'internally'. The reader takes the form of the text (including highly complex texts such as films) as guides to the meanings of the maker of the sign; form mirrors meaning, form and meaning are entirely connected, one as the expression of the other. These are principles employed by readers in their making sense of the world of meaning. Reading is not simply the assimilation of meaning, the absorption or acquisition of meaning as the result of a straightforward act of decoding. Reading is a transformative action, in which the reader makes sense of the signs provided to her or to him within a frame of reference of their own experience, and guided by their interest at the point of reading. The transformative action of internal sign-making in reading is shaped by the sign that is read, but is not determined by it. The boundaries to the act of reading/transformation, to the making of new, further internal signs are set by readers, out of their interest. The transformative action of reading includes the processes of abstraction and condensation. Lastly, the question of what is taken as a sign to be read is also largely under the control of the readers, guided by their interest.

READING AND THE CONTEXT OF CULTURE

Nevertheless, from another perspective, what is there to be read is provided by a particular culture, or by a group of cultures in one society. As the form of the object to be read is one of the crucially important aspects of reading, what is available or is made available for children to read is highly significant. So far I have focused largely on children's interest in their reading. But it is the cultural environment which determines what is available; what is available is laden with the meanings of that culture. Making sense of the world happens in a world already laden with sense.

Before turning to a discussion of texts/objects quite directly 'within' literacy, I would like to explore briefly the question of how the shape of the cultural environment shapes the interest, and hence the actions, of child-readers. My two examples come from early stages of a child's engagement with writing (Figure 3.5). One is writing in an alphabetic culture, the other is writing in an ideographic or logographic culture – namely Chinese. The 'writers' were both 3½ years of age.

As with all texts/objects, the children in their engagement with writing have to uncover for themselves the deep logic of each script. In the case of the girl learning alphabetic writing, several elements of the logic she has uncovered in her reading of print seem to me to be apparent in her outwardly made sign: this thing is linear; it has elements in sequence; the elements are connected; the elements are relatively simple shapes; they are repeatable. However implicitly this is learned, these seem to be the most fundamental aspects of writing that she has deduced from the models that she has seen. Of course, this is not the settled truth for her – these signs are subject of constant transformation, just as much as the arrangements of cushions, blankets, dolls, on the floor. But it seems the truth for the moment, and aspects of it will no doubt stay with her. Further, in fact incessant, analytic activity will change this constantly.

In the case of the girl learning logographic or ideographic writing another logic seems to be learned here. Again there is linearity; there are elements in sequence; the elements are not connected; the elements are in themselves complex shapes; they seem not to be repeated, each element seems distinctly different. As a logic about the deep meaning of written language, about writing, it is fundamentally different. I assume, though this is at this stage mere speculation by me, that the two logics have the most far-reaching consequence for notions of what language is, and what writing does. I will return to this issue in Chapter 4, though I will say here that it seems to me that the path of ideographic writing accords entirely with the meaning-making of children at this stage – the making of visual signs which directly represent the

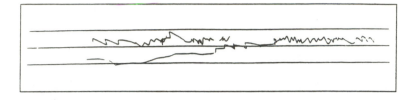

Figure 3.5 Alphabetic and pictographic writing

ideas that are of interest to them. With the increasing and rapid turn to visual communication this is also the more likely path for future forms of public communication.

However, at this stage my main point is a different one: we have here two 3½-year-old girls, one in England and one in Taiwan. Their daily experiences are set in quite distinct cultures, and their practices are shaped by what is normal in these cultures. Their *interests* are shaped by their culture. My two examples show, force-fully I think, how the already shaped cultural world shapes the interested engagement of children with their world. Both girls are keen to engage with the shapes of their culture: that is a shared interest. But that already shaped culture takes them, even at this early stage, in entirely different directions.

This is of fundamental importance. It describes and defines quite precisely the age-old debate about individual creativitiy and social determination. Both children are creative, transformative, in relation to the forms of their culture; although the early writing of children learning alphabetic writing looks recognizably similar, yet this one sign/example is unique, none exactly like it exists, I am sure. I feel equally certain that this is so for the Taiwanese girl's writing. It too, I feel certain, is unique; and will be recognizably similar to other writing by children in Taiwan of that age. The culture shapes interest, and it provides already shaped objects for that interest to work with. In working with these already shaped objects, children, like all makers of signs, are constantly innovative, creative, transformative.

As a further example of 'what is there to be read', consider the newspaper front page, produced by a 4-year-old girl (Figure 3.6). The text of the paper, read by her to her father, is 'In John Prince's Street someone got dead.' On the one hand I am interested to see what a 4-year-old thinks a newspaper is; what her 'reading' of the genre of newspaper is. In particular I am interested in knowing whether she makes a distinction between drawing and writing, between print and image. My hunch is that she does not; I do not think that it occurs to her to think: I'll first do some writing and then illustrate it with some drawing, or the other way round. I imagine that she is drawing both the print and the image; or writing both print and image. It is probably not a distinction that is sensible to her. In that she both exemplifies the normal disposition of a child of her age in our western cultures, and she prefigures accuratedly the state of public communication in the decades to come.

It is essential to become fully aware of this. We live in a world in which communication proceeds (as it has in many ways always done) in many modes, with language as writing becoming less dominant than it has been in many areas of public communication. Thinking and practices around literacy need to adjust to this fact, and become appropriate for the demands and needs of the children who will move into that new communicational landscape.

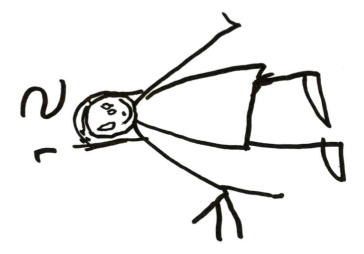

Figure 3.6 Newspaper: 'In John Prince's Street someone got dead'

WHAT DOES *READING* MEAN? A BRIEF HISTORY OF THE WORD

Ethelred the Unready is one of the unjustly maligned figures of history. His error was not that he was unprepared for the trouble he had to meet, as current myth has it; it was rather that he was un- or ill-advised. That, at any rate, is the etymology of the *-read-* in *unready*. Its contemporary German equivalents are *Rat* (said with a 'long *a*') as in advice, but also *raten* as in 'guessing', 'puzzling something out'. One of its few remaining English relatives – the unfortunate Ethelred apart – is the *rid-* in *rid-dle*, whose contemporary German cousin is *Rätsel*, something (often slightly mysterious) that needs explaining. The Anglo-Saxon form was *raedan*, 'to discern, advise, read'. We are therefore justified, I think, in taking a broad view of the meaning and the practice of reading. Our ancestors did, more than three thousand years ago, and there seems no good reason why we should be so timid or so backward as to ignore their wisdom and insight. One final word on Ethelred the Unready, who perhaps did deserve his fate: the *-red* in his first name also means 'advice'; the *Ethel-* means 'noble'. He had, it seems, everything going for him; and yet he threw it all away.

And so, with that as my justification I will turn to discussing my last example in this chapter, Plate 6. It was produced by an 8-year-old Nigerian boy, who had at that stage been in England for one year. His teacher had read the class the story of Snow White; he had then asked them to write the story and to draw a picture. As with the picture of *Jurassic Park*, this is a demand to condense the meaning of the story into a single sign – even though the production of his written version allows the child to be more specific in the drawing. At any rate, I have never seen a picture of the Wicked Queen that looked anything like this. In terms of the approach that I have tried to outline here, my explanation of this child's reading is something like this. He hears a story, from a still strange culture, in spoken language. He makes sense of it in terms of the resources available to him, which are at this stage still largely those of the Nigerian culture from which he comes, and in which he lived the first seven years of his life. Those resources include narratives and images, practices and experiences of a diverse kind, and are quite distinct from those of the English classroom in which he finds himself now.

All this – the teacher's story, the child's resources, the teacher's demand, the child's wish to respond – all determine his interest at this point. Out of that interest he constructs his interpretations, his readings, as sets of internal signs, and from these he constructs his new sign, externally – creative and transformative, yet working with the shaped resources of two cultures. The new sign has 'translated' a text which he received through spoken language into two new media, each distinct in its own possibilities for making meaning: written language, and the image reproduced here. This transduction is an entirely usual, normal, characteristic part of the full processes of reading, even though it happens invisibly in the brain. It may be one of the most crucial of all the cognitive and affective aspects of the processes of reading. For me this image is a potent metaphor of reading, and of its constant creative, transformative actions. It shows us clearly how the reading-riddle is solved, by all of us, always; and the innovative action of doing so.

Chapter 4

Drawing letters and writing dinosaurs
Children's early engagement with print

MAKING PATHS INTO WRITING

Most parents follow their children's gradual entry into the world of print with a mixture of delighted fascination and terror. Seeing, close up, the intensely energetic, innovative, creative path which any one child makes for itself into that mysterious world which adults seem to value so much, cannot fail to produce wonder and delight. But terror is ever present, for failure looms in so many forms. Now that the child has learned to speak – and at what age did your children utter their first words, were they late (developers), or early? Did their progress match the charts provided by helpful experts? Did they fall behind or did they do far better? – now comes this new terror: will she or he learn to read and write at all, will they be slow, fall behind, or make you feel pleased at their startling progress? In England the National Curriculum now makes specific demands: at the age of 7, for instance, a child must understand what a sentence is. (Do *you* know what a sentence is?)

Fortunately nearly all children find their way into and through the maze of print and solve the mysteries of alphabetic writing, even if a disappointingly large number decide for a range of social and cultural reasons not to continue, to give up at some later stage. Their achievement is astonishing because, it has to be said, we know very little indeed about the real problems and cognitive challenges which alphabetic writing presents to someone who first learns it. This seems an outrageous statement, given first and foremost the enormous dedication and wealth of practical experience of teachers in the early years of schooling. It also seems to slight the massive amount of research carried out in various forms of psychology on this matter. But the practical experience of teachers remains just that: teachers do not have the time (and often not the inclination) to engage in a theoretical articulation of their experience: they know what they know; they pass it on to younger colleagues in myriad ways in which informal knowledge has always been passed on, whether between professionals as in this case or as the knowledge of everyday life – through talk, demonstration, anecdote, materials loaned, observation of teaching, and so on.

Given my outrageous statement, my first task here is to show just what complexity resides in the mysteries of print – because it is as *print* rather than as handwriting that children first encounter language – and what kinds of things we need to begin to ask questions about, where at the moment no questions seem to be being asked.

WHAT'S IN A NAME? PRINT AS A COMPLEX SYSTEM OF SIGNS

Like many parents, I was fascinated by how our children learned to write their names. The name, it seems, provides a particular challenge, motivation, mystique for the child: this is a bit of writing in which they are positively interested. So there is no lack of enthusiasm for writing it, no lack of energy, and boundlessly many opportunities. Names can be written by themselves, providing endless fascination, and in a society in which ownership, possession, is crucial, it is especially often written *on* something, with something, to show who did it, owns it, or who should be its owner.

In Figure 4.1 is a sequence which traces one child's constant practice, experimentation, and new shaping. It is clear to me that this is *creative* activity, transformation, and not, decidedly not, copying. There is no question of lack, error, of 'not yet good enough'; the task is to understand, by retracing it, what principles the child has brought to bear, and are at work, what processes of analysis have been applied.

This sequence spans a period of just over one year, from November 1993 to December 1994 (from the age of 4 years to 5 years and 1 month). Emily's writing of her name, over that period, represents, as I suggested in Chapter 3, her *reading* of her name. The changes recorded here are therefore the continuously new signs which she produces as a result of her transformative action in reading. Each reading, it seems, produces a slightly different analysis, which leads to new ways of writing her name. Each new

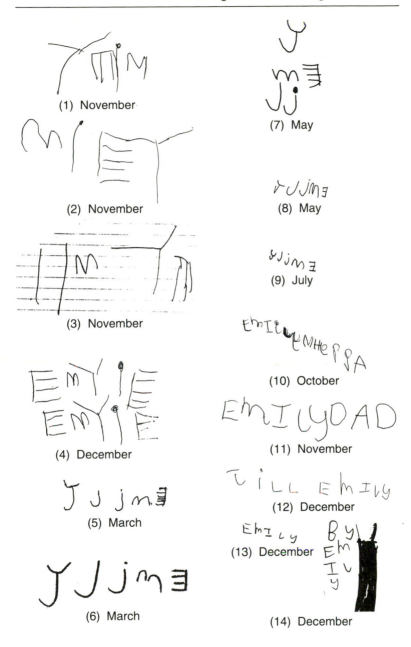

(1) November

(2) November

(3) November

(4) December

(5) March

(6) March

(7) May

(8) May

(9) July

(10) October

(11) November

(12) December

(13) December

(14) December

Figure 4.1 'Emily'

way of writing represents the insights she gained from her preceding analysis, represents therefore a change in her knowledge. Of course, and this is crucial, these writings (as are the readings) are also the product of affect; her enthusiasm and involvement is coded as much in her writing of her name, or of individual letters in it, as it is coded in the drawing 'My birthday' (Plate 4). And just as in her drawing of the camel (Figure 2.3) her excitement – 'A camel has that much humps' she said, holding up four fingers, with her thumb tucked in – is coded in the exuberantly excessive number of humps, so it may well be that her affective interest is coded in the exuberantly excessive number of bars which characterize her early forms of the capital letter E. But, and this is an important 'but', the bars on the E are quite likely to code her interest in 'numerosity': an instance which might tell us that it is impossible to separate affect and cognition.

So let me begin with that. It is a question which preoccupies her for six months at least. The important point is: what has she 'read'? Has she read something like 'There are many bars on the letter E, coming off from the longer line', in the way in which in many counting systems still in use in the world there are three number terms: one, two, many? Has she been satisfied by representing 'many' as an accurate representation of reality – as would someone in the counting system with three terms? Or has she simply not been interested enough to be precise at this point, recognizing that there were many, but not fussed about accuracy – as when the police are asked to estimate the size of crowds at a rally or demonstration? Or is it an expression of exuberance, of affect – as when I say, 'Yes, yes, yes, yes' to a suggestion that is particularly pleasing to me?

It is impossible to know; but we do know that she never has fewer than three bars, she is precise about the fact that there are no fewer than three, so there is imprecision in one direction only. She clearly has a quite specific meaning. In the absence of certainty we can do two things: insist that there is a meaning (somewhere around 'many'), which is supported by the fact that she never has fewer than three; and that that meaning represents her interest. Both force us to enquire further.

In the first three drawings of her name a number of issues seem to preoccupy her: (a) How many elements are there in my name? (b) What is their shape? (c) What is their spatial orientation? (d) What is their size? And (e) the issue of sequence of the elements, their order(ing)? The answer to the first question (a) is: either four or five. The answer to (b) will take much longer to be developed; in fact it has no answer in a real sense; it has an answer only in a conventional sense, namely that adults in the world around her will be satisfied at a certain point, not far removed from the form she produced in December 1994. In a real sense, she still has not stopped 'experimenting' now, a year on, even though adults around her may lose interest in that form of experimentation, which may seem 'merely stylistic'. The issue of spatial orientation (c) (which way is 'up' for *E,* for instance?) is settled, for *E* as for the other letters, by the following month.

There is a point which arises here: what is it that makes spatial orientation easier to settle for the child, than the shape of the letters ('How many bars on the *E*?') or of other factors? Is it a simple matter? More obvious? Less open to experimentation, clearer to read in one way only? I have no answers, but I think that this opens up very important general questions about writing, reading, perception, creativity, which apply much later on just as much as they do here, although perhaps not quite so visibly.

The fourth question, that of size (d), seems not to prove very problematic for the child. This is interesting in one way because even when she writes her name on unlined paper she is able to keep the size of the letters in approximately the right proportions to each other. The order of sequence of elements (e) is, similarly, not such a big problem, from the evidence here. It is solved by March, considerably earlier than the letter-shape, which is settled by May. I am somewhat puzzled by this: on the face of it it should be quite difficult to sort out such a relatively complex thing. (How long does it take you to remember another or a new identification number for one of your credit cards; have you ever managed to forget it, or to get the sequence mixed up?) Two possibilities suggest themselves to me; and both may in fact apply. One is that she remembers her name as a Gestalt, as a whole entity. The other is that she associates letters with sounds, and that she therefore *matches* letter-sequence to sound-sequence, matches the Gestalt of the letter-shape to the Gestalt of the sound-shape of her name. This speculation may provide us with a crucial clue about how a child can make an inroad into the connection between the visual shape of a letter, and the oral shape of a sound. The Gestalt of the sound-shape of her name, it may be, provides a mnemonic for the Gestalt of the letter-shape of her name.

So several questions are posed by the child and are answered quite quickly; with differing implications. Some questions remain, and new ones are opened up by the next sequence, the twice written name, in December 1993 (4). (The two shapes were drawn together, in the way shown here.) The two new questions opened up here are, a question (f) around directionality, and the question which seemed not an issue in November, (g) what exactly are the elements? In November the five letters of her name are established; in December the *l* is missing, replaced by a repeated *E.* The issue is not, obviously, about the number of letters, there are five here, but about *what* they are. Again we can speculate about the repeated letter. Is it aesthetic or affective considerations – either it looks good to finish this way; or, it gives a completed look; or, 'I'll have an *E* twice as it defines my name' which led her to this? Sequence is settled, even if 'wrongly' at this stage: both forms have the same sequence.

The other new question is that of *directionality*: while the sequence of the letters was an issue in November – 'Is it *Y E I M, M I E Y,* or *L I M Y E,* or does it matter anyway, as long as I've got all the elements here?' – now it is settled. The sequence is *E M Y I E,* and it is written from *left to right.* Directionality stays as an issue for the next ten or eleven months, in one form or another. In the sequences from March until October, she decides to write from right to left. This decision is, in one sense, doubly surprising: having made the 'right' decision about directionality earlier, she then changes it; and as a left-handed writer (then as now, at the age of 6), it might seem easier, more 'natural', to write from left to right.

Again, it might be said that these are 'accidents'. I find that a deeply unsatisfactory approach, for it tells us nothing; it actually prevents thought and analysis on our part, and prevents us from understanding the child's intelligent activity, and her cognitive *work.* For another thing, it is an accident that befalls very many children in alphabetic cultures. That of course could be linked to 'development', either directly through a Piagetian account, of the 'unfolding' of cognitive/mental stages, or to other forms of mental development. Again, it tells us very little: it forecloses further inquiry. It is also the case that these are accidents, or developmental stages, not experienced by all children, even in alphabetic cultures.

The 'accidental' account, and I think the 'developmental' one also, are ruled implausible by several factors. One, the issue of directionality affects not only the whole block of letters, the letter Gestalt, it works more subtly. Second, directionality, sequence and linearity, which are all closely related phenomena, are treated as entirely discrete matters by this child. Together these should force us to think that one plausible explanation is that there are particular kinds of logic at work here, kinds of thinking which we may understand in part already, and others that we have no real idea about – yet.

To deal with directionality first. When Emily decides to move from a left-to-right writing direction to a right-to-left one as in the examples from March 1994, this affects not only the sequence of letters, it affects the individual letter-shapes as well. So the 'flicks' on the bottom of the *i*, and *l*, 'should' go to the right, if they were written 'correctly'. But the principle she applies is clearly an over-riding one here – 'one thing to the left, everything to the left' might be the slogan, at this stage at least. This happens even when linearity is ignored, as in the first of the two examples from May 1994 (7). The direction is still right to left. In the example from October 1994 (10) she has made the decision to change directionality (though she still writes left-handedly), for letter-shapes and for letter-sequence. The 'flicks' on the *l* and the *y* now go to the right, even though this is 'wrong' in the case of the *y*. By November, directionality is beginning to be settled; for both letter-shapes and letter-sequence (11). The 'flicks' go where they should, and the words are written from left to right. This clearly needs to be settled finally, as an issue for each instance, and so in the example from December 1994 the capital *J* is still pointing right (12). The second December example (13) convinces me that she now has this issue fully sorted out. Again, as in the example from May (7), linearity is ignored (because there was a painting of a candle on the right which blocks the space, a similar situation as happened in May, where there was a drawing to the left), but sequence *and* directionality is preserved: the writing-sequence is left to right for the *By*, for the first two letters of *Emily*, *Em* for the next two letters, *il*, underneath, and in an imagined continued sequence, for the last letter *y*. All the 'flicks' go in the right direction.

It may be that when she initially switches from the left-to-right to the right-to-left directionality that that happens because direction isn't something that bothers her as a factor. If that is the case we know that when she changes back, to the 'right' order it *is* something that she has focused on. In either case, there are things to be recognized here, and understood.

My second point is about the separateness of linearity, sequence, and directionality. In the first March example (5), even if not in the December 1993 one (4), she has established the sequential order of the letters. And that sequence stays. The examples of May (7) and December (14) may suggest that this is not so; in fact they demonstrate that sequence is absolutely established, and not just as a specific concrete feature; it is now a cognitive fact. Both are written in the sequence *E m i l y*. In the May example she went below the line for *i, l*, and then, as there was no further space below that, above the initial *E, m*, to write the *y*. And the same happened with the December example. 'Sequence' exists now, for her, as an abstract cognitive/conceptual category: its 'mere' implementation on a page is, very nearly, an incidental matter.

My arguments about directionality are exactly the same. Right-to-left or left-to-right are established in the May and the December examples as abstract cognitive/conceptual categories; the fact that she has to start several times (three times in May, four times in December) in the direction she wants to go, simply illustrates how firmly *and abstractly* this is established.

There are issues of style that might be discussed: for instance, why does she put that 'stick' on her *m*s from October (10) on (a fashion which persisted for another year!). These issues should be explained in the same terms as I have attempted here: 'style', in other words, is not an explanation. Is that stick a question of 'affect', another way for her to assert her identity?

But I want to conclude this section with two other comments. One is to point to the complexity of factors involved, most of which are generally overlooked, as are the questions that follow from them. Of course teachers will point out that the 'hook' on the *l* or *y* go in one direction or another; but that is not focused on as a highly significant, abstract, cognitive/conceptual matter. That approach leaves both the problem and the achievement unrecognized. The other point is to say that any explanation of this process which points towards notions such as copying, imitating – and its very many versions: 'acquiring knowledge of the shapes', 'practising the shapes', even some versions of 'learning the letter-shapes' – is misunderstanding the intelligent actions of children in a deep way. The actions, the processes, the cognitive and affective *work* done here is deeply transformative, and creative. It represents each individual's own path into the convention-laden system of lettered representation, shaped by the individual's work with the already culturally formed stuff around them. It explains why reality may be so different for each individual even when the surface of their practice often looks the same.

DRAWING PRINT: A CHILD'S VIEW OF THE WRITTEN ENVIRONMENT

The child's engagement with print reveals a complexity in the medium of 'print' which has gone unrecognized and unremarked. Instead there has been a focus on the quite abstract idea of 'language', or on 'writing', in most theoretical (and political) debate, as though there could be such a *thing* as language independently of its material appearance, whether in sound or in print. If much, perhaps most, of the complexity of the system of writing goes unrecognized, it is not surprising that modes of teaching may not be able to help all those who have particularly marked problems. Of course, as I said earlier, most children manage to find their way into and through the perceptual and conceptual maze of print, only for some to give up later for a variety of cultural and social reasons. But all of them might find the whole process much easier if the complexity of their task was understood by those whose job it is to know – academics, 'educationalists' – planners, policy-makers, teachers, and yes, politicians.

Children make signs and read them out of their interest, and make signs which reflect the meanings they want to convey in the form and the substance of the sign. They make signs which are founded on a motivated relation between meaning and form, signified and signifier. That is the overriding principle with which they approach the world of alphabetic writing. And then they come up against the brick wall of a system which in a number of ways and at a number of levels resists an understanding in those terms. There simply is no reason, no 'motivation', for a shape such as E expressing the sound of e as in Emily. No one's interest is expressed in that particular relation. At this point the child's logic does not work. Nor does it seem to work when she or he seeks to understand how or why *crocodile*, or *car*, or any word means the things they do mean.

Because we are dealing with cultural systems of very ancient histories, the step, the connection, the principle is not easy to see, not immediately graspable. We are dealing with cultural materials which have accreted around them layers and layers of meaning, and these richly meaning-endowed objects form the substance out of which we make new meanings, by the processes of metaphor. When an English speaker asks for a light bulb in a shop, or screws it into a lamp, she or he does not remember or remind themselves that the word *bulb* is a metaphor, made quite some time ago, using an existing word, encrusted with its meaning (spring bulbs, onion bulbs) to act as the vehicle for a new meaning, that of the glass and metal object fashioned by a new technology. Once pointed out, the metaphor is of course visible: the motivated character of that sign becomes apparent – as it is with the German *Glühbirne*, except that here the word for a fruit, the pear ('glowing pear'), was used as the vehicle for the new meaning. Both are motivated signs; clearly not arbitrary, even if the 'vehicle' for the new meaning was a different one in each case.

Children try to persist with their logic, and with their principle, and in the process they reveal more of the complexities of the medium of written language. The question, as with the images, texts and objects discussed in the earlier chapters, is: what do the children see; what do they regard as central; what are they interested in representing? Looking at the things they produce as a result of looking at print, leads me to say that unlike adults – whether linguists or educators – children see complex objects, and not 'just language'. In fact they constantly switch focus; they change their point of view; and in that process they 'see' different things, 'print' takes on different forms. It is these different things I will now examine, in order to discover what children think this thing 'printed language' or 'writing' is, and the manner in which they may make sense of it.

All of the kinds of things considered here are entirely usual products of children in the course of their move into writing. The first of these is Figure 4.2. It is this which made me think that the child is focused on print, rather than on writing. Compare this

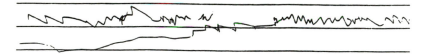

Figure 4.2 Writing as a 'block of letters': 'doing my work writing'

Soon everyone in Pontypandy was out looking for Rosa. But there was no sign of her.

Figure 4.3 Fireman Sam caption
Source: Alison Boyle, *Fireman Sam and the Flood*, London: Heineman, 1990.

with Figure 4.3, a caption from a page of a *Fireman Sam* book. The one-and-a-half lines of print take up about a thirtieth of the page, the majority of which is given over to a coloured picture. That discrepancy must be puzzling to a child: why is it that adults pay so little attention to this huge part of the page, and so much attention to this tiny part of the page? That in itself makes print intriguing – it must be important if so much is made of so little! It is not unreasonable to think that the child is imitating precisely the object 'lines of print'. As a visual object, the one-and-a-half lines do have the appearance of the child's drawing: elements of a similar kind, running together, across the page, with some more of the same underneath. A painter who was asked to draw the *Fireman Sam* page as an object in the background of a bigger picture might represent the print in quite the same way.

Focus on writing produces an object, 'line of print' or 'block of print', in the child's reading. It does not provide an answer to the question of what it is, for the child, other than 'parents treat it as by far the most important bit of the page, they "read" it, it makes meaning'. That is a complex and important meaning, and provides another stepping stone on the path into print. Children produce other analogues and forms: the headlines of the 'newspaper' (Figure 3.6) are an example; here the child had 'read' those elements on the page which have significant bold letters, as a noteworthy object, and represented them.

There are many other perspectives on print. Figure 4.4 shows a common set of forms, where the child is practising, it seems, the shape of particular letters. Over the page I have put together a few examples.

While in the Figures 4.2, 3.6 and 4.1 the child's focus seems to have been on a whole, larger unit: 'line of print', 'headline', 'my name', now there is a new focus, namely on the constituent element and its shape. Or perhaps it is still the line of print, but now with a focus on the individual elements in the line of print, showing both the shape of elements and 'regularity' as a feature of writing.

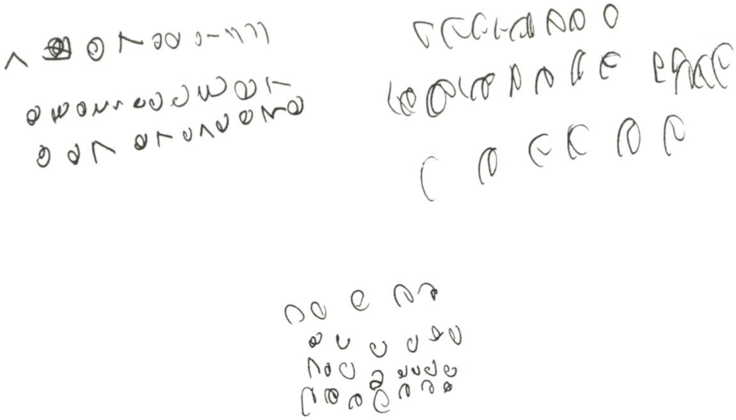

Figure 4.4 Practising letters

A sideways glance at a child writing 'numbers' may be instructive in the search for understanding their view of and perspective on writing. Figure 4.5 shows 'numbers' written by a 4½-year-old girl, about 6 months after she had drawn the letters in Figure 4.4.

There seems to be a difference in shape for all these numbers (which had been written on separate scraps of paper initially) compared to the shape she uses for letters. Whether she has, at this stage, a sense of the difference between letter and number is hard to say, though the shapes shown here may mean that she is sensitive to a difference in the characteristics of the shapes.

Yet another 'take' on writing is shown in the example of the newspaper in Figure 3.6. This is a focus on the *medium*. In the (4½-year-old) child's example several things seem to emerge from her reading: newspapers have (sensationalist) news, the caption (as read by the girl) was 'In John Prince's Street someone got dead'; they have images; and they stand in the relation of head-lines (and other writing) at the top, and image at the bottom. 'Headlines' are in big bold letters. Other captions, on other examples of newspapers drawn at the same time, are: 'They were having a conference in America' and 'There was a burglar broke into somebody's window'.

Her then 7-year-old brother's newspapers are more developed. Where her paper is made on a single sheet, he has folded the same-sized sheet, so that his papers have a front page, and inside

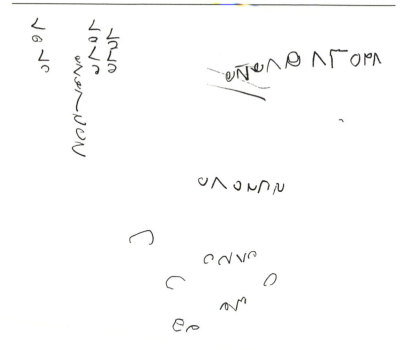

Figure 4.5 'Numbers'

pages. One of the front pages (not shown here) has an emblem, a picture of the sun, and is called *The Sun*. Its bold headline is *The Big Day*. The two inside pages are divided between 'New's' as its heading says (the right-hand page, page three so to speak) and sport, with its heading 'The mach of the day' (Figure 4.6).

Clearly, this child's reading is guided by his interest. 'News' is defined, as in his sister's paper, by its sensationalist or violent character. Sport, in the form of soccer, is the other factor that his reading and his production focuses on.

As well as a focus on the medium (the 'mass media') in their different ways, there is clear evidence also of a beginning focus on the generic organization of written materials, by content ('News', 'Sport') as much as by a beginning awareness of formal generic differentiation. The girl's 'In John Prince's Street someone got dead' was spoken in a 'newsreader' tone of voice. The boy's 'arplane cashas' is headlinese. One newspaper produced by him a year and a half earlier has this dictated text 'Someone is hanging out so much washing. Do you know who it is? If you find her/him

Figure 4.6 Newspaper: 'The mach [*sic*] of the day'

call – [and then his phone number].' Below that is a drawing of a lot of washing flapping wildly on a line. Another which was also done at that time has this heading: 'Good news just in' (spelled 'God nes just in') over a drawing of a giant strawberry, and below that 'Giant Strawberry'.

In the multiple readings which children perform, the different 'takes' they have, looking at print now this way and now that, now as 'block of print', now as 'letter', now as 'sequence of letters', now as 'newspaper as object', now as 'newspaper as message', now as 'text as genre', children gradually develop a sense of what this 'stuff' is. Each new focus, each 'take', each perspective, reveals print as a different object; and each of their readings produces a differently motivated sign. All of these are real enough aspects of writing/print. 'Block of print' is one aspect of print/writing; so are individual letters; so are the media which the children discern. Their principle of making (and reading for) motivated signs works on each occasion. As I tried to show in the discussion of the child's name, what we as adults take (too naively) as simply print or writing or language, is an enormously complex phenomenon. Children treat it as such, and uncover this complexity bit by bit. Print/writing is 'multisemiotic', in that it uses a multiplicity of semiotic means all at one time. Children have to unpick this multiplicity bit by bit. It is a process that takes years. The writing of the name traces a continuous analytic engagement over a period of thirteen months – but it had started before that, and it continued after my last example. The examples that I have range over many years, in the case of Michael's newspapers up to the age of 8. The analytic, transformative engagement isn't finished then. The paths into writing are many, enormously complex, and long. It is the adult's simplistic view which obscures this.

All of these many paths start unobtrusively, hardly noticeable at first. The path into generic form has already begun when the 4-year-old girl makes her newspaper. It is much more clearly formed by the age of 8; although it is the transition from primary school to secondary school which marks a crucial stage here: secondary school clearly requires generic writing in specific disciplines. But we can see an increasing focus on generic form all along that path. There are 'listings of items for sale' (much like the listings recognizable from certain forms of junk mail); there are recipes; there are cards; invitations; tickets for admission to plays; and of course, there are many stories, and many narratives.

Here are some examples of these texts: first a list from a shop. Items are written underneath each other, as in the original.

SHOP

bage's	1	(badges)
Palasmat's 10p		(placemats)
10p 2 paperarpans		(paper aprons)
kron 10p		(crown)
2p pad's		(pads)
rocete's		(rockets)
saf's 10p		(scarves)
10p neclse		(necklace)
washas 10p		(washers)
racdaer 2p		(recorder)
10p monser		(monster)
Paper		
Patnan		(pattern)

This list was posted up, as part of a game of playing shops; the goods were all made by the two shopkeepers.

Here is a 'lunch list' made by Michael, (age six years and three months)

Lunch list for Michael

Matad chese and tmotew and bacn ol on a biscat into the coca te mac a piser. and da tric of cold tholt.

This was a request for 'lunch next Saturday'; he read it back to me as 'melted cheese and tomato and bacon all on a biscuit in the cooker to make a pizza. And a drink of cold chocolate.'

In his reading back he instructed me to 'make a full stop there', where it is above, and where in fact he had placed it himself in his own written version. In other words, a part of his attention towards writing now includes 'punctuation'; this is also indicated by his lavish use of the apostrophe in the shop list just above.

Here are two stories, both illustrated. The first, 'The bii and the rinocsrs' (The bee and the rhinoceros) is produced as a book of six pages.

The bii and the rinocsrs.
[Title page]

Oaes a pon tim their wos a bii and a rnacrs.

[Pages 2 and 3; the text is on page 3, page 2 has a drawing of a bee in the top half – more or less opposite the word *bii* –, and a drawing of a rhinoceros in the bottom half of the page]

Won day the rinosrs met a bii.
[Pages 4 and 5; again drawing of bee and rhinoceros on the facing page, 4]

And the bii sdg hem sow the rinosrs poct the bii. And thats The End.
[Page 6]

This book moves from the 'back page' forward; that is, its directionality is the opposite of western convention; the writing itself is from left to right.

The second story is 'The roadrunner' (my title). This is written as a story on a page; with the story more or less across the top of the page, and the illustration more or less across the bottom of the page. 'Once upon a time a roadrunner lived. The roadrunner was chased by coyote. Coyote was dumb but he thought he was clever. He called himself a genius because he made so many traps. But roadrunner ran through his traps.' This is my transliteration made from his reading of the story to me. The original was written something like this (I say 'something like' as it is not the neatest writing in the original – a point to contemplate in itself in the question of writing as a medium of transcription: writing may be too slow or cumbersome for the child's needs in telling a story).

ensc apon atam a rodraunar lad
the rodranauar was shast bi e cioti
the cioti was damb bat he thot he was cava.
He coot hersalf a genas.
Be cas he ma soman trrapps.
But radranur ran thaw hes traps.

The child read the story to me (it was written on the 26 December), on the 5 January, when I transcribed it (making the note that *himself* was read as *he:self*); he had read it to me also on the previous night, and three days prior to that, that is, on the 1 January each time in the same form. I make that point because there seems some uncertainty generally about the extent to which these early forms are reliably written, or are simply more or less serviceable mnemonics for the child. I assume that there is a slow development in this, but that by this stage these forms represent accurate transliterations of sound into graphic form. In a sense this is the end of drawing: it is the beginning of real writing.

But having said ' in a sense' I want to hedge this statement even more. I think that this represents yet another, a crucial point in the observation and analysis of print/writing from so many foci, so many perspectives: the crucial point where the letters are drawings of sounds. Now the graphic form *letter* is used to carry the meaning of (a particular kind of) *sound*. This shift, like all the metaphors that I have traced, is of great complexity and cognitive subtlety: a visual form is linked to a sound meaning. It is the linking of two fundamentally different media: of sight and sound; that of the spatially expressed and that of the temporally expressed.

Throughout this long process as I have presented it here, a period of at least four years, the child applies the idea of the motivated relation of form and meaning. In this process, 'meaning' has very many very different guises, as I have tried to show. The signs children make, in 'writing' as in 'reading', are expressions of their interest; it applies to their drawing, their making of objects, and their engagement with print. In this they act like all makers of signs, children as much as adult.

DRAWING IDEAS, OR DRAWING SOUNDS: THE LOGICS OF WRITING

Figure 3.5 shows a contrast: two girls, both about 3½ years old, engaged in writing/drawing. One, Sarah, living in Taiwan, has as her model a form of writing, that of Chinese characters, which differs fundamentally from that which Emily, living in England, has as hers, alphabetic writing. Both forms of writing are of ancient history, of about four thousand years. Both derive from picture-writing. In the case of Chinese that mode continues to this day, though of course four thousand years of use have superposed layer upon layer of abstraction and convention. Nevertheless writers of Chinese can, even now, show the pictorial/meaning origin of the characters they use. In the case of the (Roman form of the) alphabet the mode has changed. In the move from Egyptian hieroglyphic writing, and its successive borrowing and adaptation/transformation, first in the immediate vicinity of Egypt, and then around the Mediterranean, to the north and the east towards

Persia and India, a continuous process of abstraction moved the system from a picture-script to one in which (abstracted and reduced) images came to stand for sounds. Given that the script was borrowed continuously by people who spoke quite different languages from each other, this process of abstraction is understandable. In the case of the Japanese borrowing of Chinese script this did not lead to such a change, but preserved, in many fundamental ways, the pictographic nature of the script (though the development of Kanji is the same kind of move as is the move from hieroglyphics to alphabet). The point is that children start as pictographers: they have an idea – loosely speaking – and they look for some concrete, physical form of its expression. The 'pillow-car' on the floor is an instance of that as much as the dart-like car of Plate 1; or the camel with 'that much humps' (Figure 2.3).

If we compare the two kinds of writing in Figure 3.5 many differences are immediately apparent: the objects which the children engage with are so different that necessarily their readings are entirely different; Figure 3.5 represents the signs produced by them on the basis of their reading. What do their readings show about their understandings of the meaning, of the logic of each writing system? For the girl learning writing in the alphabetic environment, five characteristics of that logic seem quite clear: linearity, sequentiality, repeatability, connectedness, and relative simplicity of the individual elements. That is, relatively simple elements are repeated, they stand in a linear sequence, and are connected. The contrast with the girl learning writing in the environment of pictographic (or ideographic, logographic writing systems) shows that what may go entirely unnoticed by staying in one system alone, is in fact a fundamental issue. The logic here seems to be quite different: linearity, sequentiality, discreteness, not repeatable but individually differing units, and complexity of the individual units. That is, individually complex units, which are not repeated, are in a linear, sequential arrangement, unconnected to each other though 'adjacent'.

As a logic about the deep meaning of language each differs fundamentally from the other. I imagine that each produces far-reaching assumptions about the deep characteristics of language. The difference that seems most crucial is this: pictographic writing is a transcription of ideas; alphabetic writing is a transcription of sounds. For the one child language/writing is about ideas; for the other, language/writing is about sounds. Only at a second step, does pictographic writing associate sounds with those meanings. Similarly, it is at a second step that alphabetic writing associates meanings with sounds. The deep logic is fundamentally different: one writing system is oriented towards representing *ideas* in the visual form of pictures; the other writing system is oriented towards representing *sounds* in the visual form of abstracted graphic symbols.

The bodily act of making marks in the two systems differs considerably. In one it involves the repeated action of simple movement; in the other, the action of individually differentiated complex movement. In so far as 'full command' of a system depends on the fully habituated, 'grooved' chain of action from brain to muscle, to that extent the coding in the bodies of these two children will be entirely different. One body is oriented towards regular repetition of similar, simple units; the other body towards the individually differentiated drawing of distinct and complex units.

It might be thought that individual ability plays a part here, in that the child learning alphabetic writing may not have the drawing skills of the Taiwanese writer. Figure 4.7 is a drawing she produced at about this time. It shows both enormous powers of observation in making sense of the principle of construction of the model dinosaur, and great command in the execution of the drawing.

Pictographic script provides a path which enables the child to move from the drawing of ideas to the drawing of characters; from dinosaur drawing to dinosaur character. This is a move with great abstraction and conventionalization, but one where the child remains on the same perceptual, cognitive, productive path. Alphabetic script forces the child to start again: the drawing of ideas has to be abandoned (for most children permanently), in order to learn to draw the various forms characteristic of alphabetic writing, the letters. Letters are pictures of sounds, not pictures of ideas. That opens up a vast conceptual–cognitive gap which is very difficult to bridge. That children manage to do so nevertheless is testimony to their persistence and tenacity, and their relentless application of the principle on which they base their meaning-making.

The pictorial representation of ideas is, it seems, the obvious, perhaps the natural form of representing ideas other than by direct use of the body – as in speech, gesture. Breaking that obvious mode brings with it great difficulty for children in their learning of

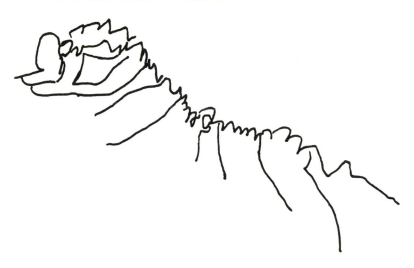

Figure 4.7 Tyrannosaurus rex

writing. The question is: what advantages does it bring? What advantages does the natural mode bring with it? The answer lies somewhere in the domain of cognitive, affective distance, and in consequent forms of logic and rationality; those characteristics which we regard as archetypally characteristic of 'western' modes of thought and action. The real question is: although they served us well in the past, will they be sufficient in the decades ahead?

DISPLAY AND VISUAL SPACE: THE DESIGN OF THE PAGE

In Chapter 3, I discussed an image produced by Michael after seeing *Jurassic Park* (Plate 5). The image covers the whole page; it is symmetrical, and the elements that he wished to show are spaced in a design across the page. A rainbow divides the bottom from the top, and fields with animals in them are divided off from the jungle. While there are some texts and objects produced by children in a seemingly random fashion, with no apparent interest in design – letters or sequences of letters written in the free space of a page – very many others, and in fact the very great majority, show a clear concern for design. That applies to the symmetry of the Lego car (Figure 2.2) as much as it does to the pillow-car (Figure 2.6), with its clear three-part structure. Looking at the arrangements produced in children's play, the very same is evident. Yesterday I noticed, casually, three 6-year-old friends turning our living room into a house: the kitchen here, under the plant stand; the living room over here by the easy chair next to the basket with magazines; the dining room over here; and so on. Each room had a careful arrangement of items, appropriate to its function. Each arrangement – at least initially – was carefully devised 'interior *design*'.

In relation to the page, the skills here displayed and constantly developed are a part of the path into writing. One of the factors the child needs to learn to control is precisely the display of the text on the page. This is not a matter dealt with in most discussions of writing – the page is not considered as a meaningful or significant element in writing (though it is in journalism) – but it has a number of quite central functions. And so the books, lists, images, newspapers, cards, invitations, tickets, and so on, which children produce are important from that point of view among many others. The spatial unit of the page is a significant unit in itself – it provides the measure of the length of a line, for instance; it suggests the size of an image; it apportions space between story and picture. Folded, the page can become a new medium, either book (especially as several folded pages put together with sticky tape or staples, or just placed one inside the other) or newspaper; or birthday card. With the change in medium comes a change in generic form; and with that demands for different kinds of writing.

Badly displayed written text produces an effect, as does a well-laid-out page. This is therefore a skill that needs to be consciously fostered, a meaning which cannot be ignored. As public communication moves with increasing intensity to greater use of images together with written language, the means of handling the relations of elements on a page becomes an essential skill for all who need to communicate through the use of the page.

Chapter 5

'You made it like a crocodile'
A theory of children's meaning-making

DEVELOPING A FRAMEWORK

The 4-year-old who said 'My Gawd, I made it like Australia' was clear about her agency in her production of meaning; another 4-year-old was equally clear about her father's deliberate intent in shaping a crocodile in taking bites from his delicately held toast when she said 'You made it like a crocodile.' Whether in describing and commenting on their own making, or their reading of the making by others, meaning is at the forefront of both of their concerns. It seems a reasonable, and I would say *essential* task to develop for ourselves a theory, a working account, of how children make meaning. Of course children tend not to engage in extended theory-making, though frequently they make comments which are so incisive that we can only wonder at the precision of their insights.

In this chapter I will draw together the various points raised so far in the discussion, in order to put together a consolidated picture of what children do in meaning-making, to describe, in effect their 'practical theory'. From that I derive my theorist's theory. The chapters following will then build on that composite theory: rethinking the concept of literacy and of theories of language; considering, in detail, the question of transformation in reading and writing; putting forward a new view of literacy; and, finally, speculating on social and economic futures in the light of the whole book's argument.

Here I consider several issues in turn as they emerge in a close look at children's meaning-making: 'interest'; the motivated sign; tranformation; multimodality; representation; reading; resources for making of meaning; imagination, cognition and affect; the limits to imagination, representation; and the question of synaesthesia.

INTEREST

The traditional, and in this century commonsensical view of meaning is that there is a stable system of entities which are available to a fully competent user of a language for the expression of their meaning. These might either be entities which name objects in the world – words like *cat* as the name for an object in the world; or they might be entities which get their meaning through our competent knowledge of their place in a whole system of related entities – *cat* as the entity whose meaning is that it is not dog, not horse, not guineapig, hamster or whatever domestic pet there may be. This is a gross oversimplification, but it works reasonably, nevertheless, at one level. One corresponds to the biblical story of Adam naming the animals in the Garden of Eden; the other corresponds to a post-Renaissance view of 'man' as the maker of his own world.

In this view there is a system, however it may have been developed, which an outsider has to learn, has to gain competence in – whether this outsider is a child newly born into the group which 'has' this system, or an adult outsider – an adult learner of the new language. There is no suggestion that the individual who uses a language – or other system of communication – has any effect on that system. This view may have developed for any number of cogent reasons: children do seem to end up speaking or writing the language of their parents – even if, and this contradiction goes unnoticed, the same elders have always been known to complain about the changes, deformations, corruptions, degenerations, introduced by the new generation. 'Foreigners' are either marked out by speaking differently to the 'locals', or have learned to 'blend in' perfectly, to adopt to the forms of the new community. There are of course issues of power in this, namely the question as to who has control of the language.

It may also be that the real focus of theory has always been on adult users and uses of the language; and where the focus has been on children it has been in order to see how, or to demonstrate *that* they 'move into' the adult system. In other words, children's meaning-making has been seen from the viewpoint of the adult, which has not permitted an understanding of their actions in their terms. Children's interests have been invisible because of the dominant power of adult interests.

When we struggle to see the situation of meaning-making from

the child's point of view – and extend it as a means to explain
the adult's world also – the picture changes radically. Children, as
all will admit, are not competent users of adult systems; and so we
can see what it is they do to make their meanings in the absence
of the routinized, practiced, finely honed and quite 'natural'
competence of adults. We see that they have 'interests'. Too often
these appear as a nuisance to the adult: the child who 'throws
a tantrum' because *she* wants to choose her own clothes in the
morning – at remarkably young ages, as young as 1½ or 2 in my
own wearied experience – is expressing her interest in how she
looks, how she will feel for that day. Why do I try to resist her?
Partly because there is *my* routine – though my routine would be
less interrupted by giving way early. In large part, and at bottom,
it is, I think, because I cannot actually imagine that the 2-year-old
can have a 'real' interest, real dress sense, real knowledge, real
understanding; perhaps because she has far less power. Once I
concede the right to the child to express her or his interest, and
observe, I find that there are meanings; that they express and
intent; as well as systematic design.

Another serious obstacle to the adult's perception is the fact that
children's interests change. The maker of the cars in (Figures 2.1,
2.2, Plate 1) made one car in which it was crucial to show the car
in action: but he also made (among many others) a car which was
meticulously produced to be an object devoid of context, so as
to express the potencies of the object *and* to give it a different
status in terms of realisms. The two girls who made *their* car on the
floor of the bedroom wanted a car which was mainly made for
getting into and sitting in. So their car became a very different car
– without steering wheel, without gear lever, without wheels.
Children's interest changes; and as it does, that which is regarded
as criterial by the child *about* the car changes; and so what is
represented changes. The girls' gendered interest sees cars differently from a boy's – usually, though not necessarily. One of the girls
who made the pillow-car was making a car with cardboard cut-out
wheels stuck on to a cardboard box a week later.

'Interest' is a short-hand term for an enormously complex set
of factors. My reason for using the term is to find a way out of a
seemingly irresolvable difficulty in educational thinking. It is the
difficulty of reconciling the apparently total opposition between
individuality, meaningful individual action on the one hand,
and social determinism on the other – the view that our actions are

circumscribed by social convention, constraint and convenience, to such an extent that we act as simple socially determined beings. Neither view is attractive or plausible to me. So I want to ask 'Why did this person make this sign at this point?', and have a better answer than either: 'She (or he) just felt like it', 'They were just expressing their feelings', 'I just say what comes into my head'; or, on the other hand 'In this context the rules/conventions of politeness, power, and so on are such that you must do such and such', 'The best form to use is this', 'The correct (or standard) pronunciation (or syntax) is this.' Even in conditions of heavy social constraint people can and do act out of their interest; equally, what seems merely individual is socially constrained – why is it that my 'individual' taste is satisfied by interior decor which can be found in thousands of houses in England and in Australia, to some extent in Germany, and less so in France and Portugal?

Interest as an explanatory category comprises at least the following for me: we see the world from our own place, and that place differs from that of our neighbour. One reason 3- and 4-year-olds draw adult figures with such enormously long legs topped by a short body and large head is not just limited competence, but the fact that from *their* height adults do look like that. Throughout our lives we have had *our* view of the world: that world is the same for millions of others, and that produces commonality of view; but I always see it from my position, and that produces difference of view. There is no need to go here into the usual statements about social and cultural differences: they are obvious.

Interest is a composite of my experience; but it is also a reflection of my present place, and an assessment of my present environment. With my experience – whether as a 5-year-old or a 55-year-old – I stand here now, in a social place, in a physical place. My experience, personally constructed out of my incessant readings through all my life, makes me assess my present position, and its potentials and responsibilities. It makes me read my immediately present social environment, now at this moment in a certain way. These readings are my transformations, my signs made from what is to hand, out of my experiences and in my present social environment. That includes the person or the persons with whom I am communicating. I assess my relationships with them in terms of my wishes, of their and my power, my affective responses, and so on.

All of these together are the source of my making of signs in communication – not simply what has come into my head, because what has come into my head has come from prior cultural and social places; and then, on the other hand, is it neither simply what society, convention, power, constraint tells me I must do, because I act transformatively in my making of signs.

To what extent is this an apt description of the meaning-making of children? I wish to maintain that the principle is the same. The difference is that when children make signs at a young age, necessarily their experience of, and exposure to, social and cultural forms is less, and so it forms a lesser part of their making of signs. Affect is a much greater part of the signs of very young children, and because it is a greater part it is more readily visible. That has led to the mistaken view that the signs of young children are 'merely expressive'. Also, what children 'have to hand' differs; very often what they 'have to hand' is what they have found – objects and materials not considered materials for making signs and messages by their parents, teachers, or carers – and so often entirely unconventional, like the empty box of Panadol. In consequence, their objects and texts often resemble the objects and texts of naive art and as such are easily overlooked. What they 'have to hand' also differs conceptually, but the influence of the society and of its culture exerts itself from the earliest stage – much earlier than my experience of 'Lean Tomato'.

MOTIVATED SIGNS

Signs come about as the result of human action, usually in the context of culture, often with an intention to communicate that sign. The traditional view of the relation of form and meaning, of signifier and signified, is, in the now clichéd words of Saussure's *Course in General Linguistics* (1974), conventional and arbitrary. That is a view which holds that there is no intrinsic connection between the expression of a meaning, and the form which is used to express it. Two examples will illustrate this by now seemingly unassailable common sense. In German the word for the meaning expressed by the English word *tree* is *Baum*; in French it is *arbre*. So there is one meaning, but three forms for its expression. No one can (now) pretend that there is a real reason for the connection between these forms and the meaning. The second example is adopted from the writings of Ludwig Wittgenstein, the Austrian philosopher. If you and I are playing chess (or draughts) and we lose one of the pieces, then it is no great matter to say 'Look, we'll just let this match, or this button, "stand for" the piece – perhaps a pawn in chess – which we need.' And, as these examples are entirely persuasive put like this, they have passed by without (very much) challenge.

When we look at the etymology of *Baum* (the nearest English relative is *beam*) we find that it is related to the present-day German word *biegen*, 'to bend'. It seems that the original meaning of *Baum* was that it was that conspicuously large plant which bends in the wind. Once we know that, then the relation of form and meaning is less arbitrary – we can see the reason, the motivation for calling the plant after an outstanding characteristic. Given that the ancestors of the people who now say *Baum* came from somewhere in the steppes of southern Russia (some four thousand years ago or so), where trees might have been scarce and thus conspicuous in the landscape, it makes even more sense.

In the case of the button/pawn we can argue in the other direction. Assume that I have lost five or six pieces of my chess set, two pawns, a bishop, the queen, a rook. If I have five identical buttons the idea of substituting the buttons for the lost pieces begins to become problematic. I will need distinguishing features: size for instance. But if I had buttons of different sizes, I would not use the biggest button to substitute for a pawn; I would use it to replace the most valuable piece, the queen: size would become a signifier for value, which is a motivated relation. We could then establish *by convention* that size will signify value. Therefore, in our game, the second largest button would become the rook, and so on.

Now we have a clear situation where there is a motivated and conventional relation between meaning and form, namely that the greater the value of the chess piece, the larger the button that is used by us to substitute for it. Making *larger size* mean *greater value* is a matter of a motivated relation of meaning and form; and that latter feature is established by us as our convention. In the signs that I have discussed in the previous chapters, there is at all times a meaningful relation between the meaning conveyed, and the form which plausibly or aptly expresses it. The people who named trees after their characteristic of bending in the wind focused on a particular, noticeable – perhaps to them unusual and astonishing characteristic – and they named the whole thing by it. Their *interest* was reflected in their combination of meaning and form. In the case of the 7-year-old's newspaper (Figure 4.6), his interest in the team he supports (an affective meaning as much as a factual description) makes him draw the one player taller, wearing boots with bigger spikes, coloured bright red, and so on.

The combination of form and meaning in the signs made by all humans is motivated: *being tall* as a signifier of *power*, but also as a signifier of the child's great affective investment in the star player, his hero, in the football team that he supports. The child selects – no doubt unconsciously – those characteristics which he regards as most important for him in the thing he wants to represent, and he finds the best possible means for expressing them – size, colour (and in this image, the ball in the net of the opposition's goal!). The relation which unites form and meaning is one of analogy: *size* (of the player) can be the analogue of (this player's or his team's) *power*; *the intensity of the red colouring* can be the analogue of *my affective involvement*. This relation of analogy leads to metaphors: *size is power*, *intense red* equals *my affective involvement*. Motivated signs are therefore always metaphors; formed through the process of analogy; which itself is motivated by the sign-maker's interest.

The older children are, the more their signs are likely to focus not just on expressing the things that they want to represent, but to focus also on communication. This involves a recognition of the presence of the people with whom they are interacting; and that recognition increasingly involves attention to the communicational environment: 'with my teacher I need to communicate in this way', 'with my friends I communicate in this way'. In this manner, the sign-maker's interest also begins to include considerations of the needs of the audience as part of the complex considerations in making signs. Signs have to represent adequately what I want to say; *and* they have to say it in such a way that they pay due attention to what I think I want to achieve in this act of communication.

Signs therefore have a double social motivation: once because of who the sign-maker is, and what her or his history has been; and another time because of what the sign-maker assesses the communicational environment to be, and how consequently, she or he adjusts their making of the sign.

This issue is important because it affects notions of what *learning* is. In a theory founded on the assumption of arbitrarily constructed signs, the task of learning is conceived of in one broad direction: as the cognitive ability to acquire abstract systems of high complexity, which are, in their characteristics of make-up, in their logics, extraneous to the person who needs to acquire them. Language is seen as one such system, and teachers therefore inevitably hold that view of what the child's task in learning is: 'mastering' this complex, abstract system (whether in speech or in writing). 'Failure' by a child in this task therefore is explained as a failure of precisely that kind – an inability to cope with abstract systems, a 'cognitive disability' defined in terms of the logic of this assumption.

Teachers, along with linguists and educational specialists, have a firmly settled notion of language as a system of arbitrarily constructed signs. Their common sense coincides with the specific difficulty which children face in learning to write, namely the move from drawing picture-ideas to drawing sounds, which I discussed in Chapter 4.

I will return to this question below, when I discuss learning.

TRANSFORMATION AND TRANSFORMATIVE ACTION

The cultural world into which children slowly have to work themselves is a world which already has form. So children's making of signs takes place in a world which has the complex shape produced by all the previous sign-makers of that culture, in a particular society, all of them always expressing their interest in the making of their signs. As a result, with few exceptions, members of a culture end up as 'acculturated' – all having what appears as the same cultural knowledge, the same values, the same, recognizably similar traits and dispositions. All speak the same language, make signs in all the modes which are available in that culture, in quite similar ways. To all intents and purposes, it looks as though the culture has imprinted itself on us, or we have actively acquired the culture in the sense of making a copy of it for ourselves.

Against notions of copying, imitation, acquiring, however implicitly they may be held, I would like to propose the idea that children, like adults, never copy. Instead I wish to put forward the view that we transform the stuff which is around us – usually in entirely minute and barely noticeable ways. Consider again this simple example, which I first mentioned in Chapter 1. A 3½-year-old child, on a walk with his family, is climbing a steep hill; it is difficult for him to get up, and he says 'This is a heavy hill.' My transformative view of meaning-making leads me to say that he had a meaning, something like 'this is really hard, it takes a lot of effort to walk up here'. The closest experience that he may have is lifting or carrying something heavy, for which he has a word. So he uses the word which is available to him as the means of expressing his meaning. In the process he has made a new sign. In this sign the combination of meaning and form is motivated: *heavy* was the form which best expressed his meaning 'this is really hard, it takes a lot of effort'.

But now, *heavy* has a new meaning for him; it is *no longer* the word it was before. In his own use he has transformed it, *conditioned by the practical experience in which he had to make the sign*. He has transformed his own language; the fact that no one around him will follow his use in their sign-making means that no *convention* will develop which will sustain this usage. In other cases, if there is a group which does follow such a use, a convention will develop, as in the 1960s use of *heavy* in youth-culture: 'Heavy man, heavy.'

This is not a view which treats *heavy* as an error, a sign of a mistake in the acquisition of the adults' system. To me it is clear that the child was not attempting to copy *steep*, which is an attribute of *hill* (*a steep hill*), but saying something about his own experience (which was produced by the attempt to climb the hill) and expressing that experience. So while the adult syntax focuses on a quality of the hill – something external to the speaker – the syntax of the child's sign focuses on his experience, internal to him, from which he then makes an attribution to the thing outside of himself: *a heavy hill*. He had other possibilities available to him for making a sign, *hard* perhaps, but he chose *heavy* as the best for his meaning. This is one of countless times when he will use *heavy*, each time to express a new meaning; and as he grows more and more into awareness of his culture's conventions, his uses of *heavy* will come closer and closer to those of that culture. As an adult speaker of the language, his use of *heavy* will come to resemble that of other members of his cultural and social group; and in everyday communication it is most likely that neither he nor those with whom he is talking will find anything at all unusual about his use of the word. To all intents and purposes, he has grown into society, he is, linguistically, fully acculturated. Yet in my view *heavy* for him will bear the traces not only of that one use which I remember but of all others: his *heavy* will be different from the *heavy* of all other users of the language. He has made his own path into that bit of the language.

So, an approach based on the notion of transformation suggests that we arrive at a stage which is sufficiently similar to that of other members of culture, and yet is never identical with it. The former makes communication possible, the latter opens the possibility of individual differences, even for fully socialized and acculturated adult users of language – and of all the systems of communication. What the culture and the society in which I am makes available to me, becomes necessarily the stuff with which I (have to) engage constantly; but how I engage with it is a matter of my *interest* at a particular moment in communication, and in engagement with that stuff. For me, the two examples of the girls engaging with the scripts of their respective cultures are a telling metaphor in this respect: both are learning to write, acting out of their *interest* in wishing to come to terms with the logic of the scripts of their culture, and are producing transformed versions of those scripts. Neither of them are copies; but the powerfully shaping influence of the characteristics of each script is there to see.

A view of meaning-making as transformation allows me to give an account of how *we* make *our* paths into language as into all cultural systems. And even though we arrive at very similar places, we have got there by quite different paths, *our* paths.

MULTIMODALITY

Throughout the preceding chapters I have tried to give a sense of the multiplicity of ways in which children make meaning, and the multiplicity of modes, means, materials which they employ in doing so. Many of these means and materials are not recognized by the adult forms of the culture, and so tend not to appear in theoretical discussions of learning, the learning of writing included. At the same time I tried to show that the signs which children make, whether with conventional or unconventional means (coloured pencils bought for them, paper supplied; or bits and pieces assembled by *them*) are themselves multimodal. The shiny red cut-out car involves paper, pencils, sticky tape; and needs scissors for cutting out. Paper as a material offers the potential for being drawn on, coloured, stuck together and cut out. As a material, it opens certain possibilities, which cardboard offers less readily. Cardboard offers the possibility of being turned into container, shield, sword, objects for relatively robust physical handling.

All of these offer the possibility of representing through a multiplicity of means, at one and the same time, in the making of one complex sign. Children are therefore entirely used to 'making' in a number of media; and their approach to meaning-making is shaped and established in that way. Children act multimodally, both in the things they use, the objects they make; and in their engagement of their bodies: there is no separation of body and mind. The differing modes and materials which they employ offer differing potentials for the making of meaning; and therefore offer different affective, cognitive and conceptual possibilities. The opportunity offered by paper for being cut out is a physical opportunity, as much as an aesthetic one: it allows the maker of the subject to heighten, to intensify desirable aspects of his or her represented object; to make his or her imagined shapes physical, concrete, objective; to bring them into the world of potential action. It is also an opportunity to perform, physically that highly abstract conceptual/cognitive transformation from flat representation to concrete object, from represented object to real object, and with it the transformation from potential to action.

The discussion, in Chapter 3, of children's engagement with print shows how essential this capacity for multiple engagement is. It enables them to treat print, which is too often seen as a unidimensional medium, as multimodal, as a complex semiotic system; and it is this disposition, which makes it possible for them to make inroads into the great complexity of alphabetic writing. For children, alphabetic writing is clearly multimodal: it is blocks of print; letter-shapes; media – such as newspapers, birthday cards, books; genres; it is an aesthetic object which can be used in design; a medium of meaning; a drawing of sound; and so on.

Here we can clearly see how all children make their own paths into literacy. Given the intense multimodality of writing as print, two aspects in particular lead to differentiating paths into writing. One is simply this: in a multimodal system, the child has a choice as to which aspects, angles, features, to focus on, to highlight for herself or himself. This will have a potent shaping influence on that path. The other is the question of 'what is to hand'. Clearly, if the child is in a 'rich' environment of print from the earliest time, the stuff of print will appear to her or to him differently from when it is relatively absent. This has been commented on in great detail, and is well understood. Perhaps slightly less well understood is the issue that I am focusing on here: that of the relation between the kinds of things that were or are to hand for the children in their meaning-making, and what habits of practice, of cognitive and affective engagement they led the child to develop. For me pillows and blankets are in this respect as important as coloured pencils and paper: the former encourage a disposition towards taking everything as being potentially meaningful, and as being capable of use in representation and communication. The latter are important in providing the means of representation and expression of that more distanced kind which I discussed in Chapter 2, and which is a necessary part of the path into writing.

Pillows and blankets also enable children to develop their sense of arrangement, display and structure. Transforming a room into a whole house requires and fosters high degrees of both abstract and concrete structuring at the same time. Arranging the furniture in a room in this house – setting out the items in the 'kitchen', for instance – requires planning, classification, design and display. All of these are essential in writing; the page, mentioned in an earlier discussion (Chapter 4), is a space that needs to be designed, managed. It is also a space which, like the room in the house, can be transformed. A sheet of paper unfolded is one kind of space, with one kind of potential – to be a picture perhaps, or a space on which to list things, or to write a story on. Once it is folded it can become a newspaper – with front and back page, and inside pages; or a birthday card; several sheets folded become a book.

Equally important is what is to hand conceptually. And here parents' views of language and writing, are crucial. Here it may be that middle-class parents are as limiting for their children as parents who are less focused on writing, less anxious about success in literacy. A view of writing as too abstractly 'language' may prove as limiting as the absence of a view on language altogether.

Two further considerations are crucial. When we think about writing, it is necessary to ask 'What for?' Even in an era when writing dominated the communicational landscape, it was essential to focus on the purposes of writing. There have been countless deep debates about this – arguments which have ranged from personal expression, development, 'growth', to highly specific pragmatic arguments about 'effective communication' seen in a strict and narrow economic context, with many other versions in between, about pleasure, desire and fulfilment. Now, in a thoroughly multi-modal context, where in many domains of public communication language is no longer central, the purposes, benefits and limitations of writing (and of reading writing) can be and must be newly examined. As visual modes of communication have become more dominant, language has not just been pushed off the centre of the page (literally – if you look at any tabloid in Britain today, you will *see* the literal meaning of that phrase) it is also changing in its 'internal' form, and in its uses in relation to readers.

The effects of multimodality are far-reaching, and deeply affect the paths into literacy of the children who are growing up in this – for me, new – communicational landscape. They form their paths into literacy unencumbered by nostalgia about the place of writing which besets so many of their parents and grandparents. But in my view it is not just unhelpful, but damagingly limiting to burden them with my nostalgia. It may very well be that the technologies of communication just as much as the information-based economies of the day after tomorrow will actually need, demand, visual modes of representation and communication. 'Information-overload' may be an effect produced by the continued reliance on verbal representation, on writing, as the central means of communication. It may very well be that the solution to information-overload is not to produce less information, but to handle it visually. This book is not quite the place for this argument, though it deserves some elaboration, and I will state my ideas on this in the final chapter.

REPRESENTATION AND COMMUNICATION

In the late 1970s I went to a new job, in Adelaide in South Australia, at a college which had a course in journalism. As it was my task to develop new courses, broadly in communication studies, at the college, I had to become very interested in this course. It was a transition point in the media, and in communication, though I wasn't then fully aware quite how significant that transition was. It involved, on the one side, the introduction of word-processing into the journalistic production process – what soon became more generally developed into 'desktop' publishing. On the other side it involved ENG – electronic news-gathering. The technology which had made that possible was the development of relatively small-sized video cameras. That technology has since developed, though by involving a number of distinct routes, into multimedia production. The quaint metaphor of 'news-gathering' – like collecting seaweed or shells or wild mushrooms at the right moment – gave rise to a vast debate around *bias*, because underlying the metaphor is of course the assumption that just like seashells or mushrooms, the news was out there to be gathered.

This debate very quickly developed the understanding that news is 'manufactured' like all messages and signs, as we now think. It is therefore manufactured by particular social actors, in particular social institutions, and inevitably represented their interest – just as, I would say, all signs do. This debate never quite or fully reached the point where the notion of bias was dropped, as it needs to be: if all news (or signs) always reflect the interest of its markers, all news is biased – and not biased.

I am interested in drawing out one further point in this argument, which bears crucially on children's making of meaning, and their learning of writing. The older view of *representation* rested on an assumption of a relatively clear and stable relation between the world 'out there' and the ways of re-presenting that world in systems of signs, whether as words or images or gestures. That assumption could and did sustain particular kinds of beliefs in the characteristics of truth, questions of fact, possibilities of doing things correctly. News-gathering – whether by the stenopad clutching newshound or the video-camera-equipped reporter – has been replaced by multimedia production: in the latter I can actually *make* the news. The theoretical metaphor of the 'manufacture of news' is now reality. I can have, in my data base, images, words, music, background noises of all kinds for a soundtrack, and I can literally *make* the news. I stick together sounds, images, words which I have in my system of representations. Now of course it is becoming possible to make images (and sounds) in an even more radical sense. The consequence of that move however is that I cannot possibly sustain a notion of news-gathering, and nor,therefore, of older notions of truth, fact, objectivity, correctness. *I* make the representations, out of *my* interest. The older notion that my representation refers directly to something in the world has gone, probably for the next several centuries. That of course leads to new metaphors – those of virtual reality for instance. My best possible attempt at making news now is to construct a parallel text – but a fictive text – to events which I think are happening in the world.

My point in introducing what may seem like a somewhat abstract theoretical debate into this book is to try to point forcefully to an inescapable characteristic of the communicational and representational world into which children are moving, and in which, to a considerable extent, they already live – in which they make their paths into literacy. Their communicational world is already one in which the relation between the world and its representation, a relation which was an unshakeable common sense as recently as thirty years ago, no longer exists. That common sense was founded on representation as reference, the stable relation between the world of signs and the world of reality, 'out there'. The new common sense will be founded on representation as sign-making, with a more difficult link to the real world, 'out there'. It seems to me absolutely essential to understand that new world – even if we may not approve of it. Without our understanding, the paths of children into social sign-making, whether in writing or in images will become more difficult. Above all, that path, that process, will become the domain for carrying out deeply unenlightened, nostalgic and pessimistic moral and ideological struggles – with children inevitably as the losers, unless we are clear about what is happening.

READING

My brief excursion into the etymology of the word *reading* in Chapter 3, was to make the point that it is legitimate and necessary – and supported by history! – to take the most generous approach possible to an understanding of reading. This does not mean, for me, lack of attention to the detail – the most minute detail – of textual form; quite the contrary. Without such attention we cannot hope to 'read' in any sense. Equally, without the most generous sense of the multiplicity of factors involved in reading, the scope of relevant elements that are drawn into the reading process, I will remain with an impoverished, disabling approach to reading. So let me be clear: it is neither authoritarian formalism, nor unconstrained anarchism that I'm interested in. Reading is a complex activity, and demands to be understood with the greatest seriousness. A text is a riddle, but it is a riddle absolutely strewn with clues!

Reading is our means of engaging with the world. That engagement takes place in a multiplicity of ways, in a multiplicity of dimensions, as I attempted to demonstrate in Chapter 3. Children take print to be a multisemiotic medium, and then subject that medium to the most rigorous and sustained analysis imaginable. Certainly, speaking for myself, it was only when in hindsight I looked with some care at the 'developmental sequence' of Emily's writing of her name, that I became aware of the meticulous analysis that she had performed, and which all children perform, in their engagement with print as with other semiotic modes.

In 'taking in the world' we transform it, on the basis of a few fundamental principles: form is the best possible guide to meaning (because makers of signs seek to find the most apt form for the expression of their meaning); the internal organization of the sign is the best possible clue to the organization of the meanings of the sign-maker. In the transformative act of reading we all constantly form signs which have an 'internal' representation, and these internal representations then function as the basis of new 'externally' represented signs. This activity changes the reader's own internal representational system, and it enables the reader to participate in changing her or his culture's system of represen-tation. If children are unable to make signs externally, in some or many modes, they are cut off from participating in the constant remaking of their group's systems of representation and commu-nication. Equally seriously, they are cut off from the benefits of 'objectification', which enable me to see, when I have written something, what it is that I know or think, and to take a distanced relation to it.

The internal making of signs in reading changes not only the representational system of the reader, it makes her or him able to act differently as a result of that change. A child who has developed – from energetic, enthusiastic expression of circular 'scribbles' – the shape and idea of circles, is now able to use circles to make new signs: wheels for instance, and from wheels 'car as wheels', snow-men, ghosts, pumpkins. Of course all these newly made signs further transform the sign of circle, much in the way in which I described the transformation of the word *heavy* earlier in this chapter. The ability to act differently has a transformative and con-structive effect on who the sign-maker is, and becomes: from the ability to do, to a different sense of being. Words such as *liberating* are often used, though other words such as *competence, potential,* even *skill, ability* name important aspects of what I think happens.

Reading is therefore one central component – in literate cultures – of the formation of who we are and can be. That does not mean that non-literate societies produce lesser humans: many so-called 'oral' cultures have a wider range of representational and communicational resources at their disposal and in everyday use than so-called 'literate cultures'. The etymology comes in useful here to remind us that we are always talking about '*rid*dles', and riddles can exist in many media. I think here of my (extremely) marginal knowledge of Australian Aboriginal societies which use a complex variety of means of representation as a matter of course – in different domains at different times: speech of course, organized often in complex narratives; drawing, whether in the sand or on bark, or on a rock face, with different colours or not; the body as expressive, in dance, mime; or as object for decoration; message sticks. All of these are elaborated into highly articulate means of expression. The fact that such societies can still be called 'illiterate' is a problem of western language- and writing-focused cultures; though it has of course been made into a problem for those societies, through the power of western colonizers.

The sign-making process in reading is, at one level, the same as the sign-making process in writing. Readers make signs out of their interest; that is they draw from the object or text in front of them the features which correspond to their interest, and form their new internal sign on that basis. The important *social* difference is that writing is the making of a sign externally, which therefore can act in affecting others in being the reason for their making of new signs. This becomes amplified through the effects of media for those who do have access to them.

Because the signs formed in reading are made out of the interest of the reader, when that interest does not coincide broadly with the interest of the writer, readers may shift their reading, so to speak, into an oppositional or *resistant* reading in which formal aspects of the text that is read are read as signs of the writer's ideological intent, which is to be resisted. This introduces the issue of the boundaries to reading, one aspect of which is the question of the boundary of the sign. One common-sense assumption is that writers do, and have the right to, fix the boundaries of the sign, so that reading beyond those boundaries is not legitimate. There are important considerations here for the teaching of reading. The effect of different approaches can be to produce readers who *will* consider it improper to exceed the boundaries of the sign made by the writer. This does not imply that their reading is not transformative none the less. Other approaches may produce readers who habitually refuse to accept these boundaries. There are deeply significant social metaphors at issue here – and the potential to produce more authoritarian or more liberal personalities.

The implications for a curriculum of reading are therefore vast; and the fierce debates which surround this specific matter bear testimony to the fact that they are well enough understood at some level at least.

RESOURCES FOR MAKING MEANING

We commonly tend to think of resources for making meaning in quite abstract terms. In Michael Halliday's theory of language (1985), grammar is seen as a resource for making meaning. In this section I would like to be more encompassing, and talk about the quite abstract as well as the very concrete. I will start with the very concrete.

Throughout the previous chapters I have referred to 'what is to hand'. What the childish eye falls on as materials for making exceeds in entirely unpredictable ways the conventionalized expectations of any adult. I have mentioned a considerable range of materials and objects already, and the list could be extended: in my room now I have a helmet made from a barbecue-bead box, for instance; but the list if I wanted to reopen it would be an open-ended one. The real point about this voracious appetite for semiotic recycling is the child's ever-searching eye, guided by a precise sense of *design*, both for material and for shape. The materiality of the stuff out of which they choose to make their signs is in itself meaningful; the buttons on the coat of the Panadol-man were made from material that lent itself to represent the button: shiny, firm, plastic, white, and above all, three-dimensional. The child could easily have drawn buttons on the body of the figure, even used white paper stuck on. But that would not have given the same meaning. The pillows in the girls' car suit better than the upturned drawer because they represent the comfortableness of cloth-covered car seats. The strong cardboard, with its shiny exterior, of the barbecue-bead box is ideal for a helmet, in a way in which an ordinary cardboard box could not serve. For young makers the materiality of the stuff from which they make their signs matters; it is a meaning-carrying element of their complex signs.

From this point of view it is revealing to see how these selections change with age; and how they may be influenced by gender. Predictably enough the choice is wider and freer at earlier ages; and it seems to be less gendered – in my experience at least – but it is not free of its influence. Children are drawn into the semiotic web of culture through a vast array of signs – in which the family and its practices and values are centrally important. But there are countless other messages, and again not only those usually focused on. Toys, for instance, are sign-objects which code meanings about a society's view of different ages of childhood: soft plastic, or furry, in bold colours early on; perhaps simple shapes in polished or painted wood. Then, as the ages of children for whom the toys are designed increase, the materials change: metal might appear – they become harder, more angular; the colours change. Of course the range of things which are drawn into the world of toys also changes. The domain of toys constitutes a communicational system, in which differing ideas of being a social human are suggested, and forms of social life explored.

I made the point earlier that there are deep logics at work in the materials of meaning-making – with effects on the conceptual, cognitive and affective organization of children. But children act on materials also. Consider again, the example of a sheet of paper discussed earlier: it can be used as a flat sheet, for drawing on or writing on; once it is folded its potential changes. If it remains a material object, it offers opportunities for cutting out regular patterns along the newly made spine – producing complex symmetrical shapes when they are folded flat afterwards: snowflakes, trees, but also 'Australia'. If the folded sheet becomes a surface for receiving representations, then the folding changes its generic potential – to book, newspaper, birthday card. That change may seem both obvious and simple; it does, however, have far-reaching consequences: if the now-folded sheet has become a newspaper, then it requires the child to produce whatever text it is that makes a newspaper; Similarly, if it is a card.

In other words, the simple act of folding the sheet has implications for the child's exploration of what texts are, what layout is, how newspapers actually look and what is done with them. These are transformations of the material stuff which have effects well beyond the merely material. Another way to think about this is to say that the separation of material stuff and non-material, abstract conceptual stuff is untenable in the actual making of signs, by children at least.

But there are also abstract, cognitive/conceptual materials which are to hand. Children have to make these for themselves, in slow, persistently energetic fashion. The preceding chapters are full of examples; nevertheless I'll allow myself two examples here. One, Figure 5.1 is visual, the other is verbal.

Figure 5.1 illustrates both the notion of 'what is to hand' and the child's own action in developing his (in this instance) resources of representation. The three images represent a sequence that took place over about a year and a half. The top image, circular scribbles, was made at about the age of 1½. The child's energetic circular motion seems to be merely expressive, though even at that age he would often accompany his drawing with some descriptive commentary. By the second image 'circularity' is clearly apparent; the third image represents circles which he had drawn, each on a separate sheet. There is clearly a constant development going on; from one instance to the next (with very many instances between the ones shown here) there is transformation, with a gradual refinement of the abstracted and generalized circle-shape. Each of these instances represents 'what is to hand' for the child, which can be used in the development/transformation to the next. Once the circles are 'what is to hand', the child can use these to make a complex sign, for example, the car of Figure 1.1 discussed earlier. His commentary, as he was making it, illustrates metaphor, design and deliberateness, intention.

My second example is from a child at the age of 5½. On vacation with her family in France, travelling in the car in a small town near where they stay, she said 'The thing I hate about France pedestrian crossings is / the cars get to choose. / But its great when you're in a car / because then VVRRAAAM . . .' It seems clear enough what is to hand, and what is being made entirely newly out of what is to hand. She wants to say things which I understood to have been something like the adjective *French*, the noun 'priority', and some exuberant, and joking expression of her sense of the relation of pedestrians and cars, and her pleasure at being in a car at this moment. She fashions these signs from what she has to hand, namely, the noun/name *France*, which she makes into a different syntactic sign, an adjective; the meaning of *priority* is analysed by her, and expressed in terms of its analytically derived components (changing, in the process from the possessive *have priority*, to the action *get to choose*). And for the expression of her affective meaning she changes mode, using sound and other physical expression as a material to express her feeling directly.

The point here is not to list the kinds of (abstract) resources which are available to her, but to make clear what these processes

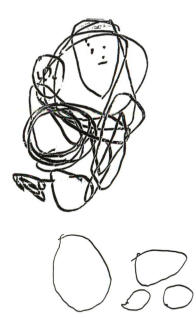

Figure 5.1 From circular scribbles to circles

are, and what their effects are. As with the material aspects of 'what is to hand', here too the different resources have differential potential and effect. It is by starting from that realization that we may be able to construct curricula of representation to meet our aims, and the needs of the younger generations.

IMAGINATION, COGNITION AND AFFECT

Imagination is an aspect of the processes of sign-making; of necessity it is always 'internal', for when its effects are expressed as 'outward' signs it has again become a part of public social semiosis. Imagination is a form of sign-making in which the boundaries to sign-making, the chains of signs, are potentially unlimited, and are not subject to the usual social constraint. It is dependent on and enhanced by the ability to engage in free movement among forms of (internal) representation – not confined, for instance, to staying within language, or the visual, or the tactile, but able to range freely across modes. The formation of signs described throughout this book is clearly the same kind of activity as that which we call imagination; a sign is a metaphor; metaphor involves the new expression of individual interest, and is therefore always in a sense a facet of imagination.

Imaginative activity takes place in any medium, though it is the case that society, perhaps particularly in formal education, in its focus on written language, acts to inhibit or suppress that activity of 'free ranging across' for most members of that society. That does not apply to the Arts, but the very fact that they are treated as a quite separate domain indicates the extent of the separation. The different media make different kinds of imagination possible; and impose their limitations on imaginative activity. The difficulty of translation between texts and signs in different media is evidence of the different potentials of the various modes.

One question to ask therefore is precisely about the limitations and possibilities of each medium. The visual, for instance, seems to permit in many cases much more subtly graded expression than the verbal. Language has to make do with units, such as words and sentences, or units with particular meanings, such as nouns and verbs and adjectives. In the visual semiotic there is a rule, for instance, about the meaning of *distance* between viewer and object viewed – something broadly like familiarity, solidarity, intimacy, formality; but clearly variation of distance is infinitely variable. In language I can say 'quite far', 'quite close', 'very close' and use a range of other forms, but there is a clear limit to the number of such variations. In the visual mode there is no such limit: the distance between myself and the object I look at is infinitely variable. Similarly with the possibilities of signifying meaning through colour: the range is infinite in the visual semiotic; and limited, relatively in language by the existence of colour terms.

Forms of teaching, as much as other social practices, can, over time, engender dispositions which impose limits to imagination, yet forms of teaching could equally be designed to open up its possibilities. At the moment the easy move across media 'mentally' – synaesthesia – is discouraged. The brain's capacity for translation from one mode into another is not seen as a quality to be fostered. If it were, the imaginative capacity of humans in western culture would be entirely different.

If cognition is the same kind of mental activity as that which we consider to be imagination, then the freeing of one will have positive effects on the other. This is entirely traditional thinking; but it may be possible to think freshly about this in the light of a theory which treats both as the same activity: one, cognition, is dependent on the existence of articulations of units and their relations in a particular medium, the other, imagination, is dependent on actively moving across media and modes, always going beyond the boundaries set by convention in a particular mode. In my view imagination and cognition are entirely and closely related. What we have learned to call 'cognition' works with established modes and their elements, and stays – in so far as that may ever be possible – with one mode. What we regard as imagination works across all the modes – in so far as it is not suppressed by socially induced 'habits of mind'. Cognition works with, and depends on, sign-making by using established kinds of units and their relations, respecting what can be generally referred to as the established boundaries; and where it does not, it is clear about the transgression of boundaries. Imagination goes beyond units and exceeds boundaries as its normal mode of action.

Lastly a word about affect. It seems to be the case that, as biological beings, we have different dispositions towards the world, differential preferences in relation to our senses. One child might prefer physical three-dimensional representation, another the distanced representation of drawing or writing. Another child might prefer to express herself or himself through the body, in dance or gesture. Compelling a child to forget his or her preferred mode will have affective consequences. Cultural groups have developed preferences in relation to modes and forms of expression. School necessarily imposes some further selection. These all have their influence on the child's affective disposition towards modes of representation and communication. In thinking about affect it is important to be aware of the relatively fine distinctions between cultural groups, within broader categories such as 'Western European', or even 'English' (rather than 'British', or 'Welsh' or 'Scottish'). Within multicultural 'English' society there are cultural groups strongly oriented towards writing; and not oriented strongly towards bodily forms of expression. Other groups within that society are much more oriented towards spoken language, and are freer in their use of the body as a means of communication. Children from both kinds of group can end up in the same 'English' classroom. The very broad distinctions of 'West African', 'South Asian', 'Mediterranean' may be too uselessly general, but they allow us to think, for instance, about the different cultural uses of the body as a vehicle of representation and communication. The difference between 'South Asian dance' and 'African dance' may suggest the distinctions I have in mind. In multicultural Britain or Australia or Germany, all these appear in one classroom. The consequences for the affective response by children in that classroom are impossible to calculate, but need to be imagined by a teacher.

Beyond that, there is the question of affect generally. The affective state of a child coming from her or his home to school in the morning will influence how that child will and can respond to an explanation, a task, given or set by the teacher. Affect 'colours' all activity, and cognitive action in particular. Again this is simply restating, in some ways, what is commonsensical: a warm, supportive, encouraging atmosphere in the classroom has positive effects on the ability of children to learn; and equally the opposite will be incontrovertible. Affect can dampen or enhance our performance, and the transformative tasks and processes of synaesthesia may be particularly prone to that. At the moment we know very little about all of this; and we know very little because the issue is not quite respectable on the public agenda. As I'll explain in Chapter 8, it may well be that we can no longer afford the luxury of such disdain.

Chapter 6

Literacy and theories of language

THE PRESENT COMMON SENSE IN THEORY AND IN PRACTICE

Ideas around literacy are intimately connected with, and often derived from, theories of language. They, in their turn, can and do come from very many fields: from linguistics of course; but also from psychology, anthropology of certain kinds, literary studies, sociology, media theory, and so on. Given that literacy is very much an applied activity, its practitioners can be highly pragmatic in their uses of theories: they are not in the least bit worried about borrowing eclectically: a bit from here, a bit from over there, and some other bits from somewhere altogether different. The current common sense about language in literacy is an amalgam of forms of anthropology, sociology, literary studies, with strong influences from psychology, media and cultural studies, and in fact with remarkably little contribution from linguistics itself. 'Phonics' of course derives from a branch of linguistics, namely phonology and phonetics, but otherwise, linguistics is noticeable largely by its absence.

The focus, generally, in contemporary literacy theory is on *use*: who does what with it; under what circumstances; for what purposes? What status does literacy have in community *x*? How are youngsters brought into literacy? What values are attached to it, by whom, under what circumstances? What groups are excluded from literacy, with what effects? These are all questions which concern anthropologists and ethnographers much more than they concern linguists, or even sociologists. In teaching, especially in the upper years of schooling, the effects of literary influence are noticeable – here the questions circle around aesthetic issues, 'good writing', matters of style. The influence of media studies is noticeable in the focus on 'what is done with' literacy: how do young men and women use certain kinds of texts, 'popular romance' for instance, and what do they do with them? While issues such as comprehension, complexity, recall and memory are treated in psychology.

There are two highly significant influences from psychology which it is worth mentioning even if only briefly, namely, the influences of Piaget and of Chomsky. They are, in one sense, related. Both, in different ways, assume a deeply located disposition towards language. In Piaget's case, much more than language. Human 'development' follows a given path which maps pretty well, on the basis of inherent patterns of the human brain, identifiable developmental stages. In Chomsky's case, language is seen as resting on an innate disposition in human brains towards language, which itself is seen as a highly abstract phenomenon. The evidence, for Chomsky, lies in the fact that all human languages can be learned by any human brain, an ability which he assumes must point to an underlying common organization of the brain. The facility to learn language – in a seemingly regular fashion for children in one language and even across languages – he attributes to what he has called in earlier forms of his theories a Language Acquisition Device, familiarly the LAD.

Remarkably, many or most of the approaches to literacy are characterized by an avoidance of the material itself, the 'stuff' of literacy. It is a little like talking about a house and the building of the house without talking about bricks, walls, concrete, plumbing, electric wiring or window frames. Instead, the talk is all about what the house should do, how it matches the wishes of the new owners, when the sun will come in and where, and so on. Clearly, both perspectives are important, and equally so. Architects have often been accused of not talking enough about these very things; but then no one wants the house to collapse either: no good having the sun come into the right window if in the meantime the roof is starting to cave in.

Ideally a theory of literacy should be based on a theory of language in which what people do with literacy is closely linked to an explanation of what it is 'made of' and how this mode of representation actually works; or, conversely, to explain what is or what is not really possible with this medium, and in this mode. In the preceding chapters I have tried to develop such an approach, where the *interest* of the maker of texts/messages is the engine which constantly reshapes the very stuff of the representational and communicational mode. Socially and culturally given interests do make us act in certain ways which are not mere accidents but have to do with the structures, purposes and values of the groups in which we lead our lives. My aim is to develop a theory in which all these concerns can be accommodated in a single integrated approach. As I have attempted to show so far, in the meaning-making practices of children there are a number of underlying and integrating principles at work, which they apply no matter what the stuff is that they are working with in their communicational and representational practices.

There is for me also a political purpose. It concerns the role and status, the 'standing' of the child (and indeed, later that of adults) in the processes of representation and communication. If Chomsky's notion of the LAD is correct, the *work* of the individual in 'acquiring' language is entirely different from the work which I have described. In my view children act energetically, intelligently, perceptively, out of their *interest*, innovatively making for themselves their means of communication and representation. Yes, they do it with the stuff which their culture has provided for them – this is the force of my examples of the children learning alphabetic and pictographic writing; and yes, *they* find *their* logic in those systems, and act transformatively on them. But in the Chomskyan description, the story has already been told, so to speak: the Language Acquisition Device has a structure, which is already there, as part of the brain's organization, and the child 'acquires' language in accordance with this structure – which is the same for all humans. Chomsky's account is the miracle of the unfolding structure of the brain, a miracle that happens to all humans every-where, and which leaves language (and the cultural world) as it is. My account is the story of the active engagement of bodily humans with all aspects of their cultural environment, which constantly transforms language, individuals, and their cultural world.

In *my* story we all get to what seems like the same point – say, we all speak a certain language competently – but the similarity is only partly real, and in part it is apparent. My example of the child's 'heavy hill' (Chapter 1) shows that the use of *heavy* on this occasion, and its conjunction with *hill*, was entirely the child's, and it means that *heavy* will for him never be exactly what it is for his neighbour at school; and that applies to all linguistic form. In the

Chomskyan story the shared structure of the LAD ensures that we end up as we started – largely the same; without much effect from the energetic innovative action of the individual child. In his story, the child's 'interest' (not a term Chomsky would use) would be to do everything possible to aid the unfolding of the structures of the LAD – a structure which is, however, already there.

Both the Piagetian account and that of Chomsky are motivated by a belief in the importance and dignity of human beings; yet both in the end underplay the energetic, interested, intentional action of children in their effects on their world. In each case our attention is focused on a pre-existing schema, and we are asked to look for evidence which shows the unfolding or the appearance of that schema. For me it is much more important to attempt to understand what children are doing out of their interests, actively, with intentions and interested in making their meanings. In the next two chapters I will develop some thoughts on the importance of this approach for curriculum and pedagogy, as well as for much wider social and economic considerations.

Many of the actions and many of the things produced by children that I have and which I have seen elsewhere simply do not match the Piagetian predictions, or their existing descriptions. The pre-existence of the strong theoretical schema holds the danger of blinding researchers to what is actually going on. The real task can become to find what the theorist knows that she or he should find. And unlike Chomsky's refusal to acknowledge the importance of the social and cultural environment it seems to me simply incontrovertible that children – and adults – make signs whose form can be shown to be their response to that environment. Of course, as I mentioned before, the LAD has no conceivable place for questions of *affect*.

Two aspects of current theories of language produce particular problems in thinking about and working in literacy; and here I wish to draw attention to both. One is that, with few exceptions, linguistic theories treat language as an autonomous system – autonomous from society in all its various, messy aspects; and autonomous also from individuals as makers of the system of language. Individuals are seen as *users* of an existing system; not as transformers and remakers of it. This autonomy makes it impossible to see language as social and as historical, as dynamic and as constantly changing in response to different and changing social environments. But it is patently obvious that language changes, with changes in the 'environment' in time – over history. One response to that glaring paradox has been to pluralize the term 'literacy', and to say that there is a plurality of *literacies*. This often gets extended to saying that we all have many literacies available to us, to meet the varying demands of social life.

However, this paradox only exists if, in the first place, we assume that language is autonomous, unaffected by the social, and therefore *stable*. If we assume that language is *dynamic* because it is constantly being remade by its users in response to the demands of their social environments, we do not then have a need to invent a plurality of literacies: it is a normal and absolutely fundamental characteristic of language and of literacy to be constantly remade in relation to the needs of the moment; it is neither autonomous or stable, and nor is it a single integrated phenomenon; it is messy and diverse, and not in need of pluralizing.

The second aspect concerns a different kind of pluralization, that is, the extension of the term literacy to other areas, not just of communication, but of general, broad, cultural interest. These 'literacies' proliferate: visual, media, cultural, computer, mathematical, emotional, and so on, and so on. The problem stems from a fundamental unwillingness or inability on the part of those who develop these metaphoric extensions of the term as serious concepts, rather than as quick, rhetorically effective uses (or as glib or lazy as with 'emotional literacy' and its cousins) to see language as just one of many modes of communication. Because it is seen as *the only real mode*, as the most highly developed, the one that sustains thought and rationality, all other modes of communication, or for that matter, all cultural *systems*, have to be described as being a literacy. This devalues the term, so that it comes to mean nothing much more than 'skill' (as in keyboard skills) or competence. It also prevents the possibility of examining the actual function of other systems, as systems in their own right.

As I hope my analysis of children's analytic engagement with print in Chapter 4 shows, literacy is a name for a complex of quite disparate phenomena – print, text as block, letters, text as genre, letters as sound, directionality and spatial dispositions, media, layout. It is in fact no more than a theoretical and ideological convenience to lump all these together as *literacy*. This is problematic enough. The term becomes more and more problematic the more elements are lumped into the meaning of 'literacy'. In reading, as I suggested, there is a fundamental question both about boundaries of the unit to be read; and of the limits to reading, of the end to the chain of signs produced in reading. So one can legitimately ask: where does literacy–competence stop? Does it include the ability to conjure up my nostalgic memories of Bondi Beach from a 'reading' of the 'Seagulls' print? Does a 'proper aesthetic response' to a literary text form part of a fully developed literacy competence?

WHAT *IS* LITERACY? UNRAVELLING SOME COMPLEXITIES

Among European languages, only English has the word *literacy*. Romance languages, French, Spanish, Portuguese, use *alphabetism* (or variants of it) to name the ability to read and write. Most western European languages have words which are relatives of the word *letter* (French *lettre*), as in *literary*, *literature*, but they use them to name the product of the use of letters, rather than creating an abstract noun to name a complex of disparate factors brought together as a skill. That has the advantage of retaining a relative precision in talking about this area, and avoids what is inevitable in English, namely the attachment of far-reaching stigma (un-educated, uncivilized, unintelligent, and so on) to those who do not 'have' literacy in *any* of its senses. As it happens, these other languages are experimenting with loaned versions of 'literacy' – for instance *lettramento* in (Brazilian) Portuguese, or *Literarität* in German.

In my own practice I use *literacy* only for the mode of *lettered representation*, and for the products which result, which are fash-ioned in its use. This forces me to pay proper attention – as I see it – to a number of things: to the full characteristics of writing and 'print'; to the distinctions between print/writing and speech; to an examination of the full set of factors that make them different from other modes of representation and communication (and here I want then to bring in the anthropological, sociological, media-theoretical approaches and others). It also forces me to say how and why visual communication does not function like writing; what *its* characteristics are; to try to develop ways and means of talking about that in as full a way as it is now possible to talk about writing/print. And it forces me to think and act similarly in relation to all other communicational systems.

Other questions, some of which I have mentioned in earlier

chapters are: what are the potentials and limitations of each mode? What cognitive and affective effects do they bring with them? And, importantly in a world which is moving towards multimedia production as an everyday form of sign-making, how do all these interact? How are they read as a complex by readers? How, in other words, do we make sense of texts which consist, simultaneously, of a number of quite distinct semiotic modes?

Here I will focus on what I regard as some central aspects of the 'stuff' of literacy; this will not be exhaustive, but focuses on the one hand on aspects which I regard as quite central, and on the other will show in a reasonably clear form ways of thinking about this issue, and a way of proceeding in describing and analysing this whole area. The aspects I will consider are: the sound–letter relation – what I might call 'drawing sound'; the issue of the visual shape of letters; which is related to the whole complex question of the spatial aspects of print/writing, and layout; the relation between modes of speech and writing; *text* as the central and criterial unit of language study, literacy studies included; the sentence as a textually motivated unit rather than a syntactically motivated one; the issues surrounding the characteristics of a text, namely its generic form, its discursive make-up; and lastly, the question of the significance of the page.

If we see language and literacy as social and cultural phenomena – as I do – the *text* has to be the unit which we focus on first and foremost. This is so because when we speak and write, we always do so in a social context, and it is the characteristics of the social context which shape our language use, and which provides its boundaries. This approach to language may seem rather shocking, given that we have been taught for so long to focus on (words and) the sentence. But a very brief reflection should be enough to convince you that we do not talk in sentences: we do not utter a sentence, then another; then someone utters another. That is the stuff of certain kinds of comedy sketches. Rather we speak, write, interact in tightly integrated, coherent units, which are much much more than a mere jumble, or even an orderly list of sentences. As a small test of this, take any paragraph of more than seven sentences, and then try to rearrange them – say, putting sentence 3 in first place, sentence 7 in second place, sentence 1 in third, and so on. The tight integration and structure of the previous structure will quickly become apparent. You will find that sentence 7 had a structure which fits it precisely for that place, and so does sentence 3, and so on. It is an aspect of our competence as writers (and speakers) that we are quite unaware of possessing.

Texts derive their sense, their order, their coherence, their logic, from the logic, sense, order, of the (structure of the social) environment in which they were produced by one or more speakers, or by a writer who had her or his absent audience nevertheless closely in mind. That order is what I mean by generic form, by genre. Every occasion of speaking and writing, of listening and reading is a social occasion, in which the people who participate in it are quite well aware of their social roles; are aware of their obligations and rights; aware of conventions and the strength of conventions; and are aware of the possibilities or otherwise of contravening these conventions, and of the penalties (and in some cases, the rewards) which follow from such contraventions.

An interview, for instance, has a clear structure. If it is a job interview, there is a clear purpose, on both the parts of interviewers and interviewed; the roles are clear, as are the rights and duties associated with them, as well as the manner of carrying them out; from the welcoming 'Thank you for coming here today' to the 'And do you have any questions to ask of the panel?' It is understood who asks the questions, except for that brief bit at the end; and so on. If it is a media interview, the structure is somewhat different, because the social purposes, the social relations and structures are different: but not different enough for us not to recognize it is an interview. All texts are made in social occasions where the participants – if they are 'practised', experienced, competent members of the group – do understand quite clearly what is at issue, what the forms and conventions are, and how much transformative activity is wise or unwise to engage in.

Children, especially younger children, are not practised, not experienced, in their social occasions and their meaning, either in spoken or in written language. These are precisely things they must learn. It is important to bear in mind that these are simultaneously linguistic and social facts, linguistic and social organizations, which they are learning; and they probably do not make that distinction between language and social practices which seems so clear and important to us as adults.

Genres are the effects of the social organization of the occasions in which we interact whether through language – spoken or written – or with any other media or mode (though very little work has been done on this issue of textual organization in forms other than language). Genres are one aspect of textual shape: we recognize something as an interview the moment we turn on the radio or the television; and this knowledge enables comedians to use it for humorous effect, often through the merest perceptible exaggeration.

As I tried to show in Chapters 3 and 4, children have to learn these forms as part of their move into literacy. However, my examples also show, from how very early on they are aware of this level of organization, and how very early they begin to take those aspects into their transformative action. The newspapers (Figures 3.6 and 4.6) are clear instances. Neither are copies: no newspaper looks like any of the pages produced by the children; they are new signs made from their reading of the logic of these forms of media. Both children, one at the age of 7, and one at the age of 4 years and 9 months, produce pages which have linguistic text at the top, and visual image at the bottom of the page. Both seem to have read that as a fundamental structure: clearly they are aware of *layout*, as early as 4 years of age. Both have produced headlines: the younger child through the visual means of bold lettering; the older one through that means, *and* through forms of language. I will discuss this in detail in Chapter 7 and simply point to the fact that generic form is something which children are aware of, even if it has not entered everywhere into the common sense of literacy theory.

The same two examples are also evidence of the fact that children understand well enough that *content* has a shape. News – as genre – has as its content 'violent events': whether as an aeroplane crash, or as the death of a woman in the street. The sports pages similarly show evidence of this: the language used by the 7-year-old shows evidence of generic form, and of an organization of knowledge in specific ways: as 'mach of the day', and in the conventionalized form of 'Man Utd v Asnal'. Later, in the children's move through primary school, and particularly in their transition to secondary school, when the school subjects appear in their fully specialized form, that aspect of language and of writing, will become particularly important. I refer to it as 'Discourse' (as in medical discourse, legal discourse, the discourse of geography, and so on), to draw attention to the fact that what we usually think of as 'content' is organized in socially given ways, and that this is something children have to learn as a part of their move into literacy.

Again it is quite astonishing to me from what an early age they seem to have an awareness of this factor. In Chapter 7 I will give a number of examples, and relate them to the further question of children's differentiated interests, and their effect on their paths into literacy. By this I mean not much more than the commonly understood fact that children are not interested in just everything, but are selective in their interests; that boys and girls may be selecting differentially from an early age; and so on. These selections lead to specialisms – one child may become an expert in one range of issues, and another in a different one. One effect of such specialization is the establishment of gender. These specializations appear in their selections through language, and through all other modes as well. Some selections seem to be quite gender-neutral (in my experience both boys and girls seem to be interested in the maze as an object, for instance), others are not. But these specializations are highly significant in that they lead to differentiated forms of expression, and they are therefore aspects which we must consider with great attention.

Writing is a visual medium; both the printed page and the hand-written page are visual objects. They have features of spatial design. Even in the older forms of literacy which, for some of us, still define literacy, when the page was covered in print (*the densely printed page* as Theo van Leeuwen and I have called it in *Reading Images* (1996)), there are aspects of design: indentations for paragraphs; spacings of letters on the line; the distance between the lines of print; the form of letter-shapes chosen; spacings between words; the size of the white margin around the block of printing. These kinds of things drift uneasily in and out of definitions of literacy: from a linguistic point of view they are clearly *out*; from a designer's point of view they are definitely *in*. Contemporary technologies of writing are in favour of designers, and expose the linguist's view as having always been too narrow and too abstracted.

Certainly the control of the design of the page will be a central aspect of the productive aspects of writing/print: the page as visual object; the spatial distributions and arrangements of printing on the page as meaningful – as indentation for paragraphs is, for instance; or as bullet points are, or size and distribution of paragraphs, bold sub-headings, and so on.

These features are of course meaningful now. I have before me a page from a history textbook for children in upper primary school. The paragraphs are relatively short, never more than three lines; the letter-shapes are sanserif and are relatively widely spaced, as are the words; the lines also are not densely packed one on the other: the text, as visual object, looks 'open'. It displays, visually, in all these features, what view the designer of this page held about child readers: views about their ability to engage at length with material; about their attention span; their ability to deal with complexity; and so on.

As school textbooks are becoming more and more visual rather than verbal objects this trend will intensify – leaving aside the problematic question of the future (or even present) function of the textbook. But that move mirrors, in any case, the shift in society in and around the school, towards visual forms of communication. In Chapter 4, I mentioned another aspect of the page which it may be useful to repeat at this point; it is the relation between size and form of the page, and generic content. I suggested that when children fold the single sheet, they suddenly have an object with new (meaning) potential. The size of the page often has a close relation with the structure of the text through the simple link to the size or extent of the text. This is well understood in journalistic practice, where the length of a 'story' and its internal structure are governed by the available space on the newspaper or magazine page. (The same is of course true also of any other medium- whether television or radio news; or television documentary; or feature film; or of the book that I am writing now.) Neither the significance of the size or the shape of the page has so far had the increasingly essential attention in our thinking about competence in literacy.

Children do often show awareness of this factor: not only in the page designs which they produce in their image-based texts – though often these are designs incorporating language and image – but also in the attention they give to the *line*, for instance. Frequently, especially in their earlier writing, they experiment with the visual/spatial unit of the *line*, as a means of giving shape to their writing, before the line develops into the grammatical/syntactic unit of the sentence, which then takes over as the relevant unit. This in itself signals a conceptual/cognitive shift of considerable complexity and abstractness: the move from a *spatial unit, the line*, expressed through the material boundaries of the width of the page, to *a conceptual unit, the sentence*, expressed through the abstract organization of elements – clauses usually – in an hierarchical order.

SPEECH AND WRITING: 'DRAWING SOUNDS'

An earlier move of equal significance also involves a move across from one fundamental semiotic/conceptual/cognitive mode to another, namely that from speech to writing. Speech as a mode derives its structure from a large number of factors – psychological, physiological, social and semiotic. I will briefly touch on these, but start with what is perhaps the most fundamental aspect, namely the fundamental shift from *sequence in time* (one sound after another, one word after another, one clause after another), *to arrangement in space*, to organization on the page. When I am listening to someone talking, if I miss out on hearing or understanding something, it is gone, unless of course I feel able to ask the speaker to repeat what was just said. In writing I can retrace my path on the page without great difficulty. Speech has therefore evolved a structure which aids the listener's comprehension – one clause at a time (which means, broadly, one sense unit at a time), one after another, like beads on a string. Writing has a structure which is much more like a set of Chinese boxes, clauses stacked inside each other, as well as clauses attached in a more speech-like fashion to each other. The fact that in writing I can recover information, by backtracking, means that writing can afford to become very complex in its structure. Using technical terms, speech is *paratactic* (one thing arranged with another), while writing is *hypotactic* (one thing arranged below another).

Writing has a hierarchical structure (one main clause, with subordinate clauses which may themselves have subordinate clauses); and it is a mode which therefore has, metaphorically spatial characteristics. But writing is also literally visual and spatial. Short paragraphs may be visually attractive to certain readers. They give a particular look to the page as a spatial unit; but they also affect what kinds of sentences will be used in such a paragraph. Spatial design has effects on the actual grammar of the sentence; so the increasing prominence of visual images on newspaper pages exerts a pressure on language not only in that there is less space for it on the page now dominated by images, but also in that language – in the form of literacy – changes in fundamental syntactic ways.

The structure of speech is also shaped by its physiological and psychological origins. So when we breathe we take in a certain amount of air, which can be formed by the 'vocal organs' into speech sounds when we slowly let it out again. This means that your speech stops when your breath runs out. In a conversation that fact may give others a chance to 'come in' if they are quick, before you had time to draw your next breath! As a consequence the basic units of speech have – perhaps unsurprisingly – the same length as breath-units. In English that common unit, shaped by grammar and physiology, is the clause, roughly speaking. Psychologically, it is the case that our short-term memory, which we use in planning what we want to say before we say it, is limited to holding about the number of units which usually make up a clause (seven, plus or minus two). The same limitation applies to the brain in listening, when we have to store incoming sounds, words and grammatical structures until we have made sense of the whole unit.

These limitations on the size of the units of speech and on their organization, have far-reaching consequences: it means that those of us who are used, habitually, to their structure, develop cognitive and conceptual structures which mirror the structuring of speech. The logic of oral cultures is to a large extent determined by the logic of the structures of speech. When children go to school they meet – and have to accommodate to – the logic and structure of writing, irrespective of the structures of communication of their home background. The logic of speech is one of sequence, of repetition, restatement, reformulation, of slow development; the logic of writing is one of hierarchy, of compression of meaning, of complex syntactic interrelation. Both logics have real strengths, and both have limitations. The important point is that the logic of writing has ruled, and still does rule, in the domains of power in our societies – business, finance, technology, education, bureaucracies, politics, the law, and so on.

These differences of speech and writing shape central characteristics of literacy, even though they are now in a process of rapid change. However, those who hold sway in these things – politicians, the business community, but also educators – still have that older form as their relevant model. The newer form, as it appears in electronic forms of communication for instance, is moving in the direction of the structures of speech, in its basic syntactic and grammatical organization: less complex, less hierarchical syntax; shorter units; simpler sentence structures; and so on. The reasons for these changes are complex and probably impossible to know fully at the moment. They are likely to have to do with social factors, and to be accentuated by new technologies. If writing has been the medium of communication at a distance, temporally and geographically, speech is the medium of proximity: the person to whom I'm speaking is visually co-present. The telephone introduced the first disturbing ripple into this, because the 'other person' was co-present in time but not present in my immediate space. Electronic written communication is like that also. I find myself writing to someone who is, or may be co-present in time and yet be thousands of miles distant. The solution adopted at the moment is to use the grammatical forms which have been used for the relative informality of speech, but using lettered representation.

At times, the relation of letters and sounds, has been seen as central in defining the relation of speech and writing, and therefore central to what literacy is – as that factor which seemingly enables us to make speech permanent, to record it; to transcribe speech into visible, storable, permanent form. (The fact that this perception pre-dates the invention of various other forms of recording speech – from phonograph to tape-recorder is not important for the moment.) Children meet this relation of sound and letter in the form of 'spelling'. The etymology of the word *spell* points back to the meaning 'narrate', 'tell a tale'; and our contemporary word is related to *spell* as in 'a magic incantation'. In other words, the original meaning of *spell* does not at all refer us directly to the letter–sound relation, but rather, perhaps, to telling the tale in a permanent, or memorable form.

Children take this relation of 'drawing sounds' extremely seriously, and seem to spend great analytical energy on trying to make sense of it, judging from the constant 'reanalysis' of the relation which we characteristically meet in their writing. This issue is well known, and has had much discussion under the label of 'invented spelling'. To give just two examples here: one is a recipe, for a 'Prune Split'; the other is a story 'The roadrunner', which is given in full in Chapter 4.

Recipe for a Prune Split

Proon Split	Prune Split
1. Graps cut	1. Grapes cut
2. Amands	2. Almonds
3. Wanuts crushe	3. Walnuts crushed
4. Rasens cut	4. Raisins cut

5. Proons – split	5. Prunes – split
Sureces	Sugar
1. wite wanuts crushe	1. white walnuts crushed
2. sugar	2. sugar
Put in to proons	Put in to prunes
Put sucre on top	Put sugar on top
Miks	Mix

Here we have an absolutely ordinary example of 'invented spelling'. The cues which the child has to work with are the sounds of speech, which come to him in the form of quite different dialects, so that the 'original' form – if we think of spoken language as the source – is itself not stable but is likely to be an amalgam of many dialects and accents. One thing that children must learn clearly, is to ignore the wide dialectal variation of spoken English, or to normalize it for themselves. For instance, one person who is very prominent in the daily interactions of the writer above speaks a form of northern English, in which *crush* sounds close to *croosh*. Other cues which children have are the 'names' of letters: 'this shape a is the letter *ei*'; and rules, more or less complex: 'this letter a sounds (like) *ei*'; and so on. With this equipment, and with an acute sense of sound discrimination, children make their attempts at unravelling the mysteries (the other meaning of *spell?*) of spelling.

In the 'Roadrunner' story there are three occurrences of the word *roadrunner*: as *rodraunar*, as *rodranauar*, and as *radranur*. It seems astonishing that even in the middle of the absorbing task of composing and writing down the story, the child seemingly has the cognitive energy to reanalyse this word three times. The principles he applies in these reanalyses seem different in each case. Transcribing *road* as *rod* seems to rely on 'this letter's name (o) is *ou*'; whereas the principle of transcribing *road* as *rad* seems to rely on his own phonetic analysis: 'this word sounds to me, the way I've heard it, as *rad*' (as it might, if it was said quite quickly, with the vowel entirely unaccented, unemphasized). If that is so, we see here not merely evidence of detailed analysis and the transformative process of remaking applied to the sound–letter relation, but we see also the application of quite different principles in the analysis. In this sense this is like the child's constant reanalysis of print – is it block of print, letter, word, and so on, which I discussed in Chapter 3.

The term 'invented spelling' is an attempt to avoid labellings such as 'mistake', 'error'; but it itself obscures the processes that children engage in in making their sense of this bit of the semiotic world. It is *not* invention in the sense of plucking some solution out of the air, 'making it up'; it is invention – in the sense of new making – based as always on the children's attempts to understand the logic of this bit of their world by the application of the principles of the motivation of signs, and of the integral coherence of meaning and form (where in this case meaning is the 'sound-meaning' in the sense of 'what is the best way of expressing the characteristics of this sound'). Children continue with this rigorous, analytic examination, until they are satisfied, for a while at least, that they have a plausible solution.

If they can't make full sense of the system, it is because the system *does not make full sense* when seen from any one single perspective. You need to have a high level of knowledge of the historical formation of all forms of contemporary English; of the layers on layers of different languages piled on each other: initially different germanic dialects; then later scandinavian languages; then two distinct layers of French superimposed on all that; all with constant liberal dashes of Greek and Latin; then the massive remaking of English in the sound changes of the late fourteenth century (which have made Chaucer difficult to read for us now); knowledge of conflicting principles applied over the last five centuries by generations of quite differently motivated phoneticians, dictionary compilers, grammarians, writing regulators; all this in order to begin to make sense of the logic of this system. Few 6-year-olds have that kind of knowledge at their fingertips. To them it must seem, so many times, that they have glimpsed and grasped *the* sense of the system, only to find on the next occasion that it has yet again eluded them.

Children love puzzles; so it is not their lack of interest, lack of intelligence, or lack of energy that is the issue. In my own observation there seem two types of children: those who say: 'This is a code; I can crack it', and those who say 'This is too messy, I'll not try to make sense of it.' The latter group divides into those who are prepared to learn spelling by rote, and those who can't be bothered with a non-sensical system. But the first group, the code-crackers, those with the most rigorously logical minds, can be more or less guaranteed failure. If teachers understand the real historically complex constitution of this system of contradictory principles, derived from a most chequered history, then they might be able to devise strategies to deal with the problems faced by both groups: reassuring the first that logic can't get them all the way, so that they need a heavy dash of pragmatism; and showing the second group aspects of the differing, contradictory logics, perhaps with little bits of this fascinating history thrown in as intellectual yeast.

DESIGNING MEANINGS

In my brief description of literacy just now I deliberately adopted an order that went from text to letter, from a large unit to a small unit, from a unit which is directly governed by larger social factors to a unit in which that influence is present but perhaps a little less directly visible. I did that for two reasons: one is to go against one common-sense view of language, which might be called the bricks-and-mortar view, or the building-blocks view of language. That is a view which says that language has small units, *sounds*, which make up larger units, *words*, which make up larger units, *phrases*, which make up *clauses*, which make up *sentences*, which make up *texts*. (The theorist's version of this would be somewhat more complicated, but there are versions that are quite close to this.) As a theory of how we actually use language it obviously doesn't hold water, though that has not led to its demise.

The building-blocks view also corresponds in no way at all, and this is my second reason, to children's production of their sign/messages, whether small or large, simple or highly complex. Children's designs unfold in much more complex and much more subtle ways – and when one attempts to retrace the path of their sign-making one can only come to one conclusion: it is planned in very many instances in great detail; it shows all the features of *design*; it is done with full intent. The example of the 'Panadol-man' was one instance; here I want to give another, to foreground the issue of the child's planning and design of complex semiotic objects: complex both in their cognitive/conceptual content, and in their management of several different modes in the making of one sign. My new example is as follows.

Emily, at that stage 6 years old, had noticed that her brother had fashioned a shield out of a rectangular piece of cardboard, about 1 m long, and 35 cm wide. She asked if she could have a similar piece of cardboard. When I next saw it it had been transformed into a screen *and* movie, propped up on two pillows, below a light in the living room. When the curtain was drawn and the lights went *on*, a pillow which had hidden the central section was removed, to reveal the 'movie': a large chocolate egg on the left, a small chicken on the left; two clouds with faces above; the sun in the top right corner. The chicken was conducting (the voices emanating from behind the screen) a verbal exchange with the sun. Sun: 'A happy day'; chicken: 'No'. One of the clouds commented 'What is that' in reaction to a bolt of lightning nearby (one of two, one near each cloud). In the bottom right corner, a cut-out white paper boat nearly covered a blue lake. On the top left margin there is a printed 'BBC 15', which was announced as 'BBC Channel 15' (Figure 6.1).

While I do not know the degree to which this design was *fully* planned, in all detail, it is clear that when Emily asked for the cardboard – which she had encountered as a *shield*, made by her brother – she knew what she wanted to make. This whole 'production' process, including the 'staging' and narration, is, if we are prepared to treat it seriously, in every way as complex a task as any form of writing. In my estimation it is a more complex task. Some process of prior internal representation has to precede the execution of the design. Often, as in the case of the Panadol-man, and as here, the process starts somewhere in the middle, so to speak; and certainly it is not a process of gradual 'building up', going from small or large, or from simple to complex. It has much more a feeling of the child's sense of a whole *design* from the beginning, as a kind of Gestalt.

In fact, curiosity got the better of me, and I asked the movie producer what made her do it. She said 'I wanted to do a show, and I thought about what season was coming up, and so I made the Easter egg, and an Easter show. If I had thought about your birthday, I would have made a birthday show.' This was said at the end of January. *Show* is an established genre in her and her friends' repertoire. *Movie* might have been introduced because the previous day she had been to see the film *Babe*, which may or may not have had an effect.

The point of introducing the concept of *design* is to draw attention to these factors, which go by unnoticed, even in considerations of play, and of games. And that is significant in order to dispel a naive but persistent view of meaning-making. This is that when I speak I wish to express a meaning; which I encode in a word (which more or less 'fits' my meaning), and on

Figure 6.1 At the movies

uttering that word – or a string of words – my meaning gets across to the person to whom I am speaking. But when the two girls playing their game came to a point where they needed a car, there wasn't the object-equivalent of a car, or even more importantly, the equivalent of the car which they needed, around. In the three-dimensional multisemiotic world of objects there are no 'words'. So they had to make a car, one which suited their needs. They constructed it on the basis of a design which existed well before the drawers were removed from the chest of drawers to serve as the foundation for the central seat and the doors of the car. It existed as a clear design: it included a sense of what materials would be used; to fulfil what function; a selection of other materials from what was available; all before the first object was placed on the floor.

The realization that there are no ready-made tokens, no 'words', to carry our meanings in these modes, should make us more serious in our regard of these objects; to consider the processes of design seriously – and the implication of that decision for our view of childish semiosis and cognition. It might also make us somewhat more sceptical towards currently accepted notions of language, and of our making of meaning in language. They look seductively like that; and in theory as in common sense they have been treated like that. The four cars which I mention in Chapter 2 are all fundamentally different from each other – and they are made to express those differences. In language they are represented by the single word *car*. Words are not, in my view, ready-made objects or tokens of meaning, which we can simply insert into the chess game of our social interactions. Words are materials out of which we can fashion new signs; and these new signs express our meanings. That shift in thinking suggests that the notion of design applies to verbal text also; it could be useful to explore the consequences of using it in our approach to children's (and adults') verbal texts.

STRUCTURES AND MEANINGS OF VISUAL COMMUNICATION

If the world of meaning is becoming more and more visual the question arises whether images are a system of communication, or whether they express reality directly, in some way. Photography seems at times to be simply transmitting external reality, like a mirror: and images in mirrors are not seen as systems of communication. Generally we now understand that lenses transform reality, and that the chemistry of photographic emulsions, of processes of development, and so on, change reality significantly. Added to that are the structuring efforts of the photographer.

The first question to answer is this: what is a fully-fledged communication system, or what should it do? The common-sense view is that communication is the passing on of *information*, in the transmission of *messages*. If we want to stick with that view we need to extend our definition of information. The messages which we send contain a variety of information. There is – and that is at the centre of the conventional view – information about what has happened, what is the case, what things are like. 'Bill might have smashed his car last night' informs me that perhaps someone *did* something, to an object, at a specified time. This message also provides me with specific details: the object was a car, the someone was Bill, and so on. This is information in the most traditional sense; 'content'. It has often been called 'propositional content', or 'propositional meaning'. In fact I don't think that we communicate 'propositions' – we communicate our ideas, our experiences. And so I will call it 'experiential content', which links it tightly into social life. The sentence above also tells me that the person who says it has some doubts; she or he is uncertain. Maybe they are uncertain because of *me*, they don't want to be definite in order not to hurt, upset or offend me. Maybe if they were talking to someone else they might say 'Bill smashed up his car again last night.' That is also information, but not in the usual sense. It is information that tells us about the speaker's state of mind; and about the speaker's sense of her or his relation to me. We can call it 'interpersonal content or meaning'.

Lastly, it is most unlikely that this sentence would be said unless there was a context for it. The context in the widest sense might be a history of Bill's drinking problem, and of previous accidents. More specifically the context might be a statement by someone: 'I'm so worried, Bill hasn't shown up yet.' In other words, sentences have a coherent relationship with each other, in a text, and also have a coherent relationship with a larger context. So both statements tell those who are engaged in this interaction – but also someone who might be overhearing this exchange – about the structure of the immediate and the much wider context, and even give us hints about the contents of that context. That is information too, also not in the usual sense; but it is vital information. It locates the utterances, it locates me as hearer, and the speaker, in a particular, relatively well circumscribed world. We can call it '(con)textual information'.

My assumption is that a fully functioning communication system must always convey these three types of meaning: telling us what bit of the (social) world we're in; telling us about the relations of speaker and hearer (or writer and reader; or image-maker and image-viewer); and telling us something about the states of affairs and the objects in that world. Not all these will always be equally in the foreground, but all three must be there. So when I say to my neighbour 'Lovely day today', propositional meaning is not so significant, but interpersonal meaning is; and (con)textual meaning is, too – it locates both of us in the social world, as people who want to be friendly.

We can now ask if visual communication forms such a communication system; and we can ask the same question of all the other semiotic objects I have so far described or mentioned – the cut-out figures, the pillow-car, the 'movie', and so on. I will stay with visual communication, largely because texts composed of visual and verbal means form such a significant part of children's meaning-making activities, and partly because they form such a rapidly increasing part of the adult society's textual/communicational environment.

Consider Figure 6.2. Its title, given by the then just 5-years-old maker is 'The toy-museum/mouse, turtle, doll, Jack-in-the-box/me looking at all the toys'. Clearly this image has 'propositional content'; and using the term 'experiential meaning' links it precisely with the child's experience of a visit to the toy museum in London's Bethnal Green. The figures are arranged in order, probably in *an* order of significance to the child: size is one ordering principle, though it may be being used to form signs which are about her interest in the different kinds of toys. There is a classification at work here, which in its turn rests on a prior analysis which she had performed 'internally'. It may be that there actually *was* a display case, or a shelf, with this ordering of toys; it is equally or more likely that there was no such case and that it is her transformation of a part of her experience of the whole visit. In any case it is as a set of objects, shown spaced at equal distance, on a surface between two borders.

Figure 6.2 'At the toy museum/mouse, turtle, doll, Jack-in-the-box/me looking at all the toys'

There is also the figure of the child – the self-portrait – in the foreground. The experiential content is therefore 'Me, and the toys, in the toy museum'. The two elements of content – what was viewed, and the viewer – are represented in a clear order: the foregrounded author/viewer; and the backgrounded viewed objects.

There is clearly also an interpersonal meaning being expressed. Although the spoken caption says 'me looking at the toys', it is, visually, '*me*, looking at *you*', establishing precisely the relation with the viewer, a relation which is so strong in western art, whether in seventeenth-century English miniaturists, in Rembrandt's look over his shoulder at the viewer; Dürer's self-portrait; or more recently again, in Woody Allen's direct address of the viewer in the film *The Purple Rose of Cairo*.

Lastly, the contextual meaning: the relation between the two major elements of meaning (the toys and the girl) is handled by a visual syntax – a foreground–background relation. Because she does not have the representational means of perspectival drawing at her disposal, she has used height on the page to make the sign of that relation. This is quite often used, so that even in perspectivally drawn representations, more distanced elements are higher on the spatial unit – page, canvas, wall. The foregrounding of the major figure is of course another textually achieved feature, and gives the foregrounded figure greater salience – particularly as it is surrounded by empty space. There is also a contextual relation, with the visit to the toy museum, though that is not strongly represented, other than perhaps by reference to the drawing of the display case, and the orderly arrangements of the toys: as 'objects on display'.

In the Easter-egg 'movie' which I described a bit earlier, there is clearly experiential content: the egg, the chicken, the clouds. They are given a 'setting', a landscape, so these elements are contextualized experientially. The basic mode of representation is the classificatory one – the 'there are' relation (or the 'it has' relation) 'there are clouds, sun, chicken, a boat', and so on. Unlike the toy-museum drawing there is some (inter)action in this image: this is done via speech bubbles. The sun makes a pronouncement 'A happy day'; one cloud asks a question 'What is that'; and the chicken answers back to the sun 'No.' There seems therefore an attempt to introduce interaction into this image, to go beyond classification alone.

Interpersonally there is again the direct look at me, the viewer, by the main character, the chicken. The ordering of elements also has, though more implicitly, an interpersonal effect: these objects are displayed for me, the viewer; although the child's affective, cognitive interest is also at work here. 'Display' may be the visual analogue to 'statement' in language. Textually, the elements are arranged in symmetrical form across this space, with a bottom–top (earth, sky) and a left–right structure (egg–chicken) rather than the foreground–background relation of the toy museum. Contextually, this movie was placed in a frame of pillows, propped between two armchairs in the living room – the picture theatre, under a lamp, which was used to dim the lights or bring them back up again. The curtains of the bay window immediately at the back were manipulated to suggest the raising of the curtain in the picture theatre. The inscription BBC 15 in the top left corner was used to establish this contextual link; and there is the larger contextual link with the previous day's visit to the movies – possibly the chicken (a substitute for the duck character in *Babe?*), and the genre *movie* itself.

I have no doubt that these images function as full communicational entities, as messages. The visual does act as a system of communication, and so has to be learned like other systems of communication, such as language for instance. This is where too little thinking has been done, so that the generally held view – at least as it appears in the evidence of practices in schools – is that images are decoration, expression of feelings, emotions; pretty or not so pretty; but *not* explicit communication. That appears clearly in the comments of teachers on the early writing of children, which nearly always have images with the verbal text. Teachers will usually comment on aspects of language: 'Must put full stops!', 'Not too many *ands*'; and teachers will 'correct' spelling. By contrast, teachers' comments on the images are never 'corrections': they may be praise, 'Lovely picture'; or they may be encouragement, 'Try to do neater colouring-in', but they are not corrections. If the visual was seen as communication, then in my opinion, teachers would be 'correcting': 'Move your central figure more clearly into the foreground', 'Make your displays more evenly spaced', and so on.

In children's visual images there are relatively few instances of the representation of *action*, and even rarer, of *interaction*. There are some instances which can be seen as the representation of action: the cut-out car with its environment has action as a theme – the wheels throwing up sparks and dust from the road; the rocket which has just been fired; the flames coming out of the exhaust at the rear. Yet it is action which we, the viewers, have to imagine 'on to' the representation. Even so, this is a rare example. The crashed aeroplane in the newspaper of Figure 4.6 is not about present action, but about the effect of a past action: it has crashed, it is a crashed plane. The footballers in the same newspaper – on the sports page – suggest *interaction*, but it is represented indirectly by the portrayal of two players, in a flat, classificatory form ('there are two football players'), and the suggestion of interaction by the fact that they are drawn side-on, facing each other.

In the example of the toy museum (Figure 6.2), the child's drawing is analytical (these are the kinds of things you see in the toy museum) and classificational (there are mice, turtles, dolls, Jack-in-the-boxes and visitors). Her verbal *caption* is actional:

'me looking at all the toys'. This is a common strategy adopted by children – to use language to express action: either as spoken commentary on the visual text, or as written caption.

A fundamental question arises from this: is it that children are 'limited' cognitively and do not therefore represent action in the visual medium; or is it that the visual medium is not 'naturally' oriented towards the representation of action, and is naturally suited to analytic, classificatory representation, in the spatial arrangements of 'display'? This question is a fundamental one, not only in relation to children, but also in relation to the orientation of cultural groups. Also, given that 'narrative' seems so important in all human cultures, and has acquired a mythic status in certain approaches to language teaching, we need to understand this more clearly; or at least understand that there are difficult questions here.

The children who do not represent actions in their visual representations have no difficulty telling stories. It is clear, there-fore, that it is not a matter of limited cognitive development. A better assumption might be that this has to do with the 'stuff', the material through which we communicate and represent. Two-dimensional visual communication has to take place via a (flat) surface – a page, a wall, a screen, a bit of earth in front of us, a rock face, or a computer screen. (This shows of course that written language, print, is, in one of its guises, a visual medium.) The medium is *space*, a flat space, on which I arrange the images that I want to show. Before I can depict them, I have to decide what I want to show, and in what arrangement. That requires the double action of analysing the reality I want to represent, giving me a sense of *what* is to be represented; and the action of deciding on the best way of arranging them, according to *my* interest, giving me a sense of *how* it is to be represented – the act of displaying my classificatory schema.

Narratives are not spatial; their 'natural' medium is speech – which happens in time, as one thing, one action, after another. Therefore the order of narrative – events happening in time – runs parallel to the order of the medium of representation – things said in time. From that point of view writing is also a temporally ordered medium; we read one thing after another. So there seems to be a 'natural' coming together of the medium of space, with (spatial) analysis and classification; and the medium of time, with actions, and the succession of events unfolding in time.

Children's use of the visual mode is therefore in accord with the inherent potential of that medium, as is their use of the temporal medium of speech. It may be that this insight illustrates another of their problems: for children who learn to draw Chinese characters, the path into writing is from drawing images to drawing (abstract, conventionalized) images, a path in which they stay in the same medium, space and spatial display. For children who learn alphabetic writing, the path is from drawing images to the drawing of sound, a path which takes them across a chasm which not all manage to negotiate, a shift from spatial display to sequences in time.

One educational consequence is, yet again, the question about the potentials of the various forms. If the spatial lends itself 'naturally' to processes of analysis and classification, does it do so more effectively than the verbal does? If the verbal lends itself more readily to the representation of action and of dynamic events, to representation in the narrative form, does it do so more effectively than drawing does? There are famous visual narratives: Trajan's column in Rome tells the story of that emperor's wars and victories; and the Bayeux tapestry does the same for William the Conqueror's famous battle. Giotto's frescos in the church of Assissi tell the story of Christ's life though more as a succession of set pieces: scenes from the life of Christ. But they all do so in space with its limitations. Verbal narratives might do it more effectively (though the visual form has lasted better than most verbal narratives would have done).

If there *is* a specialization, should we make do with second best – representing classification, analysis in language, and action in images – or should we be prepared to use each medium to the fullest of its potential? I will return to this question in the last two chapters.

In this context we can now think about the pillow-car, and all the other objects, texts, arrangements which children make. The three-dimensional productions offer the opportunity of *entering into* action even if they may not represent actions themselves. They enter into action, are acted with and acted on by children; in their arrangements they can be structured to shape the course of action. A track laid out on the floor as a road or railway, also shapes the course of consequent action; as does a building-block airport, or multistorey car park.

Multimodality is an absolute fact of children's semiotic practices.

It is what they do; it is how they understand meaning-making; and the complexities of that mode of production are not a problem for them. The problem lies in our current firmly established common sense about literacy and what it is. Only we can fix *that* problem.

Colour plates

Plate 1 Car as object

Plate 2 Halloween (6-year-old girl)

Plate 3 Halloween (8-year-old boy)

Plate 4 My birthday

Plate 5 Jurassic Park

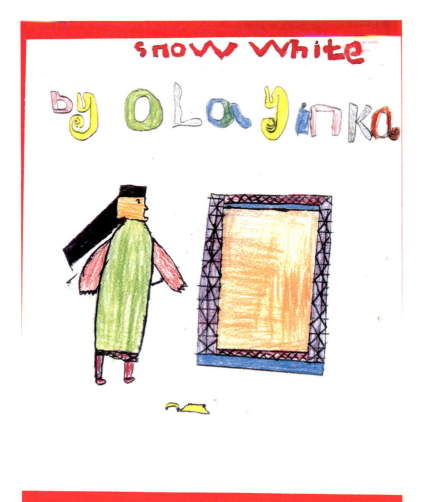

Plate 6 Snow White: the Wicked Queen

Plate 7 Tableaux: 'My family', Monte Mar Brazil

Chapter 7

Teaching literacy, learning literacy

'MOVING INTO LITERACY': CHILDISH PRINCIPLES

This is not a book about 'the gradual development of writing'; it is not an attempt to document, in detail, the gradual evolution or development of letters, even though this could be done in the terms of the approach which I advocate. This is a book about principles: an attempt to see if we can come to learn and understand the principles which children employ in their making of meaning. It is a book about all their meaning-making practices, even if I have been able to focus on only a very few. for instance, I've said nothing about children making their own tunes, their own songs, their jokes, nothing about dance, their use of their bodies as vehicles for expression and communication. All of that is another book – or two.

Nor is there anything to 'move into': literacy, as I have tried to show is no place, no thing, no stable set of forms to be copied. Nor do children see it that way. Their approach is a multiple one: things are always more than one thing, and have different logics, different uses, depending on where you stand when you are looking. At the same time, to adults it clearly is an enormously big thing, and children understand that too. It provides one motivation for them to explore this part of their world. But as I have tried to show, and as all of us know already, they experiment, explore, analyse with boundless energy, things which no parent and no school demands. The relative degree of energy and amount of time spent by children in their engagement with print is probably more than the average for the adult community, but it is not, by any manner of means, more energy or time than they devote to their other meaning-making activities. In large part my own focus on their visual and their verbal products has to do with the very simple fact that I can pick up a stack of things left lying around at the end of a session where they have been producing them, when the makers have departed to watch television, or play outside, or go to bed. If I could pick up and store the other objects as readily, not only would that change my collection fundamentally, it would also force me to devote more attention to these objects; and I simply do not know what change that would make to my understanding. So, what is recordable and storable and therefore analysable at leisure, shapes my view of children's meaning-making, even now when I am trying to think freshly.

Here I will briefly consider some examples of their meaning-output, in order to draw out some things that we might discover about the principles which children apply; or rather to discover where the principles might be derived from which children apply in their own analytic work. For instance, in Emily's engagement with the letters and the sequence of letters of her name, where did she get the principles of analysis that she seems to have applied?

To illustrate my point I will examine four issues: tracing, experiments with three-dimensionality, the representation of action visually, and the matter of content and interest.

Many children trace – around their hands and around objects. Obviously, at the beginning there is an interest in the thing traced; but the tracing also quite clearly establishes a difficult complex relationship between the flat object produced by the tracing, and the original, often three-dimensional object, say a hand. A relation of a highly abstract kind is established between the object which has volume, and the tracing which does not; between the three-dimensional object and its two-dimensional representation. This opens up precisely the issue of the relation between the object that is represented, and the representation: how is my hand like its traced outline? What has been preserved, what has been lost? What is essential, what is marginal? A large number of cognitive and conceptual principles are involved in this activity; and questions are posed for a child. So, for instance, when children make three-dimensional objects – I'm thinking of a 'recorder' made from paper, stuck together with sticky tape, and with the holes drawn in pencil – are they not examining exactly one of these issues? And similarly, when they cut around the tracing of the hand, they are reinserting the flat two-dimensional object into a three-dimensional world, though now significantly transformed.

In what seems a straightforward, trivial activity there is a series of conceptual, cognitive and semiotic transformations. The idea that a flat shape can stand for something that has mass, volume, in which the child has invested emotional, affective energy, is not a trivial one. The outline of the triceratops in Figure 7.1 points for the child to an object of quite a different kind. The child had started to colour it in, but then left that; the colouring in of the shape would have added some of the features which the tracing around could only barely suggest. From this point of view a stencil becomes an interesting object, even though it does not, seemingly, engage the imaginative faculties of its users. But it points precisely to the difficult relation of 'abstraction' – representing only the elements which are thought to be essential.

My question is this: for a child, a letter is a visual entity, an image. Is it useful for her or him to have developed the notion, through all kinds of practice with all kinds of objects, that a bare outline shape may *be* an abstraction, may have quite other, further, different characteristics associated with it; is it important to know that it may be a reduced representation of a much fuller object? Will that help her or him to make better sense of what a letter is, and how it relates to other aspects of the meaning-environment?

Figure 7.1 Triceratops

The way in which I have discussed three-dimensionality so far, was to suggest that the three-dimensional object offers different potentials for use, for interaction, from the two-dimensional representation on the page. The possibilities of engagement with the body are different; and if different bodily engagement has different affective and cognitive consequences, then this is a fundamental issue. The possibility of full tactile, sensory engagement is a precondition for a (re)development of a fuller synaesthetic response.

The argument I wish to make here is somewhat different. While tracing is a move from three-dimensionality to two-dimensionality, many children actually try to represent three-dimensional objects in three dimensions. The recorder I mentioned above was made as an object – a commodity – for sale in a game of shops (as were a large number of other objects – in themselves an interesting issue: what do children see as most commodity-like?) The objects in this 'shop' are all semiotic objects, they *are* representations just as much as a drawing of a recorder would be. They are there as representatives of the objects in the cultural/social world of children. The recorder/sign is made according to the same principles of sign-making: the relation between form and meaning is a motivated one, and this motivation arises out of the young maker's interest.

In other words, the child sees the world of objects as fully meaningful; it is as much a part of the world of signs as are spoken or visual signs. But the child also sees these different kinds of signs as entirely connected: the game produces the motivation to produce the objects; the objects need to be advertised, so that posters have to be produced on which the names of the commodities are displayed – with prices indicated. This world is fully, entirely connected; a sign in one medium produces another sign in the same or in another medium, which produces a sign in the same or another medium, and so on. All are tightly integrated. In the already present age of multimedia these are clearly essential skills and dispositions. The cognitive disposition which is produced is one that sees the connections of all parts of the semiotic world; realizes that for different tasks different modes may be better; encourages ready, unproblematic translation/transition from one medium to another; and so on. The world into which children will move will be a world of multimodality, and multiliteracy. It will demand such skills and dispositions as part of an adaptable innovative workforce.

My third point is that of the difficulty of representation of action in images, or better, the use of visual and verbal means combined to achieve the communication of action in visual form. As in the toy-museum instance above, children have no difficulty in 'narrating' a story through images. However, what they do, typically, is to produce a tableaux of figures and objects as in Figure 6.2 and Plate 7, which serve as a mnemonic, a kind of prompt, for the teller of the narrative, who does tell it, using language.

Children see this as 'telling a story', and as they have no difficulty at all with this, it seems that visual display combined with verbal narrative is a perfectly proper mode to them. Whether they are aware of this as 'using the right medium for the right job' – images to show the elements of the story, and language to relate the action – that is, as specialization of mode; or whether they see it as a single mode of expression, at a certain age at least, is not quite clear to me. I do think that up to the age of four, perhaps later, drawing and 'writing' are not clearly distinguished: the image of the *Tyrannosaurus rex* (Figure 4.7) may be 'writing' the wooden model and 'drawing' the alphabetic script (Figure 3.5). The inscription on the newspaper page (Figure 3.6), 'In John Prince's Street someone got dead', may be drawing the caption. But what is most likely is that these children make no such distinction. It seems to me, in looking at their 'texts' at this stage, that they see these pages as integrated objects.

The effect in the children's move into literacy may vary. For one thing, my generation's valuation of language as primary may no longer be shared by younger generations. In fact to say 'my generation's valuation of language as primary' is certainly wrong, in so far as it suggests that there was then some kind of question 'Is it language, or is it the visual?' There simply was no such question. It may also be that to children now in schools, letters are entirely different things from what they were for me. I learned to write them in long lines, on my slate. I did *not* see around me, in the visual environment of my culture then, the proliferation of images characteristic of contemporary western visual culture among which letters figure as images, as icons, as logos, nearly as frequently as other images do – whether the M of a restaurant chain, or the C of a brand of soft drink.

To return to the representation of action in images. On the one hand, the visual aspects of language, whether as letter, or as block of text, are beginning to be used as elements in the visual design of a page layout, equating language and image on one level. On the other hand, in school textbooks there is now an increasing tendency in some subjects – science, for instance – to treat verbal text and visual image interchangeably in giving an account of a particular object or set of objects. A paragraph of writing may say something about a task which a group of 14-year-olds performed. An image follows, which provides further information; this is followed by more text; by image; and so on. The two are treated as being elements of the same kind in one code; on the same level, communicationally.

If this is a reasonable assessment of the contemporary state of the landscape of communication, then whatever the view that children have constructed for themselves of this, they are entirely justified in proceeding in the way they do. If literacy is now a fundamentally different thing from what it was when I learned to read and write, then their paths into literacy are bound to be fundamentally different also.

It may seem unusual to introduce the matter of content here. In looking at the images that I have, one lot made by a boy from the age of just over 1 year up to the present, 8½; and those of his sister, from about the age of 2 up to the present of just over 6, it is impossible not to speculate constantly on their differing interests, and specifically to ask about the issue of sex and of gender. I made the point in earlier chapters that children, like adults, act transformatively on the cultural stuff that they have to hand. But the stuff to hand already has a structure. It matters therefore, inasmuch as there may be a choice, what stuff they engage with, for its structure will set the context of their trans-formative action. Children's interests act as a device for selecting such materials: perhaps one preferring these modes rather than those; mechanical forms rather than natural; linear rather than circular; action more than display.

These selections, however unsystematic they may look, will lead nevertheless along a particular path; and because 'interest' in this individually made and socially formed whole, each individual's path will be different, however slightly so. And so each child's path into literacy will be differently made, even though the appearance is one of relative uniformity as the end result.

Content, in a sense, goes hand in hand with affect. Figure 7.2 is a page that shows a child practising the spelling of *Tyrannosaurus rex*. As for many children, both boys and girls (but perhaps

Figure 7.2 Spelling *Tyrannosaurus rex*

differently for each?), dinosaurs are a source of fascination, in which there are also some elements of fashion involved. Affectively this child seems fully engaged with this topic.

After the first few attempts at the top of the page he seems not to have been satisfied with his own efforts, and so it seems that he engaged the help of an expert – who also seemed to have had a problem with the spelling of the word! – and then he has his final attempt. One can only speculate why on this occasion, the child's 'invented spelling' wasn't good enough for him; is it that the matter was too important?

A NEW LITERACY CURRICULUM?

In the first section of this chapter, I have set out some principles which children may have developed in their meaning-making, and which they bring to their engagement with print. On the one hand it is clearly important for us to understand these because without such an understanding we cannot really hope to develop new thinking about writing and the teaching of writing, never mind the necessary new curricula of public communication. On the other hand it may just be that these principles reveal, in any case, some central aspects of literacy, of theories of language, and of meaning-making, which will have to inform our own theories and practices. The emphasis in that section has been on the path into literacy, seen as the paths into writing. In this section I put forward some thoughts about the paths into the new literacy which, as far as one can read the runes, is likely to be the state of the world of communication over the next few decades.

I have two aims: on the one hand, to keep a clear focus on print and writing, always aware that both are subject to constant social and historical changes. On the other hand, I want to put emphasis on the new multiliteracies, their forms and function, and their likely effects and implications. Language, like all forms of communication, is part of the whole system of modes of communication; and as all parts in the system change, so language will change and so will the other elements change too. This change is on one level invisible to us, because we all live our lives in this stream, and because we are part of that change it seems that there is a relative stability around us. The last decade has begun to make people of my generation feel that the pace of change is now such that we no longer have the ability to cope. At this stage, this seems to me to be more than the usual response of those entering into 'late middle age'.

It is easy enough to get immediate evidence of language change, and we do not have to go to Shakespeare or to the King James Bible to see the distance the English language has travelled. Here are two short extracts from two science textbooks; one written in the mid 1930s, the other in the late 1980s, a distance of fifty years, less than my own lifetime:

1930s text

The simple electric motor consists of a coil pivoted between the poles of a permanent magnet ... When a current is passed through the coil in the direction indicated in the figure we can show, by applying Fleming's left-hand rule, that the left-hand side of the coil will tend to move down and the right-hand side to move up.

(McKenzie, 1938: 76)

1980s text

CIRCUITS
In your first circuits you used torch bulbs joined with wires. Modern electrical equipment uses the same basic ideas. But if you look inside a computer there are not many wires or torch bulbs. The wires and bulbs have been replaced by electronic devices like transistors, chips and light-emitting bodies.

(Coles *et al.*, 1989: 140)

Both are aimed at 14- to 15-year-olds. The first is aimed, according to the author's preface, at 'the boy who will find this text interesting'. The second, and here I am making an assumption, is meant to be read by girls and boys equally. The difference in the language needs no real discussion; it is obvious enough. What does invite discussion is the question about the reasons for this shift. I imagine that the attempt to make science more inviting to girls is one; the attempt to make science generally more 'accessible' is another. A further reason is the use of large numbers of images in the second text; as I mentioned above, it uses images and texts as elements of communication on the same level, although I should mention that the earlier book had been renowned for its 'enlivening use of images', which is not however what the contemporary eye regards as particularly interesting, visually.

Writing will remain an important medium of communication, and is likely to become more and more the medium used by and for the power élites of society. This makes it essential to facilitate the access of every child to the maximum level of competence in this medium, which is a clear and absolute aim of my own project. Schools may remain focused on writing as the most valued form of communication. These things will depend on the political/ ideological climate in society generally; on ideas about who should have access to what; on ideas about values, whether reactionary, conservative, or progressive. It seems equally clear – and the massively increasing volume of writing on this issue is perhaps the best evidence – that other forms of communication are becoming prominent, sometimes dominant in the communication environment. So a new literacy curriculum will simply have to deal with that fact. But in any case, the principles which apply are the same in either kind of curriculum.

A first question has to be that of context. What is the context in which thinking about a curriculum has to be conducted? English is now a world language; mass-media culture is rapidly becoming globalized; economic production is already globalized – or transnational at the very least; financial markets are global markets: the value of any country's currency is not decided in that country; populations move in numbers probably not seen before in the history of human kind; and so the list goes on. 'Think global, act local' may be an essential precept. But is globalization merely a glib slogan, based on facile analysis? What effect could it possibly have on literacy curricula? I'll mention three points, without going into any detail. (a) Electronic forms of communication make English an internationally usable language, but will also lead to inevitable 'local transformations' of English, all over the globe. Electronic forms of communication are at the moment moving writing in the direction of more speech-like forms. (b) Globalization will inevitably produce new social situations and therefore new forms of writing, new genres. (c) Electronic forms of communication will make greater use of directly iconic signs, and will, inevitably use multimodal texts – the multimedia products already available will seem relatively simple in a few years' time, and will become generally available modes of making texts. To me there is simply no question: it will be impossible to ignore the global context in the locally necessary curricula. The locality will produce necessary local inflections: 'local transformations' of a globally defined set of essential elements and characteristics.

A second question, which arises directly from this dichotomy of local and global, is that of the function of the literacy curriculum. At the moment it is, in many places in 'the West', a battleground for competing interests: business interests demand competence in written (and spoken) communication; other business interests ask for adaptable, innovative, creative young humans, equipped with generally usable skills of analysis, critique, design. The literacy curriculum is crucial in this as a tool. To take one instance, we cannot encourage unreflecting application of rules – whether of grammar, speaking, making of texts – in one important part of the curriculum, and expect reflectiveness, critique, innovation from these same young humans who have been subjected to authoritarian teaching modes, in the most fundamental area of communication and representation.

The shape, aims and purposes of any education system are a matter of public debate and public policy. The education system has to be responsive to legitimate demands of that society; and it has to serve the needs of that society; it has to be instrumental in relation to social goals. That, to me, is not an issue. For me the issue is the conception of social needs in terms of which literacy becomes instrumental. The literacy curriculum is therefore inevitably a domain of political conflict. These points will be discussed in more detail, in particular in the final chapter.

Where in the overall curriculum is the literacy curriculum to be accommodated? In the 1970s there was a quite strong movement in many English-speaking countries of 'English across the curriculum'. It was founded on a realization that *language* was crucial in all subject areas in the curriculum. The movement had significant effects, but in the end probably failed in its objectives of making English a central issue in all curriculum areas. With the benefit of hindsight it seems clear to me that one reason for that failure was that 'English' meant the subject as it was conceived of by English teachers for the needs of the English classroom. So for instance, narrative as 'story' became the central form, for strong pedagogical and ideological reasons. Narrative is important in science, in many ways, but it does not have the same function there as it had in the early 1970s' English classroom. And so even those science teachers who were deeply interested in this issue, in the end turned away from the colonizing designs of their English colleagues.

The force of this issue remains. In the context of multiliteracies if anything it becomes stronger. It may be that now it can genuinely become a cross-disciplinary movement, as it should. Whether the school subject 'English' will be its location rests to a very large extent on the future development of that subject. In the earlier years of schooling this institutional question does not pose such a sharp problem. The constitution of infants'- and primary-school classrooms invites in any case transdisciplinary, multimodal work, conducted in a multiplicity of forms of representation. In both primary and secondary school the central task will be – differently for each – to explore and implement the consequences of a fully multiliterate environment.

This is a political issue with a capital *P*, though there are different politics involved in different societies. In England the school subject English carries so many ideological burdens, as well as its many 'real' tasks, that a change is not easy to envisage, without a large-scale struggle. In Australia 'English' is rapidly taking on different meanings and differing functions as part of economic restructuring, as well as a widely based effort at the construction of a new multi-ethnic identity. The social and political situation in the United States looks, to me, from the outside, as being different yet again in fundamental ways, with one huge factor being the growing influence of Spanish as a language of everyday interaction. Everywhere there are possiblities of a kind which are difficult to calculate, and they include the real possibilities of reactionary moves.

THE SHAPE OF THE NEW LITERACY CURRICULUM?

Anyone who has taken even the most fleeting interest in issues of literacy cannot help but be astonished by the ferocity characteristic of current argument. At the same time these arguments seem strangely inconclusive: no 'evidence' worth the name is brought forward on one side or the other; whoever carries the biggest political clout wins the day, aided by the massed ranks of the media. Two conclusions can be drawn from this: 'literacy' serves as a metaphor for social and political life – 'discipline' vs 'freedom' broadly speaking. At that level the argument can lead to no satisfactory outcome. The other conclusion is that the terms of the debate are fundamentally flawed, misconceived. 'Literacy' consists in more than the acquisition of technical competence, skills; it is a set of practices, forms of knowledge, which form deep-seated dispositions in the person who is literate. So we need to ask: what dispositions are we aiming to foster, and why? The issue then becomes one of the elaborating our views of the mid-term futures of a society in which people will need particular kinds of dispositions in order to function fully. Or turning this the other way around, we can say that by shaping the dispositions of young humans, we are suggesting and influencing the future paths of our society.

This is the subject of the last chapter. Here I want to explore some of the elements which can form the foundation of a literacy curriculum conceived of in these terms. The elements that I will focus on are: theories of meaning-making; the potentials and limitations of forms of representation; multimodality; the question of desired human 'dispositions'; 'design' or reproduction; multi- or interculturalism; and the reshaping, the transformation of the resources of communication and representation.

In Chapter 6 I explored some of the issues which surround theories of meaning-making. The central point, for me, is that a theory of meaning-making, a theory of semiosis, has the most far-reaching educational and social consequences. It does much more than to say: this is what language is and this is how it works. It suggests actions and practices which follow from that description. If language is – as it has been thought to be, generally speaking, throughout this century – a stable or even static phenomenon, with fixed rules, in no way affected by individual speakers or writers, then the educational task clearly is to ensure that children learn this system and conform to its rules.

That defines a particular task for the individual. It is clear how this task reaches into all of social life. Language is such a potent metaphor for everyday life – 'slovenly habits in speech' equals 'slovenly habits in other areas of life' – that common-sense understandings of language can serve to become models for common-sense understandings for social conduct.

If, by contrast, language is seen as a dynamic, organic, fluid phenomenon, constantly shaped and reshaped by those who speak and write it every day in accordance with their needs and wishes, then the educational task becomes quite different. The educational task then becomes focused on the answers to the question: what are the needs and demands which are likely to be made of language or literacy in the coming decades, and how can we make sure that these young people have the necessary resources to participate fully and productively in the making of their meanings – and in their remaking of their literacy resources? That defines a quite different task and status for individuals, one in which they have to be fully competent in the use of the resources of making meaning, but in which they are seen as creative, innovative, productive, acting out of their perceived needs.

My preference lies clearly with a theory of semiosis of the second kind: not because it suits my politics – which it does – but because it accords better with the facts of language, the facts of meaning-making in other modes, and in literacy. Whether I look at the changes now happening in response to the new electronic technologies; or whether I look at the changes to the forms of writing which seem to be a result – among others – of the increasing use of images in textbooks; or whether I look over the four or five hundred years of writing in English; what I see is constant change, flux, a dynamic at work. That change reflects, broadly, the changes of the society of the time.

In the book so far I have given numbers of illustrations of the innovative production by children. It may be that we all agree that children innovate, and act creatively – that, after all, is one still current view of the creative potential of 'the innocence of childhood' – but if we wish to do so we can see and hear these innovations every day, everywhere, all around us. Simply to make this point I'll mention two such instances out of many which I have jotted down and kept during the last year. The first comes from a train journey from London to Lancaster; it is an announcement made on the train's intercom:

The next scheduled station-stop will be Preston.

I had never heard the phrase *scheduled station-stop* before; but the motives and processes for its production seem clear to me. As investment in the infrastructure of the railway system in Britain has diminished; the reliability of tracks, of signalling equipment, and rolling-stock has declined. Consequently there is now a need for a set of new words to name new events *unscheduled station-stop*, *unscheduled non-station-stop*, and no doubt others. A new set of words is produced in response to changing political and economic conditions.

My second example comes from the printed menu distributed on board a flight:

Owing to prior passenger-selection the menu of your choice may not be available.

Prior passenger-selection was new to me; and its production easily explained – countless complaints from passengers in rows 37 to 58, who had wanted the fish and not the beef . . .

The first characteristics of the necessary theory of meaning-making for the new literacy curriculum is that individuals have full understanding and command of the meaning-making potentials, the meaning-making resources of their systems of communication. They use these representational and communicational resources in their interests, and in doing so take part in the constant making of these resources in their community. This is a theory which combines the existence of social convention and of history, with the active, innovative practice of all individuals in that community.

The second characteristic is that in representation and in communication we always use a large number of modes of representation. Each such mode has particular potentials and limitations. In earlier chapters I have pointed to some of these. For example, there is the fundamental opposition of the potentials of space-based modes and time-based modes. In the former the possibilities offered by a flat surface seem to lead in children's early representations to a predominance of analytic and classificatory representations, arranged as displays. In the latter, in language, children of the same age produce stories which have actions shaped into basic narrative structures. In the adult forms of spatial and temporal communication modes, it is possible to represent actions and narrative in the former, and display in the latter, yet it seems that there is still a fundamental difference: one is better suited to one range of tasks, and the other to a different range.

At the moment literacy curricula pay no attention to this. The visual representations which children produce as a matter of course in the early years of schooling are not developed and built on as a means for future communicational use. Some children do become interested in art, but in that school subject, representation and communication are not foregrounded. It is devoted to aesthetic development; and it is therefore quite separate from the needs and interests of a literacy curriculum. In the new literacy curriculum serious attention will need to be given to the visual as well as to the verbal mode of communication. Its potentials and uses in current communication practices will need to form part of the competence of students passing from school. This is a minimum requirement, given that multimedia modes of production already go beyond these two modes, for instance also involving sound.

The third characteristic follows from the first two, namely, multimodality: a taken-for-granted assumption that texts always make use of a multiplicity of modes, simultaneously, and that consequently children will need the facility of producing texts which are based on the use of a multiplicity of modes. Principles of selection of modes for the necessary functions will need to be clearly articulated: what kinds of information are best handled through visual display? What are the available forms of visual display? What does each such form permit the text-maker to communicate? A full understanding of the children's own practices and the principles implicit in these will be of great benefit to teachers, and will form an essential prerequisite to the devising of curricula.

In all this it is important to stress that print/writing must not be sidelined. For instance, an awareness of principles and practices of display will become an absolutely essential requirement for the production of verbal text. The technology of desktop publishing and printing now makes production to a professional standard possible for most even quite small businesses and organizations. The texts produced by desktop publishing methods are more and more becoming primarily visual objects, in which language, as 'blocks of language' forms one part of the elements of a visual composition. Font choice is now easily available; as are many other visual transformations of printed text: bolding, spacing, letter-size, and layout in general. But at least as important are two other considerations. If all modes offer their distinct potentials and possibilities, we cannot without serious loss, give up real attention to the mode of writing – and of speech. From a political point of view, it seems clear to me that writing will continue to be used by the powerful, by the élite as *their* medium. Issues of equal access to power and its use therefore demand that all children have full competence in this mode and its possibilities.

It is essential that in their paths into literacy, children are encouraged to develop their already existing competence and interest in these aspects; and are encouraged in their fundamental disposition towards multimodal forms of text and meaning making. At the same time it will be essential to develop these dispositions so that they are available as clearly usable resources for the child text-makers. Above all there will need to be particular emphasis on developing their awareness about the dynamic interaction between the various modes, and their awareness that all modes are constantly changing in their interaction with other modes; and through the sign-maker's use.

This brings me to the fourth characteristic, that of *design*. In literacy curricula of the present there is an assumption that what is to be learned is *competence in the use* of an existing, stable system. At times, in some relatively rare instances, this is supplemented by elements of *critique*, in order to give the learner skills of analysis on the one hand, but also a kind of affective, cognitive, cultural and theoretical distance from the technology of representation on the other. The issue of *design* goes beyond this entirely. It assumes that competent use is not sufficient. What is needed is competence in design of new, innovative forms, which are a response to the maker's analysis and understanding, and allow the designers to go beyond the forms which exist. The older versions and under-standings of literacy regarded it as a central cultural technology which was crucial in the performance of culturally and socially required tasks. *Design*, by contrast, points towards the intention to produce *change*; the kind and direction of change imagined by the designer in response to her or his understanding of their own needs, and those of their community.

Design presupposes analysis: it rests on it as one requirement, and goes beyond it. It presupposes full knowledge of the communi-cational resources, as I have described that just now; and above all, it presupposes imagination of different, new, possibilities. It rests on the theory of meaning-making as I have elaborated it here, and elsewhere in this book. Above all, the introduction of the idea of (and the active fostering of) *design* changes the valuation of the maker of a message or a text, no matter in what mode. As in my earlier examples, the 'Panadol-man' say, it forces us to acknowl-edge the amount of cognitive work, and the kind of work, which is involved in all semiotic production. It forces us not merely to ask about intention, interest, motivation, but about the *principles of design* which were applied, and which give the text the features it has. *Design* is oriented towards change, towards future needs, wishes, demands. It refocuses literacy from a concern with the present to an essential concern with the future.

'What is to hand' never quite matches the needs of the designer, and so design is a constant pressure on 'what is to hand'; and it transforms 'what is to hand' in the direction of the design. For, after all, what is to hand has to satisfy the needs of a design. Designing implies that one's eye is firmly fixed on a future – for which the design is being made. A designer has to be absolutely clear about the environment for which she or he proposes to make objects/texts; and so design demands greater overt clarity in thinking about the shape of the future than we are used to. Currently we are used to demands to meet some immediate aim, whether in spelling, or in syntax – 'school-leavers can't speak (or write) in sentences'. A 'design approach' focuses on producing change; it asks: 'What do we need in order to act productively tomorrow?'

A focus on design is therefore a call for much more precision in relation to literacy – both in the designer's command of resources, and in the construction of designs. Some of the argument of this book may be read by some readers as a restatement of progressivism. It is neither that, nor is it a dismissal of some of the fundamentals of form-centred approaches to literacy. Rather it is an attempt to say that neither offers a sufficiently appropriate approach, and neither offers a fully plausible theory of meaning-making. The suggestion offered here tries to put on to the agenda what is essential now, and will be more so in the future, in the context of a set of principles which may allow us to move beyond the unproductive swings from one extreme position to another which mire the current debate on literacy in the public domain.

Chapter 8

Futures

THE CURRENT SITUATION

We know that tomorrow will not be like today. That is one of the few certainties of the present period. We can perceive only dimly what the day after that tomorrow is likely to be like. That wasn't always the case, as I suggested in the preface. I knew, in my early teenage, that I would, once I'd finished my apprenticeship as a furrier, become a journeyman in 'my trade', and that I could become a master craftsman if I chose that path. The fact that things turned out differently for me did not challenge the certainty: it was just a thing that happened, which could easily be accommodated in that rock-solid edifice of how we knew things were. Of course, the event that made things different for me was my parents' emigration, from Germany to Australia, which was itself a tiny part of the unmaking of the postwar world. It dislodged me from certainty, even though I continued working in 'my trade', some-what incongruously in hot Newcastle, New South Wales, for another ten years. Emigration, if anything, cemented certainties in those days: one moved from a place of social insecurity to a place of social security – which in the case of emigrants then meant from a place of no (reliable) work to a place of (reliable) work. In the era preceding the Second World War, immigration did not unsettle anything. Immigrant groups formed relatively closed-off, self-contained cultural islands in their new environment. By this they confirmed the continuity and stability of their ethnic and cultural identity, and reciprocally confirmed the stability and continuity of the host society. The certainties in that area of social life had their effects on curricula. If we knew that tomorrow would be as today, we also knew what it was that the young should learn and know.

Broadly, they should know what we knew; and value what their elders valued. Curriculum had the function of ensuring that the future would be like the present, which itself was much the same as the immediate past. We could be relatively clear about the aims and needs of today.

Other stabilizing factors have also begun to fade or to disappear. The social stability of that period – even if it was a relative myth – allowed curricula to be relatively inexplicit; indeed the implicitness of curriculum in central areas was a guarantee of its success. The stability of the social system was guaranteed by the stability of the nation state, which attempted to foster a national identity, which was itself a function of the state's school system to produce. For that identity to be produced smoothly and successfully, it was essential that the core of the value system should not be the subject of overt teaching; and not subject therefore to analysis and critique.

Given that these certainties are no longer with us, the questions around curriculum have become much sharper. At the present they are posed in what I regard as fundamentally misconceived ways by politicians and by certain education experts, not just here but in all anglophone countries, and not just by those of 'the right'. There exists now in this as in many other political areas a broad consensus, within which the range of opinion and of options is actually quite small. That range stretches on one side from purely ideological demands around moral values, cultural unity, of 'standards' variously described or not described, to nostalgic calls for the reinstatement of the forms of that former period of mythic or actual certainty. On the other side the calls are for a closer alignment of education with the demands of business and of industry; for higher and measurable levels of skill; for the lifting of levels of efficiency in communication – with spelling, punctuation, sentence construction being cited as indicators of performance.

But these are responses which seek to cope with present insecurities and uncertainties by proposing a return to past forms. I am entirely in agreement with calls for the education system to be socially responsible and responsive, and for me that includes without question a responsiveness to the economic, social, political and cultural demands and needs of a society. That seems to me absolutely legitimate, and beyond debate. The question is: what *are* the economic needs of society? What are its cultural, social, political needs for the near to mid-term future? Clearly, if past elements of the education system were attuned to the demands of the society and the economy of *then*, their reintroduction cannot serve any other purpose than the assuaging of uncontrollable nostalgias by those who advocate their return. Britain will not, for the foreseeable future return to the form of the economy which existed pre-war, let alone in the nineteenth century. There are no plans to rebuild steelworks, reopen coal mines or shipyards, to rebuild other once great industries. So the forms of work, the kinds of jobs, those aptitudes and dispositions are no longer needed because they are no longer relevant.

The curriculum clearly has to address the future needs of the society in which it operates. This involves a deeply searching attempt to speculate about that future. What can we know at the moment, about the shape of things to come – the economy; forms of society; the future of nation states; globalization; the media; cultural and political developments? While this book does not propose a specific curriculum for any part of schooling, it does attempt to say something about what dispositions schooling should attempt to produce. But that presupposes some clearer sense of what will be needed for that future, so that a curriculum can be developed along the kinds of principles that will be required. So here I will indulge in some very broad speculation, and then relate that to principles of curriculum construction.

Three factors seem central to me in remaking the shape of the future: the continuing and intensifying pluriculturalism which now characterizes all the so-called developed societies; the globalization of economies, of production, and of finance; and the changes in the technologies of communication and of transport. Other, associated factors of great significance are the globalization of the media, and the consequent internationalization of culture.

Pluriculturalism is dissolving what formerly seemed like the settled identifications of cultures and nation states, and in doing so is proving corrosive of that web of values, beliefs, knowledge, structures of identities and practices, which underpinned and seemed to guarantee the stabilities which I mentioned above. This is happening at a time when in these same places the economies which had provided relative security for the largest proportion of the population are faltering – as older forms of production are taken elsewhere, to places of much lower costs of labour, and finance capital moves at the speed of light to where 'returns' promise to be highest. This makes everywhere potentially a low-wage economy. Changes in the modes of communication are undoing more local structures of communication, and undermine local, geographically based communities. The foreign exchange dealer who leaves home at 6 a.m. to go to work has a daily routine of communication which binds her or him more tightly into a global network than into the former community of the local neighbourhood of schools, social clubs, church, and so on.

This is accompanied by a changing landscape of communication, in part produced by these factors, and in part with its own dynamic. Quite different forms of communication are needed globally from locally; electronic communication makes the person with whom I am communicating co-present in time and distant in space. Electronic media – as well as new technologies of printing make images into a much more available, accessible and *usable* mode of communication than they have been – in 'the West' at any rate for several hundred years. That is having far-reaching effects on language, especially in its written form, which have only just begun and are likely to alter the place and valuation of writing in far-reaching ways.

Written texts are becoming much more visual than they ever were even though they have always been visual objects. But the pages of novels, textbooks, manuals that I was used to reading as recently as the 1960s and even 1970s, with their dense lines of print, have given way to pages where visual images dominate in many domains of communication. Contemporary science textbooks in secondary schools are a very good example. They are no longer objects to be read page by page by page; they consist of sets of pages which make information available in writing *and* in the form of visual images of diverse kinds: they are collections of resource materials. This of course presupposes, even if only implicitly, greatly changed ideas about reading, and fundamentally different reading practices.

The now available multimedia technologies of CD-ROM go well beyond this, with moving images, sound, as well as spoken and written language. The new texts exist in a plethora of semiotic forms, and demand skills of production and design never before envisaged in any curriculum of communication.

They also change our approach to knowledge, and will radically remake our conception of what knowledge is, and the place of education in relation to it. Hypertext, CD-ROM, the Internet, are no longer organized in the sequenced, hierarchical structurings which still characterizes our common sense of what knowledge is. The sequentiality and linearity of former textual structures is replaced by a web, which can be entered at any point of my choosing and explored with neither a pre-given point of entry nor a pre-given point of departure. Like the new science textbook it makes available information for me to use in my new structures: it is a resource, which is not pre-structured in readily discernible ways.

The skills demanded here are those of (*information*) *management*; and that is rapidly displacing the *production of knowledge* as the central aim of formal institutionalized education. In England this is evident in the debate over forms of qualifications: whether A levels, the former 'academic' qualification, or NVQs (National Vocational Qualifications) or GNVQs (General National Qualifications), the new overtly practical, pragmatically oriented qualifications. The older aims of distanced critical reflection are replaced by the new aims of management and organization of (existing) information.

But new forms of social organization will still demand the production of new knowledge: we have not come to the point where we have enough knowledge for the ever-changing demands that will continue to face humankind. Economies based on 'information' as their raw material will be fundamentally different from those we know now, and I assume will demand specialized forms of representation and communication in which language will have a lesser place, the visual a much greater, and which may need the skills of moving from one mode of representation to another, using the possibilities of each to the fullest. Innovation, as a taken-for-granted requirement, will rest on attitudes to (cultural and other) difference and change unlike those fostered now, whether in schools or in society at large. The distinctly different modes of engagement with the world which inhere in the different semiotic modes and media – two-, three-, or four-dimensional, temporal or spatial, visual verbal or tactile – can lead to quite distinct logics and rationalities (and do so now), and the school curriculum will need to foster and develop them as essential requirements for the economic, social, and political demands of the near future.

NEW CURRICULA, NEW AIMS

I suggested earlier that the education system can no longer follow the lead of those who form opinion in society: there is no clarity, no unity of purpose, no plausible vision for productive futures. The likely futures held up now as *necessary* futures are those of 30–40–30 societies: 30 per cent of the population well off; 40 per cent who barely get by; and 30 per cent who have been thrown on the dump. But these are projections; they are not (yet) realities. They assume present distributions of work and of wealth; they assume declining economic activity (in the developed countries). These are visions produced not by the bottom 30 per cent, but by the élite among the top 30 per cent, whose interests may well continue to be protected in those futures.

But we do not have to remain with our present common sense about work, about pleasure, about what provides fulfilment, about distributions of economic, social, political resources, a common sense which was developed over a century and a half ago, in the earlier period of the industrial revolution. Nor do we need to accept predictions that our economy will deliver satisfying jobs for only 20 per cent of the workforce, which entails that the education system needs to be remade so as to produce that élite, and to produce dull submissiveness on the part of the other 80 per cent. It is possible to think that with the still vast resources of countries such as Britain, Australia, the United States, Germany, a rethinking can take place, which sets a quite different course for the future. We can imagine as a present task the production of a culture of innovation – in the economic sphere, in technology, in social theories, and in everyday common sense; we can work for new notions of pleasure, fulfilment, responsibility, which will lead to futures that are not as starkly, as desolately bleak as those envisaged now by the prophets of certain forms of capitalism, and accepted by their critics. The essential resources for that future are the people of a particular society, in their cultural diversity.

In this the curriculum of representation is crucial. It will need to be founded, first and foremost, on the theories of meaning-making which I have developed. Such a theory treats every individual as innovative in every respect, and as fundamentally so. It therefore encourages the development of naturalized dispositions towards innovation and change, as a taken-for-granted condition of every-day practice. In the new communicational landscape of texts made out of a multiplicity of modes, forms, and materials, the emphasis will be on *design* rather than on reproductive competence (or even critique). That is, the valued and necessary disposition will be one in which individuals have the knowledge, the skill, the ability, the willingness as a matter of course to produce the representations which fulfil their needs and demands in the contexts in which they are made. *Design* is oriented towards competence in innovative production in a full awareness of the complex conditions of a particular environment.

This curriculum will exist, necessarily, in a pluricultural society. The primary economic, cultural and political resource of such societies is the difference in cultural systems of all the groups in a society. Each culture represents the long history of the engagement of a group of people with their environment, and in its structures, forms, values, it presents the solutions which that culture has developed to the challenges of its environment. The plethora of such systems of solutions presents the single most important resource for the so-called post-industrial societies of the world. It is the ingredient out of which – given the right political and cultural conditions – a culture of innovation can be built. For that to happen the curriculum of communication will also have to develop specific attitudes to *difference*; precisely those which understand difference positively, as the essential material from which to fashion a culture of innovation.

The first aim of the new curriculum of representation and communication is the acceptance of a theory of meaning-making in which individuals are the makers and not merely the users of systems of communication. The second aim is the development of the principle of *design* as the central category, and the essential aim for all who experience the curriculum. The third is the development of productive dispositions towards cultural difference.

The fourth is developed out of one of the main themes of the book – namely, that we need to rediscover and reinstate the different possibilities of engagement with the world which are open to us as bodily humans, for all of them offer different, essential modes of being in the world – emotionally, affectively, cognitively. We cannot continue to afford to waste human abilities in the ways in which we have done. This will be and will become an economic as much as a cultural need. The rediscovery and reinstatement of synaesthesia as a desirable characteristic will be essential in this, so that humans will be deliberately free to move from one form of representation and communication to another, and in the process, circumvent the limitations of each and explore the cognitive, affective, innovative potentials of that constant movement.

DESIGNING FUTURES: WHAT DO WE WANT?

It seems to me that we are at one of those points in the history of humankind when decisions need to be made, and can be made about the shape of the future. There is no shortage of voices willing to advocate possibilities. Most of them do not appeal to me. The 30–40–30 society is one which takes anger, violence and despair for granted, it has 'factored them in' and makes its calculations on that basis. This is too bleak a future for me to accept silently. New technologies, dressed in fancy metaphors – whether of surfing or of virtual reality, threaten a new wave of alienating distance from ourselves as physical beings, and from our neighbours as full humans. At the same time a new cult of the body is developing rapidly, perhaps presaging a social split often foretold by the dystopian writers of this century.

My own aim is simple enough. I would like a future for my children in which they can lead productive lives, in a society which is positively engaged with the challenges of its time, and in which despair is, at the least, balanced by hope, difficulty by pleasure. I happen to believe that the possibilities of communication are an essential foundation for that. As I am working in an environment in which it is my responsibility to think about that, in general, and in the specific terms of curricula, it is, as I see it, my responsibility to do the kinds of rethinking that I am engaged in, and to put my ideas into the public domain for examination and debate. I think that the meaning-making practices of the young humans which I have observed are a very good starting point for that rethinking, and for such a debate.

Sources and contexts

The issues explored in this book are not by any means a part of educational common sense. Yet these same ideas have fascinated and concerned very many people over a very long time. There isn't at the moment a sense of a consolidated 'area': not like 'reading' or 'writing' or even 'child development'. I have found my own way to these ideas, and no doubt this is everywhere apparent. However, I found my way with the help of many who have had these or similar ideas before me, and often and equally importantly, those who have had quite different ideas which helped me in forming my own strong response.

At a conference in New York in July 1995 I went to a workshop in which a bibliography was handed out. It was entitled 'To draw is to write: on the restoration of drawing as a tool for writing' compiled by Mary Kennan Herbert. It is a goldmine of information on works precisely in the area of my interest. Six months before, I had published a small book *Writing the Future: English and the Making of a Culture of Innovation* (1995) in which I had used the phrase 'writing a dinosaur and drawing print'. It shows how ideas are 'about'. I have picked up ideas from three different areas: first from looking at what children do; from the 'literature' on children, inspired by the writing of Vygotsky and of Piaget; and from a broad and messy area, which I will call 'communication and representation' – which ranges for me from art history to linguistics, with many stations in between. Here I will very briefly give a sense of the work of some people in these two areas of academic endeavour, mentioning two or three names only in each case.

But first, the exhortation to look at what children do. In her book *GNYS AT WRK: A Child Learns to Write and Read* (1980), Glenda Bissex says

what I have seen here has come mainly from looking again and
again at my material in all its details, and trying to find its form
while respecting its irregularities . . . What I hope this study offers
. . . is encouragement to look at individuals in the act of learning.
And I do mean *act*, with all that implies of drama and action.

(Bissex, 1980: vi)

In the same preface she also has a brief discussion of the issue
of parent/researchers; one point among several that she raises is
that 'Parent-researchers may be long on sharing and short on
distancing. I have tried to provide enough raw material so that
readers can compensate for my lapses through their own analyses.'
I would add only that maybe it is at least as good to 'be long on
sharing' than it is to be long on distancing. The latter, I feel, has
not always served children well.

GNYS AT WRK offers a richly illustrated account of one
child's engagement with print, pertinent to the issue of 'invented
spelling'. Her work, and that of Charles Read, constitute a detailed
exploration of that, though, from my point of view, somewhat too
focused on form alone. In a different vein, the writings of Ann
Haas-Dyson are examples of the benefit that is derived from
attempting to look at what children do as closely as one can do
that, unencumbered by theoretical preconceptions.

The work of Piaget has informed common sense in this area so
strongly that it is difficult for many researchers to take a look at
children's actions other than through the lens of his powerful
schema. This is so in relation to language as much as it is in
relation to images. My own strong reservations about his work are
less with the content of his schemata than with their application
which lead, in my opinion, to misdescriptions of what children do
and are capable of doing. So my own preference is not so much
for a theory to replace his, but for an approach that says: 'Well, if
we were to accept that there are such mental structures, then
the real interest might still lie in seeing the enormous variety of
representation produced by these active young humans in their
engagement with the stuff of their cultural environments.'
Maureen Cox's book *Children's Drawings* (1992) is a highly readable account in the Piagetian tradition. *The Child's Conception of
Space* (1956) is Piaget and Inhelder's own statement. Ferreiro and
Teberosky's book *Literacy before Schooling* (1982) covers some of the
same area as I do here, from a Piagetian perspective.

In this book I have conflated Chomsky's writing with that of Piaget. The concept of the 'Language Acquisition Device', the LAD, comes from the early period of his writing, specifically the book *Aspects of the Theory of Syntax* published in 1965. This suggests that brains have an innate structure disposing us towards language, which has a universal form at a deep level. The concept has a seductive appeal. In Chomsky's own philosophical and political project it enables him to assert the equality of all humans because of the equality of their mental capacities; that at least is my interpretation. It is a fine project. In the hands of those who have taken up this notion it has too often become an excessively appealing tool, wheeled on or off the stage as a substitute for, and too often an obstacle to, fresh or any clear, thinking. It is a box that promises to offer all the answers – if only we could look inside it! I mention it here because its baleful presence is discernible in so many discussions even where the name of Chomsky or the name of the box are no longer mentioned – or even known.

My own strong preference is for social accounts of cognitive action. And so in the intertwined area of meaning-making and thinking, the writings of Vygotsky and Bakhtin are important, as is the work of Halliday. Lev Vygotsky connects social action with mental action, treating the latter as a result in strong measure of the former; his *Thought and Language* (1962) and *Mind in Society: The Development of Higher Psychological Processes* (1978) have powerfully shaped approaches to learning, cognition, language, seen as social action. James Wertsch's *Voices of the Mind* (1991) is a contemporary, so-called neo-Vygotskian treatment of these issues. Mikhail Bakhtin's writing focuses on meaning-making in social interaction in a socially diverse world. Whether in his writings on literature (*Rabelais and his World* (1968)) or on language (*Speech Genres and Other Essays* (1986)) the emphasis is always on socially formed and socially located individuals and their active remaking of their environment. Michael Halliday's emphasis is also on social action: on meaning as choice in context. That is, in a particular context I, as a user of language, want to say something, and, aware of the context and of the meaning resource of my language, make a choice to use these resources (this word, this syntactic form, this modal particle, this genre) to make my meaning. His *Language as a Social Semiotic* (1979) provides a rich introduction to his ideas on language in social life, while his *Introduction to a Functional Grammar* (1985) is both a grammar, and an extended philosophical account of language. His account of 'Nigel's' learning of language, *Learning how to Mean: Explorations in the Development of Language* (1975), focuses, as the title says, on *meaning* as the child's guiding concern.

On the side that I have earlier labelled 'communication and representation' I will mention just a few salient names: Halliday fits here, of course. Saussure and Peirce are originating figures, for much of our thinking, standing at the end of the last century and the beginning of this. Both sketched out broad and generous projects around meaning – even if very differently, and both were quickly stuffed into the straitjackets of twentieth century modernist thought. But there are figures who stand out: above all, in semiotics, Roland Barthes, whose writings on all aspects of cultural life illustrate the scope of his theory in accessible and enlightening detail. Art critics and theorists such as Rudolf Arnheim and Erich Gombrich have given us insight into the psychological, affective and social characteristics of works of art. In a somewhat different direction, two books are enormously insightful about the issues of literacy: one, Walter Ong's classic *Orality and Literacy* (1982), and one, a very recent book, David Olson's *The World on Paper* (1994), are both highly readable and most rewarding.

In the book I have stressed the importance of that neglected, forgotten and suppressed activity, synaesthesia. In the *New Scientist* (1994) there is an article by Alison Motluk 'The sweet smell of purple' on this question (which was only recently sent to me by Sharon Goodman of the Open University); Howard Gardner's work on 'multiple intelligences' is somewhat in this area. His *Frames of Mind* (1983) sets out his ideas.

Perhaps somewhat oddly for many or most readers of this book, I have drawn on recent writings on futurology and economics, management and management culture, to establish one frame for my ideas. This is certainly not 'academic', and it may prove offensive to some. I happen to think that it is now impossible to debate educational issues seriously without such a frame: for one thing, if we don't have our own ideas in this field, others do, and they will shape the future for all of us. For another, we cannot plan if we don't consider what we're planning for – and what plans others are making for us and the new generations. So, although I disagree profoundly with them very often – and often find myself benefiting from their speculations, I have started to read the work of 'gurus' such as Peters, Senge, and others. Above all I recommend the still recent *The State we're in* by Will Hutton (1995): a thoughtful, provocative, profound analysis, with proposals for change.

And finally, something about my own writing which may be of relevance or of interest. My earlier book *Learning to Write* (1994) traces the period from the age of 6 to about 12; it is focused on language. *Social Semiotics*, co-written with Bob Hodge, is an attempt to say something about the plethora of cultural meaning-making, and to establish a theory for doing so. *Reading Images: The Grammar of Graphic Design* written with Theo van Leeuwen sets out to show that the visual is a systematic, articulated means for making meaning. *Writing the Future: English and the Making of a Culture of Innovation* (1995) tries to make suggestions for a remaking of the English curriculum.

Bibliography

Arnheim, R. (1969) *Visual Thinking*, Berkeley and Los Angeles: University of California Press.

Bakhtin, M. (1968) *Rabelais and his World*, Cambridge, Mass.: MIT Press.

―― (1986) *Speech Genres and Other Essays*, Austin, Tex.: University of Texas Press.

Barthes, R. (1973) *Mythologies*, London: Paladin.

―― (1978) *Image–Music–Text*, London: Fontana.

Bissex, G.L. (1980) *GNYS AT WRK: A Child Learns to Write and Read*, Cambridge, Mass.: Harvard University Press.

Bruner, J.S. (1990) *Acts of Meaning*, Cambridge: Cambridge Unviersity Press.

Chomsky, N.A. (1965) *Aspects of the Theory of Syntax*, Cambridge, Mass.: MIT Press.

Coles, M., Goff, K. and Thornley, T. (1989) *Active Science, Book 3*, London: Collins Educational.

Cox, M. (1992) *Children's Drawings*, London: Penguin.

Dondis, D.A. (1973) *A Primer of Visual Literacy*, Cambridge, Mass: MIT Press.

Ferreiro, E. and Teberosky, A. (1982) *Literacy before Schooling*, Portsmouth, NH: Heinemann Educational.

Gardner, H. (1983) *Frames of Mind*, London: Fontana.

Gombrich, E. (1960) *Art and Illusion*, London: Phaidon.

Graham, J. (1990) *Pictures on the Page*, Sheffield: NATE (National Association of Teachers of English, 50 Broadfield Road, Sheffied S8 0XJ).

Haas-Dyson, A. (1989) *Multiple Worlds of Child Writers: Friends Learning to Write*, New York: Teachers College Press.

Halliday, M.A.K. (1975) *Learning How to Mean: Explorations in the Development of Language*, London: Edward Arnold.

―― (1979) *Language as Social Semiotic: The Social Interpretation of Language and Meaning*, London: Edward Arnold.

―― (1985) *An Introduction to Functional Grammar*, London: Edward Arnold.

Herbert, Mary Kennan (1995) *To Draw is to Write: On the Restoration of*

Drawing as a Tool for Writing, Mary Kennan Herbert, 20 South Portland Ave., Brooklyn, New York 11217.

Hodge, R. and Kress, G. (1988) *Social Semiotics.* Cambridge: Polity Press.

Hutton, W. (1995) *The State we're in*, London: Jonathan Cape.

Kress, G.R. (1994) *Learning to Write*, 2nd edn, London: Routledge.

—— (1995) *Writing the Future: English and the Making of a Culture of Innovation*, Sheffield: NATE (National Association of Teachers of English, 50 Broadfield Road, Sheffield S8 OXJ).

Kress, G.R. and van Leeuwen, T. (1996) *Reading Images: The Grammar of Graphic Design*, London: Routledge.

McKenzie, A.E.E. (1938) *Magnetism and Electricity*, Cambridge: Cambridge University Press.

Motluk, A. (1994) 'The sweet smell of purple', *New Scientist*, 13 August.

Olson, D. (1994) *The World on Paper*, Cambridge: Cambridge University Press.

Ong, W.J. (1982) *Orality and Literacy: The Technologising of the Word*, London: Methuen.

Peters, T. (1992) *Liberation Management: Necessary Disorganization for the Nanosecond Nineties*, New York: Faucett.

Piaget, T. and Inhelder, B. (1956) *The Child's Conception of Space*, London: Routledge & Kegan Paul.

Peirce, C. S. (1940/65) *Collected Papers.* Cambridge, Mass.: Belknap Press.

Read, C. (1975) *Children's Categorization of Speech Sounds in English*, Urbana, Ill.: National Council of Teachers of English.

Saussure, F. de (1974) *Course in General Linguistics*, trans. Wade Baskin, Glasgow: Collins.

Senge, P.M. (1991) *The Fifth Discipline: The Art and Practice of the Learning Organization*, New York: Doubleday.

Vygotsky, L.S. (1962) *Thought and Language*, Cambridge, Mass.: MIT Press.

—— (1978) *Mind in Society: The Development of Higher Psychological Processes*, Cambridge, Mass.: Harvard University Press.

Wertsch, J. (1991) *Voices of the Mind*, Hemel Hempstead: Harvester Wheatsheaf.

Index

NATIONAL UNIVERSITY
LIBRARY   SAN DIEGO

OKANAGAN UNIVERSITY COLLEGE
LIBRARY
BRITISH COLUMBIA

Playing with time: mothers and the meaning of literacy

Jane Mace

© Jane Mace, 1998

This book is copyright under the Berne Convention.
No reproduction without permission.
All rights reserved.

Published in the UK in 1998 by UCL Press

UCL Press Limited
Taylor & Francis Group
1 Gunpowder Square
London EC4A 3DE

and

325 Chestnut Street
8th Floor
Philadelphia
PA 19106 USA

The name of University College London (UCL) is a registered
trade mark used by UCL Press with the consent of the owner.

British Cataloguing-in-Publication Data
A catalogue record for this book is available from the British Library.

ISBNs: 1-85728-890-4 HB
       1-85728-891-2 PB

Typeset by Best-set Typesetter Ltd, Hong Kong
Printed and bound by T. J. International Ltd, Padstow, Cornwall

DEDICATION

This book is dedicated to:
Daisy Pethick, Cynthia Whiskard, Eileen Whiskard, Gladys Mace and Mary Sommerville – my grandmothers and mothers; and to my father, William Sommerville, who reminded me that "of making books there is no end; and much study is a weariness of the flesh". (*Ecclesiastes, Chap. 12 verse xii*)

Contents

List of figures and boxes

Figures

Boxes

Acknowledgements

I would first like to thank Dorothy Sheridan and her staff at the Mass Observation Archive for the scholarly and careful way in which they accepted and worked with my research idea; and to the 267 correspondents of the Archive who wrote in response to the Directive No. 46 (Part 2), and the five of these whose interviews with me, appearing under pseudonyms, are quoted in Chapter 2.

At early stages in this research, done on the edges of much else, I was truly grateful for the time given to me by the following friends and colleagues: Maureen Cooper, Zelda Curtis, Mary Kennedy and other members of the London Older Women's Education Group; Anna Davin, Liz Laing, Ruth Lesirge, Mary Wolfe and Judy Woodman; and members of the London "Women Connect" group. All these conversations helped me to hang on to a thread at times when I thought it had broken.

Ideas arising from the research were shared at papers I gave at the following events and conferences:

The British Education Research Association, Lancaster (September 1996); Goldsmiths' College Faculty seminar (November 1996); Social History Society Conference on "Time and the construction of the past", Lancaster (January 1997); Open University School of Education seminar, Milton Keynes (May 1997); and the Research and Practice in Adult Literacy (RaPAL) study conference (June 1997).

At each of these, comments and questions gave me stimulation and new perspectives. I am grateful to all those who participated; this, as I see it, is the idea of "academic community" in action.

Bev Campbell and Mary Hamilton have my warm appreciation for giving detailed comments on a draft of the whole book; as does Jenny Spiegel for her labour in preparing the final text for the publisher.

To Fie van Dijk I owe a special debt of thanks; for her intellectual and domestic hospitality and for the generous way in which she supported and developed my thinking. Thanks also to Sandra Morton, colleagues and participants in the Swansea Family Learning Programme for their enthusiasm in the project we undertook together; to Sylvia Appleton and co-members of the South East

ACKNOWLEDGEMENT

London University of the Third Age group and Joan Firth and her brother Fred for the inspiration and time they gave me.

Research for this book was supported by grants from the Nuffield Foundation and the Standing Conference on Studies in Education Research.

Picture credits

Every effort has been made to contact copyright holders for their permission to reprint material in this book. The publisher would be grateful to hear from any copyright holder who is not here acknowledged and will undertake to rectify any errors or omissions in future editions of this book.

With thanks for permission to produce:

Educate a woman . . . you educate a nation: The Federal Ministry of Education and Youth Development, Nigeria.
Time-sharing: Sally and Richard Greenhill Photo library.
Wish you were here . . . : Rupert Besley.
Too much of a good thing can be wonderful . . . : Catherine Jackson.
Meaningful relationship: Cath Tate Cards.
Knit your own orgasm: Grizelda Grizlingham (Catherine Phillips).
Signing off: Mass Observation correspondent D2402 for the page from her aunt's autograph book. Copyright the Trustees of the Mass-Observation Archive at the University of Sussex. Reproduced by permission of Curtis Brown Ltd, London.
Madonna and child, Sandro Botticelli: Museo Poldi Pezzoli.

Chapter 1
Introduction

But then she was not just a city woman, but a pom, the kind of person who has to put things down on paper before she can see what they mean.[1]

This book is a study of literacy and its meanings in the lives of mothers. Among its origins are two sets of conversations, over 20 years apart.

The first took place in 1973 during two separate initial assessment interviews at the adult literacy scheme where I then worked.[2] The interviews were with women who defined themselves as "no good at" reading and writing and were looking to remedy this. What they said seems to me to encapsulate a kind of self-disqualification by women that bothered me then and has haunted me ever since. The first woman, Milly, in her fifties, worked as a home help. She said: "Reading and writing is something I do when everything else is done". The second woman, Iris, who had been nervous when she arrived, was putting on her coat to leave when she said: "I don't want to be greedy. I just want to read what's on the walls".

Milly had always felt that it was she who had to make sure that "everything else" got done; and, too often, it never did. As Iris saw it, being fully literate would have been more than her fair share: wanting it was excessive greed, not justifiable appetite. Both women had (till then) disqualified themselves, in different ways, from a literate life. Their role was to do "everything else".

On International Women's Day 1995, I had another set of conversations, this time with a group of older women, to whom I had just given a talk on the subject of "women and literacy". In the discussion that followed (a discussion which is elaborated in Chapter 5), two of the women present revealed that their own mothers, growing up to adulthood in this country earlier this same century, had also been illiterate. Both women, now in their seventies, referred to themselves as having led an active literacy life of their own – enjoying a variety of reading and writing over a long period and currently being active participants in adult education opportunities. Later, they wrote me letters with their own accounts of their mothers' lives.

This second set of conversations caught my imagination by making me see something I had not seen so vividly before. A population of adults in the UK (and elsewhere) who are literate today are familiar with illiteracy; they grew up in households where mother, father, or both could not read and write. Children of illiterate parents, they have grown up to enjoy a full and wide-ranging life of reading and writing. (I am deliberately setting aside the educational "achievements" they may also have enjoyed; this is a book about literacy, not about certificates and degrees.)

My contention in this book is that, more than at any other time, mothers today are assumed to be essential to other people's literacy, yet are the objects of contradictory messages about their own. My purpose in writing it has been to unravel the tangled knots of assumptions from which these messages have come; assumptions that imply an over-simple causal link between the illiteracy of mothers and that of their children. As I see it, the slogans used to promote the "family literacy" programmes of the 1980s and 1990s illustrate the problem this raises.

The slogan "Educate a woman . . . you educate a nation" originated in campaigns for the equal rights of women to literacy in developing countries where, historically, girls have had dramatically less share of elementary education than boys.[3] The wording of this slogan was chosen to urge long-overdue attention to the needs of women's education. Used before and during International Literacy Year (1990), it grew out of a global concern with the low levels of literacy among women as compared with men. As numerous women's organizations and feminist commentators have observed, however, this apparent encouragement for women conceals a continuing contradiction for mothers across the developing world.[4] Without radical change in traditional forms of production and labour, the time for mothers' education can only be found by subtracting it from the time and energy necessary to sustain basic subsistence for their families. Literacy for mothers (particularly in the rural areas), unless accompanied by other reforms, remains a prize achieved at the cost of economic necessity for the communities in which they live.

During the same period, in North America and then in Britain, a similar slogan became fashionable, with subtly different wording. The exhortation was to "Teach the mother, reach the child": an explicit call, not to improve the opportunities of the mother to gain education for herself, but to lay on her alone (above all other family members) the responsibility for her children's literacy. Behind this call was a perceived crisis in the standards of literacy produced by national systems of schooling. Mothers were to be taught in order to ensure that they in turn taught their children; their own interests in literacy of any kind subordinated to that of equipping their children to succeed in the literacy of the school.

Both these slogans only thinly conceal pragmatic objectives, in which mothers as women and people with their own literacy interests are secondary to mothers as agents for others. Mothers will educate children; children are the future nation. (And, after all, what is wrong with that? Mothers are often the first to agree that their children's needs come first.) So money and slogans are addressed to the education of children's mothers, without altering the economic position of mothers or allowing for the possibility of other members in a family network to

Educate a woman . . . you educate a nation
Federal Ministry of Education, Lagos, Nigeria 1985

support children's literacy development. In North America and in the UK, this policy interest channelled funding during the late 1980s and 1990s into something that became known as "family literacy education".

For those of us who by training and experience are adult educators rather than school teachers, these messages jarred uncomfortably with what we had seen in

classrooms and discussed with colleagues in conferences and professional development courses over some 25 years. Women who have been our students have also
been mothers; all too often they have agreed with the idea that their only
justification for seeking an education in literacy has been "to help the children".
All too often, too, these women have spoken of "not having the time" to read and
write for their own pleasure or education. It was precisely because these limited
aspirations were not only being echoed but made the subject of public policy in
this way that the language of this policy struck a discordant note.

The conditions of adult literacy education are not glamorous. Classrooms are
shabby, secondhand; women students such as Milly and Iris come in all weathers,
against other pressures. Yet these are the people who, even in these conditions,
have found it possible to transcend cautious hopes; whose spirits have quickened
as they recognize their own powers as storytellers, and their capacities to be
"reading readers" and "writing writers". Such women (who, temporarily, would
forget that they were also mothers) were no longer there merely in order to
"educate a nation" or to raise the measured literacy standards of their school-
children, but to discover new levels of understanding in themselves.

The literacy of children, then, is not the concern of this book; there is a huge
literature on that subject, written by others more expert than I. Children feature
here, to the extent that children's literacy may sometimes provoke mixed feelings
in their mothers; and the childhood of women who grow to be mothers and later
grandmothers is part of the story, too. Sometimes you will meet children acting as
readers and writers for their mothers; and there are reports of families in which
sisters and brothers, fathers and grandparents may influence the way in which
young children find interest in writing and reading. But the main focus is on
literacy as a lifetime activity, not only something learned in childhood, and as
something shared in several directions between generations, nor merely a one-
way traffic from adults to children. And the protagonist is mother.

There have been, for several decades now, some engrossing and detailed studies
made of the uses and meanings of literacy in everyday life, in a whole range of
cultures. In this book I refer to some of these; at the risk of minimizing the depth
and scope of this research, I suggest that the key messages it has offered us could
be summarized as follows. First, literacy is only one means of education; secondly,
literacy is far more than what goes on in school; thirdly, there have always been
multiple uses of literacy; and finally, only in a society that assumes itself to be
literate is it possible fully to conceive of the illiterate as strange. For those of us who
live in one of the industrialized countries, in Northern Europe, in North America,
in Australia, in New Zealand, such a society is the one we live in. Those of us who
are literate in the dominant language of that society find it disturbing to conceive
of anyone who is not. So in Britain (to take but one example) the illiterate – those
adults who find reading and writing difficult or impossible, for whatever reason –
are seen variously as odd, deviant, worrying: they are *problems*. Their existence
poses a threat to the national economy – an economy in competition with others,
on the global stage. (The supposed "cost to industry" or the "cost to business" of

"poor basic skills" has been one of the less attractive aspects of the British and American campaigns for adult basic education in the 1980s.) The need to ensure that children become fully literate is an international preoccupation. The evidence of a literacy "problem" in industrialized countries with mass schooling systems has revealed that schools cannot alone meet this need. Families must therefore be recruited to do their bit, too. This is where the spotlight falls on the mother. She it is who must ensure that the young child arrives at school ready for school literacy, and preferably already literate.

It is in this setting that the prospect of illiterate mothers looks most alarming; and the myth that illiterate mothers "cause" illiterate children has subtly gained ground. The historical evidence, however, poses a challenge to this "causal fallacy". Mothers alone, whether literate or not, do not cause their children to grow up illiterate; on the contrary, an adult population of fully functioning members of a literate society includes some who are the progeny of illiterate parents. To put it another way: you and I, habitual readers and writers, are very possibly the descendants of illiterate grandmothers. Some of us may even have had illiterate mothers. In short, it is still within the reach of the living memories of literate adults to have had illiterate antecedents in their family histories.

All these observations led me to a decision. I decided I wanted to understand better what literacy means to mothers themselves. But I also decided that I wanted to cherish the possibility that illiterate mothers could be included in this understanding. To do this, I set out to find through living history some accounts of a time when illiteracy and literacy co-existed differently and when to be illiterate might have been ordinary, not strange. My curiosity was to learn more about the meanings that everyday reading and writing activities may have had for another generation of mothers, at a time when there was a different set of political and cultural assumptions about the role that they should play in relation to the literacy of other members of their families. And my purpose, as I have said, was to disentangle present-day knots of assumptions and stereotypes and release some fresh insights into the meanings of literacy today for women negotiating their identities through the excitement and fatigue of motherhood. As someone who gains enormous pleasure from all sorts of writing and reading, I also wanted to have something more to say about this pleasure to women like Iris and Milly, who continue to hold back from reading and writing.

Using a historical perspective to re-examine these assumptions, my search has been for stories and pictures of the lives of mothers and grandmothers bringing up children in the first decades of this century; mothers like those of the elderly women who had talked to me in March 1995; born in the 1870s or 1880s and bringing up children from the 1890s onwards. The choice of period was determined by the reach of memory rather than a decision made in advance that it was a better one than any other for exploring a research question. It was only when I had done the arithmetic of years that I realized how rich in significance for women's literacy this period might be. Transformations in the worlds of education, politics and popular culture during these years suggested potentially radical changes of literacy experience from one generation to the next. This was a time, following Forster's Education Act in 1870, when a universal system of education providing equal opportunities for girls as well as boys was still coming to life. For a woman born in 1880, the franchise was out of the question; universal suffrage would still not become a reality until she was nearly fifty years old. Information essential to mothers, such as contraceptive advice, was only just becoming available in print; by the 1920s this too had changed. Public transport; the penny post; the growth of the newspaper industry; later, the telephone and the radio were already transforming the possibilities of connection and communication between individuals and communities.[5] The immense technological revolutions in domestic management introduced by electricity were yet to come (arguably a revolution of greater importance to women than the more recent changes in new technology). A system of free libraries and an industry of cheap magazine publication were bringing affordable reading material into homes whose book collection, till then, had consisted of a copy of the Bible.

In short, this was a period, like any other, when opportunities co-existed with impossibilities, and when literacy had different social and cultural meanings than it has now. My hope was that by thus turning the lens on the past, there could be new insights to offer to debates in the present; and since at the heart of the argument in this book is the idea that the very uses of literacy may alter and transform our understandings of time, I see this effort to look back as a means to re-conceive how we look forward.

My sources are three. The first has been oral interviews and reminiscence discussions with elderly women. The second has been some 260 texts written by correspondents for the Mass Observation Archive (M/O). These, received in response to a directive I had written, offered a range of accounts about lives, researched from family history, personal recollection, and public records. Thirdly, I turned to literature itself – to fiction, poetry and autobiography; and to research studies in social and cultural history.

The core of the book is the evocations of the mothers and grandmothers themselves offered by interviewees and M/O correspondents. These are indeed imagined lives, refracted through the memories of their children and/or grandchildren who, in turn, offer reflections on the influence (negative or positive) of these histories on their own. The activity of remembering and imagining has itself entailed a willingness to "play with time" – and there is some discussion at intervals through the book on the issues of memory and loss it entails.

In terms of a commentary on present debates about mothers and literacy, one theme which emerges from these accounts is that of mothers' ambivalence towards their children's reading and writing. By no means all the mothers revealed in the recollections of their children felt pleased at the manifestations of their children's literacy. At times, it seems, there is indifference; at others, an active hostility to reading and writing and the world they represent. There is also a sense of yearning or longing for literacy or the time to enjoy it. Sometimes, but not always, the indifference and the longing are connected. For some women, literacy never held any promise; for others, it was an indulgence only possible in childhood and old age, but, during the years of childbirth and childcare little more than a snatched pleasure or an essential means of maintaining links with older children or relatives who live far away.

The chapters, in outline, are as follows.

Chapter 2: Literacy, mothers and time

In this chapter, I set out some ideas about my two central themes of the book – literacy and time; and consider how the experience of mothering interconnects with them. The main body of the chapter then teases out three such connections. These are:

- reading as a means of transcending temporal realities;
- literacy as an activity "snatched" out of other time; and
- the varied meanings and uses of literacy across a lifespan.

The chapter ends with a profile of Eliza, a woman who, illiterate all her life, chose to seek out literacy in her seventies.

Chapter 3: Observing and remembering

This chapter presents the work of the Mass Observation Archive and the written and oral sources this archive provided for the study of mothers' literacy in the period chosen. Of the 260 texts submitted on this topic, five are examined in some detail, via oral history interviews carried out with their authors. The story of a family literacy "drama" from one (named Gwen) will be returned to in subsequent chapters.

Chapter 4: Domestic reading and writing

This chapter picks out three uses of domestic reading and writing most frequently reported in the M/O data: letters/postcards, library books, and women's magazines. The chapter connects anecdote and story provided by the M/O writers and by other oral history interviews with evidence on the systems of communication to which they relate – postal, public library service and magazine publishing. In the latter half of the chapter we shift the spotlight to the relationship between reading, learning and writing through two present-day accounts of library and postcard use by women literacy learners. Here, too, is presented the concept of writing as a means of imaginative "play" and the obstacles to this playfulness posed by mothering work.

Chapter 5: Hide and seek

The main source for the chapter is data provided by women interviewed about their mothers; its focus is on the elusive boundaries between literacy and illiteracy. It begins with the idea of oral history as composition, and some reflections on the creative work of talking and listening. The idea of the *literate accomplice* is illustrated by two stories of literate mediators between illiterate and literate lovers; a *spectrum of literacy* is represented by the mothers depicted by elderly members of an adult education group; and a series of *silhouettes* of illiterate mothers are provided by M/O reports. There remains more to be done to reveal powerful images of the illiterate.

Chapter 6: Family is more than mum

There are two parts to this chapter. In the first part, we look at "the dark side of the rhetoric" around family literacy – including the deficit model of family, in which blame for inadequate literacy falls, by implication, on the female parent. The second part moves into the creative ways forward adopted by family literacy educators, including the continued use of community publishing as a means for mothers to articulate their own experience and histories. The story of the Swansea Mothers' Writing Group and the genesis of the community publication they wrote about their mothers and grandmothers offers an illustration.

Chapter 7: Images and certificates

Throughout the book are a number of illustrations depicting mothers reading and writing. The visual arts and media provide another source for our understanding of the meanings of literacy for women, and in this chapter, with thanks to the Dutch cultural studies writer Fie van Dijk, I begin with a discussion of two images of "family literacy". To quarry out the shape and meaning of our mothers' lives we may also turn to what historians call "documentary evidence"; and in the second half of the chapter we follow two writers (Eavan Boland and Margaret Forster) in their search for certificates and epitaphs.

   These are official documents, with a permanency about them – in contrast with the ephemeral and disposable forms of literacy often associated with women. The book ends with some reflections about these differences as they relate to ideas of time and temporality.

   This is a book which has grown more like a honeysuckle than a eucalyptus tree; it twists and turns and sprouts flowers and drops leaves; it does not grow up in a straight line to the light. In writing it I have felt alternately frivolous and solemn; I imagine that in reading it you will alternate moods, too. "Play" is a serious business as well as a delightful one. It calls for concentration and a willingness to be surprised; there is much here that I had not expected to write. The intention is to present a set of ideas, stories and pictures rather than drive an argument to its conclusion. My hope has been to make something entertaining as well educational; there is much to learn about our grandmothers, about class, about inequality, about injustice and about power. In late-twentieth-century Britain, we are just two or three generations away from a time when to be unlettered, illiterate, or simply without the daily routines of reading and writing would not have been extraordinary: or, to return the negatives into a positive, a time when habitual and pleasurable literacy was just one of what Alice Walker calls "the creative sparks" which mothers could pass on to their children.

Notes

1. This is a line from a novel by the Australian writer, Rodney Hall. The words are the thoughts of Tony, a resident in Whitey's Fall, a remote and disintegrating mining community. Tony has reached desperation point with the Englishwoman Vivien's failure to understand him and his community. He has been trying to explain to her why they want a road. She has not understood, and then he remembers why: she was not just a city woman, but a pom. When I read this book I was living in Australia; this line gave me a sense of ironic acceptance. That's me, I thought: I am a city woman, and a pom – but I'm a little proud of it, too. For me, as for Vivien, writing is about putting things down on paper – a burden to be laid down, but also a treasure to be displayed, a pattern to discover (Hall 1984: 344).
2. Cambridge House Literacy Scheme, in South London. At the time, this scheme operated a one-to-one system of teaching; each learner being allocated to a volunteer tutor. Milly and Iris were among the many hundreds of others which I and other adult literacy organizers undertook that year with men and women arriving for the first time, spurred by publicity in the media to seek a local centre where they could gain some "help" with their reading and writing difficulties.
3. "Educate a woman – you educate a nation" is the slogan used on this poster published by the Federal Ministry of Education, Lagos, Nigeria, 1985; reproduced in the UNESCO catalogue of their 1990 exhibition of literacy campaign posters (Giere 1992: 91).
4. At the Fourth World Assembly on Adult Education held in Bangkok, Thailand in January 1990, a group of participants drew up a list of fourteen "major obstacles for women becoming literate", beginning with "the link between illiteracy, poverty and marginalization" and including the "double burden" of childcare and work, the low priority given to the education of girls and women, and the incidence of sexual exploitation and oppression (Yarmol-Franko 1990: 80–81). Lalita Ramdas put the problem succinctly:

   Central to any discussion on the reasons which keep 70 per cent of women illiterate the world over, is a thorough examination of those structural arrangements which serve to keep women subjugated – namely patriarch, which alone seems to unite diverse women in their struggle for justice across the barriers of social and economic class, regional and national disparities. (Ramdas 1990: 34)

5. Joanna Bourke considers how far these changes also altered people's sense of identity during the period. Historians seem to have agreed that a growth in "national conscious-ness" accompanied both the growth in communications and in educational opportuni-ties; but they are divided as to how far this increased sense of "being British" crossed class barriers. Some, as she shows, regarded the radio (or wireless, as it was then called) as the single most powerful medium for promoting "the 'we-feeling' " (Bourke 1994: 187).

Chapter 2
Literacy, mothers and time

In this chapter are some broad brush strokes across the canvas I have chosen. There are some thoughts, first, about literacy and about time, and how the two seem to be mixed up with each other in contradictory ways. (Since I have chosen to suggest in this book that literacy has something to do with "playing" with time, a few of these contradictions needed to be near its beginning.) From these we move on to look at how these contradictions might be connected with the experience of being a mother at home. For her, the present is dominated by other timetables – those of school (the regulator of literacy), of paid and unpaid work, and of everyday life. We consider how reading provides a means of *transport out of the present time*: excursions not only out of the home, but outside its timetables.

The second connection is between *family time and literacy time* – focusing particularly on working-class mothers in the period 1890s to 1930s, and on the tension between ideas of work and "leisure". When certain kinds of literacy behaviour simply looked like "play" in conflict with the work of mothering, literacy for the mother is characterized by many women as a "luxury" and an "indulgence". Like many other "leisure" activities, literacy for mothers is something saved for the time before or after the years of childbearing and rearing. Thirdly, under the heading *literacy and life time* I consider with you how moments in the life of a girl and an old woman allow for literacy pleasures not available to the same person in the years when motherhood is her dominant preoccupation. In this section, too, there are examples of a daughter turning to literacy to find answers that her mother refuses her; and of how literacy itself has been silent on the experience of women's sexuality.

In the second part of the chapter we glimpse one mother who came to literacy in old age. The story of Eliza is told by her daughter, now herself a mother and grandmother, and her son: the story of a mother who lived through the first six decades of her life without literacy of her own (she was "illiterate"), and who, at the age of 78, for reasons unknown to anyone, chose to learn to read. Since Eliza herself is no longer alive the story depends on the "memories of memories" carried by (now elderly) children. The portrait they have of Eliza the mother is of a woman "always on the go" with no time to spare from the many roles she fulfils in her home and community. The portrait changes to another picture entirely when as an old woman, motherhood and its responsibilities no longer her prime concern, she is found turning the pages of a library book.

Literacy

"The single most compelling fact about literacy", writes Sylvia Scribner, "is that it is a social achievement: individuals in societies without writing systems do not become literate" (Scribner 1984: 7). This is an idea which is at the heart of this book.

Literacy is *one way in which people relate to each other* and to the world; to "achieve" literacy means to achieve a place within a literate culture. Just as learning to read and write is not done (either by child or adult) in a vacuum, so the use of reading and writing happens within the many textures and colours of social relationships. Sylvia Scribner, who spent five years studying the social and intellectual meanings of literacy among the Vai people of West Africa (Scribner & Cole 1981), is among a number of scholars who have argued that literacy is not one thing (as it used to be thought), but many – varying with place and time; and that each of us engages in several varieties of literacy throughout our lives, depending on the social and/ or cultural purposes we wish to fulfil. In their research, she and her colleagues found much to surprise them; not least that in the multiliterate Vai society, non-literate co-existed almost casually with literate, and one of the key literacies in use among the Vai people was propagated with no reference at all to a school system.

The question of defining literacy has puzzled people for a long time. At national and international meetings seeking to decide policy and funding for literacy programmes, it has been important for those sitting round a table to arrive at some common agreement about it. They have needed to know what it is that public money can pay for. Is it to fund some people to learn just enough to be able to write "a short simple statement about their everyday lives" (the definition favoured by UNESCO in 1958)? or will it do if they just learn to write their names (the measure used to gauge literacy in England and Wales a hundred years before)? Sylvia Scribner suggests that this worry about *definition* – and the disagreements and controversies that inevitably accompany it – might be a diversion. The useful question to start from, she suggests, is not "What is literacy?" but "What are the social motivations for literacy in a given country at a given time?" In her view, these motivations seem to fall into three groups, each of which carries its own metaphorical meaning. The first she calls the *literacy as adaptation* group, in which literacy is understood as a tool to enable people to respond to given demands or circumstances (so-called "functional literacy"). In the second group she sees an idea of *literacy as power*, in which literacy is associated with efforts at mobilizing poor communities for their own development and growth. Finally, Scribner sees some policies that appear to conceive of *literacy as a state of grace*, by which its "self-enhancing" effects of personal growth and discovery are emphasized. Each of these metaphors, Scribner suggests, implies a set of sometimes unexamined value judgements; for the purposes of educational planning, any one of them may be equally valid.

Literacy understood in this way is literacy which is a *relative* matter: it varies with who people are and where and when they are living. Relative views of the world are always less neat and tidy than absolute ones; the absolute "either–or" view of literacy ("*either* you can read and write *or* you can't") – referred to by the anthropologist Brian Street as "the Great Divide" theory (Street 1995) – sees the literate and illiterate as fundamentally different people. According to this view, the illiterate are ignorant, superstitious and backward, while the literate are rational beings with a logical turn of mind and a greater capacity for conceptual thought. Within the "Great Divide" theory, illiteracy is associated with darkness and ignorance, isolation and stigma: a gloomy place from which literacy provides rescue. Like Scribner, Street rejects ideas about "the Great Divide" and argues for a richer and more complex account of reality: one that recognizes literacy not as a singular but as a plural activity. Of course, this view can be irritating as well as illuminating; for those people sitting in policy-making meetings having to deal with practical decisions about funding, some common definitions are essential. However, the big attraction of relativist understandings of literacy is that, at a stroke, it not only does away with the notion of a single literacy, it also eradicates at a stroke the notion of "illiteracy" as a singular matter, too. Given the wholly negative association of the word, this seems a thoroughly good idea.

If literacy is understood as a way in which people relate to each other in all kinds of settings throughout their lives, another misconception may also be ditched: namely, that literacy is the same thing as schooling. In a lifespan which (with good health and good fortune) may last several decades, the time spent within classroom walls is small. Add the notion of different *domains* in which we live, and school life, as a feature of an individual's whole literacy life, shrinks smaller still. Grouping a life into different kinds of domains – home, community, education, work, and interactions with officialdom – is one way some researchers have found to express the concept of the social contexts for literacy. As a means to put school literacy in its proper proportion, Roz Ivanic and Mary Hamilton set out a memorable diagram in which they listed these "domains" across a horizontal plane and marked five-year periods of an 80-year life up a vertical axis. The resulting image – in which the slice of time occupied in the "education" domain from age five to age sixteen is set beside all the other ages and domains – reveals "how small a place compulsory schooling occupies in a person's whole life" (Ivanic & Hamilton 1990: 10).

> We scan, shun, love, copy, list, ponder the written word from the cradle to the grave and in many corners of our lives. School is only one of those corners and occupies only a very short span of time. (Ivanic & Hamilton: 17)

As historical research has shown, the equation *schooling=literacy* is relatively recent. There is a popular misconception (which I once shared myself) that the introduction of mass schooling at the end of the nineteenth century ushered in

13

literacy and that literacy levels increased with industrialization. Far from this being the case, it seems the nineteenth-century campaigns for a school system available to the mass of the population were not promoted in order to provide literacy, but in order to *control* it (Cook-Gumperz 1986). Scribner & Cole's work was just one of many studies which also showed that, in all societies, for a long time, people have acquired literacy independently of school systems.

Meanwhile, as David Barton has pointed out, whether literate or illiterate, all members of a literate society have literacy thrust upon them: junk mail is no respecter of persons, and packaging is covered in words (Barton 1994b). Everyday tasks entail all kinds of apparently trivial kinds of "literacy events" in which reading and writing form part of other activities. This concept is credited to the influential research carried out by the American literacy scholar Shirley Brice Heath (1983). Her ethnographic study over a period of nine years, in two working-class communities in the Southern United States combined the disciplinary strengths of anthropology and linguistics, and shed light on the rich everyday mix of talk, reading and writing. More recently, members of the Lancaster Literacy Research Group in the UK have published other studies of literacy use in homes and communities (Barton and Ivanic 1991, Hamilton et al. 1993, Barton & Hamilton 1998).

In the late twentieth century the achievement of literacy has become necessary to a sense of wellbeing both of individuals and of nations. Literacy campaigns invoke the language of human rights in publicity (indeed, the very idea of a "campaign" puts literacy into the realm of social justice). As an adult literacy educator for some years, I saw it as my business not only to enable people to have their share of it but also to see reading and writing as both desirable and possible. Yet, of the several hundred women and men I met in interviews and/or class-rooms during the 1970s and 1980s, not a single one of them had any sense of reading and writing as something they might *enjoy*. I do not recall one coming with an expectation of pleasure. What they came for was "improvement", with many hesitations as to whether they had the ability to achieve it. (Do you think I am too old? too slow? too late?) Few, if any of these prospective students used the word "literacy" itself; but many referred to themselves as "illiterate". Once in the literacy class, pleasure came as a surprise. Among much that seemed unreadable, something could be read; that which had seemed impossible to put on paper became written; and this experience, repeated little by little over time, revealed literacy to be something that just might become interesting and pleasurable, not merely as a solution to other problems, but in its own right. The stops and starts of the journey included moments of enjoyment, even fun: moments which, for someone to whom any call to read or write had until then spelled certain failure, were an unexpected bonus.

In the years following a public "campaign" designed to "eradicate" illiteracy, the other campaign in which students and educators in classrooms up and down the country were engaged was to transform the dominant view of the "adult illiterate" as a social outcast. Adult literacy educators were out to abolish the concept of "illiteracy" itself; and the focus of our energy was in persuading our students that a fuller literacy life was within their reach. We were there not only to teach our students how to read and write, but to persuade them of their abilities to do so. As historians of the adult literacy movement in the UK and other countries have suggested, this alternative campaign persisted against a continuing social view of the illiterate as isolated and backward (Mace 1979, 1987, Withnall 1994, Hamilton 1997).

For me, it has only been in more recent years, with the increased detachment that an academic job has given me, that I have been free to exercise a more dispassionate curiosity in literacy itself. From the defensive position of an adult literacy educator challenging dominant ideas about illiteracy, I began to think more about what it means to be literate (Mace 1992). It became important to me to separate the use of literacy from its acquisition; to distinguish between what literate people do with literacy and how people may become literate.

In considering the idea of a "literacy life", which any one of us may have (along with a social life, a spiritual life, a sporting life, and so on), I am happy to see literacy as plural and various, and certainly something far more than skills that may be achieved and assessed within a system of education. I also want to persist with the notion that literacy engages our imaginations, intellects, emotions and memories: and as such, is a matter of enormous mystery, beyond simple measurements. In this book I hope to show that any researcher who accepts this and who seeks to find out what literacy may mean to an individual or a group, has to go beyond mere observation of what could be called "literacy behaviour"; for while such observation can tell us some things, there is much that it cannot. If, for example, I watch someone else reading a newspaper on a train, I can notice which page they turn to, or how long they take to read an article; but I cannot tell what mental images or lines of thought their reading sets up. If I see someone writing a postcard in a cafe, I may notice that they are left-handed, using a felt-tip pen, and pausing over every other word; I may even – when they go up to the counter to buy another cup of tea – catch sight of a word or two of what has been written, and get a sense of what they are writing about. But I have no idea of the unwritten words that they have decided not to write.

This line of thought meant that in order to understand something of the mystery of literacy in the lives of the women I was thinking about, it became important both to learn something of these outward behaviours and contexts (when, how often, what, where and why this person reads or writes, with what skill or ability, and with what materials and apparent purposes); and also to glimpse something beyond – the person's inner life: her "mind's eye" as she read or wrote.

Time

There are two contradictions about time and literacy. The first is that there is an inequality between the *labour time* of the reading and that of the writing. The time that you take to read this chapter may be an hour or so, at one or two sittings. The time it has taken me to write it has been several days, at several sittings, several weeks apart. The choice of every phrase and connection is one that the writer may have struggled over and re-worked many times; the reader who is familiar with reading will read it in minutes. (Reading and writing, in that sense, are rather like cooking and eating. The writer (the cook) may spend several hours in planning, preparing and seasoning. The reader (the eater) devours it in minutes. This analogy between literacy, appetites and nourishment will recur in later chapters.)

The second contradiction is partly expressed by Raymond Williams's idea of "the paradoxical community . . . of a shared isolation" between reader and writer (Williams 1984: 116–17). Every time we read we read alone; the room may be full of others, but only I am reading the page in front of me (reading aloud by one person to others today being the exception, rather than the rule). The writer, while she may be writing in the middle of a throng of people, writes in similar conditions of solitude – the pen or keyboard only respond to her touch, the choice of word and sentence being hers alone. The meeting of published writer with reader is an invisible encounter, yet depends on both having a sense of a plural readership. While she writes for one reader only, the published author – not to mention her publisher – hopes and believes that there will be many. The isolation that is shared is also one of time; at the very moment of their meeting, writer and reader are living in different epochs, because of *the time that elapses between original composition and its reading* – which may be months, years or centuries. As I write this paragraph late on a Saturday April evening in London, I have no control over when and where it will be read in the future. Yet you and I conspire in an idea which assumes that, during the time you spend reading this, we are together; with common as well as different personal, social and historical circumstances in which each of us is choosing to be in each other's company.

Time is also a commodity, to be calculated, bought, sold, wasted, saved and spent. We speak of it like a possession, so that there is the idea of "having" or "not having" it. During the two years of researching this book, this possessive view of time kept reappearing. Over and over again, in interviews or writing about women bringing up children in the 1910s, 1920s or 1930s, the speaker or writer would say that she did not think she ever "had time" for her own reading or writing. Such a woman is no longer alive to speak for herself; but family history saw her as *having no time* for her own literacy life. This was not said of the woman with servants to do the housework; nor of the mother whose children no longer lived with her. But (according to these accounts) the majority of mothers at home in the early decades of this century, caught up in a multiplicity of timetables, *had no time* for all sorts of things that they might have wanted – among which, literacy and its pleasures could have been one.

"Time" for reading and writing conjures up time for being still, for pausing and considering: the kind of time which is unimaginable for most women at home, today as well as in the past. (Do women have leisure? asked Rosemary Deem, in her influential study on the subject; replying, in short, that "the experience of 'free time' remains unknown to the granddaughters of the women I have been studying" (Deem 1986: 51).) It is true that there are some occasions in a day's housework when this pondering is possible – waiting for the water to boil, the iron to heat up, or the baby at the breast, perhaps – and it is also true that women are said to be "good" at doing two things at once, the experience of motherhood having trained us to be constantly interrupted. This being the case, women's lives are less easy to describe in the conventions of time-measurement. They are asked to fit into measurable episodes and timespans, into cause and effect, and they will not. The sociologist Karen Davies described the problem like this:

> If a young infant or senile individual needs to be fed, it is hard to push this activity into a predetermined linear and clock time framework. It is hard to know just how long the activity will take. A senile person's brain and motor skills coordinate badly; it takes time to chew and swallow. Feeding the person may also be carried out parallel to other activities. The mother may help her children do their homework during the time she is feeding the baby and the employee at the old people's home may take the elderly resident with her to her coffee break and continue intermittently to feed her there, as the whole process can take more than an hour. (Davies 1986: 583)

In her survey of studies which have looked at "linear time" and women's lives, Davies discussed this problem and offered an interesting alternative. Looking back on her own research into women and unemployment she suggests that, consciously or not, researchers try to push their subjects into a "traditional chronology" that is at variance with the life experience they are describing. She argues that while plenty of people may agree that "time is vitally important for understanding our lives", the problem is caused by the fact that the nature of time itself is generally taken for granted. "Normal" concepts of time, she suggests, derive from Isaac Newton's 1687 definition of it as flowing "without relation to anything external": mathematical, abstract and context-free. If we use, instead, the idea of *temporality* we are better able to recognize that each of us lives in "a present that is made meaningful by past experience and by the person's anticipated future" (Davies 1986: 581).

Unconscious allegiance to the Newtonian, linear model of time prevents us from seeing the full complexity of life experience; the concept of temporality allows us to see it more clearly. Women's lives, she suggests, inhabit a different temporal space to men's, being characterized by "a complicated weaving of different temporal structures, times and timing" for which we need new words or concepts. One such concept, she suggests, could be that of "process time", which allows for a recognition of the mesh between time and social relations and the everyday reality of women often doing two things *at the same time*. "Process time", Davies says, "is characterized by a degree of circularity, simultaneity and waiting" (Davies 1986).

Even if we stick more closely to some idea of time passing in a linear fashion, there are ways in which we can still think more imaginatively about it than in the measurements of hour, day, week, month and year. In a collection of unpublished diaries written by white Australian women, Katie Holmes offers four different conceptions of time to help her distinguish between the way in which women may live the rhythms and interruptions of their days. One of these is close to Davies's idea of "circularity"; she calls it "biological time", by which she means the woman's monthly cycle, her periods of pregnancy, childbirth, and lactation, together with menopause, ageing and death. The other three are: industrial time (governed by the clock and calendar); domestic time (closely linked with "family time"); and "individual time" – that is, the events and episodes represented in the diaries. All of these times, she says, intersect and overlap in the diaries she is considering. The idea most directly relevant to connections between literacy and time is that of "diary time" which Holmes attributes to a writer called Judy Nolte Lensink. "Diary time", she says, is the kind of time which alternately may stretch or shrink "real time" by giving "a full page to a lover's single sentence, while describing fourteen hours of the day with the single telling phrase, 'did usual work'" (Holmes 1995: xxi).

The diary writing that Katie Holmes was examining was that which attempts to capture fragments and moments from what she calls the "eddies and whirls" of daily living. A more mundane and common use of diaries in today's society is that which you or I do when we write in for next Tuesday, or for 10 October next year, some meeting or event which we plan to attend: it is the diary as document not of the past, but of the future. Later in this chapter we shall see how a woman logging the dates of her monthly periods is using a diary both to record the past and predict the future.

I want now to see how these ideas about literacy and time can help frame some of the stories about mothers with which this book is concerned.

Literacy's transports

The mother who works at home is the family timekeeper, as well as the keeper of the place, the home. On her depends the timing of arrivals and departures, of food prepared and food eaten, of the time for bed and the time to get up. On her, in today's version of the mother, depends also the time to play with her child, to use every opportunity in the home to develop the child's language, and to enlist the child into the world of literacy. This kind of time, as Valerie Walkerdine and Helen Lucey argue, is felt differently by working-class mothers than for middle-class mothers. Their case is that the idea of a "natural" mother capable of producing "normal" children is founded on a failure to recognize different material conditions. Mothers in middle-class households appear to have more time to talk to their four-year-old children; but the appearance is an illusion. Working-class mothers, with unskilled and low paid jobs and no-one at home but them to do the housework, are "chained to time" – hence their apparent "lack" of time to do the sensitive mothering which educationalists require of them. What they hold up for us is a picture of the differences between mothers in different circumstances: a picture in which working-class mothers separate work and play, and "insist their daughters play by themselves and who insist also on getting the housework done" (Walkerdine & Lucey 1989: 30).

For women living in these conditions, literacy offers an escape: an idea most vividly conveyed by an image offered by the distinguished teacher and critic Margaret Meek. Literacy, says Meek, "is not a school subject; it does not appear on any timetable as a lesson" (Meek 1991: 226). It is nowhere and everywhere: spread all over the timetable of the school day like a veil. Her own work in lifting this veil has been an inspiration to generations of teachers and teacher educators (not least because of her engaging capacity to write as if she were having a conversation with her reader). It is her concept of reading's potential for "re-creating readers" which I find particularly arresting. The distinction she makes is between *being able to read*, and *being a reader*. To be a reader, Meek argues, is to know that writing is about making worlds, and that "reading itself is part of the text as they read it". The experience of reading in this "re-creational" way is one that is hard to convey to people who are not readers (even though they are able to read); but this passage certainly goes a long way towards conveying it anyway:

> In the process of reading a novel, where am I? at home, sitting in a chair, or in bed. But not really. I feel I am where the action is, where the sufferings are, of the people or events that the writer has made me care about, in nineteenth-century Russia, in a house in Suffolk or on the high seas, or in a quite different other world. *I am on holiday from myself, yet when I finish I know myself better.* (Meek 1991: 39) (my emphasis)

According to this idea, the reader is both present in the room and absent: utterly lost to her surroundings; and when she finally looks up from her book, feels as though she has returned from a holiday from the self that she had given to the reading.

An "altered sense of time duration" is the phrase used by two American researchers about "pleasure reading". Presented in the careful form of findings from a research project, the authors lay claim to something akin to Margaret Meek's experience: reading's capacity to lift us out of our present conditions and return us to ourselves with the feeling of a return from holiday. The purpose of their study had been to discover the factors that might decrease loneliness in later life. They interviewed 195 people between the ages of 56 and 92 living in their own homes or apartments in a Midwest American community. In undertaking the difficult task of measuring "loneliness", they drew on two research instruments: the first, a twenty-item "loneliness scale", and, as a counterpoint, the second, something called the "theory of optimal experience". According to the latter, an enjoyable activity is characterized by a state of "flow" – when we are so absorbed in an activity that nothing else matters: we have an "altered sense of time duration".

As they suggest, it is often assumed that what prevents any of us feeling lonely is the company of other people. Their sample appears to be of people who could read, even if they were not all "readers" in Margaret Meek's sense. What they found in their study of this group was that it was not a social life, but *reading* which was the most effective enemy of loneliness. Of all the activities that gave pleasure reported by those older people who were not lonely, that of reading was the one most frequently mentioned; and, taking their findings together with earlier studies, the researchers concluded that there is a positive relationship between reading for pleasure and decreased loneliness in later life (Rane-Szostak & Herth 1995).

Pleasure reading, these researchers said, is an "optimal experience"; with an altered sense of the present time, their sample of older people felt no lack of companionship. Like Margaret Meek, once absorbed in reading they are no longer sitting alone in their room, and they are no longer living a mere two hours in a particular afternoon, but two decades or two minutes in another temporality. According to this study, reading provided these older people not only with company in solitude, not only with journeys in immobility, but with a changed sense of the passage of time.

Now "optimal flow" is true for all kinds of things, as the writer Gabriel Josipovic pointed out over 20 years ago:

> I open a book and begin to read. When the book is finished I pick up another, or write a letter, go to the cinema, play tennis, talk to my friends. When the day is done I go to sleep and the next day carry on where I left off: go out to work, read a few more pages of my book, visit an art gallery perhaps, and so on. In other words I fill my days with various kinds of activities, and reading, writing, looking at pictures or listening to music happen to be among them. *These activities follow one another in time, but they also help us to pass the time – help us, that is, to ignore the passing of time.* (Josipovic 1977: 124–5) (my emphasis)

These are clearly the words of a man with what many mothers might regard as an enviable freedom to cultivate his mind and his interests. Reading and writing are among many delightful and *leisurely* activities with which he "fills his days". No mention, here, of anyone else's demands causing him to stop, leave the page for an hour or more, to return to it later having quite forgotten his train of thought. Nevertheless – for different reasons – he too, like Karen Davies, proposes that we reconsider the meaning of time itself. For there are moments, he suggests, "when something in us rebels against this linear yet timeless existence. It is as if there were unexpected knots that formed, unknown to us, in the smooth rope of our existence" (Josipovic 1977: 25). How do these connections (and disconnections) between literacy and time help us think about the meanings of literacy in the lives of mothers nearly a century ago?

Family time and literacy time

Feminist historians depicting the lives of working-class mothers in the early 1900s have set out for us a picture of determination and constant labour. Regarded by their "superiors" as the embodiments of the conditions in which they lived, they were also seen as the caretakers of the moral state of their husbands and children (Purvis 1989). The clean front step and the meal on the table were daily victories over ill health, repeated pregnancy, overcrowding and infestations of bugs or rats. As Shani d'Cruze put it: "Despite the odds, very many working-class and lower middle-class women toiled ceaselessly to achieve a clean and comfortable home" (d'Cruze 1995: 68).

In the 1900s–1920s, mothers were far more likely to be working full time at home than today. Given the conditions of paid work available at the time, Joanna Bourke regards this as more of a positive choice than their granddaughters might perceive it now; there was skill and science entailed in managing to save and forage. However, the tasks of maintaining husband and children in food and clothes, day in and day out, cost the mother at home a constant and time-consuming labour, from morning to night, seven days a week; so that there was a symmetrical equation between her time and the time of her family: "*her* work facilitated *their* leisure" (Bourke 1994: 67).

During those years of child-rearing, of providing food and shelter day after day, week after week, year after year, the woman who is a mother lived in an intricate web of timings and timetables that seems to leave little daily time for her own musings or adventures. The dirty linen must be washed. The vegetables must be bought and peeled. The water fetched and boiled, and the floor cleaned. The shops reached before they closed. The dinner removed from the oven before it burns. The table laid, the table cleared. The beds made and the beds changed.

Washing, "one of the most detested but most implacable of tasks" for women up to the 1930s and beyond, demanded "copious supplies of water and energy": and in many homes, water was by no means easily available. Whether for washing children or washing clothes, for cooking or for cleaning floors, water had to be fetched and carried up and down stairs several times a day. Even by the early 1940s less than a quarter of working-class homes had piped hot water; each batch of washing meant soaking, scrubbing, boiling, rinsing, wringing, mangling and hanging up to dry, often in cramped conditions. (Zmroczek 1994). How much working-class mothers may have longed for a holiday from all that: let alone from themselves. How some, despite interrupted and limited opportunities for formal learning, still "wrought their education" through reading and writing, must stand as testimony to a fierce determination to nourish an appetite for something else.

For thousands of women working at home in these conditions, there was little or no time for any relief from immediate pressures. It is, however, in the midst of washing that a rare first-hand picture emerges of a mother reading. It is from among the writing sent in to the Women's Co-operative Guild in its campaign for the state benefits for mothers, that one anonymous writer begins: "I was married at twenty-eight in utter ignorance of the things that most vitally affect a wife and mother". During the years of "weariness and hopelessness" and an "utter monotony of life" with five childbirths and a constant struggle to make ends meet, this woman says, "I could give no time to mental culture". Yet somehow, as she scrubbed, she snatched a kind of time:

> I bought Stead's penny editions of literary masters, and used to put them on a shelf in front of me washing-day, fastened back their pages with a clothes-peg, and learned pages of Whittier, Lowell and Longfellow as I mechanically rubbed the dirty clothes, and thus wrought my education. This served a useful purpose; my children used to be sent off to sleep by reciting what I had learned during the day. (Anon *c*.1900, in Horowitz Murray 1984: 190–91)

The reading this woman chose to do was the product of an increasingly competitive industry in cheap fiction. In 1896, Newnes' Penny Library of Famous Books had brought out its first unabridged versions of classic works, with Stead and others following soon after. The historian David Vincent suggests that, while this industry opened up new possibilities for reading enjoyment, it also posed new pressures for the reader. Poetry, classics, fantasy, periodicals and newspapers were more affordable to this woman than they would have been to her parents, providing her with brief excursions beyond the endless round of work; they also presented her and her contemporaries with added strain: "The problem was one of finding a consistent focus for their mental perspective, and of readjusting their sights when faced once more with the material realities of their daily lives" (Vincent 1993: 211, 277).

It was with an idea about *mothers' reading* that the Women's Co-operative Guild found its origins. In their account of the history of the Guild, Jill Liddington and Jill Norris quote the article in the "Woman's Corner" of the January 1883 issue of the *Co-operative News*, which stimulated the start of the *Women's League for the Spread of Co-operation* (as it was then called). The article was written not by a working-class woman, but by Alice Acland, the wife of an Oxford don: which probably goes some way to explain the suggestion of *reading* as a means for women to become politically involved. Acland urges her women readers to take a cue from the men ("Are we not as important as the men? are we not more than half the nation?") and calls on them to get together, suggesting the form in which they could do this would be in "co-operative 'mothers' meetings' where we may bring our work and sit together, *one of us reading some co-operative or other book aloud*, which may afterwards be discussed" (in Liddington & Norris 1978: 40). (my emphasis)

Alice Acland, in the 1880s, would have had greater access to schooling than the readers she sought to persuade. By the early 1900s, opportunities to gain literacy via a mass education system were still unevenly spread:

> In 1900, the first generation to feel the benefits of Forster's Education Act was just reaching middle age, and those children who had finally been forced

into school by Mundella's Act of 1880 were only in their twenties. The men and women whose childhood had been passed without the benefits of universality or compulsion still comprised a substantial proportion of the adult population. (Vincent 1993: 28)

The school, initiator and regulator of the child's literacy, marked time by lines drawn between lesson time, play time and home time, between term time and holiday time, with little mercy shown to the demands of other children to be washed and dressed, and errands to be run. Outside the kitchen, the clock of the wage-earner's life as well as the clock of the school added other summons. For the mother who worked at home, these indirect controls multiplied the other rhythms of her labour. The cycle of seasons and of menstruation, overlaid with the careful timings of cooking, washing, cleaning and care had to be meshed together with the linear diagrams of the school day and the work shift, to which her children and her husband were called. No wonder, as Anna Davin suggests, that many of those children, particularly girls, did not always meet the school's demands for punctuality, or even attendance. Since "girls' intended future was domestic", it was their schooling, more often than that of their brothers, which was disrupted: "If girls did not attend regularly it meant that family need was being put before education" (Davin 1996: 111).

The weariness of years of childbearing left not only little time, but little energy for "mental culture". Later in this book we will think about women reading fiction, in magazines or library books. Women of course also read, and have always read, non-fiction, too (not least in magazines themselves: a source of important reference on health, nutrition and local and national politics, among other matters). One non-fiction best-seller of the period was a book which has been described as "probably the most influential sex manual of the twentieth century", Marie Stopes's *Married Love*. Two weeks after its publication in 1918, over 2000 copies had already been sold, and five years later sales had totalled over 400,000 (Bourke 1994). This was women's (and men's) reading on a large scale: and a text which of itself offered a first opportunity to working-class mothers to conceive of finding time or energy for themselves. The author was a woman who offered all kinds of other reading material for visitors to her clinic: "On the desk, beside a flowerpot, was a collection of books on mothering and contraception . . . maintained as a library for patients" (Cohen 1993: 98). The first of eight Mothers' Clinics established by Stopes around the country was in Holloway Road, London. The queue of women who waited outside its door on the day it opened had been attracted by a variety of media, not least of which were the posters in Marlborough Road.

A cruel reality for many families of the period was the number of children who died in infancy; to which, for many mothers, had to be added the incidence of miscarriage and stillbirths.[1] So, while a woman's family might have been small, the number of her childbirths might have been many. Birth control campaigners in the 1920s argued that birth control information was just as necessary for those who appeared to have no families or very small ones, as for those who had a large number of children (Cohen 1993). Miscarriages, abortions and infant deaths were an invisible factor in the arithmetic of maternity and many women turned to the clinics as a last resort, when they had already had numerous pregnancies (Gittins 1982). Campaigners for women's literacy education today, as in the past, have recognized an important connection between the value of information such as that provided by Marie Stopes and the opportunity for women to control their fertility. Here, I am not wanting to draw any conclusions. I want simply to make the observation that mothers' interests in literacy engage her body as well as her soul and that the imaginative sweep of a non-fiction text could be as great, if not greater, than that of a fictional one.

Between 1918 and 1928, thousands of women wrote letters to Marie Stopes as a result of her books and articles. This extract is from one written in 1921 by a Mrs RGH, in South Wales:

> I hope you will excuse me for taking the liberty of writing to you in this way as I know no other way of doing so I was reading *Lloyds News* on Sunday and I read about what you were going to do and about the Mothers Clinic that you have opened what I would like to know is how I can save having any more children as I think that I have done my duty to my Country having had 13 children 9 boys and 4 girls and I have 6 boys alive now and a little girl who will be 3 year old in may I burried a dear little baby girl 3 weeks old who died from the strain of whooping cough the reason I write this is I cannot look after the little one like I would like to as I am getting very stout and cannot bend to bath them and it do jest kill me to carry them in the shawl . . . I was 19 when I married so you can see by the family I have had that I have not had much time for pleasure . . . (Hall 1981: 14)

Literacy and life time

Menstruation, like the seasons, is expressed as a cycle. The bleeding of the womb comes round again and again, month after month, in cyclical regularity. Then comes the interruption. Pregnancy is a growth measured in linear terms: it lasts (usually) nine months, starting with conception and ending with labour. There is a beginning, and then an end (itself a new beginning). Every woman who has experienced this, has experienced the change from something regular and cyclical to the uncertainties of becoming an "expectant mother" guided, now, by the calendar. Just a few, like this one, make use of writing to manage these uncertainties:

> I had my first baby at the age of 16. I remember, when one year passed after my marriage and I didn't get pregnant I started asking my mother, "Why is it that I am not pregnant yet?" Then on December the 17th 1950, I had my

last period; I mentioned the date *because I always kept my monthly dates in writing.*
January 1951 came, and went. I knew that I was expecting. (my emphasis)

The months ahead must be measured and calculated; and then the measure
changes from weeks or months to hours: "I woke up at 2 o'clock in the morning.
I felt some pain in my stomach".

It is no longer a month, but a time in the night which marks a change. The pain
is timed by the clock; the contractions of labour reduce the timespan not to the
hour, but to passing of minutes within it:

No, the pain didn't go. It started to get worse. It started to go and come every
20 minutes, so my husband knew it was a delivery pain. (Hackney Reading
Centre 1980: 37–8)

Three hours later, for this woman, the agony was over: she is delivered of a child.

The contractions of labour refuse a regular measure. Once in the world, the
infant embarks on a "life cycle". It is our cultural norms that converts this
biological term into a chronology – a "lifetime". Each year, the day (though not the
moment itself) of that birth is recalled and celebrated. At intervals over the next few
decades, the child is construed as arriving at points on a journey: infant, school
child, adolescent, worker, student, partner, parent, pensioner. Autobiographical
writing, looking back to our lives, chronicles the events, episodes and experiences
of that journey: but only the mother recalls the moment of its inception, as the
original interruption to another time in her own life. Few may find (or make) the
time to capture in writing the minutes and hours of labour: it took the work of an
adult literacy class in East London to offer the published account quoted above.

From the time of her first childbirth, the time for writing or for reading in a
woman's life is circumscribed. "Living with contradictions is not easy", writes
Maud Sulter in her "Portrait of the Artist as Poor, Black and a Woman". Hers is
a "creative challenge" to these contradictions:

Our priority must be to give ourselves space to create ... No one
else . . . can. So if the laundry needs to go to the launderette, or all you and
your two kids have to eat for tea is a tin of beans and some stale bread, make
a conscious decision. Either you go to the launderette or supermarket or you
don't. If so, DO IT NOW: if not, stop dithering and get back to work. (Sulter
1987: 149–50)

Since she is both a writer and (in Margaret Meek's sense) a reader, it is not
surprising that when Maud Sulter urges other women to "let others help you" she
gives as her own inspiration another writer (Audre Lorde). Her message is that
literacy, for mothers, offers liberation: but the opportunity is not given – it must
be seized. For women with no space to give themselves space, the resolution to
their contradictory lives is to be found in insisting on a "space to create" with the
encouragement of other, invisible women.

Such encouragement came to me one morning in the post, in the form of a book of poetry sent to me by an old friend in New Zealand. Leafing through it, I was met by these words:

> I want to tell you about time, how strangely
> it behaves when you haven't got much of it left.

The poem is about ageing and time; it speaks of another time in the life of a mother. This is not the 16-year-old mother giving birth; nor the other mother, at home with clothes to wash and children to feed. This is the mother now in her sixties or seventies, telling us of a different sense of time; no longer the urgency of labour to be endured, nor the desperation of meals to be found, but the contemplative possibilities of a later life, where the timings of her children's demands are now a distant memory:

> The rules change, a single hour can grow huge
> and quiet, full of reflections like an old river,
> its slow-turning eddies and whirls showing you
>
> every face of your life in a fluid design –
> your children for instance, how you see them
> deepened and changed, not merely by age, but by
>
> time itself, its wide and luminous eye; and you
> realise at last that your every gift to them – love,
> your very life, should they need it – will not
>
> and cannot come back . . . (Edmond 1996: 11)

Time changes all of us; we grow older. By reading or writing we may reverse the process: ourselves changing time.

The metaphor of time as an "old river" offers an attractive prospect not only of the present, but also of a future: of life and time yet to come, as an old woman. Like the women at Hackney Reading Centre and Maud Sulter, Lauris Edmond uses writing both to reflect on past life experiences and conceive of future ones. As women and as mothers, each had to contend with the temporal pressures of their lives to give meaning to the changes in them, using writing as a means to measure time itself. Maud Sulter urges women to seize the present moment; Lauris Edmond evokes the twist and bend of a river to imagine both future and our past. The woman recalling her labour recalled, too, the use of her diary to record her monthly bleeding.

When you think about it, it is extraordinary how silent literature has been on this most common of human experiences. Period pains, throughout history, have been routine experiences for more than half the population (and more frequent than gunshot wounds); yet until the second half of this century, little or nothing of this experience would be found in fiction, let alone poetry or drama. From her research into women's fiction during the period 1914–39, Nicola Beauman reports that the first mention of "the curse" that she found was in a novel called *Four Frightened People* by E. Arnot Robertson. This novel was published in 1931. As to the phenomenon of pregnancy sickness, one with which Mrs RCH in South Wales would have been sadly all too familiar, the first novel found to make any mention of this common malady was Rosamond Lehmann's *The Weather in the Streets*, published five years later, in 1936 (Beauman 1983).[2]

In writing her textbook on women's sexuality, Marie Stopes was part of a campaign for sexual reform (which some say, in her case, had been directly inspired by two years of unconsummated marriage). For this, she drew on her own reading in three languages of every book on sex that she could lay her hands on (Beauman 1983). The publication of *Married Love* opened up the possibility of choice and control for women over their bodies; it appeared at a time when public taboos and silence around menstruation, sexuality and reproduction could make puberty and childbirth a terrifying experience. Some research (and a lot of life history experience, too, probably) suggests that such taboos continued to result in ignorance of female contraception among working-class women as recently as 1945 (Cohen 1993). The imposed silence on these topics made for barriers between mother and daughter in the same period.

It is an autobiographical account of a Glasgow girlhood in the 1940s that suggests how literacy provided the way out, for some. The cosy intimacy of mother and young children sharing reading is in stark contrast with the later hostility, by the same mother, to her adolescent daughter's need for information. The author, Fiona MacFarlane, portrays her mother as a woman who, having had little education herself, was determined that her five children should have "the best of everything", and above all, achieve respectability. Fiona's father, recalled as a heavy drinker, was mainly absent – particularly in scenes of domestic literacy pleasures:

> My mother used to bath us all, we would be in our night clothes, and naturally my father was never ever there, and she would gather us round her at the front of the fire, and as we ate our toasted cheese sandwiches . . . and hot milk, she would read to us things like most of A.J. Cronin's work, she was very fond of them. She would borrow them from other people or maybe even got them from the library, although she seldom went out except to do shopping; and we got all these tales told to us. They were really tremendous stories, a chapter or so each night.

"I think this is why we all read without apparent effort so young", she goes on; "my mother always was reading and she read these marvellous stories to us at night that we were desperate to get our hands on books and start reading too" (McCrindle & Rowbotham 1983: 217, 221–3).

This is a happy picture, showing a mother nourishing her children with both warm food and "tremendous stories". Reading and being read to is set in a scene of safety and warmth, with the erratic male presence well out of sight and mind. A very different scene between mother and daughter follows later. The girl is now thirteen; she has discovered her first bleeding:

> I woke up one morning and blood was streaming from me – and I was screaming through to my mother in the kitchen. Nothing was sore, I felt nothing, but I thought there must be something wrong with all this blood about. All my mother said was, "Stop that nonsense, that's you coming a woman now", and that was it.

At this very different moment between mother and child, literacy fulfilled another function. The mother's reaction to the child, now "coming a woman" constituted so stern a censorship that the daughter kept hidden from her the subsequent monthly bleeding for a year. During that time, it was from her reading, not from her mother, that she gained some sense of the changes in her own body which had so frightened her:

> Through reading women's magazines – they never did mention it in those days, this would be 1945 to 1946, it just wasn't mentioned – I gradually worked out that these periods must happen regularly, because look at all the advertisements for sanitary towels there were, and if it only happened once in a lifetime you wouldn't need this massive advertising campaign. It was then I realised that this must happen regularly. (McCrindle & Rowbotham, 1983: 219)

It was advertiser's copy that provided Fiona Macfarlane with some partial understanding of the education she needed; an education for which she, like others before her, assumed the proper responsibility belonged, not to teachers, but her mother. (In fact, the day of her first bleeding was the only time this woman recalled she had ever taken a day off school.)

I have said that women, too often, were seen as "having no time" for reading or writing. I have also said that their children can only guess at how they themselves experience this lack: were they indifferent or were they frustrated? The story that follows gives us some clues; the woman at its centre also retains her mystery.

The mother comes to literacy

This is the account of a woman who, illiterate all her life, nevertheless raised two literate children, and two years before she died apparently decided to become literate. It came to me from three sources: from a "fictional biography" of her early life, written by her daughter; from an oral history interview with her daughter and son; and from letters which her daughter wrote to me later. The story itself is incomplete and will always remain so, for the question of Eliza's interest in literacy can only ever be answered by Eliza herself.

Eliza Harrison, née Fairfax was born 1892 and died in 1973. She married Harry Harrison in 1913, when she was 21. Their first child, Fred, was born a year later; Joan, his sister, was born twelve years after Fred, in 1925. In April 1996 I talked with Joan and Fred at Joan's house.

Fred, sitting back in his chair, recalled their mother like this:

> She was never still, me mother. Never still: baking, washing, cleaning, going out bringing babies int' world, helping to lay people out that had died. Anyone that were poorly, she'd go and see to. No matter what it were, "Fetch Mrs. Harrison". That's how she was. As recently as last week, I had someone come up to me and say, "By gum! your mother, she were a worker, weren't she!" And she were!

In 1995 the Stocksbridge Writers' Group, of which Joan had been a member for some time, published the book she had written about the first 20 years of Eliza's life, *A Time to Trust* (Firth 1995). Drawn from "tales told and remembered of working class life in Sheffield and Stocksbridge", it is, in the words of the author, a "biographical novel in three parts": dividing Eliza's life into three kinds of time – "Time to be a child", "Time to grow-up" and (referring to her courtship and marriage) "Time to be together".

Joan, like Fred, was struck by the continued reputation of her mother in the community where she herself still lives:

> The most surprising thing that's happened since my book is the number of people who have rung up to say "I wanted to tell you not only have I enjoyed your book, but I remember her so well and your mum nursed my sister or brought me into the world" or you know, things that I knew nothing about. I knew she used to disappear in the night and help people have babies and lay them out. A little boy who used to have fits regularly used to always ask for her as she was the only one who he thought that he could trust.

Eliza's mother and father, Phoebe and Jim, had eight children. Eliza never went to school and for most of her 81 years, never learned to read. Her own mother and father had been illiterate. The account of her daughter and son, looking back in their own later years, is that Eliza came to reading when she was 78 years old. The question we discussed in Joan's sitting room that morning, over 20 years after Eliza's death, was this: what was it that had made the idea of reading both possible and attractive to Eliza, after a lifetime of doing without it?

Certainly her childhood had given her little opportunity. She had been kept at home to help her mother in the everyday tasks of errands, washing, fetching and carrying for her younger and older brothers and sisters, and nursing her father after a major accident at work where he had endured burns. She also helped her mother with at least one of her younger siblings' births. Her childhood, then, though not without its pleasures, had not been a carefree one. Joan said: "She once said to me that she never remembered playing without having a child with her; and if she didn't have a child with her, she'd be in trouble."

At the age of 13, Eliza went to work as a "scrub girl" at the local butcher's; and then, to work for an older woman in the village; from there, she went into domestic service. Eventually she met and married Harry who, after a hard time of unemployment, had got a job as a cold steel roller in the firm of Samuel Fox's, in Stocksbridge.

As for Harry, with only three years of schooling himself, he had nevertheless acquired an appetite for reading that lasted all his life. Throughout the next 50 years or so of their marriage, he made efforts to include Eliza in the world of papers and books that he evidently so enjoyed. Joan's portrayal of these efforts in her book about Eliza has Harry, in the early months of their courtship, seeing literacy as the means to "still" his "eternally busy" Eliza:

> She was eternally busy. It irritated him and he found himself begging her to sit with him, especially when he wanted to share something he had found interesting by reading it out to her. When he protested she would just laugh and say, "I can't Harry love. My bottom's too round for sitting, I'd slip off the chair".

Joan has Harry then offering reading as a carrot:

> "Look, Eliza", he said. "You need to have some peace in your life, everyone needs some quiet. What about having a go at trying to read? I'd help you."

She shied away from the painful subject. He went on.

> "I'd find you a book you'd enjoy. I've got one called *Mrs. Haliburton's Troubles*. It's written by woman, a Mrs. Henry Wood. I'm sure you'd like it. I could read it to you and every now and then, when you felt like it, you could try an odd line until you felt able to do a bit more. How about it?" he asked anxiously.
>
> "Well, I'm not sure, but if I ever do learn to read it will be because of you, Harry. I know that and I don't mind trying", she laughed nervously, "and I do like the title, *Mrs. Haliburton's Troubles*. It might end up being Mrs. Harrison's Troubles."
>
> "Come here, love, and make time to give me a kiss." (Firth 1995: 150–51)

Harry wrote a good copperplate hand and later won more than one handwriting competition. Before they were married, he taught Eliza to write her own name, with the result that her signature was, according to Joan, "almost identical to my dad's writing".

In summary, then: according to both Joan and Fred, Eliza, as wife and mother, found literacy less attractive than her practical skills as wife and mother (cooking and washing, cleaning and caring) and her identity as the person to whom neighbours turned when there was sickness, childbirth or death in the family. She had taken in lodgers; had had soldiers billeted in the First World War; had earned a few pence doing others' washing, as well as her own; and had been a member of the British Legion for many years, distributing food and help to people who were in difficulties after the war. For most of her life, she was, indeed, "never still".

Phoebe's other children all acquired literacy to a greater or lesser extent; and Eliza's two children, Joan and Fred, both became enthusiastic – and, in Joan's case, avid readers and writers. Both Joan and Fred had known, as children, that their mother could not read, but neither recalled it having bothered them. It was Harry, their father, who was the reader in the family: father dealt with letters, father ordered books by post, father read the daily newspaper, and father ensured that both got on in their education. In 1969, at the age of 87, Harry died. Eliza was 78.

It was at some time in the next two years that Joan came upon her mother reading. Visiting one day, Joan noticed a book on the table. On questioning her, Joan discovered that Eliza was learning to read. This was how Joan recalled the scene in conversation with me. I had been asking her about the portrait she had made of Eliza as a young woman in her "biographical novel":

You said that your book is a memory of a memory, so you are remembering what your mother told you about her life. Several times in it, you make the suggestion that Eliza regretted not being able to read. There is a feeling you gained from her that she really minded. Now, is that what you got from her? did she mind?

Yes, she did mind. She minded so much that after my father died when she was 78 she actually taught herself to read, which was amazing. I went one day, and there on the sideboard was a book; and I said "What's this then?", she said: "It's mine, I'm still only halfway through it. I've had it three weeks from the library and I'm struggling but I'm going to finish it" and I said "Are you really?" and she said, "Yes". After that for the last three years of her life (she died when she was 81) she actually attended the library and took books out.

It would take a long time to read one book for she was very insecure about reading. For instance, if she received a letter, she would struggle through it but when I called, I mean we used to call three times a week because she had a little flat then, very near the school and so the girls, my girls Helen and Gillian and myself used to go three times to have lunch with her . . .

With a letter, she would read it but she was very insecure – especially if it was sort of an official letter and she would say as soon as I came in the house: "I've got a letter, will you read it to me?" So she needed that sort of underpinning that my dad had always given her.

These are memories of Eliza "minding" now that she is no longer accompanied by Harry; an Eliza who is now less physically able to fulfil the busy and useful social role she had held all her life; an Eliza who, perforce, was at last *sitting down*.

Fred's memory of their mother "minding" is of a dimly remembered sense of longing he thought that she had felt in relation to his own reading as a schoolboy:

> I could feel it, more than anything else. When I used to tell her things about school, she'd be trying hard to understand what I were doing, you see. She'd never done it, so she didn't know it. It were foreign language to her.

When it came to her daughter's reading, as Joan remembered it, Eliza felt not so much wistful as exasperated:

> When you read, it used to annoy her. She tried not to get annoyed, but you know how you get lost in a book? and she would take a book off me sometimes and she'd say "I've spoken to you three times" and I'd say, "I'm sorry mother I haven't heard you". She found it very difficult to understand this fascination that my father and I had for books.

We may imagine that the daughter's reading irritated the working mother more than the son; and of the two of them, it is Joan who spoke most passionately of her childhood pleasures in reading:

> One of the jobs in the house that I would always volunteer for was to do the paper and magazine cupboard out. We'd keep some of them in there probably because some of them would be used for the fire (they were all coal fires) and I would sit there all Saturday going through them – and she used to get really annoyed: "You've been at that hours! Whatever are you doing?" Of course, I was reading. My father taught me to read before I went to school I think, I never remember learning. I was only three and a half when I went to school. To me, it's always been an essential; to my mother, she could never quite understand this love of words. I think it was a sort of protection she should have to push it out of her life.

Both recalled their father reading to Eliza from the *News Chronicle* newspaper or the weekly *John Bull* magazine. "He'd say, 'Listen to this, love', or, 'Listen to this, mum'."

Both, too, saw their parents' relationship as a romantic one. As Joan saw it: "They obviously loved each other intensely . . . They were very much in love all their lives . . . I think that is very important and helped to boost her confidence".

Harry was remembered as a very shy "sober, god-fearing man" who had "a way of shutting himself off from people" – and of enjoying reading. As Joan put it, he had been "a great sender-off for books": *The Wonders of the World*, Dickens' novels, and "Harman's Dictionary", in parts. Possibly among the second-hand books he often bought from a stall in "the rag and tag market" in Sheffield were the detective stories in which, as Fred recalled, he took particular pleasure: "Me dad got a Sexton Blake and a pipeful of baccy, and he were happy".

The source of Joan's book was Eliza's stories. She was, as Joan recalled her, "a natural story teller" who "would tell me her stories, sort of casually" – and, unlike the mothers of Joan's friends, she also told her daughter about sex. Eliza's own education about her body from Phoebe had been abrupt, cold and uninformative, as Joan had understood it. She wanted her daughter – and her daughter's friends – to have better. This story-telling is remembered with particularly pleasant associations:

> I used to have lots of friends and mother made this lovely treacly fudge. My friends called for me but I didn't realise at the time they were really calling on mum, a) because they knew she'd give them a piece of fudge, and b) because they knew she'd answer any questions that they wanted to ask her. Never any fuss about it, just tell them; never tell them more than they needed to know.

Essentially, Eliza the mother had no need for reading and writing; she had a good memory, and regularly sent her children on errands with lists they simply had to remember themselves, as she had herself no need to write them down.

The answer to the question as to literacy's attractions to Eliza, the old woman, could be several. It has been suggested to me that, unbeknownst to her children, Eliza could read, but simply did not choose to exercise the faculty. For years, she left all that to her husband and children, and got on with more important things. With the unaccustomed leisure offered her by old age, she made the choice to re-attempt an early acquaintance with reading.

An alternative (and more romantic) theory, offered by Joan, is that Eliza sought out reading as a means of bringing her closer to the husband she had loved, no longer with her:

> I think it was partly through loneliness or perhaps it was for him, perhaps it brought her nearer to Harry, it could have been that. Perhaps she wanted to know what Harry found in these books that she'd never been able to find herself.

All those evenings with Harry settled into his detective fiction might finally have come back to her as an attractive option for herself.

A third possibility is that Eliza was not reading at all, but simply enjoying the physical presence of books around her. Neither Joan nor Fred could say how well or with what pleasure she was actually reading; all they could say was that there was a bookmark in the book and that she said to Joan: "I've had it three weeks and I'm nearly half-way through it".

Reflections

In her book on working-class women in Lancashire, Elizabeth Roberts quotes one of her interviewees as saying: "The women, they worked and worked. They had their babies and worked like idiots. They died, they were old at forty" (Roberts 1984: 148).

Literacy's meanings, I have said, are deep and varied; mothers, I have argued, have been caught up in a view that sees their educational interests as inseparable from their children's; time, I have proposed, is a concept which, if released from a linear model, enables us to see experience (including literacy experience) in new ways. In beginning a search for the reading and writing lives of women in the past, we are hampered by the lack of firsthand first-person accounts and must guess and glimpse at them. What is clear from social history is that the particular meanings of literacy at the time were different than they are a century later; and that what the historian David Vincent has called "the complex structure of reciprocity" sustained and supported all sorts of literacy events, just as it supported other situations or problems faced by groups and communities (Vincent 1993).

What reading and writing means and feels like varies, too, with who the reader or writer is. Our ethnic identity, gender and class all colour and flavour the literacy experiences we engage in. While the "either–or" view of literacy and illiteracy may have been abandoned by teachers and academics, much of the world still holds on to the idea that to be illiterate is to be stupid or backward and to be literate is a mark of civilization and superiority. Literacy and class, in our society, are tangled up in each other. Working-class women living at the turn of the century quite simply had less leisure to read or write than their middle-class sisters – even though the evidence suggests that experience of repeated pregnancies and miscarriage crossed the class barrier.

Daily life in late twentieth-century industrialized society is ruled so much by clocks and calendars that it is hard for us to imagine it otherwise. Anyone who has worked in life history or biographical research is continually in the business of checking dates and estimating periods of time. The very effort to relate cause and effect drives us to seek a chronology.

I have suggested three ways in which these themes seem to intersect. The capacity for reading to take us away from here and now is one; the struggle for women to capture the time to do that, in the context of other timetables, is a second; and the way in which life changes in a lifetime may bring us to different uses of literacy is a third.

With Eliza, we are left to muse over the appeal of literacy in a life which, by other accounts, was full enough without it. As an old woman, the "optimal flow" offered by suddenly losing herself in reading might have been an attraction. A fictional account of another woman's arrival at literacy gives a sense of another change. It is another tale of flight from the present, and tells the story of a Yorkshire housewife called Maggie Gregory. A houseproud woman, given to home-baked pies, a full washing line and a scrubbed doorstep, Maggie has never learned to read and write and never particularly wanted to. She has too much to do; there is no reason. It is the local priest who persuades her son to teach her to read, which, slowly, Maggie does (at first without much enthusiasm, humouring them). But gradually, things change. She cannot stop reading. Housework is abandoned, cooking and cleaning neglected. Husband, son and priest are shocked – for although she is still at home, she has left: "Once she fell under the spell of the printed page, neither time nor place existed for Maggie Gregory" (Naughton 1961: 116). Husband and son come to accept her new identity and the story ends with their agreeing they had better get on with the washing up: a happy ending indeed, compared to that experienced by other women coming to literacy in adult life.

Notes

1. A typical working-class mother in the 1890s (writes Joanna Bourke) experienced ten pregnancies and spent about 15 years of her life pregnant or nursing a child less than one year old. By the 1960s, the average working-class mother spent only four years of her life engaged in these activities (Bourke 1994).
2. Beauman does not record similar figures for literary accounts of miscarriages or still-births; but in the language of Welsh, at least, these subjects too have been absent, as Menna Elfyn discovered: "It is difficult now to believe that it was 1977 before the common experience of miscarriage made its first appearance as a subject in Welsh poetry" (Elfyn 1994: 282).

Chapter 3
Registers of memory

Why am I discussing father when it is Eliza we are interested in? Well, it's simply that it is quite impossible to think about them separately, especially for me who met them halfway through their lives. (Joan, letter to me: April 1996)

The work of remembering is always a present activity. Where we have arrived for the moment, emotionally as well as socially or geographically, is the place from which we look around at the landscape of our own life; the story we make of it is created from what Phillida Salmon calls its "current end" (Salmon 1992). In the enterprise of attempting to re-create the life of a person who featured in her own life as mother, Joan mixed biography with autobiography, and told it from the position she was in at the time. In the effort to recall her mother, and imagine beyond what she could recall, Joan found it hard to detach Eliza from Harry – not least because, as a "late child", she had entered her mother's life when it was already halfway lived.

Of all the people I read and spoke to, Joan was unusual in that she had already chosen to write a "biographical novel" of her mother's childhood and youth: a remarkable feat of imaginative writing that ends with Eliza and Harry about to become parents. My interview with Joan and her brother Fred took up the tale from this historical moment. In our conversation, they pieced together for me their memories of the mother and father that Eliza and Harry were to become to the two of them in the years that followed. The dilemma which Joan expressed is central to the whole enterprise: namely, in asking children or grandchildren to assemble a portrait of their own mother or grandmother, and in asking them to imagine this woman's reasons for reading or not reading, writing or not writing, I was asking them to detach this woman from themselves and others. I was asking them to tease out both images and speculation on these images, both the remembered and the guessed-at; and I was asking this from the very people who, of all the people in her life, would have known this woman least well.

I chose to seek out these recollections in two media: written responses to a set of questions, and individual interviews or group discussions recorded on tape. In the past, I have often undertaken projects which invite talk first, and then writing (Lawrence & Mace 1992; Mace 1995); a practice common in the work of adult literacy education itself. Now, most of us tell a story one way when we speak and another way when we write. Our listeners may liberate or limit us: some stories we tell are what I think of as "polished pebbles" – tales that we have kept and retold many times, with a slightly different gloss at each telling. Others come out as surprises or afterthoughts in the course of a narrative about something else altogether. In writing, there is the opportunity to curtail, restrain or edit such surprises. Writing allows for revisits and recastings. And in some of the writing I have been reading, the mother is portrayed in a more favourable light than she might have been shown in the flow of speech.

The first time I had the opportunity to notice this difference was some years ago, after I had had an interview with a woman called Nora during a project in "people's history". As part of this project I carried out individual interviews on tape, transcribed the interview and returned a copy of the transcript to the interviewee. She or he could then choose to propose changes and additions with the idea of producing a text for others to read, in the form of a community publication, to add to others which the project was producing. Nora had done this, and in one detail made a significant addition. In her original narrative she had told me of how her mother, suddenly widowed, went on to bring up her five children alone in the 1930s and 1940s. In the interview, Nora had been at pains to say:

> We had quite a happy, oh, I had a happy home. We were never short of anything: I'm not going to say there weren't things we wouldn't have liked, but you couldn't get, you saved up for them – because my mother wouldn't have anything on hire purchase.

In her later editing of the transcript, Nora had made some small changes to the whole, and added an entirely new sentence: "She was a wonderful mother, and she taught us the value of things" (Mace 1995: 112). This is a complete statement. It is written with a sense of an audience, a public readership. Without the hesitation of her conversation with me, the mother she wanted to portray was a mother who was "good".

Writing allowed an authorized version of the mother to be presented; a version that may have been at odds with Nora's childhood experience of her. David Vincent, writing about nineteenth-century working-class autobiographies, notes a tendency to go further than this. Some writers, looking back on their childhood, felt the need to portray the mother as "absolutely unselfish", "beautiful, exemplary and heroic" and even "saintly". Even fathers came in for this treatment, it seems. "It may be", Vincent suggests,

> that the passage of time increased the tendency of sons and daughters to canonise a mother or father who had struggled against poverty to bring up a family. There were instances enough of parents who had failed to meet the challenge. (Vincent 1993: 66)

Some of the work for this book was undertaken via oral interviews alone; much of it, by my reading of other sources. But its centrepiece consisted of several hundred pieces of writing by people I had never met, and whose names were unknown to me. Of these, I later arranged to meet just nine people, with whom I had two or more hours of conversation, some of it taped. So the sequence of my earlier work was reversed. We were talking about what they had already written, rather than talking with the possibility of using the talk to inspire the writing.

In this chapter, I set out some of the themes this raised, both in terms of literacy and of mothers. First, I introduce the reader to the Mass Observation Archive, the source of the writing submitted on the topic, and to the ways in which its writers and readers may understand each other. I then illustrate some of the responses by Archive correspondents to my own directive. Of these, we then focus on five women who both wrote for the Archive and later met and talked with me. I pick out some of the pictures they created of their mothers (all born in the 1890s) and show how these provide elaborations of their original writing and conclude with some thoughts about literacy and memory.

Mass observation

Long before the Mass Observation Archive became a physical place I visited, it had been, for me (as for many others, I suspect) an important idea. The idea, as I understood it, had been to give recognition to the experience of "ordinary" people, in the making of histories. "Ordinary" is usually understood in the nega-tive: "not extraordinary" or "not famous"; and in the world of adult literacy education and the community publishing movement in the 1970s and 1980s it had meant "unpublished" (Morley & Worpole 1982). While writings sent in by volunteers for the Archive are not sent in with a view to publication, in an important sense they are writing for public use. Their carefully handwritten or typed pages are, equally carefully, received and catalogued. As I discovered when I began being a regular visitor there, these texts are stored in very solid cardboard boxes, and readers are required to treat them, as original and single manuscripts, with respect. None of them can leave the Archive premises. Photocopies can be made by arrangement. In the interests of protecting original documents, research-ers are discouraged from using pens in the Archive room. For this moment when reader meets writer, the researcher's tool is the pencil.

The Archive, originally founded in 1937, has long been an important source of historical documentation on aspects of everyday life in Britain. Established in 1970 at the library of the University of Sussex as the repository of surveys and records from its investigators, it has functioned since the 1980s as a national writing project. Its five hundred-plus volunteers are volunteering their writing: sometimes diaries; more often, detailed replies to questions on specific themes. These themes are expressed as "directives": directives explain the topic and give some questions to guide the responses.

Over the years, the Archive has consistently attracted more women than men as its "correspondents". Dorothy Sheridan, the archivist and a key figure in interpretative analysis of its resources, explains that this term is preferred to others (such as the earlier one of "observer") for its association with a "sense of mutual relationship" (Sheridan 1996: 30). The word also combines the two other associations of letter-writing and of journalistic reports. It is this mix of private and public, she suggests, which might explain its appeal to women (Sheridan 1993: 22). The writing is about experience, personal opinion, subjective observation; at the same time, it is received as valuable material for public use. The identity of the author is kept confidential, until and unless correspondents consent (as some did, in this project) to reveal themselves in face-to-face meetings. This anonymity for many correspondents offers a freedom unusual in any other setting: and in an important sense, represents a particular kind of generosity. These texts are *donations* in a sense which I came to admire. Sheridan (1993) reports that many correspondents do keep copies of what they write; what I found striking, in the nine people I met with, is that not one of these individuals had done so, at least for the directive I had written – so that they could not remember what they had written, and appreciated receiving a copy of it before we met.

Directives are written on a wide range of topics, issues of current interest, or questions from researchers like myself. The Archive negotiates a "house style" with the latter, combining an informal style with a framing of questions that allow for a range of response, such as "How do you feel?" "What do you think?"

> The aim is to ensure a variety of themes, to stimulate, amuse and provoke the correspondents into replying, and to create as far as possible a diverse set of multi-layered, multi-faceted life stories on a whole range of contemporary concerns. (Sheridan 1996: 17)

The full text of the directive which I wrote with Dorothy Sheridan's help for this project is found in Appendix 1. It was mailed out in November 1995. By the time of my first visit to the Archive room in the library in the grassy landscape of Sussex University, it was (although only April) harvest time.

The only reading experience that compares with this one is the reading of exam scripts and essays by university students. But this reading was not for assessment or grading. It was a reception. Opening a box, and taking out the first page of writing, not printed like this one, but written as a single manuscript, recently written, warm still, not from the press but from the hand that wrote it, was an extraordinary experience.

The average response by correspondents to a given directive is around fifty per cent: and this one was no exception. As Figure 3.1 indicates, more women than men chose to write about this topic.

Researchers can only speculate as to the reason why correspondents choose not to respond to a particular topic. For some, the question may simply not be interesting. Others may feel unqualified to write about it. For correspondents born

	Total Correspondents	Respondents to Directive 46, No. 2	Per cent
Men	178	79	44
Women	393	207	53
Total	571	286	50

Figure 3.1 Mass Observation Directive 46. No. 2 – Mothers and Literacy
Source: Mass Observation Archive

later than the 1940s, the invitation to write about women bringing up children between the 1890s and 1930s meant writing about people they had either only known from childhood as remote and elderly figures, or had never known at all:

> I have found this section rather difficult to answer. My own mother died when I was 12 and I know little about her family. My grandmother died in 1970 when she was 86, but again I am sadly uninformed about her early life. I did ask my father, now aged 83 and although he gave me some information about his own early reading, it is not perhaps relevant to this subject. (D2123)

The lack of personal acquaintance with their subject was not an obstacle to all writers, however. W2338 (a 63-year-old woman) had never known her grandmother; but found a way of creating a sketch of her life, if not a portrait. The only clue she gives as to the sources she used in writing it is a reference to "family tradition". This is a piece without speculation, keeping strictly to the "facts"; she makes no guesses as to what "pleasure" reading gave her, nor what she used her "beautiful" handwriting for. I read it several times, and as I read, I remembered Katie Holmes' idea of "diary time" (discussed in the previous chapter) – when one brief phrase has to suggest weeks, and a sentence is used to encompass whole decades:

> She lived about 10 miles from Oldham, on the moors. As far as I know, she had three brothers and sisters. Her mother was German, and changed her maiden name from Schmidt to Smith. She always wrote in a beautiful hand – learned at school and at home. There were books in the house. She went to a "Dames" School at first. On school leaving age, she stayed on as a monitorial assistant, then went to train to be a teacher – so she would be educated up to the age of 21. She had 10 children, the last one at 45. She read for pleasure – books and periodicals. Sons were away in the war and she wrote to them (1914–18). She played the piano and sang and *all* her children went to university. The eldest son was responsible for the education of the

41

younger children after her husband died. Family tradition has it that she worked extremely long hours – baking, washing, ironing, sewing, cleaning – and had little energy for anything else as the family grew, but education remained a prime concern. I didn't know her. (W2338)

Many other correspondents, like this one, tackled the task of writing about grandmothers by turning to "family tradition", or (often) to memories passed on from a mother or father. Some were able to mix this information with childhood memories, and with census or other data they had looked up in public records. A third approach was to seek out a relative and interview them specifically for this. I will illustrate these three approaches in turn, before going on to look in some detail at the fourth: namely, those who wrote from firsthand memory about their mothers.

Memory "passed on" from a parent

T2003, writing about her maternal grandmother (born 1883 died 1968) simply begins by noting that the piece was based on "information gleaned from my mother (her daughter)".

It is a short piece (two handwritten pages). She writes that the grandmother, born in Bristol of a "stable middle-class family", the third of five children, grew up to have six daughters of her own. It contains an arresting picture of family literacy:

My grandmother worked extremely hard making ends meet etc – no labour-saving devices and 6 kids to care for. Thus I gather she had little time for reading. *However my grandfather, and the older daughters spent many hours reading to her while she ironed and sewed.* Dickens was a favourite – also travel books and biographies. (my emphasis)

Many correspondents turn to others in the family for information and insights. This correspondent (also aged 44), for example, begins her "portrait" with an immediate attribution:

Margaret Strong* was born in 1887 and died, at the grand age of 97, in 1995. She was my maternal grandmother, and the information was passed to me by my mother. (H1745) *(pseudonym).

Similarly, S481, a 53-year-old woman begins her piece:

Eleanor was my grandmother, and she died when I was seven years old. Most of what is recorded here has been told me in the past by my mother, who is now almost 80.

Eleanor had two daughters, the writer's mother, and her aunt. In using the memories which both women gave her of their mother, this writer raises the issue of contradictory memories – one daughter recalling Eleanor as "always busy and impatient"; the other, as "full of fun".

Eleanor's two girls were kept at home together, away from "ruffians" in the village, and so had to play together despite their differences, except when at school which they both attended to age 14 although my mother missed a great deal through ill-health. She remembers Eleanor as always busy, and impatient, spending little time with her and always finding her jobs to do or errands to run when she was well enough. By contrast, my aunt remembers her as full of fun, singing little songs and telling her stories. Yet the mother they describe is recognizably the same person, for many of the same stories are told but from different points of view (although it must be said that the same applies to their memories of their father, to whom my mother was much closer than my aunt).

A second example of this is provided by a correspondent (W1813) reflecting on the difference between her own recollections of her grandmother, and that of her mother (the woman's daughter). In this, we can see something of the difference between a mother–daughter relationship and that, which may often be freer, between the mother (now a grandmother) and her daughter's child (grandchild):

I find it strange that different generations often see the same people in different ways. My mother's view of my grandmother is that she saw no real benefit in education and wasn't interested in encouraging her children to read and write.

There's a sense that the writer is wishing to defend her grandmother to her mother, even as she writes for the Archive:

My mother seems to forget that for most of her childhood my grandmother was blind, so I don't suppose she really knew how to help her children. She did care enough about education to send my mother to school at two, only to be told that she'd have to wait another year! When she did get her sight back, my mother says my granny didn't value anything and used to write shopping lists on the back of family photos and tear out title pages from books to write notes on.

This carelessness and lack of interest in her daughter's education is contrasted with the writer's memory of the same woman's more active interest in her own:

When I was born in the 1950s she still did that, but she also sang songs with me and played with me and helped me to read . . . She spent a lot of time

43

looking after me when I was small because my mother was at work and I do think she was really interested in education, though not much in formal education.

As her granddaughter saw it, the same woman, as grandmother, had greater freedom to support her grandchild's education than she had had to support her daughter's.

> She (grandmother) thought people should know how to read and write, but only for the practical reasons of communication. For her it was most important to know how to survive. My mother wanted to stay on at school in the Sixth Form, but my grandmother considered that getting a job to help out with the family was more important . . . This upset my mother very much . . . My mother has never forgiven her. (W1813, 45-year-old woman writing from Staffordshire.)

Just as Eleanor's two daughters had the same but different mothers, so daughter and granddaughter, here, had dramatically different experiences of the same grand/mother.

Correspondent B89, a retired typist (aged 64) wrote about a woman who had died before she had been born – her maternal grandmother – and had no memories of her own to draw on. Her mother had told her a good deal about her, but she too had died (in 1982) and the writer is therefore relying on her memory of what her mother had told her she remembered.

The grandmother had borne ten children and brought up seven. She died at the age of 44 and, having never been much to school had never been able to read or write. This summary, like so many others I read, felt almost breathtaking in its compression of life experience; so that the phrase "very busy" in what follows seems the greatest of understatements:

> She was always very busy with her household chores and looking after her husband and children and even if she had been literate, she would certainly never have had the time to help her children with their reading . . .
>
> *I remember however that my mother told me* that she and her sisters taught their mother how to write her name. (my emphasis)

Own memory, memory of parent, plus census and other data researched

This combination of sources inspired some of the more lively pieces of writing, locating the recalled woman in the lives of others and in a social context. Younger writers, with little or no firsthand memory of their own, turned to public records and their own mothers or fathers. H1705, a woman aged 44, for example, mixed direct memory with information she had gathered from others to produce a portrait of her grandmother across a lifespan, setting hearsay fact about her subject as a young girl ("as a child she spoke Jersey French which is a local patois") next to a firsthand recollection of her as an old woman: "When she went senile in her old age she reverted to speaking only in Jersey French".

Some chose to write about more than one woman. M1996, an Australian woman aged 53, offered a lively account of no less than four. Her sense of engagement with both the topic and the reader whom she imagined is conveyed in her choice of the word "talk" rather than "write" in her introduction: "I'd like to talk about several women, although I have only limited knowledge of them as regards the subject heading". Of the four women she wrote about, Miriam, her mother was still alive, and made her own contribution to the portrait of Elise, the writer's grandmother and Miriam's own mother.

The account is based partly on the writing of Miriam, written from England in response to the directive which M1996 had forwarded to her from Australia and partly on the author's commentary on Miriam's reply, drawing on her own childhood memory of Elise, as her granddaughter. The result is a multilayered picture of Elise.

Here, for instance, is Miriam on her mother's childhood, followed by the granddaughter's memory of the same woman, her grandmother:

> Miriam considers the household Elise grew up in as middle class; that is, perhaps until she emigrated and circumstances changed. However, there was always a certain gentility apparent when I used to visit my grandmother . . .
>
> When I asked her what she knew of Elise's education, if anything, Miriam told me what I've already mentioned plus the fact that Elise could sing (something I didn't know about Nana). Miriam also remembers many letters being written in beautiful handwriting by both Elise and Ollie (her husband, my grandfather).

Miriam's response for her own life is another compression:

> Miriam wrote, "I can't answer question 3 except that I can't remember being read to. I think you know about me. I started public school . . . at 6 years of age, left 14 years. Only reading done at school".

To which her daughter (writing now, of course, as a woman in her fifties) comments sadly: "My poor, dear mother. I'm pretty sure those years are just too painful to remember." Two paragraphs later, she adds: "I find it very painful to write this, it dredges up memories of the little I know of Miriam's early life."

By way of closure, however, she writes proudly of the mother she knows now:

> For all this, Miriam left school being able to read and write. And I just want to add, even though it's out of the time span you're interested in, that Miriam

and I write to each other every week and she sure writes the most wonderful, descriptive letters.

Memory of other relative: interviewed for/spoken to about this

Some correspondents took the opportunity of this directive to do some new "family history research" of their own. T2543, a 62-year-old retired library assistant, with no direct access to her own immediate antecedents, chose to turn to others as a means of researching the portrait requested:

> Having no parents or grandparents to consult on this topic, I have relied on my 71-year-old cousin as my source of information. She has provided details about her mother, my aunt, who I never knew very well, although she and her family lived locally. The woman I am describing was born in 1901 and died in 1983, and I am writing as her niece.

Another correspondent sought a picture of the woman she was writing about from her sister-in-law who, in turn, "groped in her memory". A 70-year-old retired librarian, she was writing about her husband's grandmother, born in "approx. 1874":

> I don't suppose Mary Ann had any *time* to read, let alone an opportunity to learn. I can't answer any of your questions about her. "What was she *like*?" I asked Chris, "you all talk only about your father". Chris groped in her memory. "She was kind", she said, "she never hit us or shouted at us. The only time she got cross was after going to the pub with Dad. If he'd been giving other women the eye, she'd be jealous, and not speak to him". Her grandson has inherited her gentle, silent sulks. (G1041)

She adds her own comment about myth and families:

> A woman like that, hardly remembered, can have more effect on the family myth than their formidably literary and political father. He told the truth, she embroidered it, and it's the embroidery that remains.

W633, a 53-year-old woman living in North East England wrote about her grandma, born in 1889 and brought up in Lincolnshire. She combines her own memories as a small child of this woman with recollections gained from "all her children". First, she mentions a confusion she has between her early memories of these tales with her later reading about other lives of the period:

> Although, when I was small, I often asked her to tell me about "when you were a little girl", her stories centred on the farm rather than on school. I

always tend to muddle Grandma's stories with Flora Thompson's *Lark Rise to Candleford*, but this is probably because they have so much in common. (W633)

Later, she says more about those "stories":

When I was small, I loved Grandma to tell me about when she was a little girl, and these stories carried on even when she visited me after I was married. My husband now bitterly regrets he didn't sneak in a tape recorder.

That is how I know about getting the boots mended and the two Sunday schools. She was an excellent, low key, raconteur and able to build up a wonderful picture.

This was a woman who is portrayed as central to the family "grapevine of letters and phone calls" (fulfilling a role to which we will return in the next chapter):

All her grandchildren gravitated to her house and those of us within reach went there every Sunday morning with our fathers (the three sons). Although the family is well-scattered now – Bournemouth, Redditch, Kettering, Sheffield, Huntingdon, Cambridge, Peterborough, and Darlington, plus great-grandchildren away at university in Oxford and Birmingham – the grapevine of letters and phone calls is very efficient and I think this is because Grandma inculcated the habit of keeping in touch.

From her relatives (Grandma's five children), the writer added to this picture of a "raconteur" that of a woman who also took care to listen and to explain:

All her children remember her talking to them a great deal and explaining things, with a general knowledge that was surprisingly wide. When I said I was going to write this piece, Aunt L told me that grandma had been able to answer their questions and always took time to give information and explain. (W633)

For several correspondents, as for M1996 above, the experience of writing for this directive provoked a wistfulness or regret. B2258, for instance, a retired woman teacher aged 58, after writing about her grandmother and mother, registers this in parenthesis: "(How I wish I had asked more questions of her and of my mother – but there we are!)".

Family histories and personal memories are potentially complex and painful. Many correspondents may simply have dealt with this by voting with their pens – i.e. choosing not to write to this directive at all. One or two note the decision they made to write despite the anticipation of the subject being difficult. This correspondent, a man aged 31 living in Coventry, explained why this was true for him:

You wouldn't believe the trouble this part of the directive has caused me. I hope you realize the agonies you put "mass observers" to sometimes! I asked my Mum about my grandmother (her mother). I knew it might be a touchy subject. She was born in November 1900, the eldest of four children, in Leiston, Suffolk, and died in about 1976. She went to school at about five and left at 14, when she went to work. During this time she learnt arithmetic (tables by rote), basic addition, subtraction and long and short division (I don't know where my Mum's got this information from). She also learnt spelling, composition and comprehension . . . She apparently had a very loving home, where reading was a "great" pastime. The family were "working class".

I'm afraid that's about all I got out of my Mum. The subject's a bit touchy, as I said earlier, for the following reasons. My Gran had not one but two illegitimate children. The first, my Aunt, was born in 1922, the second, my Mum, was born in 1927. (C2600)

The secret of illegitimacy depends on written records being hidden, lost, or retrieved. As we shall see later in this chapter, the social pressures that weighed heavy on mothers with children born or conceived out of wedlock may seem laughable to their offspring in later life – but were felt so deeply that the evidence (in birth certificates) had to be kept out of sight and memory for years. For those children, like this writer's mother, who had been put out to fostering, her own mother's shame meant a sense of lifetime loss. Now a grown woman in her sixties, the subject of her own mother was still "a bit touchy" – because she had never been able to know her:

I guess it's very difficult for my Mum, when I ask her to tell me about her Mum during this time, because really, she didn't know her. It must be a terrible conclusion to come to. (C2600)

For other correspondents, this roused other regrets:

My mother used to write to me regularly and her letters were very good ones; but in general she was very dilatory about letter-writing and put it off day after day. She was a very loving mother, but we never got to know one another and I am now consumed with guilt since at last I understand, too late, why the gap was so wide. She died on Christmas Day in 1969. (D996: a woman, aged 68)

Some evidently felt more pleasure from the activity, however. R446, aged 65, living in rural mid-Wales, wrote three typed pages about her two grandmothers (about whom she says she has "very vivid memories") both born in 1872 in the West Riding of Yorkshire and commented:

Writing this has been one of the most interesting exercises I've undertaken for MO. I've always been aware of my good fortune in having been brought up in a family which valued academic ability and wanted all children, whatever sex, to go as far as they could.

A wry reflection from R1227, a 51-year-old woman might express the sentiments of many others. At the end of a page about her grandmother (1870s–1956), she noted: "This has been quite a weird experience – I seem to have dredged up all kinds of half-remembered things which I haven't thought of for years".

Unwritten tales: five writers talk

Many of the texts had tantalized me, because of a sentence, or maybe two, which suddenly suggested a habit of years, or an attitude that appeared to have dominated the author to this day. It has sometimes seemed that I have been looking for the impossible: the point at which inner feelings, dreams or imaginings just occasionally surfaced or found expression in outer forms of behaviour in reading and writing. Inevitably, the older person's memories called up in answer to my question of a child's observations of these outer behaviours could only be suggestive. But inevitably, too, these observations invited further curiosity.

Originally, I had not foreseen that I would want to meet any of the M/O correspondents who had written so much. But after reading, re-reading, and beginning to detect patterns in these boxes of writing, I knew that I needed to follow up some of these compressed lives with their authors; and in the autumn of 1996, with the help of Archive staff, I picked out nine of these anonymous writers with whom I had been in company during the summer in the silence of the library's archive room, in order to request that I may meet and interview them. They were seven women and two men; chosen, in all cases, because they had written about someone they had known as their own mother, and because what they had written contained suggestive, almost throwaway images of this woman reading or writing. All of them, then, were in their seventies or eighties. Until they had written to Dorothy Sheridan to give their agreement to meet me, I knew them only as numbers.

With one exception, I met all these writers in their homes, as people with furniture, possessions and gestures: greeting me at their own front door, and offering me hospitality to something of their own present literacy lives. The interviews took place in sitting rooms and kitchens, sometimes with a table between us, always with cups of tea or coffee, plates of biscuits, or (in one case) a cooked lunch.

Each interview was preceded by an exchange of letters, sometimes phone calls, to set up the arrangements; and was followed, usually three weeks later, by a letter from me, thanking the person for the interview and enclosing a copy of an edited version of the interview transcript. Most of the correspondents wrote to me with comments on these. There were no further interviews, however. I felt I had found all that I could wish for, given the limits of my time and their capacity or willingness to share further thoughts. What follows is some discussion from five of the people with whom I spoke: Anne, Brenda, Noreen, Gwen and Eileen.

Anne

Her house is at the end of a street of houses built (I guessed) in the 1930s, with a front garden and a path to the door in Borehamwood, twenty minutes north of London by train, ten minutes walk from the station. She told me that she and her husband had moved there from South Wales six months before. The choice of home for her, she said (only half-jokingly) was determined by one key criterion: "the library must be within walking distance".

Now aged 70, Anne is a retired social worker, and describes herself as an "avid reader" all her life. (There will be more on the "avid reader" in Chapter 6). Besides her voluntary work for the Family Fund, which disburses grants for children with severe disabilities, she told me she was currently attending (and enjoying) a WEA class on biography, having had a keen debate the previous week on truth and fiction in autobiographical writing.

In her conversation about her mother, Doris, Anne lamented how little her mother had read in the last ten years of her life (Doris died in 1982). "Television took over", she said. "She'd stopped wanting to read. That disheartened me. I'm wondering if I'm going to be like that." Part of the reason for this, she surmised, had been the effect of the sleeping tablets her mother had been prescribed, which had made reading too much effort. This contrasted with her written picture of Doris as a younger woman, whom Anne had recalled like this: "She loved to read and my early memories of her show her with her feet up, lounging in an armchair, reading a novel".

That morning Anne and I talked at some length about this kind of reading; first, however, she welcomed me into her house, made coffee, introduced me to her husband, who was about to go out, and began talking, not about her mother, but about her sister:

> I am interested as to why my sister, who never reads a book, why one daughter picks up reading, and the other one doesn't. What happens? Have you done this? It's weird.
>
> I was thinking this morning about her. You know, I was going to ring her up, actually, and ask her why.

A week after the interview, I received a letter from Anne in which she said (among other things):

> I have just had an interesting phone conversation with my sister . . . We talked of why she didn't read for pleasure and we have realized that because

she was a nail-biter (still is!) and when she reads her fingers always go into her mouth, our mother used to slap her hands away from her mouth. No wonder my sister doesn't read – talk about aversion therapy!

The typed transcript of our taped dialogue, as transcripts always do, failed to convey either the thoughtful pauses or the rush of speech which characterized Anne's conversation with me that morning. Listening back to the tape as I re-read the transcript, I noticed a pause and slowing down, as Anne went on to talk about her mother's early life, before she asked a question which clearly had been on her mind for some time. In this extract, I can only mark this change of tone in her talk with italics:

She used to say to me, "Oh, I was born in Kensington". I used to think that sounded very posh, but I went and looked at the road a few years ago, after she'd died. I think my Mum had had a very hard life because she was the, you might call the runt of the family. *The way I look at it now, she didn't have the advantages that the others had. I mean, her sister, her older sister, went into an office; why was my Mum put into domestic service?*

By contrast, there was a rush of amusement and laughter as she struggled to find in her mind a picture to offer me of her mother writing. Her answer to my question came out in a tumble of words and occasional surges of laughter. A different typeface is needed to capture this different mood:

If you drew some broad brush strokes of your mother's life, and her life as a reader and a writer, what would you say about it?

I would say it took up a very small portion; although it was an important portion, so it could be quite central, really. But it could only be a small centre. She was just too busy doing other things. Too many demands on her.

Have you a picture of her – at a table like this – ever? writing, maybe?

(laughing) *Well, nothing important or interesting. I suppose I can see her at our kitchen table, licking her pencil, and writing, yes. But I don't think it would be anything terribly interesting. I think she must have been writing shopping lists or something; because we* would all be sent on errands, as they used to say in those days, and she would write it down. "Half a pound of marge; a pound of sugar."

Both the reflective question about her mother's work in domestic service and the sudden image with the pencil bubbled up in the conversation. Neither had featured in Anne's original written piece that she had sent in to Mass Observation.

When I returned, later, to re-read what Anne had written about her mother's girlhood, I read this:

The family lived in North London, the borough of Kensington, but in the northern part – not the well-to-do end. D's schooling was at the big 3-decker LCC school at the end of her road. She left school at age 14 and went into service. However, her older sister went into office work, her oldest brother was a musician in the Royal Artillery Band, her younger brother apprenticed to a plumber, and her younger sister went on the stage as a "soubrette". My mother, I feel, got the short straw in this family!

Writing anonymously as an informant for the Archive, there is simply an exclamation mark to indicate what kind of emotion "I feel" might have signified. What she said to me, in the very personal and present surroundings of her own home, was in a "thinking aloud": with the phrases "I think", "I used to think", and "the way I look at it now" all punctuating a flow of more feeling than the single line she had offered in writing, summarizing her mother's upbringing, long before she herself had been alive to witness it.

The image of the woman at the table, licking the pencil as she wrote the list at the table, is however one that she had dredged up from direct recall. Both in the interview and her text, she had also sketched in two other images: one, of her mother writing notes to the school, the other of her mother "putting her feet up" in the afternoons, to read novels. For Anne these were clearly strong pictures, seen through the lenses of her own girlhood and adolescence in the 1930s and 1940s.

Brenda

Dear Jane Mace,
Thank you for your letter. It is ideal (if you don't mind the early train) for you to get to Whitland at 14.12 on the 28th. I will meet you, and it's a country station so you can't miss a little old lady waiting for you! Lunch, talk and the 18.10 to Swansea. Sounds fine to me.
Yours sincerely,
Brenda

Not lunch, in the end: but a gorgeous home-made chocolate cake and tea, the wind outside the window gusting across the fields. Later, before driving me back to the station, Brenda drove me in the opposite direction through a gate and over a hill so that I could see the drop down to the sea just minutes from her bungalow.

Two days later, back in London, I received another letter from her:

Dear Jane,
Lovely day. Thanks. I had a restless night (I wonder why??) and overslept, so I've missed the WEA thing today . . .
At 4am I remembered the only book(s) in the household when I was little. "Golden Treasury" for children – 12 volumes in green leather, gold lettered.

Again and again I would look at the chapter on slavery and be horrified. It was this classic preoccupation with "noises off" as a child which became a sort of emotional paralysis. The same for *so many* children . . .
Affectionately,
Brenda

Across the table, by the window, with the neck mike clipped to her jumper, Brenda seemed to be holding her breath and editing her answers carefully when we began. I checked, first, the name of her mother. Annie, she said. Born in about 1886.

Did you ever call her Annie?

(emphatically) Never. *(pause)* And interestingly – I've just remembered – she wanted us all to call her "Mother Dear". The other girls did. "Mother Dear". You see it was a sort of idealized, mother thing. She was a self-deceiver, par excellence. But she had to be, you see, because she married my father, who was better class. (It's the only way to put it, really, because the classes are so complicated.) She was probably lower middle or working class. And she spent all my life trying to pretend she had – voice, you know . . . Because my father was a terrible snob. She was pregnant when she got married. That was quite something in 1910, so she had to move herself up as best she could. I always knew it was, and that sort of coloured the whole relationship.

This, then, is Brenda, the sixth of Annie and Harold's seven children, brought up in the Wirral and still, in her seventies, grieving with a mix of rage and sorrow at her own unhappy childhood and the mother who, when she first wrote about her in her bold and wonderfully legible handwriting, she portrayed as "an ill-informed and shallow woman". As in the writing, so in the talk: within three sentences, she had captured the woman who had been her mother as a "self-deceiver". There was a mocking intonation in the way she repeated the phrase "Mother Dear"; but there was also (as there had not been in the original writing) a context suggested for her mother's pretensions: the hypocrisies necessary in a deeply-layered class society, in which her mother, as a sales assistant in a drapery store, becomes pregnant by a man with prospects, a "broker" who Brenda sees now as a "complicated man [who] hated being trapped with this silly woman" and who was also a "womanizer" who would chase Brenda's teenage girlfriends and have an affair with the Irish maid. Brenda wrote to me later with other thoughts about Annie, a woman, she said, who had loved very small children and had been kind to her when, as a grown woman herself, she had her own babies; she had simply not enjoyed her own children as they grew older.

What, if anything, did literacy mean in Annie's life? In her text for the Archive, Brenda had said two things: first, that "although she was an ill-informed and shallow woman", she certainly wrote a legible and fairly well-educated letter; and secondly, that "I can't think of one single occasion when she had a book in her hand, but she could certainly read and write".

Annie, according to Brenda, was (unlike other women of her class) not short of time for reading and writing: so it was not lack of time, in the sense we discussed in the last chapter, that prevented her choosing to read or write. Having married "up", she had not one, but two maids; and always hid the fact that when she met her future husband she was serving behind the counter in a store. As Brenda reported it, Annie read little – and showed little interest in her husband reading to her from his newspaper: "He'd say, 'Listen to this, Annie dear'. And she'd go 'Hm'. Never heard a thing".

Despite her evident affection for small children (and for Brenda's, when they later came along) Annie, as far as Brenda was concerned, was no model either of motherhood, nor of literacy. The "emotional noise" of Brenda's childhood she ascribes to a family life in which there was cruelty: a cruelty of which she recalls being an observer more than a victim (watching her sister being caned for a bad school report, for instance) – "not that I didn't feel that I was involved", she wrote to me later.

There had been four children in four years and then a ten year gap before Brenda "came along", followed by another. Brenda knew that she saw her mother differently from her older sister. Like the two daughters of Eleanor, recalled earlier, Brenda and her sister experienced the same mother as two people. Equally, at different times in their lives the mother turned to each of them in different ways:

> When I say this to my sister Ruby (who's 86, you know), she will say, "But she was as soft as a kitten, Brenda". You see?

That's not your experience of her?

> No. But in much later life I was the one that she clung to, and talked to. "Nobody loves me" you know. Heartbreaking, really. But my heart doesn't break for her, because there wasn't enough there to break your heart about, really.

The portrait Brenda painted of her childhood was of a time when there was too much distress around her to be able to show any interest in sustained reading or writing, even though technically, she could do both:

> It's a killer. You sit at the top of the stairs and listen to that fighting going on down below, at night. That's what thousands and millions of children have to deal with. And they do a damn sight better than me. They're more disciplined; but hard luck. This is the way I've done it. With no help from my mother.

I asked Brenda how it was that she had come to be the habitual and enthusiastic reader and writer that she so evidently was. Her reply was to tell me of the person she remembered as a "mentor", who had been a friend in Nottingham where she and her husband lived when they were first married. This friend had lent her "things like *Catcher in the Rye*" and was "the spur" to her lively reading life since. Widowed now, with a full life and shelves full of books and photographs of children and grandchildren on the walls, she spoke enthusiastically of the pleasures of reading books and writing letters, now that there are no longer the "background noises" from her childhood which had haunted her for so long:

> So when people say to me, "How do you like being old?" I say, "I quite enjoy it". Because there's no background noises. If I want to read now, I can sit down there for four, five hours, reading. It's all come round the other way. When people say, "Oh, I read *Mill on the Floss* when I was 14", I think, well, I can read it now. It's lovely! So in a way, no regrets.

This gives another gloss on the American research we looked at in Chapter 2. The "optimal flow" of pleasure reading in her later life is not merely a solution to the possible loneliness of living alone. It is itself a pleasure only possible because, at last, there is a freedom from earlier turmoil.

Noreen

> Woman – born 1880. Died 1942 aged 62. I am her child.
> *Her childhood.* I don't know a lot about this. She grew up on a farm in Jersey. She was the eldest girl in a family of about six or seven in modest circumstances. She went to the little country school until she was about thirteen or fourteen, then stayed on the farm to help with the youngest children. I don't know if there was much reading or writing in the home – my grandparents died when I was very young so I did not visit the farm.

It's raining, and it's Monday morning. On the settee, in this small sitting room, six piles of newsletters are neatly laid out. The books in the shelves, Noreen tells me, are organized "on the Dewey system". To the left of the television set are autobiographies (H.G. Wells, Lady Sackville), to the right, philosophy, archaeology, history. "There are at least three books I have been told I should write", she tells me, wryly; one on her work with maladjusted children, another on her travels and climbing expeditions. The newsletters are for the local branch of the ramblers association. The next climbing expedition will be in Costa Rica. The room speaks of travel.

Listening back to the tape and re-reading the transcript of our conversation, three months after we met, I was puzzled at how little, in the end, Noreen was able to tell me about her mother as a reader. In the interview, I had tried several prompts, which, with others, had elicited glimpses and pictures of the mother, as with Brenda, or Anne. With Noreen, our conversation focused on her own life as a reader and writer – and, as a teacher with maladjusted children, her observation of other children's difficulties with literacy. It emerged, too, that she had interpreted the Mass Observation directive to mean a question about how either her mother or she had learned to read, as children. Her main view of her mother's life was that she simply did not have time to read; and she went on to tell me about the boarding house for summer visitors which her mother ran each year where they lived in Jersey to keep the family economy afloat. Her father was an unsuccessful antiques dealer (who was "fonder of keeping his goods than selling them"); it was her mother who had the head for business. So twenty minutes into the interview, I asked her:

How do you know your mother could read?

Noreen simply said:

Because books were coming in; she was getting them from the library.

To the question I then asked her:

What picture do you have when you think of your mother reading? in bed, maybe? or in a chair?

Noreen answered:

Definitely not in bed. Didn't ever see her in bed. *(After a long pause)*: In a rocking chair, in the evening. But even in the winter, she didn't have a lot of time.

Noreen's text for the Archive had simply referred to her mother as "Woman. Born 1880. Died 1942". In correspondence, later, she told me her name was Louisa; but her father and all her relatives called her Lulu. In the text she had written for the Archive, Noreen summarized Louisa's motherhood in a sentence: "Mother had five children, the eldest when she was 22, the youngest, me, when she was 41".

When Louisa died (in 1942, at the age of 62) Noreen herself would have been 21. This was a mother never known to her daughter in adulthood. Noreen had never seen her mother as an older woman, with the increased detachment possible for daughters no longer entangled with the mother of their childhood.

Reading and writing, for Noreen as for her mother, had been a seasonal thing: for winter evenings indoors. For her mother, the summer was non-stop work, catering for the summer visitors; for the child Noreen, it was a time for outdoor life. (For the adult Noreen, a long-standing and active member of a local rambling association, and a regular traveller and mountaineer, this love of outdoors had persisted.) So it felt natural that the one picture which she called up in the interview of herself and her mother engaged in literacy together is a picture of a winter evening.

The picture evokes a child's pleasure in reading with her mother. This is a scene in which they both read together; a scene which was subtly different in the telling (Noreen recalling it for me in her sitting room) than in the writing. In her Mass Observation text, she had written this: "Mother invested in a set of encyclopaedias, *Golden Knowledge*, I think. On winter evenings we would go through them together".

It was in our conversation in her home, in reply to the question "What do you remember of what was going on in the house in winter evenings?" that Noreen said more:

Ah, well, this was the time when we did – it was things like getting these encyclopaedias, *Golden Knowledge*. It would have been mother, paid out. We didn't have much money, but we got seven volumes of *Golden Knowledge*, I think it was called; and *I would read it with her and she would read it to me. I can remember being devoted to it.* (my emphasis)

The change from: "we would go through them together" to: "I would read it with her and she would read it to me" changes the moment from a formal activity to one of animated intimacy.

For Noreen, however, it was not her mother who was the most significant influence on her own life as a reader and writer. This influence came from her sisters, particularly Doreen, eighteen years older than she. When she was a child, Doreen was training in England to be a teacher, and it was Doreen who inspired her mother's and later Noreen's own ambitions for herself. The sense of pleasure in reading, books, and in writing that stayed with her all her life came, she felt, from other sources than her mother – from whom she recalled only "a general sense of encouragement". Nevertheless, it was Louisa, not her husband, who wrote letters to Doreen and the other sisters once they left home.

Gwen

It has been an accident of this research that four of the people I interviewed had worked with children in their professional lives; and Gwen, like Noreen, turned out to have been a headteacher in an infants school, retiring in 1981. Like Noreen, too, she had remained a single woman all her life and had no children of her own. Gwen's mother Lily will feature several times in later chapters. For this reason, an extract from her contribution to the Mass Observation directive (originally submitted in three pages of handwriting) is reprinted at the end of this chapter.

When I went to visit Gwen in her home in a suburb of Manchester, it was a cold Monday morning in February. When I arrived, she made us both coffee; later, she poured us each a glass of ginger wine. Her grandfather clock struck during the interview; the chimes interrupted and punctuated her voice. Gwen laughed often, with what seemed like a detached amusement at the pictures she made for me; of her own childhood as well as that of her mother.

Within minutes of settling down to talk, the tape recorder in place, and my warming up to a question about her reflections on the writing she had done for Mass Observation, she said:

> And, of course, we've got to take account of the lighting. There wasn't much lighting at night, was there? . . . We got it when I was eleven. That would be 1935 . . . I don't know whether my mother had gas when she was a child, or whether it was oil lamp. I know they had a little shop nearby that sold lamp oil.

What Gwen went on to tell me was this. Her mother's name was Lily. Born in 1890, she had grown up in a small village near Blackburn, the eldest of four children, learned to weave at the age of twelve and continued going half-time to school until two years later, when the family moved to a small town called Rishton. Prospects of work were more hopeful there than in the village, where the population was growing and employment prospects at the two weaving mills were diminishing. Gwen's father, born in 1889, had grown up in the same village; and his family had already moved to Rishton for the same reason. The two met in a chip shop; courted for three years; and married. Lily had become pregnant before the marriage; and this pre-marital pregnancy remained a family secret – to all but Gwen – until fifty years later. Its discovery by Gwen, as a child, was the subject of a story which she then told me: a drama of literacy at the heart of a family's domestic space.

Couples then and since kept their "marriage lines" in a box or a drawer. (I recall, in a reminiscence group some years ago, one woman showing a box in which she and her husband kept "all their papers" – it had been, she told us, a box her husband had been given when he had left the last Dr Barnardo's home he had lived in as an orphan child.) Gwen's father and mother kept their papers in a "deed box" which her father had made himself in an evening class in carpentry. It had been his "set piece" which he had made and french polished, with dove-tailed joints. The story, although told in a matter of minutes, compresses five scenes into one narrative, two in the period when Gwen was a child, and three when she must have been an adult woman in her forties.

In the first scene she depicts her father with the box open on the table and Gwen and her sister Millie watched him going through the papers. Scene two is of Gwen, a year later, getting the box down and looking again at the documents. Years later, three further scenes succeed each other in a few words. In scene three, at the fiftieth anniversary of their parents' marriage, Millie makes the connection between marriage date and the date of her eldest sister's birth and Lily "confesses" the pregnancy. Scene four shows her mother making the same confession to Gwen, and Gwen revealing, in turn, how she already knew about it; and in the final scene, Gwen reports the reaction of the daughter in question, Alice, her eldest sister, conceived all those years before, by parents not yet wed.

The whole, then, is a drama in which the mother is engaged in revealing to three different daughters the "shame" she had kept secret throughout their child-hood, which Gwen, the youngest of all, had known, and not known, for over thirty years; a secret which had Gwen, as a child, reading the evidence with curiosity but indifference (at the time), which has her adult sister Millie reacting with mild sympathy, but has Alice, the child originally conceived "out of wedlock" shocked into disbelief. The story, centred on a written document hidden in a box kept on a shelf, begins and ends with Lily's need to keep its contents hidden; a need, according to Gwen, out of all proportion to the likely reaction of anyone else, except Lily's own mother, who had indeed been "scandalized" by the pregnancy.

Here is how she told the whole story to me:

I think they courted for three years before they married; and then she became pregnant. Oh, dear dear dear. So they had to get married.

Bit of a scandal, was it?

Oh, only my mother. I don't think anybody cared at all about that. Soon after, the First World War started. She probably had Kate, the second one, while the war was on. But before my father was called up. Her younger sister told one of my sisters that my grandma was absolutely scandalized by this pregnancy. She said ever afterwards, grandma always watched the two other girls to see that they menstruated at the right time. Whether she could have done anything, I don't know. It would be a bit too late then! But mother kept this a deadly secret from us. To her dying day she had terrible guilt feelings about it.

But one day *(pause)*, I don't know, I might have been eleven, my father was looking through a deed box he had, that he'd made himself. He had been on a carpentry course, night school course or something at one time, and as his set piece he'd made this very nice wooden box with dovetail joints which was french polished. He kept all the family important papers in here – and I think it was an insurance policy he was looking for. My sister next to me, Millie, and I were watching him this evening as he was going through the papers, opening each one, while we were allowed to look over his shoulder and look at them. Then he picked one out; and I just noticed it was the marriage certificate, and he closed it up very quickly. I thought *(pause)* why?

Millie was two years and two months older than I. So I'd have to wait until she left school, till she was 14, and then I got up on the top shelf, when I was alone in the house when she was gone to work, and looked up this marriage certificate, and found out they were married six months before the birth of Alice. So I'd be twelve at that time, when I knew that. I never thought of breathing a word to *anyone at all.*

It didn't come out, but – what wedding anniversary would it be? Fiftieth wedding anniversary [1960] yes, when my parents would be 70-odd; and the next to top sister, Kate, said to my mother (pause), "It must be somewhere near your fiftieth wedding anniversary?" (you know, thinking when Alice was born). "When were you married?"

And mother just said, "March". And Kate, said, "March? That's a funny month to get married. Was Easter early that year?" So mother had to say, "Well, I was pregnant with Alice". And Kate said, "Well, you'll soon celebrate your 50th, you know".

So Mother thought, well, it was time for us to be told, you see. I was living here in Manchester then. I mean, I was far away from the hubbub. So they told Millie (the one next to me), and Millie said that Mother said, "Well, what do you think about me?" and Millie said, "Well, it makes you a bit more human!"

So then they told me when I went over. I said, "Oh well, I've known for years and years", and I told them about looking in the deed box. They were surprised that I'd known all this long time. I think Mother was very surprised that I hadn't thrown it back at her, you know, or anything like that.

Alice, the eldest, the cause of all this, she was living the other side of Blackburn, so we didn't see each other very often. I think Kate told her, or wrote to her or something. But Alice couldn't, Alice blanked out. She didn't –

– couldn't take it.

She couldn't take it. She didn't believe it.

Reflecting later on how she told this story to me, the scene which holds the most fascination for me is the second one: why had Gwen, at the age of twelve, decided she wanted to look again in the box on the shelf? Something in the way her father must have put the papers away must have fascinated her curiosity; so that, when she did get to re-open the box, in secret, there must have been a disappointment to her. She certainly noticed the dates of the wedding, and equally, from what she recalled, noted the date of her eldest sister's birth; but for the child she was at the time, there seemed to be nothing to excite anyone and she presumably put the whole thing away.

None of this story had been part of Gwen's contribution to the Mass Observation directive. Listening to her that morning, and thinking about it later, it felt another kind of donation that she had made. Lily and Gwen will reappear in later chapters.

Eileen

She had said (on the phone) that she would be wearing a red coat, and she was, there on the platform, turning the other way as I walked towards her. Her house was red, too, as promised by its address ("Red House"). She'd moved three years after her husband's death. Must have been six years ago, she said.

Her little dog has expectant ears and eyes. She worried away at various chewed old slippers in the kitchen, as Eileen turned the heat under the vegetables and I plugged in the mike to the tape recorder. One wall was covered in children's drawings. Her own mother Catherine had been born in 1896 (we calculated), died at age of 86 in 1982 (she trusted my calculations as to the birthdate those two dates implied, and laughed as she put the rock salmon on the plates and the saucepans and vegetables on the table). We talked over the lunch that she cooked.

For the Mass Observation directive, Eileen had written little about her own mother, but a couple of pages about her mother-in-law and about her grand-mothers, one, on her mother's side:

My younger brother and I stayed with Granny "Mul" when mother had an operation, and again when she got TB. I remember lapping up all the books she had, especially fairy tales. I found out years later that she had complained to my mother that I was reading too much fantasy, it wasn't good for me!

I was curious to know more, and during our conversation, elicited some basic data about Eileen's mother, and glimpsed two very striking portrayals of her reading and writing life.

Catherine had been brought up in Northumberland, daughter of a curate father and Irish protestant mother. The family was "bookish", and the children would write a magazine together, encouraged by their parents, a rather "literary" effort. "Her father encouraged the girls", Eileen said, "he really did: which other households wouldn't". Her eldest brother used to bully his brothers and sisters; one sister became a science mistress and went out as a missionary to China. When Catherine and her husband were first married they went out to India, where Eileen said "she wrote a lovely journal". Then she added: "She was always interested in writing. She did the odd poem, you know. But I'm afraid I was so scornful, you see".

The scorn of daughter for mother is not unusual. An exasperation was still in Eileen's voice as she went on:

Every time we'd come in she'd say, "What's blankety blank, something or other?" She was always doing crosswords – and I came to *hate* crosswords, I loathe them! She was so clever, you know, she'd try to race her brother to get The Times one done. You know, that sort of thing. It's beyond me.

Eileen associated her mother reading with her mother being ill or convalescent. Her mother got TB in 1938, and feared she would die, as her sister had done. She went "somewhere in the Cotswolds, high up" for a cure; Eileen's sister returned home to look after the rest of the family; and then the war began.

> So she had a lot of time to read: because they said, "You must have this rest". She really was pretty well cured; it was so irritating, I shouldn't be mad about her, but . . .

In all that Eileen and I talked about that day, one scene caught my imagination. It seemed like a tableau, a group portrait etched in the memory, the figures in it lit by an oil lamp in the middle. Eileen herself in this picture is a small child. The year, we worked out, must have been 1928. The place is their family home in Devon, where they had moved after her father had returned, wounded, from the First World War. It is evening.

> We were sitting round the table, an oil lamp in the middle, and they'd all be reading – my older sister, my brother was a baby, and me pretending to read with a book upside down. It was so annoying. I thought I was doing so well, you know, copying the parents. But my sister Helen said, "Oh, she doesn't really understand, she's got it upside down!"

The memory was, like many strong memories of childhood experience, one of humiliation. The questions it raised for me were several. What were they all reading? (Eileen was uncertain: but thought, probably her mother was reading biography and her father, a textbook on agriculture or something about birds.) How often did this family reading scene, "sitting round the table", take place? (She wasn't sure: but felt it was something other families of her acquaintance also did.) Despite my returning to it twice in our meeting, Eileen could add no more to this scene. It was a memory that had stayed with her for over seventy years, fixed and flickering in the light of the oil lamp.

Reflections

The topic I was asking Mass Observation writers to consider was inevitably a tricky one. As I suggested in the first chapter, the literacy behaviours we may observe in others can give us only the most superficial idea of what it is that anyone is *making* of what they are reading or writing. (The additional idea I offered – that among mothers whose lives spanned the period 1890s–1930s and beyond may be some who had limited literacy – provoked strong reaction from some writers. A few, as I indicate in Chapter 5, expressed outrage.) The directive I had written invited a combination of autobiography and biography, of memory and research and the results were both rewarding and disappointing. Within the genre of a "report" donated anonymously to a public record, the nearly three hundred writers had written a great deal, while mainly confining themselves to factual data. In this chapter we have seen how many used the opportunity to explore the idea of a "literacy life" by drawing on multiple sources.

The Mass Observers whom I interviewed were among those who had written about a mother, rather than grandmother; they were writing both introspectively and retrospectively.

Our conversations added depth to the autobiographical memory they had offered in writing, and in doing so, reminded me that for any of us, to disentangle a figure we knew as our mother from our own childhood is no simple matter. What mothers choose to tell of their lives children may not always choose to hear; and what it is that children retain of the mother they knew may have little to do with the person she thought she had been. The child's interest in listening may simply not coincide with the mother's interest in telling. The "process time" of the two lives make such a coincidence of timing a rare treat indeed. A witty and poignant account of a mother's selective storytelling is to be found in an essay by the Canadian novelist Margaret Atwood under the delicious title "Significant moments in the life of my mother". Her mother had an enviable capacity to dramatize and make vivid for her stories of her girlhood and youth – such that there was a time in her own life when the version she had of her mother's was one of "sustained hilarity and hair-raising adventure" (Atwood 1992: 9). At the same time, some stories were only to be told in particular company: "My mother cannot be duped into telling stories when she doesn't want to. If you prompt her, she becomes self-conscious and clams up" (p. 10).

To tell a story is to draw on our memories for incident: our *autobiographical episode memories*. To then create a person out of these memories is to draw on a more general kind of memory: our *autobiographical knowledge* (Robinson 1992). This distinction between episode and general knowledge I find useful in considering what the M/O writers were being asked to do. In order to make their own story – the story of the mother (or grandmother) – they had to integrate the episodic stories told to them into the knowledge they recalled of the storyteller. Eileen had the general *knowledge* of her mother's convalescent condition to allow her to decide she had "a lot of time to read"; to this she added her own *episodic memory* of the irritating crosswords. Noreen knew her mother had no time to read (at least in the summer season) because of the work of the boarding house; within this overall context she recalled the episode of sitting together and reading pages of the *Golden Knowledge* encyclopaedia.

The other kind of memory, less easy to classify, is that which three of the interviewees revealed: Noreen, Gwen and Anne. It is the *sudden image*, surfacing without warning, and inspired by association. My own feeling is that this kind of memory is special to conversation rather than writing. It is in any case true that all these images came out in interview and had not been offered in the written text. Noreen's was the image of her mother Laura, in a rocking chair on a winter evening. Anne's was of Doreen, sitting at the kitchen table licking the pencil while thinking what to write for a shopping list. And Gwen's was the image of two daughters leaning over the father at the kitchen table, scanning the marriage certificate.

Much of the information I found in the responses to this M/O directive fell into the category of "autobiographical knowledge", providing detail of home and street, schooling and family. Other directives on other topics are very likely to contain information of relevance to the question I was pursuing – for what seems unimportant and obvious to a writer may be of the utmost significance to the researching reader. As Alistair Thomson has showed, one "dataset" or set of responses to a single directive can be mined for a whole range of different research questions (Thomson 1995). It is in any case the mix of written and oral sources that has always, for me, represented the richest kind of literacy experience; without the texts and letters which followed them, the interviews would have had a different significance; and without the interviews, a special kind of vivacity would have been missing. In the next chapter, we will find other themes that were revealed in the writings from the correspondents before returning, in Chapter 5, to other oral sources.

Extract from E174: "Gwen" about her mother "Lily"

My mother had four daughters and I was the youngest. My father was abroad for three and a half years without leave during the war of 1914–1918 and during that time she would write him letters and I know she sent him parcels of food and photographs of the two eldest girls who had been born before he went abroad.

She also wrote to order dressmaking patterns and had a "set" letter which ended "and obliged" . . . She would buy a postal order at the post office (usually for nine old pennies) and so would need to know how to make out the postal order or to address the envelope.

If we were absent from school she would need to send a "sick note" with a well child or the note could be taken when the child recovered; and she could never remember how to spell "bilious" and would resort to the Fennings Fever bottle where the word was to be found.

When I was ten an uncle bought me a big thick dictionary which the publisher "John Bull" was selling. My mother was very cross about this purchase as she intended that I should leave school at fourteen, so should not be encouraged to get any "big ideas" so the dictionary was soon banished to the cupboard in my parents' bedroom along with all our story books.

We all went to the local library except mother but she told us to bring her books from there by Ethel N. Dell or Ruby M. Ayres. All other library books she would quickly glance through and then said she'd read them and they were rubbish.

She had a weekly order for *Woman's Weekly* so she must have read some of that. There were complete short stories and serial stories, all of a romantic nature and very middle class, while we were very working class. There was a cookery page and an agony aunt's page and an article by "The Man Who Sees". And Adverts.

The only song I recall her singing was to sing me to sleep "Peggy O'Neill". She did say a few nursery rhymes but as she worked a 48-hour week at the weaving mill from my being 3 years old, she didn't have much time or energy to spare.

Reading and writing for us, her children, was taken for granted. She would carefully take off the plain paper which the butter had been wrapped in over the greaseproof paper and give it to me to cut up to write or draw on. Paper and pencils were always in short supply at home.

Chapter 4
Domestic reading and writing

Reading and writing are temporal activities; they also enable us to shift time about. We read or write at particular moments; but in doing so, we transcend the moment. I have said that one of literacy's attractions is the possibility it offers of "transport" out of the present time. This also implies an imaginative move out of the present place. What reading and writing both offer, as well as a journey out of "now", is a means of migration out of the immediate "here". For many of the mothers in this research *here* meant home: the only place where their excursions into reading and writing could happen. Home, the place from which they had no other escape, was – and still is, for many women – anything but a place of leisure. Home was their place of work. Literacy, as I want to suggest in this chapter, allowed not only the flight from present time, but a means to give distance to the immediate place.

Unlike other cultural pastimes, reading and writing demand little space. Somewhere to sit, the corner of a table, maybe: these are minimal claims compared with dancing, painting, or football. For women in their own homes, though, such space has been hard to find. The kitchen table is already covered in dishes to be washed or clothes to be ironed; the very act of sitting down in a chair with a letter or a magazine requires a chair to be empty – let alone a room free of other people's demands on her. So those mothers in the past who lived in crowded homes, had little space, as well as "no time" for literacy.

For women caring for others at home, moments for their own reading and writing have always had to be "fitted in", squeezed between spaces as well as times demanded by those others. The homes in which they raised their children left little room for what some saw to be "flights of fancy" – let alone the "flight" offered by literacy, caught up in the endless round of domestic tasks. Even so, in the midst of gathering up dirty clothes, or ironing clean ones, tying one child's shoelaces or washing another's hair, mothers have always remained people with their own mental worlds. The brief moments of reading and writing offer us just one manifestation of these; between stirring a pot of soup or peeling vegetables, putting food on the table or clearing it, the list is written, the pages of a magazine turned. Physically caught in one place, these moments help us recognize that women in the home, just sometimes, are imaginatively somewhere else entirely.

There are three kinds of literacy activities frequently engaged in by mothers during the first decades of this century, according to the Mass Observation correspondents: writing letters, reading library books, and browsing through magazines or newspapers. As Gwen reported, Lily was someone who, at some time or another, did all three. In this chapter, I first link examples from these reports with some account of the communication systems of which they were part and then begin to suggest the connections they make with the present-day literacy environment.

We begin, then, with the letter-writing mother; the person who wrote to husband or children, who wrote notes to school or letters to mail order companies, and who also took part in the huge growth of card-writing and reading – cards from holidays, greetings cards sent for Christmas, birthday, Valentine's day – which at the beginning of this century had grown into a huge national pastime.

We move on to the mother's use of library books: often (but not only) romantic fiction; often chosen for her by her children, brought home to the domestic sphere from the public one; books from circulating libraries and public libraries brought, temporarily, into it. During the last decades of the nineteenth century and the first two of the twentieth, the idea of a national public library system had become a reality; library use had multiplied; people with little money had, for the first time, reading "for free" – and women at home could read books without having to pay for them.

We will then look at the use of women's magazines: not only for the fiction of romance and escape that dominated their pages but also for the other features for which Lily and other readers bought them; features in which mothers were not only readers, but writers too. This was the period which saw the birth of the letters or "problem" page: a literate solution to the physical distances opened up by the dispersal of families between mothers (real or ideal) and their adult daughters. The woman's magazine industry, originating with weeklies for the upper- and middle-class woman, did not take long to seize market opportunities among the working-class in the early decades of this century.

In the last section of the chapter we will consider how these three domestic uses of literacy in the past, interconnecting as they always did with many other uses of language, might connect with those of today's mothers. We will see how women's aspirations and longings for greater mental space are finding outlet within the curricula of adult education, and how this literacy activity has given renewed value both to sociable forms of reading and writing and to the oral traditions of storytelling.

Letters and other things

As her daughter remembered it, Lily wrote letters with three purposes: to confide, to order goods, and to explain. First, as a young wife, she wrote regular letters to her husband, posted abroad for over three years in the First World War. Secondly, she would write a "set letter" to order the dressmaking patterns she needed; and thirdly, when one of her daughters had been ill, she sat down (with some effort) to write a "sick note" for the child to take with them to school when they returned.

The letter-writing mother is evoked by many other correspondents to the Mass Observation Archive. This, written by a correspondent now in his late seventies, is a particularly eloquent example:

> My mother was born on 23 February 1889 and died in 1992 . . . She had two children – me and a brother nine years younger. Miscarriages restricted her family.
>
> She did not apparently read much; she was always too busy, I suspect. Her lifetime love was singing, and she attended a choir until near the end . . .
>
> She wrote copiously – letters. Her eldest sister married and went to New Zealand early this century, and my mother wrote regularly, long and detailed letters, until her sister's death. She knew everything that went on in our distant relations and she related everything that happened to us here. Her incessant letter-writing was a linking between her immediate family and distant relations and friends. When she died and the letters stopped it was as if a retaining cord had snapped and all the interchange of knowledge and gossip stopped. (R2065)

Another grandmother (born in 1878) is also reported as maintaining contact with far-flung relatives; she "had cousins living in Canada and sent regular correspondence all her life". (P1978) Brought up in Bury, Lancashire, she met her future husband while still at school, where (according to her grandson) "he used to sharpen her pencils for her". After their marriage in 1902, they had four children. Both "were keen on education", keeping a large open shelved bookcase full of books. The writer lived with this grandmother between the ages of six and sixteen (when she would have been in her sixties) and recalls that from this bookcase, she "reluctantly allowed" him to take out "one book at a time . . . *after* I had washed my hands to her satisfaction". This is a portrait of a stern but affectionate woman, who gave her grandson "a very gloomy picture of Victorian life, long working days, poverty, frequent deaths, illness, whippings, limited food".

Postcards were commonly used, by this woman as by many others, for quite brief messages; her grandson writes:

> I have lots of postcards sent between members of the family, most quite local. Postcards were used by my grandparents almost as the telephone now, and most appear to have been sent *and* received on the same day.

At this stage it seems worth putting a context on this. Writing, at that time, was not only a means to keep contact with those who had moved far away; for many people in the early decades of the century, it was a means to communicate with very near friends and relatives. In the late twentieth century, an affordable postal and telephone system is taken for granted as part of the necessities of everyday life. A century ago, there were no phones; and the invention of the penny post but a few decades earlier had introduced a change which calls on all our powers of imagination to comprehend. Today it is commonplace for daily messages to go through the letter box of rich and poor alike. These may range from bills, sales material, free newspapers, and personal or formal letters through to postcards sent from the other side of the world. While messages via fax machines or electronic mail are the experience of the minority (albeit a growing one), the majority have grown up in an era in which it is taken for granted that the receiving of a letter costs nothing and the sending of it is cheap. It is hard, then, to imagine the period before Rowland Hill's invention of the penny post in 1840, when payment for a letter was made by its receiver, and the cost was judged on the distance which the message had travelled.

The change this reform introduced makes present-day changes in new technology pale into insignificance. Between 1840 and 1915, as David Vincent reports, "the volume of correspondence increased nearly fifty-fold, from an estimated 76 million items in 1839 to 3500 million in 1914" (Vincent 1993: 33). The idea of the Penny Post was by no means welcomed by all: for it was an idea which meant for the first time that the mass of the population could engage in the "epistolary intercourse" hitherto enjoyed only by the few who could afford it: and this could, some argued, assist in the promotion of dangerously seditious ideas among the labouring poor. The argument which helped to push through the reform was one that said: making a postal system affordable to the poor would ensure a proper sense of family life, at a time when family members were having to travel away from home for work or military service (Vincent 1993). The "family literacy" argument this represented meant literacy being promoted as a means to maintain dutiful communication between children and their parents, husbands and their wives.

As things developed over the next fifty years, more frivolous uses of literacy emerged – including an industry of greetings cards (Christmas, birthday, and Valentine). The picture postcard, as Vincent shows us, enabled all classes of society to celebrate the growing opportunities to travel away from home allowed by a developing railway system. The postcard from the holiday resort was but one symbol of a change in the way in which place and distance was understood. By 1901 some 350 million of these cards were being written and received in England and Wales: a literacy phenomenon made possible by the combination of postal, transport and photographic changes in the previous half century. The result was that for the first time, for the mass of the population:

> Communication was for pleasure. It was both a consequence and a celebration of a marginal increase in prosperity. Literally and symbolically the railway and the post came together at the seaside. The working-class family

left home on the excursion train, and returned through the picture postcard.
(Vincent 1993: 49)

How far postcards during this period had become as widespread an activity
among the working class as this suggests is hard to know. Many Mass Observation
writers certainly reported mothers and grandmothers as writing them. P1009,
for instance, recalled a grandmother who wrote postcards "from wherever
she was':

> If my grandmother needed to write a letter, I think my mother used to write
> it for her. But she did write postcards a lot. When she got older, she travelled
> around the country by bus, visiting relatives. And she always sent postcards
> from wherever she was.

What does seem clear is that short notes and postcards had become easier to
transmit: the medium, if not the message, was for the first time more widely
available than it had ever been. Postcards, before the telephone, were an easy way
to make arrangements. A number of M/O correspondents recalled receiving a
card the same day it was posted. In an autobiography of her life in Luton, Edith
Hall recalled:

> Just prior to the Great War of 1914 when I was about six years old, postcards
> with the then half-penny postage were sent between my relations each day.
> My grandmother would send us a card *each evening* which we received by first
> delivery the next morning. She would then receive our reply card *the same
> evening*. If one lived in the same town as one's correspondent, an early
> morning posted card would be delivered at twelve midday the same day and
> a reply card, if sent immediately, would be received the same afternoon.
> (Hall 1977: 5)

The very energetic activity of postcard collection for this period has mostly
tended to concentrate on collecting the images on one side, rather than the
messages on the other. Collectors collect for the pictures and vie with each
other for the best collection of a particular cartoon artist, topic, or period. "Few
people today collect cards specifically for the interest of the messages", writes
one enthusiast, in a rare publication picking out the more curious and amusing
of those on cards in the "boom period" (1890–1914) (Brooks et al. 1982: 6).
Indeed, the picture postcard was only partly used for conveying messages;
at least half its attraction was to satisfy what became a nationwide collecting
craze, with the result that "the sole purpose of sending a card through the post
was often to provide another card for someone's collection" (Brooks et al.
1982: 12).

Nevertheless, they seemed to have provided a useful medium for making
arrangements:

Box 4.1 Sample postcard

London, W.C.
8 June 1905

Dear Jessie
Mama would have been up to see you only it has been so wet, but perhaps she
will come on Friday if fine. Will you write and let me know if you are going
anywhere on Monday because if not I should like to come up, but must leave
early in the evening. Your affect. niece Corrie
(author's collection)

Box 4.2 Sample postcard

Stockport
6 April 1909

Dear Ethel,
Will come round to your house, between 10 past and quarter past 8 tonight.
Trusting you are in the pink of condition.
From Willie
p.s. Tell Esther I will put on my hat tonight, so I hope she has got the
binding etc.
(Brooks, Fletcher & Lund 1982: 48)

To conclude this section on the "writing mother", two other points need to be
made. First, families and communities shared out writing tasks; and secondly,
writing letters and postcards were only one means of maintaining continuity and
contact in a family. Mothers (and, less often, fathers) are several times recalled as
scribes and readers of letters. W2338, a retired teacher, recalls her maternal
grandmother (born in 1860) as a "strong, domineering woman". The mother of
nine children, she lived in Manchester after her second marriage and was evidently active in the suffrage movement ("women's suffrage was her main hobby
horse and with it rights of women – property, etc."). This was someone who was
much in demand as a scribe:

> I think she took her own literacy for granted but did a good deal of letter-
> writing and reading of documents for friends and neighbours who didn't
> have her skills. There was a constant stream of people wanting to have letters
> read, explained or written and they all turned to her.

As Ursula Howard suggests, many of the children who were to become mothers
in the early years of this century would have grown up in a period when "both

writing and receiving letters was a social as much as a solitary activity". Some did not wait till adulthood to be the writers and readers of letters for others: "After the 1890s it was common for a Board School educated child to be the scribe for older family members who did not have literacy skills" (Howard 1991: 101).

The mother of M1571 (whom we shall call Nina) would have been a teenage girl when she took on such a role for others in her community, too. The youngest of nine children living in a small East Sussex village, Nina's father had been a gardener who had "worked up from kitchen garden boy . . . to head gardener". Nina had attended school until she was fourteen; her first job was in the village store and post office (a place which, in Ursula Howard's words, was often "an informal advice and social center oiling the wheels of working people's lives") (Howard 1991: 102). There Nina found herself called upon not only to deliver, but also to read letters to their recipients: and in so doing, being the bearer of often dire news:

> She lived in, to be available for sorting letters early in the morning, and did deliveries up onto Ashdown Forest in all weathers. Her ability to read meant that she would read the "letters to mother" sent back from the sons fighting in France, and it often fell to her lot to deliver the dreaded "official telegrams". This experience, I am sure, helped to make my mother the kind, understanding woman she was.

Letters and postcards to children away at war or relatives who had emigrated were certainly an important way in which women sustained what R2065, quoted earlier, called the "knowledge and gossip" to the family connectedness. Writing these was not the only way this connected feeling could be created. The mother (or grandmother) as the family historian, the one who tells the stories and passes down the history to her children, was a figure who appeared several times in the writing of Mass Observation writers. This grandmother, who plainly took pleasure in both reading and writing, also engaged her granddaughter in storytelling through other media, too:

> She was easy to talk to . . . I was very shy and could not talk to other adults. My grandmother gave me things to do like playing in her huge button box and telling me the history of different buttons. She was the family archivist; she kept masses of photographs of her relations and wrote on them who they were. I have inherited these, and her notes are invaluable. She used to talk about these people to me. (D826)

Library books

Lily, it will be remembered, started work in 1902 at the age of 12 in a weaving mill in Lancashire. At the age of 23 she married and her first child was born the same year. She went on to have three more daughters. It was these daughters who took turns to bring her home books from the library:

> We all went to the local library except mother: but she told us to bring her books from there by Ethel M. Dell or Ruby M. Ayres. All other library books she would quickly glance through and then said she'd read them and they were rubbish. (E174)

For us living in the late 1990s and beyond, reading material may often be "free" in a negative sense: it is unwanted and gratuitous – it is junk. Like it or not, the texts of advertising copywriters confront us on the doormat, in the street, on the bus, in shops, in every public space. Free papers are pushed through the letter box. Free magazines are thrust in our hands outside shops or stations. And libraries themselves are full of leaflet racks, poster displays and tables laid out with college prospectuses, guide books, programmes for upcoming local attractions. Anyone who is a confident reader of English is daily invited to a positive blizzard of free reading; and for those of us born in the 1940s or later the idea of a free public library service is barely commented on. Without any payment, we expect to be able to walk into a building and have at our disposal several hundred books. We can sit down there and then and begin reading; or we can borrow a few of them and take them home.

Thomas Kelly, the historian of libraries, suggests that the word "free" had "unfortunate connotations". There was, as he put it, an "odour of charity" (Kelly 1977: 101) about the first municipal libraries, seen as primarily for the working class – and, like the penny post, introduced originally against considerable opposition. The Public Libraries Act of 1850 (for England and Wales: that for Scotland was passed in 1853) provided the funding of books for the labouring classes: but this funding would mean increased taxation. The "liberal minded reformers" saw libraries as the means to ensure a sober and industrious working class; others (such as landlords and shopkeepers) "objected to paying rates for the benefit of a lot of lazy people with nothing to do but lounge about reading" (Kelly 1977: 81).

Municipal authorities were slow to institute their own public libraries; one by one, Norwich, Winchester, Manchester, Liverpool and Birmingham led the way. But others took longer. Finally, in the last years of the century, other authorities followed suit, encouraged by (among other things) Queen Victoria's Jubilee in 1887, the demands of newly instituted technical education opportunities legislated for two years later, and substantial funding from private benefactors such as the Scottish–American steel magnate Andrew Carnegie. By 1918 some 60 per cent of the population, theoretically, had access to a public library; but those living in urban areas were far better provided for than those in villages. (Kelly 1977).

The "local library", where Lily's daughters collected books for her, might have been not the municipal library but one of the circulating or twopenny libraries, stocked by the newsagent or corner shop. These, at this time, stocked between two and three hundred books, rented by the shopkeeper from a wholesaler. Both of Lily's favourites novelists were among the most popular in the stock; Ethel M. Dell's *The Way of the Eagle*, published in 1912, had been an instant success and reprinted 27 times in the ensuing three years (Beauman 1983). Set in the final days of a siege at a British-held fort in India, its main character is Muriel, the wife of a "masterful" and fearless soldier husband. As Nicola Beauman sees it, this novel was:

> The best kind of read for anyone wishing to curl up in an armchair, flu-bound and lackadaisical, and wallow unashamedly in a book that is entirely timeless, oblivious of realities and predictions. (Beauman 1983: 179)

To be able to borrow, not buy: to have several books in one week, all for free: the public library must have had a special impact on what life indoors felt like. In the last decades of the nineteenth century it offered, of course, the opportunity for uses of literacy that were more apparently purposeful and serious than the cosy escapism of romantic fiction. As Liz Greenhalgh and Ken Worpole put it, the free public library meant free public access to all, regardless of income; it ensured the opportunity for someone "to try it once and see if they like it". It also opened up possibilities for study and self-education – at least for men (Greenhalgh & Worpole 1995). During the years of the 1914–18 war, surveys of public library use as well as publishers' sales figures reported a reading "boom": more books were being sold and borrowed.[1] This was in part owing to the restrictions imposed by the war (blackouts, the closure of public entertainments, for example), which curtailed leisure activities, so that reading was increasingly seen as a cheap way of passing the time.

It was for fiction that the Mass Observation writers most recalled library use by mothers and grandmothers. Norah, introduced in Chapter 2, was someone whose reading was squeezed in between her daily work of feeding, not only her seven children, but also livestock ("pigs, young calves, hens, turkeys, ducks") on the farm where she lived and worked in rural Ireland. Like Lily, she had her library books chosen for her. Her daughter (W1835) reported how she and a friend of hers from the next farm would collect books for their mothers from a library run in a house some three miles away from their village. Other women had their husbands, rather than their children, make their choices for them. According to B2240: "My parents were *avid readers*. They belonged to Boots Booklovers Library which was their one 'luxury' expenditure. My father chose the books and rarely did my mother not enjoy his choice for her". (my emphasis)

This expression – avid reading – is used by several Mass Observation correspondents. R1025, who describes herself as a 52-year-old housewife, writes about her grandmother, born in 1890 in a village in Essex in a family where "a great deal of reading and writing went on" and in which her grandmother, as a little girl, was "an avid reader, always with a book in her hand, often shutting herself in the toilet to be alone to read".

"We all joined public libraries", writes correspondent F2090; adding "My mother did not have a lot of time for reading at that time but she was an avid reader to the end of her days". A2787, a 32-year-old woman writing about her grandmother, reports: "Nora, as I said, greatly grieved for the fact that she hadn't had an academic education, because she read voraciously – mostly library books – and loved figures".

"Avid" or "voracious" reading – usually of library books – was an activity which children engaged in, often to the torment of their overworked mothers. Thus, a retired librarian recalls her mother's horror at her passion for reading. Her mother, she writes, taught her to read when she was four (in 1929); but:

> I learned so fast, and read so ravenously, being a bored, short-sighted only child [at the time], that she was alarmed, and seemed to spend the rest of our lives discouraging me from reading . . . Appalled at my turning out a book-worm, she would not let my sister learn to read until she was nine. (G1041)

This woman's mother may have been appalled for several reasons. There were potential dangers to eyesight and health from continuous reading: especially given the danger of "germs" from library books. Books might give children – especially daughters – ideas. And daughters reading were daughters not helping mothers, or learning to be mothers themselves.

Eliza, whom we met in Chapter 2, brought up two children who were enthusiastic readers without being able to read herself. It was especially her daughter's passion for reading that "annoyed" her:

> When you read, it used to annoy her. She tried not to get annoyed, but you know how you get lost in a book? and she would take a book off me sometimes and she'd say "I've spoken to you three times" and I'd say, "I'm sorry mother, I haven't heard you". She found it very difficult to understand this fascination that my father and I had for books. (Interview with Joan: Stocksbridge, April 1996)

Libraries, then, while offering new opportunities for affordable reading to adults and children alike, held fears for mothers, as well. We will return to this ambivalence in Chapter 6.

Fictions and fantasy

To judge from both the Mass Observation writers and the interviews I have had with older people, "unashamed wallowing" in sensational fiction by mothers, at least by working-class mothers with large families, was the exception, rather than the rule. Only one person had an unequivocal view of her mother's capacity to indulge her reading appetites – whether for romantic fiction or any other kind, and that was Iris, in the University of the Third Age (U3A) discussion group we will meet in Chapter 5. "She was an avid reader", said Iris then: "It wasn't a case of, 'Oh, you've got a nose in a book'; it was a case of, 'Mother? oh, she's got her nose in a book again!'"

Avid reading and housework seem at first to be impossibly at odds with each other: to read avidly suggests to read for more than a few minutes at a time. Lily, however, enjoyed reading romantic fiction. Ethel M. Dell and Ruby M. Ayres satisfied this appetite; so did the short stories and serials in *Woman's Weekly* – written, in the words of E174 for middle-class readers:

> She had a weekly order for *Woman's Weekly* . . . They were complete short stories and serial stories, all of a romantic nature and very middle class, while we were very working class. There was a cookery page and an agony aunt's page and an article by "The Man Who Sees". And adverts.

A magazine which Lily may also have read was called *Peg's Paper* (a publication also referred to by members of the U3A group, discussed in Chapter 5). As her daughter recalled in our later interview, "a little card . . . little adverts on *Peg's Paper*" used to come through her mother's door.

Peg's Paper (as I learned later, stimulated by these references to seek it out in the shelves of the British Library) was launched in 1919 as a "really cheery paper". In its first issue, the editorial began:

> It's going to be your weekly pal, girls. My name is Peg and my one aim in life is to give you a really cheery paper like nothing you've ever read before. Not so very long ago, I was a mill girl too.

The "snippet" which landed on Lily's doormat in the Lancashire mill town where she still lived as an older woman was, as Gwen recalled it for me, a trailer for the magazine's main sales pitch: that of fantasy and romance. The titles of short and longer stories featured in the early issues give a flavour of their appeal: "Lured to London", "Her ruined beauty", "Her night of terror", "Her secret past". The print, to our modern eyes, is small; the illustrations inside, black and white line drawings. The magazine cover, however, had colour. Not the colourful glamour achieved by *Woman* magazine (launched in 1937, and the first to use photogravure); and certainly not the multi-image photo-collages and mix of graphics we are used to today in that magazine – but at least, red.

Beside my word processor on this table is a colour copy of the cover to issue No. 113. Beneath the magazine title picked out in bold scarlet letters, is a picture of a young woman in bed. Her long wavy hair spreads over the pillow and sheet. Her lacy nightdress is short-sleeved; her bare pink arm lies across the pillow, which she is clutching in evident despair. We can see at once this is a woman sleepless with love; each of her beautiful large eyes, gazing hopelessly into the distance, is filled with a huge tear. Beneath this image of tragedy we read the anguished question which is evidently its source: "Would he never speak to her of his love?" Below these words, framed with a red border, is the caption (lettered in large black capitals): "SCORNED BY SOCIETY". Above, in smaller lettering, appears another (equally irresistible): FROM FACTORY TO FOOTLIGHTS. The red border which surrounds the picture with rosettes and ribbons also embraces the proud words PEG'S PAPER (with the price – twopence – more discreetly printed in grey alongside)

The years of *Peg's Paper* (1919–40) coincided with the growth of the cinema, and a regular feature in the magazine was "photostories" of film stars such as Mary Pickford. Other features were fortune telling ("our woman of mystery") and a letters page ("My private postbag") – usually answering anxious queries on matters of etiquette. (Mabel – Richmond: bread eaten at mealtimes should always be broken with the fingers and never with the knife (No. 88, 11 January 1921, p.3); he drinks – tell him he must give it up, or lose you, dear (No. 111, 21 June 1921).) Advertisements focused on appearance and beauty secrets. (Blushing – how to cure it. Don't be laughed at. Have you a red nose? send a stamp to pay postage and you will learn how to rid yourself of this terrible affliction free of charge.) Corsets are everywhere (the "natural corset style 2" a particular favourite).

Did Lily give in to the "adverts" about *Peg's Paper* and buy one? Was her appetite whetted? According to Cynthia White, the historian of women's magazines, many thousands of women did. *Peg's Paper*, like other later publications (*Red Star*, launched 1929; *Secrets*, 1932; *Oracle*, 1933; *Lucky Star* and *Miracle*, 1935) satisfied

> The need of hardworked poorly paid girls and women to escape from their drab surroundings into a colourful, action-packed dream-world where love and riches were for once within reach. (White 1970: 98)

These, White tells us, were the first women's magazines to be published with the working-class woman reader in mind. They were the product of a period between 1875 and 1910 that saw the birth of an entirely new kind of reading material, unavailable to previous generations: the affordable, disposable weekly or monthly magazine written for women. To that extent, women like Lily (born, you will remember, in 1890) had reading material at her disposal which had been quite unknown to her own mother.

In 1921, two years after its parent paper was launched, *Peg's Companion* appeared, a "new story paper" in each issue of which would be two complete novels. In the editorial to its first issue, "Peg" is once again here to explain all:

> Dear girls – I daresay a good many of you who read this little paper will wonder about the title – why it is called PEG'S COMPANION and who Peg is? Some of you will know me, because I already edit another paper bearing my name – Peg's Paper. But to those who don't, I would like to introduce myself.

Really I am a mill girl, or rather I was before I took up journalism. It was always my ambition to succeed in conducting a paper – or papers! that give girls like myself exactly what they want to read – papers which contain stories you'll enjoy reading after your day's work is done, and which on your "grey" days when things go wrong will cheer you up.

The cover picture to this first issue shows a slightly different portrait of a woman's anguish than had appeared two years earlier. This time, there are two people. On the right stands a young woman, holding in her shawl a sleeping baby; her head is tilted back so that we can see the curls peeping beneath the brim of her hat. Her other arm is outstretched to, on the left, a fierce-looking man with a moustache. His eyes glare at her, his moustache is bushy with rage. His right arm thrusts an accusing hand out of the picture. "For my baby's sake forgive me, dad", reads the caption. It is the image of the fallen woman; the banished daughter, guilty of the ultimate sin: a child born out of wedlock.

As I sat beneath the dome of the British Library on a summer's day in 1997, turning the yellowed pages of this magazine, I wondered about the women who, in very different surroundings, would have read its issues hot off the press. If Lily did ever read this magazine, did it "cheer" her? As a young mother, unable to find comfort in her own mother's reaction to the pre-marital conception of her first pregnancy, did she ever think of writing to "My mother's pages" in *Peg's Companion*? The invitation to her and others to do so (had she read it) was cast in hospitable terms:

Dear All of You,
Although I've never really met any of you, I seem to know many of you through my girl Peg, and when she came to me with the request that I should write a letter to her chums – as she speaks of you to me – I was delighted.

In the centre of two columns of print is a picture of the fictional author: a sweetly smiling woman, knitting in an armchair. Hair parted in the middle, dark dress edged with lace at collar and cuff, she looks straight out of the page at her readers.

I've got wrinkles on my face, and my hair is white, but I can still laugh and joke, and find this world a good place to be in; I am not so old that I cannot remember when I was a girl.

How comforting she sounds! what a contrast to the agony of doomed love, let alone of an unexpected pregnancy!

I know how dreadful a heartache can be, dear girls, a far worse thing than a headache, so if ever you have a secret that worries you, come to me.

I shall keep your letters for that time. Remember that all your confidences will be sacred. You need not even tell me your name, or where you live . . .
(1 November 1921, p. 39)

Alongside this promise of secrets shared and shame confided, *Peg's Companion* provided stories with titles even more sensational than those in *Peg's Paper*. Turning the pages in the hush of the library in London, I wondered how the same pages might have rustled in the commotion of a crowded kitchen:

> *The fatal kiss*: When Lord Tony kissed her, beautiful Amber West forgot that she was only a working girl and he was rich and titled. What happened afterwards is told below in a long complete novel by MURIEL KING. (Issue No. 2, 1921)
>
> *The finger of scorn*: Gay Nicholson was lonely and longed for adventure, and when Fate beckoned she followed, never realizing that she had taken the first step down the path of sorrow and deceit. Her story is told by HESTER YORKE. (Issue No. 153, 1924)

Had I been Lily or someone like her, and read the first issue, I would have encountered a tragic tale entitled *Her mother's sin*: "the love story of the beautiful Annette Orme", by Cora Linda. The villain of the piece, someone by the name of Gervase Fortescue, was an individual prone to talking "suavely" or "coarsely". The heroine herself (I would have discovered) was virtuous, as well as beautiful. Sometimes she spoke "primly" (as in: "Mr. Fortescue!" she said primly. "Whatever does this mean?"); at other times she was "vehement" or "broken" ("'Have mercy have mercy!' the girl cried vehemently . . . 'I can't explain!' she whispered brokenly").

Had I been Lily (or someone like her) I might have been in my thirties, the mother of several children; the hands that turned the page would have been dried a moment before from wringing another pile of washing. Among the readers intended by "Peg", the supposed editor of these publications, were factory girls such as Lily had once been. Neither Gwen, nor I, nor anyone else can know if Lily read this magazine, and if she did, what she found in her reading of its pages. Whether the fictional "mother" in the columns of "My mother's page" offered her amusement or comfort, we can only speculate. The ideal mother this feature represented – always hospitable to the troubles of daughters – was a commercial product. The reality for mothers like Lily, herself still a daughter, was governed by other imperatives.

Mothers, talking and writing

Whether they have time or inclination for reading or writing, mothers have always told stories. It is partly from the recollection of some of these stories that children, now older women or men, were able to create new ones; composing imagined and/or remembered portraits to send in to the Mass Observation Archive. For some, this storytelling life was vivid indeed, and of much greater importance to the vitality of the family than reading or writing:

> On the evidence of what I saw while living in my mother's childhood home, there was little to suggest a family devoted to the printed word; but plenty to confirm that Kerry folk are great talkers, and pursue this pastime late into the night. (P2578)

In the latter part of the twentieth century we inhabit a world in which opportunities to tell and listen to stories in the home compete with other media. Children have television programmes to watch, computer games to play, and telephones on which to talk to their friends. At the same time, opportunities for mothers to explore their own literacy interests, while still far too circumscribed, are certainly greater than they would have been for their grandmothers. It is the contribution of a movement of community publishing that these opportunities have at the same time reasserted the value of oral tradition through the practices of working together at reading and writing in groups, and sharing the writing that emerges in public readings.

The following piece, first published in the 1980s, came out of the experience of the writer meeting with other women in a writers' workshop.

> Shush – mum's writing
>
> Sit down be quiet read a book
> Don't you dare to speak or look
> Shush Mum's writing
>
> She's left the dishes in the sink
> All she does is sit and think
> Shush Mum's writing
>
> Nothing for dinner nowt for tea
> And all she ever says to me is
> Shush Mum's writing
>
> But what's all this Mum's wrote a book
> Why not buy one have a look
> No need to shush now we can shout
> And tell all our friends about
> MUM'S WRITING
>
> Pat Dallimore (1978)
> (in Morley & Worpole 1982)

The writers' group of which Pat Dallimore was a member formed part of the activities of a community publishing organization called Bristol Broadsides. This, in turn, was a founding member of the national Federation of Worker Writers and

Community Publishers, established in 1976 and still thriving today.[2] I was fortunate to hear Pat read this piece at one of the readings organized by the FWWCP in the early 1980s: so in reading it on the page, I can still hear particular voice (and the defiant rise in her intonation on the last three lines).

Women in the 1900s–30s appeared to use libraries a lot – but rarely as places in which to read and write. "Shush – mum's writing" is shushing the family in the home, not other readers in a public space. Libraries – some of them at least – offer the quiet and uninterrupted place in which to compose ideas. Working in the reading rooms of reference or academic libraries has been for me among the great pleasures of writing this book; as an academic attached to an academic institution I expect to be able to browse frequently both along shelves and on screen in search of thinking that continues to enlarge and extend my own. It was on a Saturday afternoon in 1997 that I knew I wanted to find Liz Greenhalgh and Ken Worpole's study of the changing history of the public library from which I quoted earlier. In the local branch of my public library in Lambeth, London, I stared at a computer screen and adjusted the mouse to "author/title". Discovering that the library did indeed have it in stock at the reference library two miles away, I left the branch library, walked to the bus stop, and caught a bus. Twenty minutes later, I was reading the book I had been looking for: all this, "on the rates".

As it happened, that afternoon, the bus on which I travelled was full of mothers. All ages were there; grasping huge carrier bags, clutching one child and keeping an eye on another, turning to their neighbour, finding a seat; some wearing lycra leggings, others, billowing cotton dresses; some, leather trousers; others, pastel jackets. Black velvet with sequins sat next to faded brown tweed. Scarves and hats of all shapes and turbans covered the heads; sandals, trainers, platform boots, court shoes the feet. There was grey hair, wispy brown; black, glossed or stretched; plaited auburn; blonde, caught up with combs. The faces were pink-pale, brown-dark; spectacled, lipsticked, smiling, blank; crows-footed and smooth.

Such variety mocks generalization: but this is what I thought, that afternoon. Motherhood is both gift and theft. Mothers are people who, all things being equal, are given the experience of watching a small infant grow, and, all being well, receive the rewards of a needy child becoming a loving friend. However, things are not equal, and all is not always well, and in a culture which assumes them to be primary carers, mothers are also people too often robbed of their own care. Literacy, a medium with which we may create worlds of our own, is a means to care for our need to recall and to plan, to imagine and to record: to make a mark. So the expressive possibilities of writing enables a mother to give voice to her suffering, as well as such joys as children may give her, and in so doing, claim a hearing which otherwise is denied her. Many of those other mothers on the bus may themselves have been using libraries for studying, if not that Saturday, some other time in the week. Or they may not. Their reading and writing lives, like mine, are but a fraction of their other lives. But for some who choose to make the fraction a little larger, as Pat Dallimore did, they may themselves become authors of the library books, as well as readers.

Such an experience is reported of a woman adult literacy student called Suzanne in Melbourne, Australia. It was in a library near where she lived that Suzanne first met the person who was to be her literacy tutor. She felt fearful and shy. She found it "nerve-racking" to be there and "spoke very quietly", and was "frightened that someone in the library reading a book" would find out that she was illiterate. Later, much later, Suzanne contributed a piece of her writing to a collection by students in the literacy programme of which she had become a member. Her piece was "a story on my schooling and childhood". The collection was published; the library acquired copies, where they were from then on available for others to read. From being afraid of reading, of not being able to read, and of being found out as an outlaw in a library, Suzanne had moved to being one of the writers on its shelves (Campbell 1991: 12–13). Like Pat Dallimore, she had changed the distance between public and private literacies, altering the relationships between herself, her family and her community.

Both women did this through the talkative literacy work of the classes and groups in which they were participants; claiming their own time to "play around" with ideas, to be playful with possibilities. It is in an essay by the teacher, poet and feminist theorist Adrienne Rich that this phrase was used about writing and motherhood. In this essay she poses the idea of writing as a form of *play*; going on to tell how it was this mental playfulness of which she felt robbed during her own years of mothering in the 1950s. The sheer weariness of "work that others constantly undo" had put an end to the writing that she had been doing before having children:

> I was writing very little, partly from fatigue, that female fatigue of suppressed anger and loss of contact with my own being, partly from the discontinuity of female life with its attention to small chores, errands, work that others constantly undo, small children's constant needs.

In contrast to this weariness and interruptedness, she goes on, what is needed in order "to write poetry or fiction, or even to think well" is

> a certain freedom of mind . . . freedom to press on, to enter the currents of your thought like a glider pilot, knowing that your motion can be sustained, that the buoyancy of your attention will not be suddenly snatched away. Moreover, if the imagination is to transcend and transform experience it has to question, to challenge, to conceive of alternatives, perhaps to the very life you are living at that moment. *You have to be free to play around with the notion that day might be night, love might be hate; nothing can be too sacred for the imagination to turn into its opposite or to call experimentally by another name.* For writing is re-naming. Now, to be maternally with small children all day in the old way, to be with a man in the old way of marriage, requires a holding-back, a putting-aside of that imaginative activity, and demands instead a kind of conservatism. (Rich 1980: 43) (my emphasis)

The "holding-back" and "putting-aside" seem like an inner brake: once the brake is taken off, the wheels roll, the mind takes off. Day might be night and night might be day, and the mother can, simply, let herself go. It seems to me that it is for that freedom to *play*, with time, as well as with "notions", which mothers, today as in the past, must claim their own time, if literacy in its fullest sense is to be theirs.

Reflections

I write this sentence on a summer's afternoon; *you* may be reading it on a winter's morning. Writer and reader of the same text, we inhabit different times. Once any piece of writing has left its author, this has always been and will always be the case. In the literate relationship, reader and writer meet at different moments in their own lives. The experience of the text in front of them can never be a simultaneous one; the reader, reading, is living through real and imaginative times different from those lived through by the writer, writing.

While literacy had never been the sole means for women to undertake such journeys of the mind, it sets up a relationship beyond the immediacy of the oral expression of song and story. The storyteller or singer and her listeners occupy the same space; each is present to the other. Whereas, just as you and I, reading and writing this paragraph in different times, inhabit different historical moments so we also inhabit different places. I (on this summer's afternoon) sit in a specific upstairs room in a particular house. You (on your winter's morning) are somewhere else: maybe not in a room, but on a bus, or beside a river. For me, you are in the future; for you, I am in the past. What separates us is history; but what also separates us is geography. Writer and reader, while we engage in this relationship of literacy, are both physically and imaginatively located in separate places.

This physical difference is true for the briefest of literate communications as well as for the longer one of a book like this. The holiday postcard is the most extreme example, for it offers a picture as well as the writer's greeting to emphasize the geographical separation between her and her reader. This is very literally a message from one place to another place, sent precisely to enable the reader to locate the writer, at a seaside resort instead of at her usual address. The literal message may often be just a few words: but the message conveyed by the whole text is – look, I'm here! (not where I usually am). The words themselves ("wish you were here", perhaps) are there to underline how far away the reader seems to the writer; the reader, for her part, is being given a reminder that the writer is somewhere else.

"Avid reading", reading with an urgency of appetite, was certainly something which public libraries were able to offer to households who otherwise could not afford their own books. Mothers, according to several Mass Observation correspondents, found their children's avid reading alternately infuriating and worrying. A fictional account set in the 1920s offers a particularly vivid picture of the scenes referred to in the M/O reports. The mother in the scene is called Ada, a

Jewish refugee from Poland bringing up her children in the East End of London. Ada's daughter, Miriam, becomes a passionate reader; she "read as if starving, read while dressing, read at the table, read in the lavatory, and to finish a chapter would walk to school holding the book in one hand and leading Philip by the other".

Ada, struggling with the daily toil of managing home, family and shop, is portrayed in this novel as torn between pride at the school achievements of her growing daughter and torment at the effects this passion for literacy will have on her daughter's future as a wife and mother: "The girl was simply not interested in anything, it worried her to death. What would become of her? One couldn't clean a house with a book in her hand, or give it to one's husband instead of dinner" (Adler 1984: 79).

The association of reading with nourishment, hunger, and greed brings together both reading for escape and reading for learning. This chapter has focused on "domestic" reading and writing; exploring, through three kinds of domestic literacy activity, how mothers in the early decades of the century might have "played" not only with time, but with the space in which they found themselves. We have also considered how literacy – especially reading – is seen both as stimulating and satisfying an "appetite" to move beyond the present place. This metaphor of appetite and nourishment is taken to its limits in a passage describing a scene from the period in which the mothers about whom we have been reading were living.

It was in Newcastle, on a hot morning in June 1913. A crowd of women were gathered for a meeting. They had travelled from all over the country for a conference of the Women's Co-operative Guild, founded twenty years earlier. One by one, they had come up to the platform to speak, calling for reform of the divorce laws, for a minimum wage, for shorter working hours, for improved maternity welfare, sanitation and education; they demanded the right for women to vote. Many of the speakers were mothers, all were working-class, none had spare energy for their own leisure or education. Yet they conjured up the image, for one witness, of women with the "indiscriminate greed of the hungry appetite" for reading.

That witness was neither a mother nor working-class. The appetite she thought about, however, was one for which she had a particularly keen sympathy. Her name was Virginia Woolf; and as she watched and listened that day, she felt frustration at the continued powerlessness of pre-suffrage women:

> In all that audience, among all those women who worked, who bore children, who scrubbed and cooked and bargained, there was not a single woman with a vote . . . The thought was irritating and depressing in the extreme. (Woolf 1990: xxi)

Recalling the scene some years later, Woolf wrote of being inspired, as well as frustrated; not only by the "vitality" of the women she listened to that day, but by the "inborn energy" she found, some months later, reading the memoirs sent in by Guild members to its Secretary, Margaret Llewellyn Davies. What she found in these writers was a determination, against the odds, to reach out for other possibilities via literacy,

> With that inborn energy which no amount of children and washing up can quench [and which] had reached out ... and seized upon old copies of magazines; had attached itself to Dickens; had propped the poems of Burns against a dish cover to read while cooking.

"They read at meals; they read before going to the mill", she goes on; these women (as she saw it) read:

> With the indiscriminate greed of the hungry appetite, that crams itself with toffee and beef and tarts and vinegar and champagne all in one gulp. Naturally [Woolf went on], such reading led to argument. The younger generation had the audacity to say that Queen Victoria was no better than an honest charwoman who had brought up her children respectably. They had the temerity to doubt whether to sew straight stitches into men's hat brims should be the sole aim of a woman's life. (Woolf 1990: xxxv–xxxvi)

There is more: but I hope this has given you a flavour. The reading these women had done had fed an appetite and created another; an appetite for "argument", and for speaking up and writing, too.

Literacy is about more than reading, and certainly about more than reading books. In this chapter we have looked only briefly at the informal writing of postcards and letters, and imagined something of the traffic of written messages in the early years of the century. The widespread use of the telephone means that postcards today fulfil different functions; yet I suspect that the writing of cards, for condolence, celebration, encouragement, gratitude or simply keeping in touch, is still more a female than male habit. This is temporary and transitory literacy; brief (especially postcards) and disposable.

It was at a 1993 conference on women's literacy that Anne Nederkoorn offered a story of two postcard-writing episodes, which had taken place among the group of eight women in a literacy class that she taught just outside Amsterdam, in Holland. The group, who were aged between 22 and 50, met every week with her in a community centre, practising reading and writing and, what is usually known as, "basic literacy skills".

> One time (Anne told us), we had some practice with writing postcards. Most of the women had never written any postcard or letter before, so this was quite a new experience to them. They wrote a little note to each other, and the address. And they themselves received mail! All within the classroom.

One day one of the participants was absent; she was ill. Every woman wrote a little note to her, first without paying too much attention to spelling, then rewritten (as correct as possible) on the postcard. One of the participants wrote the address, another volunteered to post it. From that moment on, we almost always sent something to someone absent. We wrote letters together or put several single letters in an envelope.

Martha was the name of one of the learners in the group. She often talked, Anne told us, about her learning and change through literacy.

After about six weeks participating in the literacy group, she told me about a letter that had been sent to her and her family. Until then her husband used to read and answer letters. But this time Martha said to him: "I'll answer it". He said, "You're not able to write properly. I'll do it". Martha grasped the letter out of his hands and he had to let her answer it.

Some weeks later, Anne herself was ill. After a few days in bed at home, she received a big postcard from the group, written by Martha. "She wrote the address too" said Anne (Nederkoorn 1993).

Within this story were the elements of a kind of *affection* in teaching and learning which many of us at the conference had been speaking of with wistfulness. The hard edges of market forces, "outcome-related funding" and measurable performance indicators of literacy progress in the funding schemes of the late 1980s had been taxing the spirits of adult literacy teachers. In the words of Rosemary Fraser, then Adult Basic Education co-ordinator in Edinburgh:

Government agencies, with their emphasis on the acquisition of functional skills (divorced from political realities) are actually entering into literacy as a form of social control. This has led some educators to fear accreditation as an instrument of this control. (Mace 1993: 4)

The achievement represented in the writing of the postcard to the woman at home, at first glance, appears fairly trivial. Compared to the writing of reports, letters of complaint, curriculum vitae, application forms for housing benefit, and all the other necessary routines of adult basic education, a postcard seems lightweight stuff: inessential. But in that context its purpose – to gather and express group support for another woman – was central to those women's interests in literacy: and central, too, to celebrate their sense of pleasure in being able to use writing in more confident ways. So Anne's story restored for people at that conference the sense of *playfulness* on which serious literacy education flourishes: the kind of playfulness that women all over the world have always used to transform the "control" of government agencies.

For women coming to literacy in adult life, there are persistent and daily obstacles. Seeking to claim time or space to write anything – whether it is an essay or a postcard, a list or a poem – is making a claim to "play around": so that the imagination, however briefly, might be free to "transcend and transform" experience.

Notes

1. There is something innocent in the question used to try to discover what people actually *did* with their reading (used in Gallup Polls on the reading public in the 1940s):

   Do you happen to be reading a novel or other book at the moment? (McAleer 1992: 74)

2. The Federation of Worker Writers and Community Publishers was established in 1976 and currently consists of some 30 member groups: community based writers' groups, publishers and adult literacy organizations. The FWWCP has a website: http://www.fwwcp.mcmail.com.

Chapter 5

Hide and seek: the search for illiteracy

This chapter is about two things: talking and illiteracy. Most of it is about conversations and interviews, rather than written sources; and at the heart of it is the "taboo" of illiteracy, on which I hope to shine some calm and gentle light.

In the last two chapters, there have been examples of how one person expresses their recollection of another differently in speech than in writing; how the same person may vary their account of another when they are telling it to different people; and how two people will have different memories of that person. These are familiar experiences to most of us; just as, if we stop and think about it, we can recognize that at different moments in our lives, we retell the same experience in different ways. It is sometimes as if we are trying on different clothes, using language to experiment with different kinds of truth; sometimes the telling is "dressed up", at other times it is allowed out "any old how". But all the time, autobiographical narrative wears the ornaments of imagination.

The interplay between the remembered and the imagined is even more evident when we attempt to create a life of which we can only have ever known a small part. "To me, grandmothers were born grandmothers", one woman said to me. Within the world of the child's reality grandmothers are unimaginable as being any other age than the age they are now (which, to a young child, is simply *very old indeed*). For the child, still young, it is impossible to comprehend them as having a life beyond their own reality; only when the child has become old herself may it begin to become possible to perceive just some of the dimensions of that life beyond her own autobiography.

So when autobiography fuses with biography, when we conjure up a sketch of the person we knew, who is no longer here to give their own account of themselves, our memory has to be extended by imagination: we combine the creative effort of novelist and historian. Thus did Joan piece together an imagined story of her mother's life before she herself entered it, writing what she called a "fictional biography". Her published book about Eliza drew on "a memory of memories": her recollection of the stories that Eliza, her mother, had told her when she herself had been a child. What she wrote was a creative story-telling act, superimposed on that of her story-telling mother.

My research purpose, as I expressed it in the directive to Mass Observation Archive correspondents, was to invite others to help me "create a portrait" of women no longer alive and to discover the place that reading and writing had in their lives. These portraits were elusive; their daughters, sons, grandchildren and other relatives did what they could to imagine, as well as remember them. As correspondents for a public archive, they were both liberated by their anonymity and constrained by an unseen readership. There was restraint in the writing. The development that was possible when some of these writers consented to meet and talk was considerable; in the intimacy of interview, other recollections came to life – not because these were censored from the written account; rather, that with a present listener in the room, the tales could be elaborated with the certainty of their interest.

Oral history is the term usually used for such work: two people with a tape-recorder. Reminiscence work (as I understand it) is what goes on when a group of people meet to recollect and exchange memories with each other, usually with someone acting as facilitator. Both approaches entail a creative process – a *searching* and a *making*. Since I am by training an adult educator first, and only secondarily a researcher, my own preference is for a combination of the two: both individual interviews and group meetings, offering the opportunity for the inter-viewees to meet each other, as well as me – not just once, but several times. Because the single tape-recorded interview has so much at stake, this has always seemed more comfortable to me. With only a single meeting between interviewee and interviewer, there are considerable risks of injury to the former and confusion to the latter. Of course, with sensitivity and care these risks can be avoided. But with only a single meeting, however risk-free, an opportunity is missed. Conver-sation provokes memories; memories, once spoken aloud take on a life of their own. With time allowed for revisiting and revising things said, the interview becomes more than a useful research event for the interviewer: it is the start of an interesting communicative process for the interviewee. Offered the opportunity of reflecting on the interview – either through receiving and being invited to com-ment on a copy of its written transcript, or through a second conversation – the interviewee is also given back material for research of their own. If there is also the possibility of the individuals having the choice to meet up with others who have been through the same interview process there is the chance (if they want it) to continue the reflections and to re-situate their own experiences in another con-text. In this chapter, I quote from interviews with two individuals and use some transcript from a discussion in a group. I continue to feel grateful to these people for the time they gave me. What I hope is that the interviews, discussion and later correspondence and meetings provided a process that was useful to them, too.

I begin with the idea of oral history as a project of joint composition, in which both listeners and tellers compose together, pictures and tales. From two separate interviews then comes two such pictures, both (as I see it) portraying a "literate accomplice" to their mothers' girlhood romance, both mothers recalled as illiter-ate. From this, we move to a discussion with a group of older women recalling their own mothers, each in turn conjuring up glimpses of their literacy lives. The "Great Divide" theory is indeed of little use in making sense of these lives: instead there are shades and changes, a "spectrum" of literacy use and absence, told by women who themselves are committed readers and letter-writers and actively engaged, in their seventies and eighties, in their own education. The illiterate mother sits next to the "avidly reading" mother.

From this I have returned to those written accounts that reported illiteracy, and present some silhouettes of mothers who could neither read nor write. The chapter ends with some reflections on the debates about measuring illiteracy in the past.

Composing in talk

Interviewing others, as I was interviewing Anne, Brenda, Noreen, Enid, Eileen, Joan and Fred (in Chapters 2 and 3), is a project that is like both reading and writing. The interviewer and interviewee read each other's faces, voices, intentions. In the case of these interviews, I was also privileged to read something of their home surroundings: something interviewees were unable to do of mine. Opening the door, there stood a person. Entering her home, there were her chosen possessions, colours and textures. On the walls were paintings, photographs, calendars. On the shelves were books and ornaments; on the tables, cups, saucers, newspapers; on the floor, rugs, carpet, lino; on the pegs in the hall coats, hats, umbrellas. All these were the person who was now inviting me to take off my coat. Photographs of children and grandchildren stood on the mantlepiece. Calendars hung in the hall or the kitchen. All this was for me to read, too, as well as the welcoming smile of my interviewee.

Interviewing is also like writing. It is a composition between two people; we are partners in a conversation in which we are both composing ideas, questions and images. As co-authors, we create between us a text that pauses and hesitates and then, suddenly, leaps forward. The composition also becomes a text in the literal sense when, later, the tape-recorded interview is transcribed onto paper. The common and separate ground between written and oral sources of history, as the historian Alessandro Portelli suggests, needs to be better understood. Many interviewees, as he points out:

> Read books and newspapers, listen to the radio and TV, hear sermons and political speeches, and keep diaries, letters, clippings and photograph albums. Orality and writing, for many centuries now, have not existed separately: if many written sources are based on orality, modern orality itself is saturated with writing. (Portelli 1998: 69)

Communication between interviewee and interviewer is a two-way process. Portelli will brook no excuses: the oral historian is as much a maker of the text of the interview as their "informant". Not for him the invisible identity of the interviewer: she or he is part of what is said, too – too easy, the pretence of the detached and impartial narrator quoting their sources. "Alongside the first person narrative of the interviewee stands the first person of the historian, without whom there would be no interview" (Portelli 1998: 72).

For this writing project to be fruitful, both participants need also to be actively engaged in imaginative work; as I see it, both life history and autobiography are not only the making of narratives, but also an exercise in speculation – a puzzling around possibilities. An image from my own past illustrates what I mean; not a clear story, with known boundaries, but a blurred image:

> It is an early morning in spring. My sister and I are in my grandfather's garden, taking turns on a hammock, swung between two trees. We are there before breakfast. The perfume of the wallflowers in the garden is only just rising. The grownups are still in bed.

As I recall this scene, I hold both certainty and uncertainty together. For an instant, I am quite certain that scene happened, and happened more than once. But within the instant, there is also what I can only call a shimmer of uncertainty. The scene suddenly appears impossible. As I sit there recalling it, there is only me as the witness. Later, on the phone, I check with my sister; she agrees with me that the scene happened, and happened more than once. But in the hour or day or week after the phone call, when I try to revisit the scene, it retains the shimmer and there are uncertainties. How did it happen, that she and I ran into the garden in those early mornings? there is no name to the day (was it Wednesday or Thursday?) and no length to the hour (was it seven or eight in the morning?) The picture, at first very sharp, seems to tremble. It is a reflection seen on the surface of a pond, not in the sheer surface of the mirror. A breeze ruffles the water's skin and the outlines of the picture become blurred.

Life-history work is the work of turning word pictures into tales. For my hammock picture to become a tale, there would need to be others, so that the one picture follows another in a sequence, and a tale is told. The telling may be a private soliloquy: we reminisce alone. But once it is spoken aloud to a listener, the speaker is no longer the sole creator. When Gwen told me the story of the box and the marriage papers, I was part of the making of the story. She spoke economically, with little in the way of descriptive language, setting the stage with the minimum of scenery; in order for me to create my own picture of the scenes she described, I had to give my full attention and ask her questions that would bring them to life while she composed the drama in which they were played out.

As we sat in her sitting room on a rainy February Monday, both of us were creating our own images of the twelve-year-old girl reaching for a box on a shelf in the kitchen. For an instant, as I listened and Gwen talked, the girl hovered between us. Once she began telling me the story of her father, her sister, herself, and the family secret hidden on the papers in the box on the shelf in the kitchen, my imagination was working as well as hers. The two of us were engaged in a joint project. In Carolyn Steedman's words, I, as the "story-taker" was the "necessary collaborator" in the project of story-making:

> The one who listens, shapes the narrative by assuming that there is some-thing to be told; who takes the story, not as appropriate, but as part of a deal, so that the outcome – an entity, a story – might be placed there, in the space between listener and teller. (Steedman 1992: 171)

The listener, in this view, is partisan and participant. She, with the interviewee, is far more than simply a passive receptacle for any story that happens to come her way. She is co-author; her every signal, verbal or non-verbal, contributes to the story's making.

Carolyn Steedman's earlier book about her own mother, subtitled "a story of two lives", is not about oral history research, but about the telling and interpreting of stories (Steedman 1986). It is a fierce and painful book that has, no doubt, inspired many other people, as well as me; a scholarly work, the author carrying her scholarship through the three parts of the book as though it was a torch. Among the gifts that it offers is the possibility that we too, her readers, might be able to make some use of the disconnected stories of our own lives, if only we are prepared to allow ourselves to dwell on them. Another, is her central theme – the difficulty of *classifying* a life, and the recognition that any story of a life is a partial and ephemeral one:

> Accounts of working-class life are told by tension and ambiguity, out on the borderlands. The story – my mother's story, a hundred thousand others – cannot be absorbed into the central one: it is both its disruption and its essential counterpoint: this is a drama of *class*.
>
> But visions change, once any story is told; ways of seeing are altered. The point of a story is to present itself momentarily as complete, so that it can be said: it does for now, it will do; it is an account that will last a while. Its point is briefly to make an audience connive in the telling, so that they might say: yes, that's how it was; or, that's how it could have been. (Steedman 1986: 22)

Gwen's story began as a story about her mother Lily: about her shame at a child conceived out of wedlock. The tale as she told it to me, however, was one in which Gwen herself – or rather herselves – had a principal role. Gwen the storyteller is an old woman – as old as her mother would have been at the climax of the tale. An old woman as she tells it, the two other selves she conjures up of her own life are a young girl and a woman in her forties. Lily, her mother, is at first off stage: an absence. The people in the scene are a father and two daughters, looking through papers on a table: papers in which the mother is present only symboli-cally. Later, Gwen is alone with the same papers, again registering the mother's symbolic presence. It is when the mother is by now the same age as Gwen herself is now – an old woman in her seventies – that she becomes present in the story. To the extent that I "shaped" her narrative at all, my part in the making of this tale was to recognize that here there was something to be told – not so much something about Gwen herself (although, as I have said, her part in the drama still intrigues me) but about her mother. I was there to listen as Gwen made her own commentary on the tale. In the space between us the tale took its place, with the invisible mother at its heart.

This is a story told from inside Gwen's own experience; for her, the protagonist must be herself. For me, the search is for Lily, the elusive other woman; together, we glimpsed something of her, and speculated. The pictures that the story reveals of Lily, like those of the many other women whose lives have been composed for and with me, shimmer in waters of *imagined memory*: a combination of imagining and remembering. As we have seen, many more of these memories have been what Joan (in Chapter 3) called "the memory of a memory", using the recollection of the mother's tales of herself or of her own mother, composed and conditioned, as Gwen's was, by the listener who was present at the telling. The listener makes up her own pictures to fill in gaps left by these tales. Sometimes the gaps were left by the teller; sometimes they are gaps in the listener's capacity to hear the tale. There is something else here, too: for the story Gwen told me had also been told before, to others, by her sister, her mother and herself – each time with an audience "conniving" to its telling and to its production in the form it was given to me. (In Chapter 7 we will return to the literacy event at its heart: to the keeping and finding of certificates.)

Imagining the lives of women just over the horizon of living memory is like trying to reach the plum that is just out of reach. The other fruit is nearer; we have autobiography and living history to give it to us. But just above those that we can pick, within reach, hangs the ripe golden oval of a life whose taste can only be guessed at. Audrey spoke of her mother as having had a "very hard life". To this day Audrey is still asking a question to which she has no way of finding an answer. Why, when her sister went to work in an office, did Doris (her mother) get "put" into domestic service? The question clearly holds a fascination for her. There is a sense of a wrong done, and injustice suffered. There is also the sense of an imagination stopped in its tracks.

For me, there was another fascination, too. There sat Doris, the young mother, at the kitchen table. She is licking a pencil. Her mind is on a list to be written. Suddenly, when Audrey said "I suppose I can see her at our kitchen table, licking her pencil", I saw her too; and weeks later, when I re-read the transcript of our conversation later, I too felt my imagination halted, uncertain. I could taste the metallic stub of the pencil on my tongue, and hold its wood in my fingers: but how long would the pencil be? I felt the surface of the table: but was it oil cloth, newspaper, fabric or wood that I felt? I wanted to hear the children's voices beside her, feel the ache at the base of her skull, sense the fold of her skirt on my hips and the shape of her shoes on my feet. I wanted to know the angle of light through the window, the colour of the sky outside; the smells in the room of coal, damp, soap or cooking. I wanted to imagine being Doris, to be inside her, as her mind reached out to remember what else must go down on this list, different from the one she had written the day before or the one she would write the day after as she calculated the price and the amount and the time.

On the scrap of paper are the words that she has written: "half a pound of marge". Something must be written next. The pot is boiling; the child is becoming impatient; a decision must be made. She picks up her pencil and writes: "A pound of sugar".

And so Audrey and I both worked to move our imaginations beyond this sudden gift from her memory to create a fragment of Doris's guessed-at life which now shimmered in the space between us. This moving and telling, listening and imagining is what goes on every time a story is told: as when a mother tells her daughter the story of her own mother.

The literate accomplice

Doris's shopping list is an unromantic piece of literacy history. It is a spare piece of literature, deliberately disposable. Yet in the action of writing it, the mother whose mind is disorganized with the work around her claims a moment of order. Literacy at this moment is represented by the scrap of paper on the table and the pencil in the hand. The writing to come is both an instruction to her child and a request to the shopkeeper. Here sits Doris, the same person who, at the age of fourteen, left her own home to work as a servant in another's: the person who, at another time, has her feet up, reading of a fictional world in which poor women marry rich men and there is no more washing to be done.

What year was it that she wrote this list? Might it have been 1926, the year of the General Strike? or 1928, the year that all women over the age of 21 finally got the right to vote for those who would govern them? Doris is not here to answer, and she has left us no written account of her life to help us. We are dependent on our imaginations as she writes: "Half a pound of marge; a pound of sugar".

There is more romance in a first message between boy and girl, than in the later writing that girl has to do once she has become his wife. If one of the couple was illiterate, such a message needed a third person, an intermediary. Kathleen and her future husband met at a horse fair in Ireland, in 1925, when she was sixteen. He could read and write; she could not. The meeting had to be secret because of the prohibitions around illicit courtships in the Irish travelling community. This is how her daughter Mary Anne told me the story:

Do you know how they met?

Yes. In a fair, in a cafe. She had to pretend that she didn't notice him. He'd got a note to her – she got someone else to read it – to meet him later on . . . At that time you couldn't approach anybody. It wasn't done. And even now, with a lot of us, it isn't done. It's got to be done in a roundabout sort of a way. And if you do talk to someone, there's got to be someone there with you. So she decided to go to meet him and that was it. He was a very handsome looking man. So was she.

She had the note, that someone else had to read for her.

But that was another young girl like herself, who wouldn't squeal on her, see what I mean? Some of them could read and write, but a lot of them couldn't . . . There was very careful chaperones in those days. (Interview, September 1996).

Kathleen married her sweetheart and bore him fifteen children. Five of these children died in infancy. Her husband died in 1949, when Kathleen was forty. All of that was in the future, that day at the horse fair; and who can know how things would have turned out for Kathleen had it not been for the "other young girl like herself" to read her the invitation to meet.

Mary Ann, Liz and I are sitting in her home on a travellers' site in Bermondsey, South London. It is September 1996. We are drinking tea in a tiny kitchen/sitting room. There are paperback books on the shelf beside the cooker. Mary Ann recalls her mother Kathleen with affection, as a woman with contradictory feelings about the literacy of her children: "She'd say to me, 'Them books is putting ideas into your head! With the books you'll go blind!' And yet the only thing she ever wanted to do was to write a book about her life".

Living in her small trailer in a crowded inner city site with the voices of neighbours and children just outside the door, Mary Ann, a mother and grandmother herself, withdraws into the paperback fiction she buys from boot sales as a retreat: "When I want to forget about all the noise out here, I'd get straight into a book".

The three of us sit there sipping tea. The years of Kathleen's life, the pregnancies and the bereavements hang heavy in our imagination. But like the flicker of a candle far away in the dark there is that afternoon, before all that, when a "handsome" young man sends a note to the girl of his fancy and she and her friend huddle together to read what it says.

In a second story of literacy and young love, it is again the boy who is literate and the girl who is not. Once again, there is another girl who steps in as the literate accomplice. This time, the scene is not in rural Ireland, but in London's East End.

Kate started life in 1898, the child of a refugee single parent. When her mother made the decision to flee the pogroms in Vilna (then under Russian domination) she left behind a husband who, as a conscript in the Russian army, was unable to leave with her. Unable to speak a word of English, she arrived in London with two young children, pregnant with Kate, her third, to join the 120,000 other Russian and Polish Jews who, between 1870 and 1914 made the long journey to Britain in order to escape waves of savage anti-Semitic persecution (Frow 1996). The father who was to have followed them never did: and nothing more was ever heard of him. Possibly the young pregnant mother with her small children stayed in the Poor Jews' Temporary Shelter set up by the Jewish Board of Guardians which, between 1895 and 1914, provided two weeks' board and lodging to nearly all the newly-arrived refugees. In any case, Kate's mother made a living sewing, along with many of her neighbours, and the girls – particularly Kate, the youngest – were often kept at home from school to help make ends meet.

Abraham, later to become Kate's husband, was born in 1902, also of Jewish refugees. After his father died, he and his three brothers were sent to school in the Jewish orphanage, and unlike Kate, he became literate. The two of them met in one of the many workshops started by Jewish clothing manufacturers in Whitechapel, where he worked as tailor, she as seamstress. During their courtship Abraham wrote not one but several letters to Kate. It was not until after they married that Abraham discovered who had written the replies. It was not Kate, but her sister who wrote Kate's love letters. This is how their daughter Joyce told it to me:

I'll tell you another story. He didn't know that my mother was illiterate; because her sister used to write her love letters for her!

So they met, but in such a way that they'd exchange letters? So they weren't seeing each other every day? or he was separated from her?

I don't really know. He worked in the tailoring, so they worked in the same sweatshop. That's where they met. Now, whether he moved on, or whether there was a forced separation, I don't know. But there was letter writing. My father would have been a very romantic young man. He's a romantic old man! but he would have been a romantic young man – and possibly would have written even if he was working with her. He would have written to her: to my mother. And possibly, my mother would have felt obliged to return in the same way. So whether they were actually separated? It could have been.

So she got help from her sister?

Who wrote her letters. Not just help: her sister wrote her letters.

How do you know?

My father told me.

And how did he know?

He found out: when they were married, you see. I suppose she couldn't really hide the fact from him altogether. Also, being sisters, they lived in the same household: both were married with children – and there was great rivalry between those two. I've no doubt in one of the quarrels it came out. So he knew. He got to know, after they were married. He said it was a bit of a shock. (Interview, April 1996)

Kate and Abraham had three children. Joyce, the oldest, was born in 1926. The window of her sitting room where she and I were sitting (70 years later) looked out on a garden. The image of the young woman we both tried to imagine was overtaken by other images, of the same woman as her mother, bringing up her children with a fierce determination that none of them should have to grow up as she had done:

> No child of hers would ever have to scrub a front doorstep, as she had had to do. No child of hers would ever have to go into a sweatshop, as she had had to do. Her children were not going to be subjected to this way of life.

Kate never became literate: and, as far as Joyce could tell, she had never had a longing for literacy. We have no way of knowing how she felt about her sister writing her "love letters" for her, or whether she might have wished for the privacy of writing her own words for herself. One thing Joyce did know: Kate had certainly wanted the first literacy ambition of all: "She learned how to sign her name – very shakily. You know, like, you sometimes see very old people slowly and shakily write their name? That's how she'd write it. I watched her do it". But it was her sister who wrote her love letters.

These two stories were told me by literate daughters of illiterate mothers. Mary Ann is in her fifties; Joyce, in her seventies. Neither, as children, had found their mothers' illiteracy either shocking or strange: it was part of the life they lived. Other people, not the mother herself, could be relied on to deal with reading and writing when it was necessary. Both women, as children, learned to read and write, and grew up to enjoy literacy. For them, the stories of their mothers' courtship were known to include others who could act as the writers and readers of letters between sweethearts – the friend who could be relied on "not to squeal" and the girl who was able and willing to write "love letters" for her sister.

A literacy spectrum

In July 1996, six women sat with me in a room in Goldsmiths' College, London (where I then worked) and talked about their mothers. Rita, first, talked about her mother Hetty, born in 1898. Sylvia told us about her mother Sarah, born in 1885. Doris, next, spoke about Laura Elizabeth, born in 1896. Jean, then, talked about Peggy, born in 1886. Iris took her turn to tell of Grace, born in 1904. And finally, Dorothy told of her mother Violet, born in 1879. The women talking are active in their own education, for they are all members of a branch of the University of the Third Age, the voluntary organization set up in the 1980s to enable older people to design and run education courses to their own agenda. Our meeting had been arranged as a result of a discussion we had had eighteen months earlier, which I will briefly recap here.

On 8 March 1995, International Women's Day, I had been invited to give a talk to the Goldsmiths' College U3A branch about women and literacy. The talk I gave was about four themes: adult literacy education in the UK in the previous 25 years; the picture of adult literacy and illiteracy internationally, as revealed by statistics; the focus this had given to women, schooling and work; and, lastly, some examples of women learners growing into their possibilities as writers and readers. I spoke of how the campaigns by feminists worldwide had generated attention on the disparity between male and female illiteracy; and how it had only been in very recent years that this specific focus had been given published form (with writings from conferences and research work by Krystynia Chlebowska (1990), Fie van Dijk (1990), Jenny Horsman (1990), Lalita Ramdas (1990), Lalage Bown (1991), and Nelly Stromquist (1992) – all appearing within a couple of years). Unequal opportunities for schooling remained a major barrier to girls and women in countries of the South to achieving literacy. Meanwhile (I had continued) in the UK and other industrialized countries, while education at primary level may be longer established, the experience of adult literacy education suggested that many women remained limited in their confidence as readers and writers. The UK adult literacy campaign launched in the 1970s, I said, had been dominated at first by an idea about male illiteracy; in the 1980s, the push by many women in adult education for better crèche provision had enabled other women to take part in the classes that existed; and while women in the UK were (statistically) said to be no worse off than men in terms of their opportunities to develop and use their literacy, it remained a fact that many women were excluded from educational opportunities by reason of family and social pressures.

That is how I talked. The discussion that followed, that day in March, was one of the inspirations for this book. Some 30 women were there: all aged sixty and over. The questions at first were about the adult literacy work in this country. But right away I noticed they were not the usual questions from a "lay audience". Only one person asked the routine "How do they manage?" question, from an experience in which illiteracy was strange. Everyone else there was clearly familiar with the possibility of illiteracy. And within minutes, first one woman, then another, began to talk about their mothers. Not all recalled mothers who were illiterate. But many recalled mothers who had had little opportunity for education, and little time for reading and writing; and two spoke about their own mothers who had never learned to read or write.

A year later, the Nuffield Foundation approved a grant for me to carry out a study I called: "Literacy histories and futures: the role of mothers". The work of this book formally began in the autumn of 1996. But in truth it began that March day in 1995. For it was the first time in all the years I had worked in adult literacy

Speaker	Mother	Mother's d.o.b.
Rita	Hetty	1898
Sylvia	Sarah	1885
Doris	Laura Elizabeth	1896
Jean	Peggy	1886
Iris	Grace	1904
Dorothy	Violet	1879

Figure 5.1   Mothers recalled: July 1996

that I had been in the company of literate people who took the experience of parents' illiteracy as ordinary.

So when a group of the same women agreed to meet me again in July 1996 I knew there would be much for me to learn. During the two hours we spent together, it seemed as though I and the six of them were joined by six other women: born in another time, each different, all related to those speaking for them. Figure 5.1 provides a "map" of the speakers and the names and dates of birth of the mothers about whom they spoke.

Rita was the first to speak:

My own mother was born in 1898.

Would you tell us a bit about her? What's her name?

Hetty. She wasn't born in this country. She was born in Russia. Or Poland: she wasn't really quite sure, because it kept changing. I mean, you know . . . the borders kept changing. It actually was Russia, part of Russia.

I don't know too much about her, really, apart from the fact that, when I was aware of her, she was literate. She could read, she could write: she read newspapers, she wrote letters. But I don't know actually where she learned to do all that. She probably came over here when she was twelve. But she had enough English to be able to help other people who'd come over here with no English – to help them with their shopping. She taught them the money over here. And she would take them out the East End of London and orientate them.

But when you're, what, five or six, and your mother can read and write, you don't [know] all the questions I would like to ask, it's too late to ask her now, where she learned all those things.

Was she one of many children?

I don't really know. Probably five or six, I think. Some who may have been born in this country. And then, of course, with the interruption of the war, when I was nine years old, I went to Norfolk, and it was expected that I got letters from my parents, and it was my mother who would do all the writing.

What year were you born, Rita?

1930. My brothers and sisters were born in the twenties. All sorts of questions I would like to ask her, but it's like a lot of things: you only think of them afterwards, don't you?

Say that bit again, about the war and her writing?

Well, she would write us letters, when we were away: we would write to her. There was an expectation on our part that she was able to do all these things. But I don't think she read for pleasure, because I think bringing up three children in the thirties, most of her time was spent in domestic chores. She used to go to the theatre; she used to love going to the theatre. There wasn't a great deal of money around. But I don't remember actually seeing her read a book not for pleasure. You read the newspaper for information. You listened to the wireless. She listened to the wireless.

She wrote you letters. When you were evacuated.

Oh yes. She used to say, "My handwriting is bad". But it wasn't bad at all, it was perfectly legible. She said that when she was in her late eighties, "My handwriting's bad", but it hadn't changed from when she was young. "That's my arthritis", she would say; but her handwriting was perfectly all right, and it was very legible.

Sarah, Sylvia's mother, was also an emigrant from eastern Europe. At the age of nine (in 1894), Sarah was sewing clothes for her many stepsisters and brothers; at twelve, her mother died; at fourteen, she travelled with her family to the East End of London and "went straight into the rag trade". The language Sarah grew up with and with which she brought up her own children was Yiddish. All her five children learned to read and write in English; neither Sarah nor her husband were literate in any language.

She was born in 1885. Her father had been married three times; but the first two wives had died. And so her mother had a very large family. Her own mother died when she was twelve. They were living in Poland, and they were persecuted by the military. So they didn't go to school . . .
   She couldn't read or write. She never learned to read or write. But she spoke quite good English. Although at home, because my father spoke very

poor English, they spoke Yiddish all the time. So we didn't hear English, really, until we went to school.

She was very keen for us to learn. She was very encouraging. She wouldn't allow any of us to go into the sweat shops, which were the usual place for school leavers to go into. She was very adamant that we shouldn't do that.

She was wanting more for you?

Yes. Very much.

Did anybody take a newspaper in your house?

I was the youngest of five. And my two brothers and one sister always brought in newspapers. They started going to the library at a very early age. Course, we didn't have any books at home at all. My mother and father couldn't read or write. And I suppose I followed the tradition of going to the library.

Doris's mother was called Laura Elizabeth. Born in 1896, Doris told us, "she had meticulous handwriting . . . very clear, and joined up; spelling, perfect". But Laura disliked books, and disliked her children reading them.

She was born in 1896; and she had meticulous handwriting. They certainly taught them how to write. Very clear, and joined up; spelling, perfect. But she never read anything. She despised it; my dad was a bit bookish, and unionist, and socialist; and I got a place at a grammar school. And if we sat down at a crossword, she thought, "Oh you *two*! wearing your heads out, doing crosswords". She could speak well, and grammatically. She could write beautifully; and she could read. But she never read a book . . . She wasn't interested in books; yet she was highly articulate.

I think you said, she wasn't only not interested, she wasn't very pleased that you –

She was hostile, almost. My father used to go to auction to bring home sets of Shakespeare. He wrote off to the *Daily Herald* for a complete set of Dickens. I said, "Whatever you do, mum, don't throw away Dad's books, they're quite valuable". She had no time for them.

What did she say about it, do you remember? about book reading?

Well, she thought girls reading – she'd say, "Come and dry up!" And I'd say, "Why can't he dry up?" My brother. And she'd say, "Always got your nose stuck in a book".

Interjection by Rita: *Brothers never dried up.*

And she used to think I was awful! I remember when I was seven. I said, "Come along", I said (to my mother), "We're going to the public library to join". Because you couldn't join before you were eight. There was no children's department. And I took her along – she was a bit fed up about it, really. It would be more books, wouldn't it?

Do you think she thought they were messy? or got in the way of the –

No, it was – it withdrew you. If you were reading a book, you weren't listening to her claptrap; because, like me, she could go on for ever. Talking. And it was nothing.

"Brothers never dry up": Doris had struck a chord:

Sylvia: My brothers were never asked to do anything in the house. They used to read excessively. But if my sisters were reading, she'd say there was something for them to do. She encouraged all of us; but the daughters would be expected to do the household chores.

Jean: It was a threat, in some way. Reading books. I don't know –

Rita: I don't think that was a literacy thing. I think that was the social climate of the time. Boys didn't help. They just ate the food you prepared. And they walked away from the table.

Iris: Because they were going to mature and have families and go out to look after the families, and be the wage earners. So really your mother asking you to make the beds or wash up, was: "Well, you've got to learn to do it someday, my girls, so you might as well start now". It was almost like domestic science, perpetually every day. In the home.

For Doris, because reading was something she enjoyed doing, the double standard felt a double irritant.

*Doris, what made **you** want to read?*

Oh, I *always* wanted to read. I don't know.

Do you think it was something about losing yourself, too? The very thing that your mother didn't want you to do?

She used to read magazines. *Peg's Paper* and *Home Notes*: all those things.

Rita's mother, Hetty, could both read and write – "she read newspapers" (for information), she wrote letters (with an "expectation" from her children that she would do so). Sylvia's mother, Sarah, who never learned to read or write, was "encouraging" to her children's learning. Doris's mother (with the "meticulous" handwriting and "perfect" spelling) never read anything and was "hostile" to her daughters' reading.

Jean knew that her mother, Peggy, read romantic fiction (Ethel M. Dell and Warwick Deeping, as examples) but never witnessed her doing so: ("I can't recall her actually sitting reading"). Like Sarah and Hetty, Peggy was recalled as some-one who had had a hard life, and always wanted her children to have a better one. Dorothy's mother, Violet (born in 1879) had a happy childhood in Kent as the adoptive child of parents who kept a newsagent shop, and later went into service. Dorothy remembered her with affection. Violet had four children (three sons and Dorothy); and in later life wrote regular letters to her daughters-in-law (expecting replies by return of post: "She got ever so wild if she didn't get letters back!" Dorothy recalled).

Iris spoke of her mother Grace, as an "avid reader". The expression was uttered (and repeated) with certainty:

> She was, yes, she was literate. In fact, at home, I wish I'd brought it today – I've got a book, where she won a prize, for English, English essays: from her junior school. She was an avid reader. She loved reading . . . Novels, maga-zines, anything. *She was an avid reader.* She used to read a lot. Yes. Irrespective of what the paper or the content . . . she lost herself. Monday was wash day. She'd do all the washing. We came home from school and had cold beef and mashed potatoes. But in the afternoon, she'd sit down, make herself a cup of tea – it wasn't a case of, like Doris' mother, "Oh, you've got your nose in a book": it was a case of "Mother? oh, she's got her nose in a book again". It was the mother, yes! (my emphasis)

The "Great Divide" view of literacy (touched on in Chapter 2) would place these women, and their mothers, in one of two camps: either they could read and write, or they could not. Instead, as this discussion reminds us, reality is something much more subtle and interesting. The women portrayed represented a spectrum of literacy lives. Between us, we saw not only differences in what women did with their reading and writing, but also in what attitudes they had to that of their sons and daughters (a theme to which we return in the next chapter).

Like Kate (Joyce's mother), Sarah did not speak English as a first language. In order to be literate in English she first needed to be fluent in English. Denied literacy in her first language, literacy in her second could only come hard. Today she would be a candidate for an ESOL class (English for Speakers of Other Languages). Both women were illiterate mothers of literate daughters. Other mothers, with English as a first language, were also illiterate in English, and also raised literate children. In the end, research is about discovering the questions as much as revealing answers. And this conversation with the group of six women in South London helped me realize I needed a new one. Instead of asking: what is the meaning of literacy? Or how do illiterate mothers successfully raise literate children? I now wanted to ask: What is illiteracy, anyway? Does it exist?

Illiteracy: silhouettes and questions

The directive I wrote to correspondents for the Mass Observation Archive (reproduced in full in the Appendix) had begun with a couple of provocative statements. Re-reading it now, I am momentarily alarmed at the exaggerated claim it contained: "A generation of women in the early years of this century had had little if any schooling as children. As adults, many therefore had little or no literacy in English".

This is a sweeping generalization indeed; and on reflection, it is surprising there was not a stronger reaction to it from the correspondents who read it. "A generation" is a lot of people; and the stickler for evidence in me recoils at such an unsubstantiated assertion: a thing which, as Brigid Ballard and John Clanchy observed, is one of the punishable crimes of academic writing (Ballard & Clanchy 1988). However, my purpose in writing it at the time – one which I still stand by – was to set up a framework within which it would be possible to write freely and without inhibition about mothers or grandmothers known to have been illiterate.

I had done this because it seems to me there is a need to see beyond the simplistic stereotypes of illiteracy – not least because, in a literate society, the experience of being illiterate can often indeed be associated with shame and embarrassment. Some years ago, Mary Wolfe and I carried out a search for positive images of illiterates as people who were powerful and wise. We chose to look at fictional representations within our own culture – broadly understood to be British/American – in the media of film and novels. We thought, and still think, that the seemingly separate categories of fictional or documentary representations of illiteracy in fact inform each other and have a mutual influence on the way in which the experience of being illiterate is depicted.

What we found was depressing. There seemed to be three ways in which the illiterate men or women were portrayed, as:

- dumb animal;
- prisoner (usually criminalized); and/or as
- outsider. (Mace & Wolfe 1995)

Put in other terms, illiteracy has become a condition which, in Jennifer Horsman's words, has become couched in the "discourse of 'the other'; it is considered to create 'foreignness' . . . [which] helps to create an image of an 'outsider', unable to function in this society" (Horsman 1990: 138).

From the experience as an adult literacy worker in the 1970s and 1980s, it is clear how much this discourse was evident in media coverage. To judge from Rosie Wickert's example from an Australian newspaper report, the language of melodrama is still alive and well in the 1990s; the woman described:

> was *crippled* by illiteracy, *reduced to silent isolation* by her sense of shame and humiliation . . . Yvonne Simmons has escaped the *prison of illiteracy* but there are a staggering 1.1 million adults still *trapped inside its invisible walls*. (Wickert 1993: 31) (my emphasis)

Such images, which have for years reinforced ideas of failure and inadequacy on the part of the "illiterate", also dominated the thinking of those who chose to enrol as adult literacy learners. (More usually, this was known as "coming forward to seek help" with their reading and writing.) In initial interviews, the common phrases would come out: "I'm a bit backward, I know"; "I've always been a bit thick when it came to spelling"; "I'm probably too slow for this class"; "I've always felt bad about it". In writing published by adult literacy programmes, the sense of regret and retreat would recur whenever the writer chose to write about their literacy:

> I am a very ordinary person, and I must dress ordinary. I cannot wear a coat that has fur on it. I would feel like everyone is looking at me. I used to say that it is people who can read and write should wear those things. For if you dress up and go out in the street and someone asks you to read something for them and you can't, then that is where I would feel funny. (Minto 1979)

"I have reading and writing difficulties" is the title of a paper given to an international conference on literacy, in Sweden. Its author, Eva Karlstrom, wrote: "I left school without the ability to read and write properly . . . For eight long years nobody talked to me about my difficulties. The only thing I understood was that I was unintelligent, nothing but stupid" (Ericsson 1991: 131).

While their teachers avoid the term "illiterate", adult students of literacy all too often claim the word for themselves, marked by a sense of exclusion from a majority population perceived to be not only more literate, but more clever than they are. In an adult literacy programme in Georgia, for example, a woman called Janis is reported as insisting on using the word illiterate for herself, despite the "well-intentioned objections" of her tutor. Her fear as a self-defined "illiterate" was that her daughter would become like her:

> And that hurt me so bad when her teacher talks to me about her. Sometimes I want to cry but I say to myself I can't cry and let the teacher see me act like this . . . My heart drops in sorrow because I know that I am not smart. (Nurss & Ketchum 1995: 38–39)

It was, then, from that context – a *discourse context*, I suppose, rather than a statistically valid context – that I wrote my invitation to Mass Observation writers. For a very few, indeed, this was too much to ask. Three in particular reacted against my generalizations; two, with polite bewilderment at my ignorance; a third, with disgust and outrage:

> The response to this question has been most interesting and it has aroused strong feelings in the people I have spoken to about it. The general feeling is that the setter of this question has her facts wrong and must be thinking of the previous century! . . . My mother is sure that the parents of all the children she went to school with could read and write. (R1025)

> I have read this over and over. I really don't want to be rude but I question this statement whole-heartedly. (B1120)

> I disagree completely with the preamble, and think that JANE MACE is writing absolute nonsense . . . I made it my business to consult those of my friends, classmates (WEA) and relations of the appropriate age, and they all agreed . . . that, as today, there may well have been the odd "thick" child who was illiterate, but not their foremother, certainly not a generation . . . I am certain that JANE MACE is most comprehensively misguided, and I beg of her to reconsider her current headlong descent into the blindest of alleys. (F2693)

Fortunately, the last writer proved wrong. This was no blind alley. My invitation to imagine and remember the possibility of mothers who either did not or could not read or write released many other kinds of reflection. Some simply did not know, for sure, whether the woman they were considering was or was not literate. A woman born in 1889, for example, the mother of six children whom she brought up in a two-bedroom terraced house in Liverpool ("without electricity, no bathroom, no hot water on tap, no indoor lavatory") is introduced with these words:

> I do not think my mother had time to read or write anything.

The writer went on:

> My lasting impression of my mother who died when I was fifteen years old was of a kindly, meek, quiet lady, who would not say boo to a goose but lived in fear of offending my father . . . As she died at an early age . . . she must have been worn out looking after her family. I think she loved all of us but I am also sure that she was not very bright or clever enough to be more than just a good mother. Being the nice inoffensive person she was, she would

Name	d.o.b.	Details	M/O ref
Anne	1870	One of 9 children, brought up in "tiny mid-Wales village"; no schooling; Welsh first language	P2759
"Kathleen"	1864	Family of itinerant charcoal burners; never went to school	R1418
"Margaret"	1870s	Did not go to school but, at age of 12, was taught the 3 Rs by the "lady of the house" where she worked in domestic service	L318
"Rachel"	1868	Refugee from Russia; spoke no English, could sign name	K1380

Figure 5.2　"Silhouettes" from Mass Observation

even forgive me for daring to suggest that she might have been illiterate. (T2459)

This is gentle writing, with no sense of horror at the possibility of a mother's illiteracy. As for his own literacy education, the writer refers to the encouragement of his older sisters, who introduced him to the public library. There is no sense of the mother being regarded then or later as strange or "foreign" for possibly being illiterate.

Others wrote about women who were known to be illiterate; and while they did not all provide what Mary Wolfe and I had been looking for (namely, portraits of people who were powerful and wise) none resorted to the narrow limits of dumb animal, prisoner or outsider. In the next few pages are portrayed four such women. More silhouettes than full portraits, three describe women without any literacy at all; one is of a woman who gained basic literacy without benefit of schooling. All were born in the 1860s and 1870s. Figure 5.2 provides an introduction to them.

Recent research has shown that people who do not happen to be good at reading and writing may often have well-developed routines for dealing with literacy. This suggests that the shame of illiteracy is even today not necessarily felt by all illiterates in a literate society. Arlene Fingeret's study in America (Fingeret 1983) and David Barton and Sarah Padmore's research in England (Barton & Padmore 1991) both showed that networks of friends, neighbours and relatives exist to provide a give-and-take support when it comes to reading or writing letters or other documents. From a year's research with 43 adults who were unable to read or write at basic levels in a northeastern American urban setting, Fingeret argued that only a minority of these could be called "dependent". What she found, instead, was a careful choice of people on whom they might call when literacy tasks had to be undertaken, for whom, in return, it was assumed they

---

Box 5.1 Anne

My mother-in-law's mother, Anne, was born in a tiny mid-Wales village in 1870 and lived in good health up to her death 82 years later in 1952 in a south Wales valley town. She was brought up in the small and remote village of Bont, "emigrating" South, as so many of the people of Wales did during the late 19th and early 20th century, when she was in her early twenties.

Anne was one of nine children, with her twin brother the second oldest. Extraordinarily there were two other sets of twins among her brothers and sisters.

Not untypically the family were almost entirely Welsh speaking and although she was able to speak English it was not her first language and it was clear that she was not comfortable using the language. It is remembered that she had a very heavy accent when she spoke English and could be difficult to understand. The family was poor. By her early teens her father had died and her mother relied on parish relief to survive.

Anne did not attend school but did learn to read to some level in Welsh. There is no memory of her being able to read in English or ever writing in either language. It is thought that her brothers did go to school and gained a level of literacy in both languages.

In the early years of the century Anne had three boys and two girls, two of whom (one boy and one girl) died in infancy. The remaining children attended school, indeed the oldest child, a boy, completed school and went on to university where he gained a degree. My mother-in-law initially attended school until she was 14 years old in 1920, then she went into service. However, her older brother insisted that she returned to school to complete her education.

Anne was quite involved in the local community and was an active member of the early Labour Party in south Wales. The fact that she did not write in English or Welsh or read English at that time appears to have presented no particular social difficulties in pre-war Welsh local communities. Quite clearly, however, Anne recognized the importance of her children being able to use English as Welsh society was increasingly transformed and anglicized.

Talking to my mother-in-law it is clear that Anne was a strong, and what we would now call assertive, woman. She exhibited no embarrassment about her own lack of formal education, or indeed considered she had been denied any alternative life because of it. She appeared, rather, to be determined that her children took the advantages of education that became gradually available in the early part of the century.

Box 5.2 "Kathleen"

My grandmother, born 1864, never went to school and had no formal education at all. Grandfather, born 1861, was able to read and write. His education, though, was not entirely free. For some years after the implementation of the 1870 Education Act, parents were expected to pay a school fee of up to sixpence per week according to the age of the pupil, proceeds of which went towards paying the Master's salary. These same parents, from a deprived working-class background in an era of universal poverty, were also expected to pay for their children's books. By September 1891 school fees had been reduced to a flat rate of one penny and all books and other materials free of charge. Even so, as the Master's log for 1874 at our elementary school makes clear: "Several pupils are very irregular in the payment of their fees, although it is only a penny. It is as much trouble to get a penny as it was sixpence . . ."

Grandmother must have been very self-conscious about her inability to read. I can remember as a child going to the house and seeing a newspaper there and books on a shelf and sometimes she would put on tiny glasses and pick up the paper or open one of the books. I never knew at the time that she could not make anything of what she held. It was likely that grandfather would read aloud to her when they were alone.

I used to love going to grandma's house and seeing all the shining brass on the mantel piece, the copper kettle, the cast-iron ornaments on the hearth with its gleaming black-leaded grate, the polished floor and bright rugs, the beautiful vases and pictures, and I would be in awe of the orderliness so lacking in my own home.

It was not until after she died I knew of her disadvantage. All I know of her earlier years is that she had one sister and a brother, and because of their life style I have no doubt that they too grew up without any schooling. And it was later still I learnt she belonged to a family of itinerant charcoal burners and were never settled long in one place. English was her first language, of course, but I think she had at least one more, because of her gipsy roots.

---

would return other kinds of support or services. Such a woman was Diane, of whom her friend said:

> She listens and helps you figure out your problems. No matter how hard it gets, you know you can come here and have a friend, get some ideas, some help, so you can face it . . . sometimes I read the mail for her, or her daughter brings the paper and we sit and read it together, talk about what's going on. We don't none of us have much, but we help each other, what we can. (Fingeret 1983: 139)

Box 5.3 "Margaret"

My mother was born in 1894, had six sisters and one brother, and another brother who died in infancy. Her father was a farm labourer but early in his life served for 12 years in the army; her mother ("Margaret") was in domestic service before her marriage and although she had a large family she continued to work in the domestic field when and as long as she was able.

My grandfather could neither read nor write other than sign his name, but I thought always fairly good at arithmetic as he could always keep track and count his money. ["Margaret"] did not go to school and at the age of 12 was put into service in a large farm house. There were several servants and the lady of the house was a believer that they should all be able to read and write and as she was an educated person taught them the three Rs, so my grandmother was able to read to my grandfather.

Many years ago there was a daily newspaper named the *Daily Graphic*. It had more photographs of daily events than any other paper by far. They purchased this paper daily price 1½d (pre-decimal). Grandfather looked and studied all the pictures then grandmother would read out the captions to him and I thought that a very good arrangement. They never owned a radio although they were readily available, TV was not on the go at the time, they lived in a very old cottage without running water or electricity and the toilet was at the end of a large garden some 200 yards from the house.

Box 5.4 "Rachel"

My maternal grandmother was born in Russia in approx. 1868, arriving in England as a pogrom refugee in 1898. She came from a small country village where she received the most basic of education. Her principal ability was to do simple adding and subtraction, and almost daily reading of the Bible. She spoke no English and was almost unable to write, apart from signing her name. She married my maternal grandfather, a skilled cabinet maker, in 1899 and produced five children, three boys and two girls, the first of the two girls (my mother) seeing the light of day in 1900. Until my grandmother's death in 1931 she remained in her original home, her whole life spent in rearing her children, unpicking knotted string for a living, scrimping and saving to clothe her flock by taking in washing and ironing. Until her dying day she was never able to speak English, her tongue was classic Yiddish mixed with Russian. All her children received their education in elementary schools in the East End of London.

Similarly, Barton & Padmore found, from their study in Lancaster, that people took different roles for different literacy activity and illiterate and literate operated reciprocal networks of support, exchanging assistance in reading and writing with other kinds of help. As they point out:

> Because these networks exist, problems do not arise . . . Often it was when these networks were disrupted that people were confronted with problems, and this was sometimes given as a reason for basic education classes. (Barton & Padmore 1991: 70)

There have been many social science studies of networks of support among poor communities. In the effort by the habitually literate to imagine illiteracy, such a concept is useful: it allows for the possibility that to be illiterate might be ordinary. It helps us imagine its unimportance; for what it also does is alter the idea of literacy as merely an individual and solitary activity. In so doing, we begin to see ideas about the meaning of "family literacy", to which we will move in the next chapter, in a different light.

The following are four examples of what I mean, silhouettes again from Mass Observation writing. Reading them, we may be tantalized with what is left out; these are people for whom illiteracy and literacy were co-habitants, and whose own perceptions of this can only be imagined. Each extract is followed by the questions they raised for me. In the absence of an evidence which gives us the answers, they are here as an invitation to you, too, to *speculate* as to the possibilities.

The first shows a woman who left family correspondence to her husband, having other things she clearly did to support him (such as cook his meals):

> Grandma "Minnie" lived in a Devon village. At about 12 she was put on a tram to go as a servant to a London family . . . She could not read/write well, but had other skills she could teach . . . She could not read a recipe, her "head" was her book . . . and . . . relied on her husband for any "letters". (B86)

How did Minnie keep contact with her family of origin in Devon once she started work in London? What did she feel, later, about her husband reading and writing letters?

In the second, an "avid reading" mother is partner to a non-reading father. While recalled as "sadly called illiterate", he was also accorded the respect of being a hard worker and clever at mental arithmetic. The correspondent, a woman now in her eighties, recalled:

> My father was a hard worker and did manual work, but I can remember how quickly he could add up figures almost on his head! Yet sadly he was called illiterate! He could not read or write and today they would have said he was dyslexic . . .

My mother herself was an avid reader, and I quickly followed in her footsteps. One of the first books I read was Charlotte Brontë's *Jane Eyre*, my favourite book even to this day. I have just bought a copy. (B36)

Who was it who called this man illiterate? What did he make of his wife's pleasure in reading?

In a third extract (from a text written by a woman now in her sixties) we are shown children teaching literacy to a mother:

My maternal grandmother married when she was about 21, gave birth to ten children of whom seven survived infancy, and died at the age of 44, from meningitis I believe.

She herself was one of the elder daughters of 18 children and despite the 1870 Act was not able to attend school much as she was kept at home to help her mother with her large brood . . .

My mother told me that she and her sisters taught their mother how to write her name. (B89)

When did they do this? Were the daughters still young girls? Or adult women? Why did they do it? How?

Finally, we meet, in the same person, a considerable capacity for reading and a near-illiteracy in writing. The extract contains a family tableau: while the woman sits carefully writing her name, her family stand round her, "holding their breaths". R446 portrays her grandmother as someone who "was still reading library books into her eighties"; yet:

Although she was a great reader, her writing skills were almost non-existent. I always took this for granted but can clearly remember how, whenever she had to sign her name, anyone who was around was called in to assist and the only picture in my mind that I have of her writing is of her surrounded by a small crowd holding their breaths.

Were they there to give her moral support? or to marvel?

All of these questions are unanswerable: but each of the extracts invites us to puzzle and imagine. All four come from texts which show households with few material resources. Each one is a working-class experience, written by literate descendants, without astonishment. The U3A group that afternoon in London, similarly, had found no surprise in recalling both the "avidly reading" Grace and the illiterate Sarah as among their mothers. In these extracts from Mass Observation writers, I found a similar spectrum of literacy ability, set within a set of social relationships with others.

113

Only in one Mass Observation report did I find any suggestion that, at the time, there may have been any shame associated with illiteracy. The story is of a marriage between someone who today would be called a literacy tutor and her student. According to the writer, the romance between them caused such horror in the woman's family that they never spoke to her again. What seems to be implied here is the shame, not so much of the young man being illiterate, as of him being from the "lower classes". The parents regarded him as a social inferior to their daughter:

> My grandmother was born in 1876 and her family were quite prosperous. She was therefore very well educated and able to read and write. At the age of 19 she became interested in teaching "the lower classes" to read and write. This was done through the church at evening classes. Here she met a young man and fell in love. He could neither read or write and he worked on the railways. Her family were distraught and threatened to disinherit her if she insisted on marrying him. In the year 1897 at the age of 21 they were married at church in Plaistow [East London]. Her family never spoke to her again! (H260)

There is one other tale of illiteracy which evidently intrigued the writer. Her grandmother, she recalls, was born in 1874 of "extremely poor" family, first living in Lancashire and later moving to Manchester. When this woman married in 1896, she signed her name on the marriage register. A year later, she registered her mother's death. This time, she gave her name with the X of an illiterate. The granddaughter (now aged 49) writes this:

> Either
>
> 1. She hadn't learned to write her married name
> 2. She was too shocked and upset to write
> 3. She did not want to put her name to what was on the death certificate (it was not all correct information).
>
> When I told my mum (her daughter, b. 1916) that her mum possibly couldn't write, she had no comment, i.e. she did not know that she couldn't write but she could not say that she had ever seen her write (letters, shopping lists, etc.) so there was no proof either way. I think that writing was not very relevant to her life. Her work was always as a cleaner or a servant and after her second marriage her husband could deal with any paperwork. (J931)

Within a spectrum of literacy–illiteracy, ranging from one extreme of complete absence of literacy to the other, of total dependency, even addiction to it, there are many other gradations of experience. Of all the vignettes and glimpses offered by Mass Observation writers, one in particular is my favourite. It is an image of two people who, while literate, did not enjoy literacy: a mother who (according to the writer) read "laboriously – seldom for pleasure" and a father for whom "reading and writing always seemed difficult". This is how the writer recalls them reading the newspaper: "My father frowned at the business pages – my mother 'read the pictures'." (G1374)

What recurred throughout the reports, as I suggested in Chapter 2, was the simple *lack of time* for mothers, literate or not, to find pleasure in literacy. To this, at least one family offered a solution. The story is of the writer's grandmother. Evidently born (in 1883) into a middle-class family, the girl had done well in school. However at the age of 17 she had had to stay at home to "mind" her alcoholic mother. Once married, she had six children, whom she had to bring up in "dire financial straits" after her husband's discharge from the army on medical grounds. Her granddaughter writes:

> My grandmother worked extremely hard making ends meet . . . Thus I gather she had little time for reading. However, my grandfather and the older daughters spent many hours reading to her while she ironed or sewed. (T2003)

Reflections

What adult literacy learners said or wrote about illiteracy when they joined adult literacy programmes in the 1970s and 1980s revealed insights into the experience of being, or being seen to be, illiterate in a literate culture. They spoke of shame and embarrassment, of humiliation and frustration. And adult literacy educators like me learned to listen with a different ear and to devise ways and means for others to listen, too. For a long time it was assumed that all illiterates – all those who could not read and write in adult life for the purposes and in the ways that they wanted to – must feel like this. It was Mary Hamilton's work in the mid-1980s that suggested another possibility. Studies of adult literacy until then, as she pointed out, had concentrated on those who had come forward for tuition. This included my own book, based on interviews with adult literacy students. Hamilton's point is this:

> Such studies can be very misleading. They have typically reported on small groups of adults who do not represent the full range of adult students. In addition, there is no guarantee that those who come forward for tuition are representative of those who do not. (Hamilton 1987: 7)

In this chapter we have been hearing about women for whom such "tuition" did not exist. They were living in a period when a national "campaign" for adult literacy education was several decades in the future. If they felt ashamed, isolated or frustrated, we do not know. The speculative among their biographers tried to allow for the possibility, but could not find any evidence either way. The story of the grandmother who gave her name one year on a document as a signature and the following year with a mark is mysterious. But signatures themselves *are* a mystery. To assess adult literacy levels in the last century, they were the single measure used by historians, who based their data on the ability to sign the marriage register. On this basis, the census of 1851 placed the literacy rate for England at 69.3 per cent for males and 54.9 per cent for females; by 1900, on this measure, it was 97.2 per cent and 96.8 per cent, respectively. As the historian of literacy, Richard Altick, put it, these figures are "very unsatisfactory evidence of how many people were able to read", and other evidence (such as school attendance statistics, and house-to-house surveys) suggested that signature literacy (or what David Vincent calls "nominal literacy") was very far indeed from full literacy (Altick 1983: 170–72).

Literate observers had their own opinions as to the reasons for which some people might have made a mark when they could have signed. Altick cites one Victorian commentator who was concerned to explain away the high number of marks in marriage registers. In the 1867 *Journal of the Statistical Society* one W.I. Sargant evidently suggested that some brides and grooms, though fully able to sign their names, were so nervous that they preferred to scrawl a cross instead; or that when a literate man took an illiterate bride, "he chivalrously wrote his X instead of his name to save her embarrassment" (Altick 1983: 170).

"Embarrassment", like "shame", is a frequently used word in any discussion about illiterate people in English-speaking literate societies. In attributing it to the "illiterate bride" W.I. Sargant had only his own sentimental views of young love, or of young men's vanity, to go on. From the "illiterate bride" as from the illiterate women bringing up children 40 or 50 years later, however, we have only silence. A total of 12 such women have been discussed in this chapter: Joan's mother Eliza, in Sheffield; Mary Anne's mother Kathleen, in Ireland; Joyce's mother Kate and Sylvia's mother Sarah, in East London. We have also met Anne, in Wales, "Kathleen", from an itinerant family; "Margaret" who learned the three Rs in service; and "Rachel", who spoke no English; we have also glimpsed the grandmothers of B86, B36, B89 and R446.

Such writing as we have today about firsthand experiences of illiteracy often bears witness to pain and exclusion. Janis, who, with her tutor, wrote so eloquently in this vein, was a student in an adult literacy programme who went on to gain confidence and fluency in her writing. The understanding we have of present-day experiences of illiteracy depends on sources like her, who are by definition a specific population: people who have chosen to seek out education for themselves. The habitually literate who do not happen to live together with or near to those who cannot read or write with ease must rely on their imaginations to conceive of living with different spectacles on. Meanwhile, in the search for powerful and wise portraits of illiterate mothers, the writings of Mass Observers and the interviews with daughters offered some additional questions to consider. In the next chapter, we will see how the fear of illiterate mothers has taken shape in the form of educational policy.

Chapter 6

Family is more than mum and literacy is more than school

> It was very difficult to get accounts of the literacy work that women do in maintaining their home and families. They don't notice it; literacy is another piece of the invisibility of women's work. (Rockhill 1993: 167)

"Family" and "literacy" are two words with many meanings. In the language of educational policy, they have been joined together as one phrase, intended to represent a solution to perceived crises in standards of reading and writing. This chapter gathers together four clusters of debate around the two words. From consideration of these, we will move on to see how the experience of mothers in the past may give inspiration to the literacy interests of mothers in the present.

The first cluster circles around a negative association between mothers and the literacy of their children. It seems useful to begin with the dark side of rhetoric, even though the intentions behind the policies that it expresses have included liberatory ideas, too. The association is one of blame and of deficit, internalized sometimes by mothers themselves as well as articulated by implication in public discourse.

From this we will consider the way in which research data purporting to show the effect of mothers' education on their children's success at school has been used to signal the launch of a national initiative in family literacy education in the UK. In this section we will notice how this initiative, apparently intended for "the family" actually focused attention exclusively on the mother and the young child.

The results of the initiative (and the funding it provided) included a wide array of varied activity, developed often with imagination and creativity. Its effect, however, as its commentators have observed, has been to shift the meaning of "family literacy" itself – from the reading and writing life within families, to an educational programme. This shift in meaning is the subject of the third cluster of ideas we will consider.

Fourthly, we return to mothers: and notice how the language of rhetoric has elided the word "parents" with mothers, rather than fathers. Here, we will also consider how the idea of mothers with time for their children is an idea premised on class assumptions about *time*. The encouragement to both parents to have anything to do with the schooling of their children is a recent one. Two examples

Time-sharing.

from the interviews for this book illustrate how distant (to the mother) a school may have appeared.

Where do these issues take us? In the second half of the chapter, I offer first, a reminder of the extent to which mothers have been excluded from their own literacy. History, as Alice Walker, Tillie Olsen, and Virginia Woolf each bear witness, suggests centuries of a kind of silencing of women's creative capacities as writers. In contrast to this, we will then consider how the movement of community publishing, originating in the early 1970s, has opened up for mothers in settings of adult literacy and family literacy education new ways of telling old stories; and in so doing, offered another dimension to the meanings of "family literacy" – illustrated by the story of a "mothers' writing group" who chose to use their own literacy education to research that of their mothers.

Blame and deficit

Mothers are convenient scapegoats for our children's failures, if not the ills of society. We are only too vulnerable to the charge that any difference between our child and an assumed "norm" is our fault. Despite all kinds of evidence to the contrary, if our child learns to crawl, talk, or read later than any other child we are quick to believe that it must be something that *we* are doing wrong. If our child seems less clever, less quick, less successful than other children, it must be *our* failure. If they sniff glue, bunk off school, or steal, the cause of their wickedness lies in *us*.

Part of my research interest has been to explore how adult children perceive this view of their own mothers. Looking back as people now in their seventies and eighties, many writers and interviewees have been at pains to portray "good" mothers – and edit out the imperfect person of whom they may have felt less forgiving as children. However, as we saw in Chapter 3, this happy state of affairs is not true for all: some children, looking back on their mothers, found them to have been difficult or deficient in some crucial respect. For this, the passing of the years does not always make it easier to forgive.

Over 20 years I have read and collected the writing of many adult literacy students, from the UK and many other countries. In all this writing I have found only one example of an adult child who assigns blame to her or his mother for their own literacy difficulties; and even this is blame attached at one remove, as it were. The piece, which is published in Canada, begins like this: "This story is about my mother not having an education and her mother is to blame". As the author (Yvette Gonzales) goes on to relate, her mother's education ended at the age of five when her father died. The person who made this decision – and (Yvette assumes) thereby caused her mother's consequent illiteracy – was her mother (her own grandmother).

Yvette sent her mother a Mother's Day card and rings her up to tell her she has posted it. In a phone conversation which follows this, her mother says: "Yvette, you know I can't read because of mama Olga, I does feel so ashamed." In reply, her daughter told her: "Mommy, it's not your fault that you can't read. It's your mom's. She took it away from you by not sending you to school while your other brothers and sisters attended and learned to read and write" (Gonzales 1991: 96).

121

Mother's Day card, 1990s: "Happy Mother's Day, Mum! I'll always love you . . . but I'll never forgive you for cleaning my face with spit on a hanky!"

I find this piece striking. Yvette Gonzales is an adult student of literacy. Yet in this piece she says nothing about her own quest for learning; and makes no suggestion that her mother's illiteracy may have had any part to play in her own difficulties with reading and writing. The mother who is blamed here (the grand-mother) is being charged, not with failing to be able to read and write herself, but with failing to send her daughter to school. Yvette Gonzales' purpose seems to be both to free her mother of the sense of shame she feels about her illiteracy and at the same time – in making an accusation of neglect to her grandmother – to issue a warning to other mothers: "Don't let what happened to my mom happen to your child by stealing their education" (Gonzales 1991: 96).

Although the charge is not a mother's illiteracy, the target of her accusation is still the mother. The blame for the daughter's lack of schooling is laid, not at the economic conditions of society in which her grandmother raised her family, not at the society of the time that assumed the daughter might as well remain outside the school system, not at her mother's father, but at her mother.

As some of the accounts in earlier chapters suggest, illiterate mothers are part and parcel of the social history of families of the literate, as well as the illiterate. Yvette Gonzales was herself the daughter of an illiterate mother; she is also (as an adult education student of literacy) clearly a very active member of a literate culture. Yet this same culture suggests that this is unusual, if not impossible; that mothers with "low literacy skills" do not have children who are literate; and that illiterate mothers are dysfunctional mothers. Voiced publicly, this suggestion is most usually made obliquely, with an air of benevolence. Here, for example, is the *Reader's Digest* (a publication with a considerably larger readership than that in which Yvonne Gonzales' piece appears). The story is of the discovery of the "illiterate mother" who, in the view of the reporter, is an exception; she is a concerned and competent mother – but she cannot read and write:

> It was her son's class teacher who first spotted that Pauline Hammond might need help. Why, she wondered, did Stuart's mother never come to school to talk about the six-year-old's progress, or return forms giving permission for him to go on school trips? Pauline seemed an alert, attractive wife and mother. Could she have a reading problem? (Brown 1993: 37)

This mother is portrayed as "alert" and "attractive"; she is also a "wife". There is an insinuation here. Alert, attractive, married women are *assumed* to be literate women; it is taken for granted that they will also make sure their children do well. Tired, plain women who are single parents are clearly not. This being the assumption, the blame for Pauline's illiteracy is attributed later in the article, not to any failure on her part, but to inadequate schooling. Even so, the writer nevertheless goes on to attribute guilt to Pauline herself and makes no suggestion that things should be otherwise. "Barely able to write her name" at the age of 36, he tells us, Pauline is "handicapped" in her own right; but "worse still", he writes, "was the guilt she felt about her son" (Brown 1993: 38).

The story comes right in the end, for this mother is guided by her son's teacher to an adult literacy scheme down the road. Pauline's son, it seems, will not meet the same fate as Yvonne's mother.

In 1995, BBC Education decided to promote the social issue campaign of adult literacy. Unusually for an education programme, they decided to use an advertising agency to design the promotion. The resulting programme or "spot" was broadcast 25 times over a week in February 1995, advertising an 0800 phone number for viewers to ring up and order a free copy of a "Read and Write together" pack (part of the Basic Skills Agency's family literacy initiative). A target of 40,000 response calls was set. The programme far exceeded its target; over 300,000 calls were received. Encouraging news indeed for anyone interested in ensuring good times for children learning to read and write. The advertisers saw themselves as "doing something to stop [illiteracy] going from generation to generation"; their clients distributed a lot of educational packs; and the advertisement won an award (IPA 1997).

Less encouraging, however, were the images used. The two children portrayed were: a little girl with her doll, mimicking her mother finding reasons not to read to her, and a little boy, listening to repeated readings of a story his father has committed to memory. The picture of the girl shows her standing at a toy ironing board in her Wendy house. She has blonde plaits, and is talking to her doll. "Sorry darling", she says, "I can't read to you now. I'm busy." And in silky tones the voiceover tells the guilty viewer at home: "If you can't find time to help them, your children *may* have trouble learning to read". The parent of the girl is a mother who has no time. The parent of the boy is a father who cannot read. The father of the little boy reads to him alright; unlike the mother mimicked by her daughter, *he makes time*. His father (the viewer knows this, but the boy does not) is a good father – but an illiterate one, who has to pretend he can read.

So the bad mother is not necessarily an illiterate mother; she is the mother who is *not finding time* to help her children. Reading and writing is, today, a silent and often solitary business; the mother who does not or cannot read and write with her children casts her shadow across the Wendy house, the spectre which haunts the "deficit model" of family literacy. According to this model, the problems of children's illiteracy are created by the low-literate home and, especially, the non-literate mother; illiteracy is "passed on" from parent to child like an illness, and poor literacy is mixed up with poor parenting. The model is most starkly represented by one William Raspberry, who in a piece published in the *Washington Post* in 1989 asserted the following:

> The point is that literacy, like illiteracy, is a heritable trait; children catch it from their parents. And it may be that the best way to launch an attack on illiteracy is to treat it as a family disease . . . [Illiterate parents] also tend to have poor parenting skills . . . Illiteracy is condemning millions of adult Americans to poverty and destroying the life chances of children. (cited in Auerbach 1994: 11)

It is certainly shocking to find the *Washington Post* giving houseroom to such blatant nonsense. Elsa Auerbach, who attacked it in an article of her own, is the author of the most robust published critique of the "deficit" version of family literacy education, based on substantial research and practice carried out by a team she led in Boston, Massachusetts. In their review of work already undertaken, the team found that:

> Study after study . . . has refuted the notion that poor, minority and immigrant families don't value or support literacy development. In fact, often, quite the opposite seems to be the case for immigrants: those families most marginalised frequently see literacy and schooling as the key to mobility, to changing their status and preventing their children from suffering as they did. (Auerbach 1989: 170)

Their own family literacy programme, which worked primarily with immigrant and refugee communities, drew on the research experience of other populations too, with the aim of challenging what they had found to be the single idea which, despite these studies, dominated the *practice* of American family literacy education to date: the "transmission of school practices" idea, by which the programmes trained parents to transmit the literacy culture of the school, in order to prepare their children more adequately to engage in school-type reading and writing. This idea was founded on the idea that the "problem" of poor literacy was caused by families and the homes in which children grew up, not the schools. Auerbach's team also found that the idea of family literacy assumed, not a mix of experience across lifespans and between all age groups and relatives, but a one-way activity, from adults to children – or, more specifically, from parents to young children.

Both from other research studies and from the learners in their adult education programme, however, Elsa Auerbach and her colleagues found no simple link between the limited literacy of parents and the commitment of those parents to supporting their children's literacy. Whatever their literacy abilities, parents were encouraging their children's confidence as learners in other ways apart from actually doing reading and writing with them:

> I help my kids by staying together with them, by talking to them. I help them by confronting them and telling them what's wrong or right just as they do me. I help them when they need a favour or money, just as they do me. It's just like you scratch my back, I scratch your back with my family. (Auerbach 1989: 171)

Five years later, Auerbach summarized her argument for a progressive approach to family literacy education as being "against intervention and towards participation":

> Rather than proceeding from the schools to the communities and families, its direction is from the families and communities to the schools. It invites students to become critical readers of their own reality and authors of the changes they hope to make, so that literacy can truly become socially significant in their lives. (Auerbach 1994: 16)

The William Raspberry article compared the "intergenerational cycle of illiteracy" to a hereditary illness and had been circulated by the Barbara Bush Foundation. Two years later, I heard the same article quoted with similar concern by Professor Colin Harrison in a lecture given in London. I was only sorry he did not demolish it more thoroughly. In this lecture, Harrison offered an analysis of the efforts of the International Reading Association's Family Literacy Commission (of which he was a member) to review the developments in family literacy education since 1991 and distinguished between an "interventionist" interpretation of family literacy education (designed to improve children's literacy development in a family setting) and two others. The first he called the "intergenerational" interpretation. This aims to boost children's literacy, improve their parents' ability to help them, and increase the parents' own literacy and, as he saw it, had been the predominant version in funding policy in North America and the UK in the 1980s and 1990s. The second he referred to as the ethnographic approach, which understands family literacy to be those uses or practices of literacy that occur "spontaneously" in the home. Within this interpretation, Harrison (like others) saw Denny Taylor's study of families in a small community in New Hampshire, USA, as being the originator of the term "family literacy" itself.

Harrison reported concern among the members of the Family Literacy Commission at the ideology of what he, like Auerbach, saw to be the "deficit model" of family literacy (of which metaphors of plagues and epidemics would be an extreme symptom). According to this model, he said, three interlocking factors are blamed for national ills:

- the level of literacy skills among the population is inadequate to meet the demands of the economy;
- poor literacy skills (or illiteracy) are the cause of poverty and crime; and
- the reason for schools' apparent failure to deliver is that families fail to deliver children to them who are capable of acquiring literacy.

The solution to these ills (proposed by bodies like the Barbara Bush Foundation) had been to introduce school-like activities into the home, in order to reverse a perceived "cycle" of illiteracy.

In his lecture, Harrison then described the alternative to this: a "wealth" model of family literacy. According to this:

> There is no national literacy crisis and literacy levels are, in fact, rising steadily; poverty, unemployment, homelessness and crime are the result of economic policies; illiteracy is a consequence of poverty, not its cause; [and] programmes which recognize and use practices already in people's homes may be more successful than those based on school-like models. (Harrison 1996: 26)

From his study of the family literacy work in North America and the UK, he noted that while funders had tended to think along the lines of the "deficit" model, those who are employed as educators work with a "wealth" model. The first group tend to attract more media attention than the second: which may be why British, American and Australian teachers and adult educators (who could do more of our own media relations) have evidently been so concerned at the family literacy's association with "deficient" families.

School teachers and adult literacy educators alike would agree that literacy-rich homes offer a more favourable environment to children's interest in literacy. This is not, however, the same thing as seeing poor literacy skills as an inherited illness; an idea which still, unfortunately, seems to find echoes in the language of policy-makers. In a July 1997 radio interview, for example, I heard Helena Kennedy QC, Chair of the Committee reviewing adult and further education saying on an early morning radio interview:

> And then there is the problem of basic skills. One in six people in this country have problems with literacy and numeracy. If we don't address this problem now, *it will get passed on*. (BBC Radio 4, 2 July 1997, 7.15 am) (my emphasis).

Teach the mother to reach the child

With the exception of one day in 1993, the word "mother" was not frequently used in public utterances about family literacy education. On that day, the then Secretary of State for Education for England and Wales launched a Family Literacy initiative in the UK. Many of us present at the conference he addressed, organized by the Adult Literacy and Basic Skills Unit (soon after to be renamed the Basic Skills Agency), were caught unawares by the slogan he attached to the announcement. Like the readers of the newspapers the day after the conference, the several hundred delegates who heard him speak represented experiences of all kinds of family structures. We were nevertheless told that the "family" in mind had only one adult in it: "John Patten, the Education Secretary, yesterday announced a £250,000 grant for 'teach the mother, reach the child', pilot projects to be set up by the Adult Literacy and Basic Skills Unit" (McLeod 1993: 4).

The mystery was this. If the focus was to be limited to what Elsa Auerbach had called the "one-way" traffic of adults to children, where had the fathers gone – or indeed any other adults in the family? The answer, as we were to find out later, lay in the interest raised in the UK by a study carried out in America, which had stressed the importance to children's literacy attainment of their mothers'. The study argued that: "Parents', *especially mothers'* education levels are related to the development of children's learning abilities before school . . . during school . . . and into adulthood" (Sticht 1993: 12–13). (my emphasis)

The appeal of the family literacy approach in America, as Ruth Nickse had expressed it, was its capacity to "help prevent the debilitating cycle of illiteracy" (Nickse 1990: 13). Among the factors seen to be at the root of a perceived "literacy crisis" were: a shortage of daycare provision; the assumed difficulties of minority groups in acquiring appropriate education and job training; the low literacy of the many young families living in poverty; and – note – the large number of mothers now in the workforce. The key to reform which family literacy "programme interventions" would provide was the notion of "literate models" for children. As Nickse saw it: "Low literate parents cannot act as literate models, have trouble helping children with homework and often have low expectations and poor attitudes about schools and schooling" (Nickse 1990: 13). Like Sticht, Nickse saw the most significant person in this cycle as the mother: "Family variables, most particularly the mother's level of education, are associated with the child's school achievement and therefore the child's chances for school success" (Nickse 1990: 13).

By 1990 there were over three hundred family literacy programmes in the US, and with Even Start legislation between 1989–94, still more "coming on stream". By the time, then, that the UK launched its own initiative, in 1993, there was a groundswell of assumptions and claims from the other side of the Atlantic with which to legitimate the catchphrase favoured by the Secretary of State for Education.

Research findings, promoted with enough energy, have a way of coinciding with and reinforcing dominant views and ideologies. The idea that mothers are to blame for what goes wrong in schools finds support in all kinds of casual and not so casual discussions. The absence of fathers, for instance, appears to dominate the training of primary teachers. Among the texts assigned for undergraduate students of education, the assumption remains unquestioned: "Once a child has begun to learn to read he [sic] can bring his book home from school and *read to his mother* the same words which he read to his teacher earlier in the day" (Donaldson 1987: 91). (my emphasis)

Little wonder that some of these students reproduce unquestioningly such assumptions. Among essays I marked from a group of fourth-year students in a BA (Ed) degree programme in 1996, for example, was on the topic of "helping the special needs child with learning to read". The child under observation was described by the student writer as having parents who lived separately.

She lives with her father who cannot read, and visits her mum once a week who can read and is keen to help in the limited time available.

With a complete lack of concern as to what he was implying, the student went on:

The initial priority is to communicate with her mother, establish the value of her contribution and to make sure she understands her role and feels both positive and confident about it.

The question I pondered, reading this assertion, was this. Was it because the father was not the mother, that the student assumed this parent had no role in the child's literacy? Or was it because the father was not literate? The child lives with the father; presumably it is with this parent that she has most daily and nightly contact and most opportunity to talk, learn, and gain confidence in learning. But this is a father who "cannot read". At a stroke, the male parent is both absolved and dismissed. The student (who would soon, presumably, be a primary school teacher) took it for granted that a father, especially a non-reading father, had no part to play in the child's learning.

Family literacy: shifts in meaning

What families actually do with reading and writing in everyday ways is actually a rich area for research, as David Barton reports. His work, and that of the Lancaster Literacy Research Group of which he is a member, has done much to open up the possibilities for the ethnographic approach to family literacy iden- tified by Colin Harrison, and to support its "wealth model" espoused by many teachers and adult educators in family literacy education. In a review of research and practice in family literacy, he suggests that the most useful way of understanding the conjunction of the two ideas – "family" and "literacy" – has been to study "people's actual lives". From studies such as these, Barton picks out six observations that can be made about this conjunction. Firstly, literacy is more than book reading. Secondly, these studies take account of the fact that "family is more than mum". Thirdly, they show that home literacy is not always the same as school literacy. Fourthly, family literacy means literacy across all sorts of lifespans; fifthly, all sorts of people, literate and less so, participate in literacy; and finally, literacy itself may be supported in all kinds of ways as well as by a child (or adult) being given direct reading and writing instruction or help (Barton 1994a).

Abbreviated in this way, these insights suddenly look painfully obvious. Yet, as David Barton suggests, they remain ignored or unknown to many. He quotes Denny Taylor, writing ten years after publication of her influential study, which had first coined the term "family literacy" (Taylor 1983). Taylor voices a concern at:

> The way in which the concept of family literacy has been co-opted and used to reify deficit-driven views of families who live in poverty . . . Above all [she concludes] we need to . . . turn to the wealth of information that we can gain from educators and researchers who work with families in naturalistic set- tings. (cited in Barton 1994a: 4)

Essentially, what has happened to family literacy over a 15-year period is a shift in meanings. Peter Hannon sees this shift from family literacy as, "*A way of seeing* the interplay of literacy activities of children, parents and others within families", to one applied solely to

> Certain kinds of educational *programs* [which] used broadly . . . refers to any program which, through its content or practice, recognizes the family dimensions of literacy learning. (Hannon 1997: 1)

Hannon, whose own work persuasively argued for primary teachers to attend to "people's actual lives" (Hannon 1995), cites the National Literacy Trust as an important source of information about the wide variety of family literacy work which, funded though it may have been through a "deficit model" of families and literacy, has nevertheless celebrated the alternative (Bird & Pahl 1994).

"Now is the literacy hour": thus the *Guardian* newspaper headlined a report (7 January 1997) on the Conservative Government's announcement of its "National Literacy Project", which, among other things, was to require schools to allocate one hour a day to all-school literacy activities. This was a move (following others) in anticipation of a new general election, to show the government's muscular response to the perceived literacy crisis in schools, following the launch in Summer 1996 of a number of "literacy centres" round the country.

For their part, the Labour Party was not slow in promoting itself as the party to rescue us from the same crisis. Just a month later, its own announcement of a literacy strategy was reported in the familiar triumphalist language of "campaigns" against illiteracy. This, too, was to be a "fight" against a disease – but this time, parents are to be not the campaign's beneficiaries, but its lieutenants: "Labour to enlist parents in fight against illiteracy" (*London Evening Standard*, 24 February 1997). By July 1997, when the Labour Party was now in government, its strategy had taken on an added edge. Time, once again, is the commodity required of parents (and for parents, we must again read "mothers"). The obligation is quite specific. For 20 minutes a day, parents of primary school children were to be required to "sign an undertaking to read with their children" ("Parents told to sign reading pledge", *Guardian*, 29 July 1997).

This front page article featured Stephen Byers, the Education Minister with responsibility for schools, announcing an allocation of £1.8 million to run three-month literacy courses for thousands of parents whose own standard of reading was not good enough to provide the necessary help. The purpose of the programme was to enable the government to meet its declared targets for literacy at 11. "There is no intention of parents being sued if they do only 19 minutes of reading with their children", the Minister is quoted as saying. (Did he have his tongue in his cheek?) The sense of veiled menace implied here continues: "The government would eventually have to tackle the very small number of parents who did not act responsibly", Mr Byers said (*Guardian*, 29 July 1997: 1)

In all this plethora of publicity, from the 1993 announcement to this most recent variation on it, mothers have once again vanished: the word is "parents".

The 17 photographs reproduced in the pack produced by the Basic Skills Agency in 1993 to promote and encourage the development of the programmes, which were careful to represent an ethnic mix of children and adults, included seven featuring men, of whom several looked as though they might be fathers (Basic Skillis Agency 1993). Seven out of 17 is not a lot; but it is a lot more (proportionately) than the number of fathers who participated in the programmes that were funded. Three years later, the evaluation of the programme reported that, of the parents who participated, just 4 per cent of the total were male. To put it another way, 96 per cent of "parents" in the biggest family literacy initiative in the UK had been mothers (Brooks et al. 1996: 24).

Mothers are the only parents

Please, miss
my mother, miss
forgot to tell you this, miss:
that I, miss,
won't miss,
be in school tomorrow, miss.[1]

It is at this point that I want to reconnect with my theme of mothers and time. Twenty minutes a day may not seem a lot to a male politician. But what of the reality of mothers who, sometimes, may be single parents, who may have more than one child, and who have just got home from the part-time job at the supermarket checkout? There is a game which Valerie Walkerdine and Helen Lucey see as "beloved of psychologists and educators"; it is called "Find the sensitive mother". According to this game, the bad mother fails to prepare her young child for school; the good, sensitive mother, "tirelessly answers [her child's] unrelenting questions and makes her home, her everyday life, an assault course of developmental tasks" (Walkerdine & Lucey 1989: 22).

The game, as they set it out, is one in which researchers search the transcripts of interactions between middle-class and working-class mothers and their young children in order to detect which mother is adequately carrying out her role of developing the child's language. As I suggested in Chapter 2, the analysis that Walkerdine & Lucey offer is a direct challenge to this one, which (as they argue) is steeped in class prejudices about "normal" and "natural" mothering. Their critique has been inspirational to other feminist writers, glad of the blast of air they blow into the airless claustrophobia of the good mother "tirelessly" working at her child's play. The working-class mother has work to get on with; to see this work as compatible with the child's play is a luxury available to mothers who either have other women whom they can afford to pay to do their housework, who have a partner (male or female) sympathetic and willing to share in this work, or who have the material conditions to provide the toys and books and, simply, time, to give to one or several children at the end of a long day.

Miriam David, one of those who cites their work with gladness, offers what I find to be a really useful insight into the recent discourse to be found on "family literacy". Like Walkerdine & Lucey, she is writing before this term gained the currency it now has. What she does is pick out the move from the *explicit* focus on mothers following Bowlby's (1953) influential concept of "maternal deprivation" to one which *implicitly* refers to mothers, as a result of the 1967 Plowden report on primary education. The language of Plowden, David points out, referred to an ungendered "parental participation"; it is this language, she suggests, which permeated both official policy developments and the subsequent range of social research studies set up to evaluate them (David 1989). She points out that these developments, couched as they were in apparently neutral language, coincided with reductions in nursery and childcare provision, a growth in the voluntary organization of mothers in the form of the Pre-School Playgroups Association and an increase in home–school initiatives: all having a direct bearing on the assumed and actual pressures on mothers to take the primary responsibility for their children's learning. Despite becoming grouped with fathers as "parents" since the 1960s, David argues, "the different parental roles expected of mothers and fathers were in fact clear" (David 1989: 44).

In the 1990s, then, "mother" remains a word masked by the word "parent". In this context, John Patten's call to "reach the mother" is striking. Since his conference address in 1993, policy language has once again retreated into ungendered territory. It is as if there is a coyness about using the actual word "mother": even though she was the person precisely identified by the Minister. Once again, the word "parents" is used to mask the woman at home; and "family" too often stands as a euphemism for the maternal parent. In a study of the language used in journalism about family literacy education, Jacqui Armour noted how easy it was to pass by the stereotyping at work. From an analysis of feature articles published in seven national newspapers covering literacy programmes promoted for "the family", she found that mothers were mentioned over three times more often than fathers, that images of women outnumbered men by 3 : 1, and that 75 per cent of the "gender-encoded" phrases in the text were female gendered (as in: "welfare mums", "at mother's knee", "listen with mother"). In reflecting on this, Armour comments on how subtle this language bias can be, and how on first reading, she had been unaware of it. She concludes: "'Teach the mother and reach the child' denies any interest that women may have in literacy learning from their own development and ignores women who are child free" (Armour 1996: 36).

With the growing movement of home-school links in primary education stimulated by the 1967 Plowden Report, mothers and fathers have been able to get beyond the primary school gate as a matter of course, and if a teacher needed to know of a child's absence, the child's parent or carer could tell her in person. Parents at the turn of the century, however, were in a different position. As

Peter Hannon put it: "There was no space for parents in schools of the late nineteenth century. Indeed there was little enough space for the children" (Hannon 1995: 18). Equally, many parents then (as now) had little spare time to visit the school, let alone have conversations with the teacher; and the growing movement to professionalize teaching in the early half of this century, if anything, increased the gulf between the school and the home. Telling "miss" had to rely on the child or sibling taking a message: and sometimes a note must be written.

Once again Gwen's mother Lily helps us imagine what this might have felt like. Gwen had four older sisters, so by the time she herself started school in 1930, Lily had had some practice in solving the spelling problem such writing posed for her – and a solution:

> If we were absent from school [mother] would need to send a "sick note" with a well child, or the note would be taken when the child recovered, and as she could never remember how to spell "bilious", she would resort to the Fenning's Fever Cure bottle where the word was to be found (E174).

The writing of the note was a formal business, however, and Lily obviously took it seriously, as Gwen recalled for me when we talked:

> It was a palaver. It was a big event, this writing. It was quite something . . . "Oh, we'll have to send a note. And get organized, and get the Fenning's Fever Cure bottle out". (Interview, February 1997)

The note to school posed different problems for Audrey's mother, a woman recalled as writing little other than "birthday cards or short notes to relatives". Audrey remembered her own embarrassment when Doris "used to write notes to teachers if I was absent from school and address them 'Dear Madam', which somehow I didn't think was right. Her style of handwriting was round and carefully formed – and I could easily copy it". (B1533)

In interview, later, Audrey said: "It made me feel very ashamed"; and then added this reflection:

> You see, it was due to her life in service, wasn't it? "Dear Madam". All ladies were called Madam, weren't they? They always called teachers governesses, didn't they, too? Did you know about that? Oh yes. Always. They didn't call the teachers the governess; the headmistress was always the governess. My mother would refer to Miss Richards, the headmistress, as the governess.
>
> *You don't think she wrote "Dear madam" because she didn't know the teacher's name?*

133

Oh, she knew the teacher's name. I'd do nothing but talk about my teachers. Yes, so it wasn't that. No, it's because she was used to addressing women in a better position as "Madam". She continued in domestic work, charring, all through my childhood – and in fact long after it, during the War, too.

For Doris and for Lily, the children's school was remote and the teachers who worked in them were distant figures to be treated (at least by Doris) with deference. For both women, writing of any sort was an unusual activity; more formal writing was undertaken only under duress.

Exclusions and resistance

Historically, mothers in many cultures have been actively forbidden (sometimes by their own mothers) to read and write. I was reminded of this when, in July 1997 I came across a Website on the Internet published by a network of some one hundred women journalists in America. From a 1994 article reporting on the then imminent Fourth World Conference on Women to be held in Beijing, I read this:

> Bharati Mukherjee, an Indian novelist and professor at the University of California at Berkeley, recalls how her mother had to fight against society and her in-laws by learning to read and passing this skill on to her daughters. Mukherjee remembers her mother stashing away part of her monthly allowance to buy books secretly.
>
> "If any of us were caught reading books, my grandmother would confiscate them", she says, explaining that reading and ideas threatened her illiterate grandmother's sense of right or wrong. (Levine 1994)

In the previous chapter we saw how daughters in Britain recalled their mothers discriminating against their own literacy and learning in favour of sons. Testimony such as this reminds us that mothers themselves have often been effective censors of their daughters' literacy development. It is from another feminist writing from an Indian experience that we are reminded of the political and social context within which this censorship might flourish. The writer's name is Lalita Ramdas; the article she published in 1990 had a profound effect on me when I first read it, and I have used it in my teaching and writing many times since (for instance in Mace & Wolfe 1990). The core of Ramdas' argument is this. Literacy education for women cannot be separated from the lived realities of power relations and poverty. Too much educational planning, she says, has assumed it is possible to separate the two. And she tells the story of a national convention in Bangalore, India, at which over a thousand delegates were divided into subgroups and charged with the task of coming up with "timebound action plans" for their states. One group of women delegates rebelled. They met separately, and talked at length about the specific barriers to literacy experienced by women and girls.

When this group came to present its recommendations to the conference, they proposed that, for literacy programmes to be effective, certain conditions would need to be met. Instead of a "timebound action plan", they called for childcare facilities, a re-education process towards the traditional roles expected of women, and at least 50 per cent of decision-making bodies to be composed of women. Their proposals were greeted with "condescension bordering on disapproval". Where was their "timebound" plan of action?

In the same article, Ramdas went on to argue that any timetable for literacy can only be conceived within the lived timings of women's lives. She illustrates her argument with a woman, whom she called Chintamma – who, as Ramdas suggests, may have neither the time nor the interest for the literacy being promoted for her, let alone for her daughters. Chintamma is part of the statistic which, globally, shows that 70 per cent of the world's illiterates in 1990 are women. She is also one of many thousands whose conditions of living are such that there is not only little incentive to take up such opportunities for their literacy as may be offered, but little time. Ramdas makes the connection between Asia and Europe where, historically, "male control over female access to literacy continued in one form or other, visible and subtle, into the industrial period" (Ramdas 1990: 34).

It is from the black American writer, Alice Walker, that we are reminded of another, more thorough prohibition laid on the literacy of both women and men: four hundred years' of literacy being denied to black people who had been slaves. "What did it mean for a black woman to be an artist in our grandmothers' time? In our great-grandmothers' day?" she asks. "It is a question with an answer cruel enough to stop the blood" (Walker 1995: 233).

The passion of this essay is enormous (enough, indeed, to stop my blood). It is a piece fashioned from a poet's research and a granddaughter's rage. As a white reader, when I first read it, I felt (as I turned the pages) like a witness, allowed in to a huge gathering of black women, the readers addressed by Alice Walker. This is certainly not only a piece about literacy, and literature; her fury and grief is at the wasted talents in *all* the arts, brought about by centuries of brutality and humiliation wrought by white people on black slaves. While her subject is the whole field of artistic creativity, it is literacy and the full use of reading and writing that is nevertheless at the heart of her piece (unsurprising from someone who is, after all, an artist in this medium herself):

How was the creativity of the black woman kept alive, year after year and century after century, when for most of the years black people have been in America, it was a punishable crime for a black person to read or write? And the freedom to paint, to sculpt, to expand the mind with action did not exist. Consider, if you can bear to imagine it, what might have been the result if singing, too, had been forbidden by law. (Walker 1995: 234)

Alice Walker was the ninth child of a mother who, in the late 1920s, had run away to marry her father. She describes this mother as a woman "rarely impatient in our home" whose "day began before sunup, and did not end until late at night": a woman who was constantly at work, with "never a moment for her to sit down, undisturbed, to unravel her own private thoughts, never a time free from interruption – by work or the noisy inquiries of her many children" (Walker 1995: 238). The "punishable crime" of reading and writing, although no longer forbidden to her mother in the same way as it had been to her grandmother, was still out of reach; a pleasure in which she had no freedom to indulge, no time to spare.

How would this woman be judged by a "pledge" to read to her children for 20 minutes a day? by what kind of "standard" are we to measure the literacy of her daughter, who has the power to "stop the blood" of those who read her writing? The ticking clock of the Education Minister cannot be answered.

Tillie Olsen, also an American, also writing in the early 1970s, from her catalogue of the number of published women writers in the nineteenth century concluded that "until very recently almost all distinguished writing has come from childless women" (Olsen 1980: 31). As Olsen eloquently expressed it, history shows that for white mothers too (although to a very different degree than for their black sisters) literacy and the creative business of writing was forbidden territory. "Almost no mothers – as almost no part-time, part-self persons – have created enduring literature . . . so far" (Olsen 1980: 19).

Tillie Olsen's first book was published when she was fifty; and she gives a poignant account of her own longings, over two decades of combining child-bearing and child-rearing with such paid work as she could get, for the space and time to do the writing she had in her. Situating her own experience in the context of women silenced by men and by the social forces that insist on them caring for the needs of others before their own, she places this autobiographical narrative into a world in which mothers, historically, have been hemmed in and kept away from a literacy they craved.

> More than in any other human relationship, overwhelmingly more, mother-hood means being instantly interruptible, responsive, responsible. Children need one *now* (and remember, in our society, the family must often try to be the center for love and health the outside world is not). (Olsen 1980: 20)

In the hope of writing, during those years, she was living a daily life of "conscious storing, snatched reading". No coincidence, she says, that the first work she considered worthy of publishing was the piece that began: "I stand here ironing, and what you asked me moves tormented back and forth with the iron".[2]

What, then, does this silencing of mothers' literacy suggest about the daughters who grew up to write? If their own mothers had given them little to go on, in terms of being "models" of literate behaviour, or whose own "standard of reading" was "not good enough to give them the necessary help", how have women like these two internationally acclaimed authors been possible?

Among the answers, of course, is the radical change in educational opportunities for working-class and black girls and women over this century. Alice Walker gives another: her inspirations and encouragement to write as she does came, she says, from something else her mother gave her. Not a "model" of a literate life, nor a source of "help" in children's homework, the gift with which her mother supplied Alice Walker was instead something else. This is how she puts it:

> And so our mothers and grandmothers have, more often than not anonymously, handed on the creative spark, the seed of the flower they themselves never hoped to see: or like a sealed letter they could not plainly read.
>
> And so it is, certainly, with my own mother . . . No song will bear my mother's name. Yet so many of the stories that I write, that we all write, are my mother's stories. Only recently did I fully realize this: that through years of listening to my mother's stories of her life, I have absorbed not only the stories themselves, but something of the manner in which she spoke, something of the urgency that involves the knowledge that her stories – like her life – must be recorded. (Walker 1995: 240)

For Walker, the "creative spark" of the oral rhythms and meanings given to her by her mother had infused those she went on to use in her writing. There was something else, that had nothing directly to do with literacy, which she sees her mother to have given her. Not only was her mother a storyteller; she was also a gardener – and this, according to Alice Walker, inspired her daughter's growth as a writer no less than her use of words. Her mother, she says, was constantly working with flowers, in the house (however "shabby") and in her "ambitious gardens"; and it is from her mother's sense of artistry in planting and pruning, her "respect for the possibilities", she says, that her own creativity – as a writer, and as a black woman – was given life.

Mother-publishers

I want now to suggest how, in the 20 and more years since adult literacy "campaigns" took off in North America, Britain, Australia and other countries – and especially since specific campaigns for women's literacy in the 1990s – working-class and black women and mothers have changed the "silencing" referred to by Tillie Olsen and Alice Walker. One way in which this change has been made has been through the work some of them have done together in the setting of adult literacy and women's education groups. In these settings, women have found the means to write and become published and, in so doing, created another set of meanings for family literacy.

Publishing from adult literacy work began in the mid-1970s in the UK, America, Canada and South Africa, not long after the writing we have just been considering by these two women. The work grew out of a dissatisfaction which English-language adult literacy teachers felt in the reading matter available for teaching grown-up students. It had become apparent that the way in which this problem could best be solved would be by asking for the help of the learners themselves. The teaching method that became known (in primary, as well as adult literacy education) as "language experience" was brought in to help. Using this method, the literacy teacher acts as scribe. The learner, freed for the moment from the anxiety about spelling and wording what she wants to say, talks a little; maybe tells a story. The written version of what she has said is then the text between teacher and learner. Later, with others coming to read it, the same text may need to be changed a little, added to and shaped (Moss 1995). The technology of typewriters, duplicating machines and later word processors and photocopiers made the business of then "publishing" this text for a wider group of people relatively simple.

Out of this unpretentious classroom business grew national and then international movements in community publishing, resulting, over 20 years later, in hundreds, probably thousands, of booklets, magazines, news sheets, and even "proper books" (with spines), appearing in centres of community education as far apart as Johannesburg and Cork, Toronto and Edinburgh. They vary in appearance from the home-made and humble to the glossy and glamorous. In content, they have one thing in common. Each author in their pages is moving towards Tillie Olsen's position of being "a writing writer", and in so doing, just slightly altering their own position in the world.

Here, for instance, is a piece by a woman about why she writes poetry. What she says, among other things, is that from a position of being a woman abandoned to bring up children alone, she turned to being a writer, read by the husband who had left her. Her feelings that, in another form, had seemed mere "petty nagging", expressed in another language could no longer be ignored:

> I must have told my husband half a dozen times how I felt about him going to prison and leaving me to cope with the children on my own. He used to read my letters and dismiss them as petty nagging. So I wrote him a poem, "I've heard it all before" explaining my grievances. Suddenly it sunk in. He realized that if I felt strongly enough about it to burst into poetry, then I must be serious! (Fazackerley 1984: 51)

(I remember another woman, a few years earlier in South London, also speaking of her husband suddenly seeing her in a new light. She had had something she had written printed in a community publication. There she was, in print. Her regrets for a schooling cut short, the sense of loss after their emigration to Britain from the West Indies, and the determination she now felt – now that their children had grown up – to claim time for her own education: these things he had known about, but only (she said) when he saw them written down had they fully "sunk in": and he wept.)

Among many themes in this literature, that of what once were the taboos of women's reproduction is one. In Chapter 2, I quoted from the best-known example of these: *Every birth it comes different*, published by the Hackney Reading Centre in London in 1980. The process of producing the book had taken two years. Beginning from reading the information, pictures and poems about child-birth collected by the tutors, the work had entailed telling and listening to stories – 18 women literacy students took part, all of them with stories of childbirth to recall – and writing. At one stage, two local midwives had joined the group to talk about home deliveries and hospital births. After the book was published, one of the authors, Sue Bissmire, gave a copy to another woman as a source of reference. As one of the literacy tutors recalled it for me, Sue took the book into the nursery where her baby was cared for and gave it to one of the nursery staff who herself was pregnant. She said, "If you're going to have a baby, this is what you should read" (Mace 1983: 41).

Community publications from adult literacy work, then, have become a resource beyond the walls of the classroom; and – in this case – women's stories of motherhood and reproduction, written down, took the "creative spark" from a long line of mothers before them to pass on to others. This, then, is one way in which black and working-class mothers have taken hold of literacy to reverse several kinds of silence – including that of reproduction and men-struation. As one woman put it, in a collection of writing and discussion about the experience of "the curse":

My Mum never talked to me about this stuff. She would die if she heard the word vagina! (East End Literacy Women's Group 1990: 16)

The mothers who have taken part in "wealth models" of family literacy educa-tion have been enabled to use the opportunity familiar to women's education groups in adult literacy programmes like these to mesh their own reading and writing interests with those of their children. The publishing of their stories becomes a resource for the children. The example in which I have been able to take part myself took place in Swansea, South Wales, between January and July 1997.

The Swansea Family Learning programme began in May 1994. Set up by the Community Education Service in West Glamorgan, its declared intention was first and foremost to provide an educational opportunity for women who had always been under-represented in their basic skills and Employment Service courses. (Employment opportunities for women in Swansea has been, in the 1980s and 1990s, largely confined to part-time shiftwork as shelf-fillers, cleaners, care assistants or factory operatives.) From a beginning in two schools, the programme grew over two years into a programme working with 23 schools, on a pattern of weekly half-day attendance. Sandra Morton, the co-ordinator, quoted women reporting similar gains in confidence to those reported from literacy programmes such as those in Hackney and Toronto:

"It has made me realize that I still have a brain . . . and it works."
"I don't feel so isolated now."
"There's more to life than being a housewife and mother; there are opportunities beyond home."
"I joined a computer course last week and I never would have done it if I hadn't come here." (Morton 1996: 41,42)

When Sandra agreed to work with me to convene a group of women from this programme to explore their own experience of literacy in relation to the historical material I had gathered, I felt excited. Originally, we planned it as a two-day project, with an interval of six weeks in between for the participants to carry out some of their own research, stimulated by what I would share with them of my own. As things turned out, a sequel proved essential; for a small group of the women with their tutor chose the option I proposed to develop their work into a community publication.

Forty-eight women from nine different family learning groups turned up on the first of the two days, in January. The two crèche workers employed for the day were fully occupied with ten children to look after; five tutors, and two librarians took an important role as scribes and discussion leaders. The invitation they had responded to was headed: "Reading, writing and living: a research project with and about mothers". The day began with a presentation I gave on three themes picked out from my reading of the Mass Observation writings about mothers bringing up children in the early decades of the century, summarized in the words: *time, help* and *letters*. The idea was to offer a sense of a recent past, when mothers like those in the room that day had had (or not had) time for their own reading and writing; when there were networks of help among communities which mixed illiterate and literate members; and when mothers were often the key letter-writers in family groups. In giving them examples of autobiography, poetry and fiction during the presentation, I had wanted to suggest that history has many sources.

The women shifted the chairs into circles and within minutes the room was alive with talk. As I might have (but had not) predicted, the intended focus on literacy in the lives of their grandmothers and mothers was soon lost in the energy of all kinds of recollections. It was as if a tap had been turned on. The talk flowed; the scribes and discussion leaders were awash in words. Giving their own names to each other at the start of the talk was the easy bit. Giving names to the subjects of their discussion, was not. The women spoke of "my gran", "mum", "my mother-in-law", "granny", and that particular Welsh word, "mam": women portrayed as having many children, much washing and scrubbing to do and strong personalities. Their names – Vera, Gladys, Maud, Emily, flitted in and out of the talk like strangers. Scrapbooks, knitting patterns, newspaper crosswords, funeral bills – the reading and writing they did, at least as it was recalled that day by their daughters and granddaughters, had been fiercely practical (one great-grandmother had a straightforward filing system: the rent book kept under one cushion and the insurance under another).

Many of the women, as they left at the end of the day to go and pick up children from school, spoke of a new enthusiasm for history, hitherto seen as a dry affair. A month later, 28 of the same women returned, having carried out some of their own research. At Sandra Morton's suggestion, a "talking wall" display was put up (a long sheet of newsprint paper) on which the pictures and writing that women had brought in was tacked up and visible. Much of the morning was spent in groups with women talking of what they had learned from interviews and questions they had asked in their families. There was then a discussion as to who would be willing now to take their writing about mothers or grandmothers further, and take part in a community publishing project.

It was a group of five women and their tutor who, later, chose to develop the work in their weekly meetings during May and June, for which I joined them on two occasions. The family literacy they were engaged in now had a focus, not on their children, but on themselves, their mothers and their grandmothers. Jayne chose to write about her mother-in-law, about whom she had spent many hours in discussion and inquiry with her husband; Nazma decided to write about her mother, who had died a year before in Pakistan, for whom the process of the work provided, she said, a partial healing for her grief. Carol had interviewed her mother on three separate occasions, and learned a whole new dimension to the person she had known all her life. Lynda had written about her grandmother, drawing partly on childhood memories and partly on recollections of her aunt; and Linda had written about the grandmother with whom she had lived as a child.

Of Carol's two children, her 9-year-old attended the same school as Lynda's daughter. She had not been able to take part in the original days in January and February because of hospital appointments; but she had taken inspiration from the notes of those sessions and discussions in the group, and had interviewed her mother, Margaret – known as Peggy, now aged 83. At our meeting in May she told us this had been "hilarious": and in recounting some of what her mother had told her, she had us all laughing too. Lynda, the mother of one daughter, had come to both the first meetings, and had brought with her to this one two versions of a piece she had written about Maud, her grandmother. Her aunt (her mother's eldest sister, now aged 90) had read the first version and said, "But you haven't said about her temper". So Lynda had inserted an addition to the second version. In her first version, she had begun:

My Gran was a lovely lady who always had a smile for everyone. She was born on the 11th February 1881, one of four children, to a Devonshire Father and a Welsh Mother.

The comment from her aunt led her to insert (after "everyone"):

But she didn't suffer fools gladly and had a sharp tongue for everyone.[3]

Jayne, herself the grandmother of a child at the school where the family literacy group had started, had from the start of this project declared an interest in researching the life of Lily May, her mother-in-law, who had died aged 92. She brought to the group an assortment of notes, certificates and photographs about her, together with typed sheets of her own writing.

Nazma's recollections of her mother, in this and later meetings of the group, brought tears. This is how she described the process of writing and remembering:

> I started writing all the things *I* remembered about my mum – my personal relationship with her. At times I felt like crying. Towards the end, our relationship was a bit tense. She's gone now, and what I tried to do was to go on to think about her as a person. I kept thinking, I've got to write this down for my daughter. It took me five or six weeks altogether. Lindsay helped me a lot. She wrote down some of the things I said. And we thought about the words. What about another word for "clean"? We looked it up in the thesaurus and found "immaculate". So I used that, instead; it seemed to say it better.

Carol was the only member of the group writing about a woman still living. Asked if she thought her mother would mind reading about herself in the planned publication, Carol said:

> Oh no. When I said "I've got to interview you" she said, "Am I going to be on the telly?"

The interview, she said, had been hard:

> I sat down and wrote a list of questions, but when she began, she talked about nothing to do with what I'd written. I interviewed her several times. I found it upsetting. My mum has always been there; I hadn't realized what a hard life she'd had.

Linda wrote, first, from her childhood recollections of her grandmother, who, with her grandfather lived with her and her family. It was not till later that Lindsay herself, the group's tutor, decided that she too wanted to write about her grandmother. This was at the stage when we agreed that this could be a community publication, to be launched in the autumn as a fruit of the earlier meetings in January and February, as an encouragement to the women who had participated then and others to develop their recollections in the same way, and as a resource for the authors' children and grandchildren.

It is always hard to convey in writing the vitality of discussions like those we had together, this group of women and I. There was a tremendous outburst of anecdotes – about funerals, for instance, and the writing work of undertakers' receipts, letters of condolence, obituaries. (Jayne brought in a tin box with a 1928 receipt from the local undertaker in Swansea.) Carol spoke of her mother (now 83) keeping receipts of all kinds of things – including the pram in which she had been pushed as a baby. We discussed the question I had asked Mass Observation correspondents: namely, how do we know our grandmothers could read and write? and Lynda remembered hers reading the newspapers to her grandfather when he was going blind.

The work of the group's meetings during these weeks had sometimes been emotional. ("We've had so many tissues passed round since we started this!" said Lindsay.) There was a discussion about making the move from seeing their mothers as "mum" to seeing them as people with names. As Jayne said (of her mother-in-law) "Lily May was always 'Ma' to me". Each member of the group, in her writing, alternated between using their subject's full name and using her family name. Linda referred to Maud as "my gran", throughout; the habit of a lifetime was impossible to break. Carol alternated between "my mum" and using her name, Peggy. Nazma introduced her mother by her name, Sakina Bibi, and then moved on to writing about "my mother" or "mum".

In November 1997, the group held a publishing party, to which many of the original crowd of over 50 women came, together with families, friends, and children. By this time they had chosen a title both for their publication and for themselves. The first was to be called *Portraits in time*; as for themselves, they chose "The Swansea Mothers' Writing Group". Here are extracts from two of the pieces they wrote.

Peggy (by Carol)

Peggy had always been conscious of her lack of education, especially in reading and writing. My favourite story is one my sisters have told me about my mum writing letters to my dad at sea. It was a time they both dreaded. They would both be banished to bed and she would settle herself at the kitchen table ready for this mammoth task.

After a few minutes, Peggy would call out: "Glen, Glen!"

"Yes, Mam?"

"How do you spell *please?*"

Glen would diligently call out the letters one by one.

Next minute you'd get, "Glen, Glen!"

"Yes, Mam?"

"Which way does the P go – up or down?"

This would go on until the letter was finished.

Things haven't changed. We all dread her writing her Christmas cards, because every few minutes we get a phone call asking how to spell somebody's name. (Swansea Mothers' Writing Group 1997: 5)

Lily May (by Jayne)

My mother-in-law Lily May was born in 1898 to Sarah and Patrick Morrisey. I feel that her life through childhood, marriage and old age can be reflected by the improvement in her circumstances. I've thought of them as flagstones, lino and fitted carpets.

Flagstones

Lily was the third of five children but survived them all and lived until April 1990. Her birth certificate with a mark of "X" shows her mother Sarah Jane's inability to write her name. Although her birth certificate shows her as Lily May, on her marriage certificate she is called Lilian May. She was an exact sort of person and had wanted her name written in full. (Swansea Mothers' Writing Group 1997: 20)

This then was a group of mothers choosing to "play with time": to imagine and research what life might have felt like for their own mothers, mothers-in-law, and grandmothers. The process of making this history had included: interviews of a mother still living (Carol, with her mother); painful recollections of a mother recently dead (Nazma); gathering of childhood memories (Lynda, of her grandmother, who died when she was six years old); "long evenings reminiscing" (Jayne, with her husband about his mother); "lifting the mists" of her mother's memory through her own (Linda, of her grandmother); and sifting through family photographs (Lindsay, of her grandmother). Two women were reporting on women still living; four had searched for the other women through the traces they had left behind in their own memories and in the documents (such as they were) that remained of their lives.

Reflections

The family literacy programmes undertaken in the UK since 1993 have been creative and widespread; and I have no intention, in this chapter, to underplay either the seriousness of intent or the educational effectiveness of the whole range of projects and schemes that this initiative has encouraged into life during that time. Following a series of surveys over three years in England, Scotland and Wales, the National Literacy Trust estimated that some four hundred programmes were currently taking place in the UK "which could be broadly described as family literacy initiatives" (Pahl & Bird 1996, unpubl.). The fact that they found that the projects took place in playgroups, churches, housing schemes, libraries, day nurseries, baby clinics, family centres, travellers' sites, after-school support centres as well as schools seems to be an encouraging indication that the Ivanic & Hamilton (1990) notion of "domains" in which literacy enters our lives is more fully reflected than some have feared. The dominant model remains, however, that of parents working with young children; the Trust does not report how many of the parents were male.

My central question, therefore, remains this: why, in its inception, did the family literacy "idea" have such a central focus on the mother? This focus on the female parent ignores the other literacy networks which research – as well as everyday experience – shows us, surround the child. More important, for me, this focus on the mother, as the person responsible for carrying a message about the literate life to her child, poses a serious risk to that woman of denying her any interest in literacy for herself. Teaching the mother solely in order to reach her child excludes her from reaching herself.

That morning in a room in Swansea, as we ate the sandwiches and cake and coffee that the women had brought, we talked of women with no names but the name of mother, mum, gran, and ma. In the talk, the use of their names began to become a custom; and in that use, other people were revealed: Maud, Lily May, Violet, Sakina, Peggy. People who had been girls, as well as old women: people with voices of their own, and possibly – like the women there that day – with literacy appetites, too.

In the last chapter, I wrote about the networks of support to which those with limited literacy might resort when there is literacy work to be done. Such networks are not always simple, however; and among the pleasures for women in gaining their own self-confidence as readers and writers is the pleasure of no longer having to rely on a literate partner. Many years ago I was reminded of this by a woman called Sarah, talking to me in her flat with her volunteer literacy tutor, Pam. Sarah – the mother of eight children – had had constant paperwork to deal with in the struggle to gain a passage to this country for her son in Jamaica. She spoke that day of the sense of pleasure she had in Pam's meetings with her. She also spoke of the pleasure she had in no longer having to depend on her husband to deal with her letters:

> Before directly I couldn't read. I feel a fool of myself, you know? Like I doesn't have no sense. You know, but since now I picking up, you know, no one can fool me directly so much again. Even my husband, you know. Sometime when I get a letter, sometime when me and him don't agree, you know? I have to still force on him to look at the letter. But now I can directly look at it and see the words, and I don't have to ask him. Sometimes when the kids them take letter, form, from the school, I can sign it and write so-and-so on it. (Mace 1979: 103)

For Sarah, at the time, to be literate was to become independent – a position of pride. The women in the group in Swansea were already – in a technical sense – literate, certainly more able to read and write than Sarah was. What they stood to gain from our project together, as I hope Sarah has gained since then, was the sense of being members of a writing community, mother–writers as well as mother–readers. What they revealed, too, was the existence in their own histories of some mothers who chose to conserve and treasure the paperwork of family life. Jayne's mother-in-law Lily was such a woman:

> As I was clearing her home following her death (writes Jayne), I was struck by how much she'd loved writing and had hoarded anything written. She kept many documents such as the rights of burial for her parents, dated 1913. I also found a letter from her son David John dated "Sunday 1944 – 5.30" sent from France during the war. All letters from (her sister) Elizabeth and her friend May were neatly stored away in a chest. (Swansea Mothers' Writing Group 1997: 24.)

The theme of "mothers and literacy" assumes, as one colleague put it to me, "the idea of mothers helping their kids to read and write". In this chapter we have, instead, considered how it can mean mothers imagining their own mothers' lives through the lens of reading and writing. This suggests one alternative to the one-way, mother-and-young-child version of a "family". Another is offered by the Family and Community Literacy Electronic Network, announced at a 1997 conference on the subject: "A 'family' can be construed as any small constellation of adult(s) and child(ren) committed to living closely together for an extended period, potentially including a very wide range of carers" (Savitsky 1997: 50).

Notes

1. The bounce of two balls against a wall created the rhythm for a playground rhyme on the subject, which my daughter Jess, like thousands of other girls in playgrounds all round the country, chanted with her friends in the mid-1970s.
2. Both Alice Walker and Tillie Olsen add their own gloss to Virginia Woolf's earlier diatribe against the silencing of women. Woolf had written: "Genius of a sort must have existed among them, as it existed among the working classes, but certainly it never got onto paper" (Woolf 1981: 48). Olsen footnotes this with: "Half of the working classes *are* women" (Olsen 1980: 11). Walker's parenthesis, to the same passage is this: ". . . among the working class [Change this to 'slaves' and 'the wives and daughters of sharecroppers']" (Walker 1995: 239).
3. It was a change that for me related to others, described in Chapter 3, in which talk with others may extend the written account of one person's memory.

Chapter 7
Images and certificates:
traces of a life

Sources for understanding the past may be written or oral. They can also be visual. This chapter pays a little attention to this, and begins with the possibility that pictures and photographs offer as sources for imagining mothers in the past.

Most of the written traces of mothers' lives consist of what historians call "ephemera": transitory writing, not intended to last or be kept – the kind that, if it is kept at all, clutters up the kitchen drawer, is stuffed behind a clock on the mantlepiece or forgotten in a box: postcards, shopping lists, bills, messages and scrapbooks; written for a time, but not for all time. All these are important evidence of everyday literacy practices, the place where private and public selves meet: intended only for the self or the single other reader, for light entertainment, for arrangements or as a prompt to the memory. Until now, these are the only written "evidence" we have considered.

There are also, however, the official documents of a life, designed to last as a permanent record, and providing a public record of the individual's existence. Certificates of birth, marriage and death and the inscriptions on graves are literacy at its most solemn: the search for family histories depends on their preservation in archive record office or stone. This chapter tells of a poet and a novelist who both seek to become the historians of their grandmothers' lives through sources such as these.

At the beginning of this book, I considered some thinking about two of the book's themes: literacy, and time. Literacy is not an absolute: its uses vary with context. Similarly, in lived experience, time is a conditional matter. I conclude with some reflections on the identity of "mother" herself, and on how this, too, is a relative matter. With this, I recapitulate the main strands of the book as a whole.

Images

Several times in the research for this book I found myself asking people: When you see your mother reading, what do you see? when you picture her writing, what is the picture?

When I interview myself with this question, I see at first nothing. Then, I see two things. First, a sheet of blue notepaper, address in capital letters centred at the top; and my mother's low, round handwriting. Her letters to me always began with the same words: "Darling Jane". (But still I do not see *her*, for by definition the letters are symbols of her absence.) Then, I see her reading aloud to my daughter, years ago, when she was maybe six or seven years old, both of them curled up on the sofa. (But still I do not see her *reading for herself.*) She read, I know, in bed at night; she used to say she could not contemplate going to sleep without first reading for at least half an hour first. She bought and read magazines, I know; she borrowed and read library books; she read and consulted knitting patterns; she wrote shopping lists – and more letters. For the last 17 years of her life she was a volunteer transcriber of braille; she would sit in the afternoon in the spare room upstairs and translate all kinds of texts, from O-level exam questions to cookery books, for a transcription service.

But I cannot *see* her reading or writing. My mother's name was Mary. To the extent that her literacy life was a time of play, Mary, in adult life, played at a time and a place when this child of hers at least was not there.

In the second chapter I said that, to understand anyone's literacy life, the observation of their literacy behaviour is not enough. Looking through other windows and between the curtains of other people's memories, it has been possible to catch glimpses of other mothers, at different ages throughout their lives, snatching moments of reading, pausing over writing a letter, alone and with others. With that information we can piece together a partial idea of their literacy: but we can still only guess at what they made of it. In order to create some kind of portrait of mothers reading or writing, the writers and speakers in this book have searched their imaginations as well as their memories. Some of them also searched through the written documents of a life; and a few of them referred to photographs.

On the pinboard in front of my desk is the photograph of another woman: half-lying on a sofa, her arms flung in the air, her face wonderfully animated: an image of warmth and voice captured by a camera, one Saturday morning in June 1997 in her house in Holland. The woman is Fie Van Dijk. The occasion is a conversation: she and I are talking about women and literacy. Beside me on the table, here on a dark London autumn evening six months later, are some of the postcard reproductions she lent me from her collection.

Fie Van Dijk's work in collecting and analyzing the gendered representation of reading and writing has illuminated the thinking of literacy educators across Europe and beyond. In the UK, her work first became more widely known at a conference convened by the national Research and Practice in Adult Literacy (RaPAL) network in 1990.[1] Papers from that conference were later published (Hamilton et al. 1994) and included six reproductions from Fie's collection alongside the summary of a discussion on women and literacy. Her own account of the origin of the collection later appeared in a number of papers, notably in an article she published in an issue of RaPAL Bulletin (van Dijk 1994):

The start was quite simple: now and then I got postcards with love from friends. I don't remember when it startled me that a certain pattern showed up in the pictures of reading and writing. And that pattern is that women are reading and writing in quite different ways from men. (van Dijk 1994: 1)

Two examples she gives of this difference are: men read newspapers, women read or write letters; and:

Most postcards depict women in subordinate positions. They look up (often in a very provocative posture) at the man who gives them orders, they type their texts even literally blindfold, and above all they read the letters of their lovers; they never study. (van Dijk 1994: 2)

The collection is one of postcard reproductions; from that early start somewhere around 1983, the collection has since grown to over a thousand. Selections from it have been displayed at conferences in England, in Germany, in Holland and in France; and the thinking that they have provoked has inspired and contributed to cultural studies in those countries and beyond. These are pictures of women and men reading and writing, in many different settings: outdoors and indoors, in hot and cold climates, alone and with others. They are reproductions of drawings, etchings and paintings from across the world; as well as photographs and cartoons (usually European or American). As such, they are commercial products, themselves designed for literacy use; and the very fact of Fie sending and receiving them is an illustration of one of the roles in which she found women most often depicted: namely, as readers and writers of letters (of which the postcard, as we discussed in the previous chapter, is the most abbreviated and least "important" form).

In the next two pages are three cartoons lent from Fie's collection that offer an ironic look at the kinds of reading and writing we have seen that mothers engage in. Out of duty or pleasure, with grim determination or delicious luxury, these women write the holiday postcard, make yet another shopping list and soak indulgently in fiction.

Two other images follow: images at the opposite extremes of "family literacy": the first, a sentimental and domestic scene which portrays both parents with a child, the second showing three women (any one of whom might be a mother, we don't know) very clearly reading with nobody's interests in mind but their own.

Bourgeois literacy: France, 1920s

The woman is sitting in the armchair, one bare arm resting on the arm of the chair, the other embracing her child. For her part, the little girl seems to be half sitting, half standing close to the mother's crossed legs. The mother is turning the page of a magazine. The magazine has a picture on the front of what appears to

Wish you were here . . .

Too much of a good thing can be wonderful . . .

Meaningful relationship

be a child-fairy, with full-skirt; the figure is clasping a baton and staring laughingly out at the reader. Above the picture is the magazine title; indistinct, the first word, the second (blurred) appears to be the word "Ouvrage". Mother and daughter smile at the magazine. Their hair is carefully waved and brushed; the mother is wearing a short-sleeved silky shirt and a round-necked plain dark dress, and the kind of shoes that were fashionable in the 1920s, with bars across and low heels. We cannot see much of what her daughter is wearing, except her white socks. The two of them smile, eyes lowered, at the magazine. And at the mother's elbow, lying on the arm of the chair and casually touching the skin of her forearm, are four roses.

Who is this, standing behind? dressed in three piece suit, his tie pierced by a neat tie pin, his glossy hair smoothed flat either side of the careful parting, leaning over mother and daughter: who can he be, but father? The three of them, looking down at the magazine held lightly in the mother's fingers, form a triangle: entranced, as it were, by the magazine – which, held at the distance it is from the mother, must be all but illegible (as it is to the viewer). The smiles are unanimous. The message is: we are a unit, united at the lowest point of our triangle by the prospect in front of us. None of the three has their mouth open. No-one is speaking, still less reading aloud from the page in front of them. The rose petals just touch the skin of the woman's arm; the man's finger just brushes the silk of her shirt. How happy they look! how transfixed! what an image of family bliss!

151

Bourgeois literacy

It is a photograph, in sepia; all it says on the reverse, is "fabrication francaise". We do not know the identity of either photographer or subjects. Fie's comment on it as I picked it out of her box of cards was: "It is so *bourgeois*!"

Knit your own orgasm

Many Mass Observation writers mentioned that the one thing they *did* remember their mothers reading was knitting patterns. Both my mother and my mother-in-law were fine knitters, prolific producers of garments large and small, fine and chunky, from girlhood to old age, over six or seven decades. Knitting is also the single thing it is possible to do – if you are good at it – at the same time as reading or talking. To the outsider, or non-knitter, knitting is homely, knitting is sensible, knitting is the good housewife and mother; it appears to occupy no intellectual or

Knit your own orgasm

emotional energy; out of the context of home and hearth, it is faintly absurd. What is deliciously funny about this picture, then, is the association of the knitter with sexual delight. The secret is out: women who knit also have bodies. Beneath her motherly apron, the reader on the right is capable of lust.[2]

In the search through Fie van Dijk's collection, I became struck by the representation of family literacy offered by European paintings of the "Madonna and Child". While, at first sight, the pose appears to be that of mother reading to child, it holds other significance. As an interesting aside on my main focus, I have included a note on this in Appendix 2.

Most of this book has focused on memories as a source of information about the lives of mothers. These have been a mix of episodic memories – tales and anecdotes – and something referred to earlier as "autobiographical knowledge". In addition, we have noticed that some memories have been of pictures or scenes. The following is another such image; its power lies not so much in the visual scene it presents as in an atmosphere which it recalls. It comes from my interview with Gwen:

> I remember, I think it would be just before my 4th birthday, the Christmas before I was 4. And we went to my Grandma's on Christmas Day. My Uncle Joe and Aunty Lena lived there, of course; they'd provide most of it. Father Christmas had come to Grandma's before we arrived – and I remember that

I'd been given this beautiful nursery rhyme book. It were the colourful, stiff back kind, and it was thick. It was big. My mother was sitting on a chair, and I was standing next to her with this book open. And there were pictures – on every page, there was a nursery rhyme and a picture – very, very nicely done. It would have cost a lot of money. It perhaps cost 5 shillings, which was, you know . . . and I was trying to attract my mother's attention: "What's this about? what's this about?". But she was, of course, in conversation with all the adults.

I remember feeling great pleasure with the book and with my mother being there, because my mother was working otherwise, you know. The whole, the warmth of the room, and everything was absolutely smashing – even though I didn't get my mother's full attention – it was all absolutely magical, and this book was part of it.

(Interview, February 1997) (my emphasis)

Lily had had little schooling herself; an "unbookish" upbringing. All Gwen's childhood she had been a working mother, working at the mill. In this picture of mother, child and book, the book is incidental. Its importance lies not in who was reading and what it was about, but in the intimacy and warmth of atmosphere. It was "magical"; and in that sense, it is a picture which neither painting or photograph could adequately capture. It is the context of the image that keeps its importance for Gwen – a context which is absent from the sentimental cameo of family literacy provided by the "bourgeois" threesome in the postcard.

Certificates

For Carolyn Steedman, the discovery of a photograph on the mantlepiece was also the discovery of her father's first wife and child. It was after her father's death that she and her sister learned they had been illegitimate; in this learning, a multitude of details and incidents from their lives took on a different significance and meaning than they had ever had before. (The fact that the two girls had had "proper" birth certificates is one which, she says, gave her (as a historian) cause for concern: if her own certificate had been fake, what did it mean for "the verisimilitude" of any others? (Steedman 1992: 41).) The certificates lied: or rather, her parents had. She follows this discovery with that of another certificate – one she had always thought would exist, and which turned out to be nonexistent. When she was a child, her mother had told her that she had been baptized, in Hammersmith, and that they had "lost touch" with her godparents. After her mother's death, years later, she found that this story was a fabrication: "It was a genuine shock *not* to find a baptismal certificate with my name on it after her death, among all the papers stuffed into drawers and old handbags" (Steedman 1992: 71).

As well as memories, Mass Observation writers and the other sources for this book also turned to documents to make some sense of their mothers' lives. Just as literacy itself represents a hidden life, so the hidden lives of mothers may be revealed through written documents discovered long after the event they record. The Irish poet Eavan Boland and the English novelist Margaret Forster both sought to find an understanding of their grandmothers via "written evidence". Their published accounts of these searches mix poetic description with autobiographical narrative:

> In a summer dusk, when I was seventeen (writes Eavan Boland), my mother told me a story. I was leaning across a chair, facing a window. Back out towards the river, which ran behind the house, the sky was still bright; everything else was still darkening. The fruit trees were spare and dark – a child's drawing. The apples were black globes.
>
> The story she told was about her mother. She had been born into a family of millers and had been one of thirteen children. She had married very young, a seaman who became a sea captain. She had died after the birth of her last child – my mother – at thirty-one in a Dublin hospital.

"It was a short conversation", Boland goes on:

> Of a woman she could not remember. Who had been deserted by good luck and had left five orphan daughters. There was nothing heroic in her account, and she offered no meanings. Instead she did what innumerable human beings have done with her children. She told me what had happened. (Boland 1996: 67–68)

The scene is between mother and daughter – a scene when, briefly, the mother is herself a daughter, passing on the "facts" of her own mother's life. Elsewhere in the same book, Eavan Boland takes the reader on her journey to fill in the gaps in this picture: gaps left both by her own listening, as well as by her mother's choice of telling. Her search takes her to the Dublin hospital where she attempts to discover the woman who, at the age of thirty-one, had gone there to die; and to a graveyard, where this woman, her grandmother, had been laid to rest.

But her grandmother's name was not to be found. In that graveyard outside Dublin, through a long cold afternoon, she peered through unkempt grass at stones, some with inscriptions, most without; reading the few with words and names on them, and searching the others, she finally had to give in and recognize that her grandmother's name was not there, and she grieved – both for the name and for the woman it belonged to: "She had turned her head for it, come running to it as a child, hoped for it on a letter and answered it in moments of love. And now she had no memorial because she had no name" (Boland 1996: 23).

With this, Boland resumes the narrative of her own life as a young poet, of how she had felt herself to have no name; a woman reading men and finding no place for her own experience in their writing.

This had been a quest for a grandmother whom the granddaughter had never met but who had always been part of her life. Reading it recalled a similar search

I had made myself, not long before. In 1995, I too sought my grandmother's grave. Like Eavan Boland, I had never met this woman: she had died before I was born. Unlike her, I found her name, carved in stone, and I read the words that had been composed by her grieving husband, my grandfather. On the wall at home I also have a black and white photograph of her, taken in 1919 or 1920 holding my mother (aged three) on her lap. In a box I have just one letter in her handwriting, written to her son, my uncle, a few months before she died. These three pieces of "evidence" are all I have with which to imagine the life of someone called Cynthia Salome Caroline, "born January 12 1893, married August 28 1915, died July 30 1940". I know she had three children; I do not know how many other pregnancies she had. I know she had a brother and a sister, a father and a mother, and a husband; I do not know who else she loved. I know she suffered from asthma, played the piano, grew up in London, died in Canberra, Australia. What I do not know is how she saw the world or her place in it. What I am told, by the inscription on the gravestone, is that "she was much loved".

When my grandmother wrote to her son, my uncle, she was 47; he, 15. As the mother of a son who is now 26, I feel sympathy for her. Yet, despite the phrase "my grandmother" I can feel little claim on her. Our lives are separated by deaths: her own, that of her husband, my grandfather, and all her three children, including Mary, my mother, the eldest. It takes a conscious effort to name her in her own right – Cynthia – a similar effort to that of the women in Swansea or in the U3A group in London. But at least her name was visible to me, that day in the churchyard in Canberra.

Boland found no stone memorial for her grandmother; but she did find her death certificate, marking "the death of a young woman, far from her home" in the National Maternity Hospital in 1909. Here, Mary Ann's name is written "in a sloping, florid hand . . . the letters of the name thick and thin by turns, where the calligraphic nib pressed down and eased up" (Boland 1996: 29).

In Margaret Forster's case, the search was also for written names. She sought not only her grandmother, but her grandmother's "fourth unacknowledged daughter". She too went looking for the *name written down* – the name of the mother, and also of the daughter who was never allowed to be named. In her search, she checked registers of birth, marriage and death. Knowing her grandmother's birthdate (1869) and her name, she was able to track down the record of the daughter's birth:

> Immediately, it was there: to Margaret Ann Jordan, domestic servant, aged twenty-three, on 12 April 1893 a girl, named Alice, born in Wetheral, the village Tom (Margaret's husband) took his girls to, but where Margaret Ann would never go. (Forster 1995: 48)

The book Forster writes is not an autobiography (or not in the sense of the author's own lifetime alone) – although she enters it in the first person two-thirds of the way through; it is, rather, a combination of fictional and documentary narrative, woven with the skill of the practised novelist. The search it represents is not for her own life, but for her grandmother's: for Margaret Ann, mother of an illegitimate daughter, had herself been illegitimate.

Its magic, to me, is the way in which Margaret Forster steps from one literacy drama to another. Beginning with the birth of her grandmother, she moves to a day just over 60 years later when a woman (who turns out to be Alice) stands on the doorstep asking to meet Margaret Ann, the mother who had abandoned her as a child. From there, Forster shifts the scene to another day, after Margaret Ann's death and funeral, when Alice reappears seeking to know what may have been left to her in her mother's will. This document, pulled out of a drawer by shocked middle-aged daughters, makes no mention of Alice. Ten years later (in 1946) we are in a church hall where eager young Brownies (of whom Margaret Forster herself is one) are being encouraged to go home and research their family history, ask questions of relatives, and write down their family trees. The child, "goes straight into her home and begins asking for names and dates, pencil poised, sheet of paper ready" (Forster 1995: 11)

Thus began (as a good storyteller might say) a lifetime's search, culminating (but not ending) in the discovery of Alice's birth certificate. So the grandmother *had* given birth to a fourth daughter: a daughter whose name she had caused to be recorded at the time of giving birth, but refused to recognize at the time of her dying.

In 1930 Jean, Margaret Ann's daughter, married and moved. It was as if she had emigrated. The mother grieves; the daughter promises to write. Letters would be small consolation: "Facts had to be faced; this daughter was leaving the family and that was that. The ninety or so miles to Motherwell might as well be nine thousand for all they would now see of her" (Forster 1995: 79).

As things turned out, the letters to and from Jean *did* provide consolation – not for Jean's mother, but for her sister, Lily (Margaret Forster's mother). The picture she gives of Lily sitting down to write each week to Jean (so far away) is of a ceremony:

It was a formal business, this letter-writing and it impressed me. My mother looked so important doing it. She would spread a felt undercloth on the living-room table and put a sheet of blotting paper on top of it and then a bottle of Quink ink and a pad of blue Basildon Bond notepaper, and then she'd pick up her blue and black Conway Stewart fountain-pen and start. (Forster 1995: 141–2)

Lily, once a doctor's secretary in an office with letters to type and be signed, brought the formality of the office into her living room. The letters themselves, according to her daughter's recollection, did not satisfy their author; but the replies (each Tuesday) were "a treat, kept for the afternoons, when the washing and cleaning were done" (Forster 1995: 142).

The "bare facts" of the life of Eavan Boland's grandmother had been given to her one summer dusk when she herself was 17 years old. Years later (in her early thirties) she set off to a graveyard in her car to try to find the headstone of this woman, and finds none. At the age of 49, she writes about these two episodes, and about her reaction to the handwriting on the one document where she did find her grandmother's name written: the death certificate. The handwriting is "sloping"; the letters of the name "thick and thin by turns".

Facts and handwriting go hand in hand. Pencil in hand, the eight-year-old Margaret Forster sat poised to elicit "facts" about her family history. Her mother Lily, writing to her sister, set herself the task of telling her some of the "facts" of her life that week. And at the end of the letter, she signed her name, as a sister would: not with the formal signature she might have used for more official purposes (like the marriage register) but in her everyday handwriting. Cynthia, my grandmother, wrote the word "Mummy" at the end of her letter to her son: the sign of a tie of love and affection, but a word which also puts limits around what he could ever have known of her. When, years before, she had signed her name on the marriage register, she would have written, instead, the word "she would have turned her head for".

Mothers are relative

A mother, of course, is only a mother to her children. It is a relative term. The mother of my niece is also the sister of my husband; my own mother was the sister of two brothers; while I am the mother of my two children, I am also aunt to my brother's sons; and so on. My own mother was not only "mine": she was the mother of my two brothers and sisters, too. More important still is the fact that a mother is also a woman with other identities. In different contexts she will introduce herself as different people: in one, she may say she is the chair of the meeting; in another, she is the receptionist in an office or surgery; in a third, she is the singer of a song. She may be able to fix a broken engine; she may be good at speaking three languages. She may be black, she may be white. Being a mother is a relative condition, not an absolute one. But as soon as we put "mothers" and "literacy" side by side, there seems to be a common assumption that what we are talking about is "mothers helping their children to read and write".

The business of mothering has itself been the subject of a mass of writing, in the last century as well as this. Since the 1950s, for women becoming mothers for the first time, or for mothers of infants and pre-school children, an "explosion of books, pamphlets and magazine articles" had become available, advising on every aspect of child development (Urwin 1982). New mothers have been subjected to advice since time began; advice on the best way of bringing up children has never been in short supply. The special feature of advice to mothers in the late twentieth century, however, seems to have been this focus on *literacy*.

There is such pleasure to be had in knowing we can help our children; the confidence that mothers gain from feeling we are competent to enable them to grow and bloom is immeasurable. That children flourish in such a relationship of support is well known. Meanwhile, every mother has her other identities and lives; each one holds within her adult, maternal self both the girl she once was and the old woman she is yet to be: regrets and relief mix with anticipation and dreams. When one or other of her other selves seeks to find expression, her family may protest:

> I announce to my family that, in future, I am claiming time off from domestic chores to read and write, in preparation for an O-level in English! "Mum's Career" has long been a source of merriment, and notes left on the table or cooker are referred to as "Mum's literary efforts", without any action being taken on their contents.
>
> Now I am in earnest. Other mothers belong to clubs, play bridge, golf, bingo. This Mum wants to read to some purpose. The hour between the children's tea and preparation of Father's dinner shall be devoted to Keats, or Hardy, or Macbeth. I shall go into the lounge, away from the television noise. My books are already in there. "MUM! is something boiling over on the stove?" (Stanton 1986: 40–41)

Women who leave home to engage in their own writing and reading via family literacy projects can and do meet in their own right, as well as in their capacities as mothers to children at school. Such a group met for two years in Moss Side, Manchester, telling stories about their own families, childhoods, and the countries they had grown up in – as part of learning to speak English more fluently. The women had grown up in Somalia, Tanzania, Bangladesh and Pakistan; for most of them, learning English had also been their first opportunity to learn to read and write – and the magazine and anthology they produced was published in their first languages as well as in English. Ten of the women contributed to a book of these texts published by Gatehouse, the established publisher of writing by adult learners. Both the process and the publication represent a fine example of a family literacy strategy that gives voice to the women in their own right, not merely in their relative roles as mothers (Fitzpatrick & Mumin, 1996).

"Teaching the mother to reach the child", without attending to the woman in her own right, is to continue to subordinate women to being mere agents of reproduction. It should hardly be a surprise that mothers who have been denied the opportunity to reach their own literacy interests have had mixed feelings about their children's.

Ambivalence

"She wanted us 'educated', so that we could get safe jobs", recalls one Mass Observation correspondent (E1510). His mother had been born in 1894, the eighth and last child of a tailor, in Devon, who grew up to have four of her own children and whom he recalls as "literate, intelligent, politically-minded . . . but not an avid reader". Also described as a "tough, Amazonian woman", this mother, according to her son:

> Would have snorted at such words as "literacy". To her, education was a means to an occupational end. And who could criticize her, given her years-long struggle keeping us fed, clothed and together during childhood?

Other mothers felt impatient or even hostile to their children's schooling:

> Maud ruled her family with a rod of iron, and I believe, was afraid of her children being "cleverer" than her. She believed that school work should be done at school . . . Maud would not tolerate their homework and once threw Elsie's homework on the fire. (R1321)

The sight of a child lost in reading or writing is assumed to be a delight to parents: in practice, it could be the last straw. Eleanor (in an account derived from stories told to the writer "by my mother, who is now almost 80"), was a woman who had brought up a large family in a remote Lancashire village. She had, according to the writer, "an antipathy to reading":

> She felt it was "a waste of time when there's work to be done", and my mother remembers her throwing books on the fire, or lighting the fire with their pages, with the remark that "It's all they're good for".

Eleanor's "antipathy" to books co-existed with an equally passionate sympathy towards other kinds of literacy. She enjoyed what she saw to be "real life" reading. She valued receiving letters from her family in the village 12 miles away and regularly read the newspaper, which she said "had some point to it": "It was about real life and not the fanciful stuff of books" (S481). Several people (including Gwen) wrote about mothers who, at one stage, were apparently sympathetic to their daughters' literacy and at another stage opposed to their education.

If at the heart of literacy's pleasure is the pleasure of playing, both with time and with what Adrienne Rich calls "notions", then who should be surprised if a mother "in the old way" – a mother managing home and family with little space or time for herself – should feel contrary emotions at her daughter's withdrawal into this play?

It is difficult to draw an accurate picture of my mother's childhood. I know what her parental home was like, because it was still where my grandparents lived during my own early childhood, an upstairs two-bedroom flat in a mean, brick terrace where the housewives proudly whitestoned their front steps daily, where there was always a smell of damp and decay along the downstairs corridor, where a single room always served as combined kitchen-dining-living room and where you washed yourself in the shallow kitchen sink with water heated in a big kettle on the coal-fired range. The loo (unlit) was in the back yard alongside the scullery. It was in this setting that she shared her formative years with her sister (two years older) and her brother (two years younger). (J2520)

After a day's reading texts such as this in the cool shade of the quiet Archive room in the University of Sussex library, I was struck by the contrast between what I had been reading and the scene that faced me when I walked outside. Students, women and men, were strolling across the grass, leaning against the wall, meeting and talking, resting or hurrying. After the descriptions I had been reading of crowded basements and kitchens steaming with clothes drying and meals cooking, the sunlit scene was a sharp contrast.

The lifespans summarized in some of the texts lingered in my head as I walked down the steps from the library:

Jinny (born 1874) went to school and I remember her telling me that at the age of 12 she went part time and paid twopence (or a penny) a week. She could definitely read (she died reading a newspaper). All I ever heard about her home life was how poor the family was. There was never any suggestion that anyone (mother or father) read or had any education. From age 12 she worked as a servant. (J931)

The scene before me had the illusion, at least, of freedom. Had I not been aware of the growing fears of debt and poverty facing university students since the 1980s, I would have assumed that the people I saw that afternoon were living a life of luxury of which their grandmothers could only have dreamed. Once mothers had become grandmothers and (with good luck) were enjoying a relative freedom from the round of daily housework endured when they had been raising their own children, many were reported as swelling with pride at their granddaughters' educational achievements. But indoors, in the home, when those daughters were "*in the way, not helping*" or "*doing the dishes*", with their "*nose in a book*", many of the mothers recalled in the typed and handwritten pages I had been reading, under the constant pressure of "work to be done", had felt maddened.

Teaching the mother

Literacy is a very ordinary, everyday business; it also confers status and power. Ethnographic studies of reading and writing in daily life have offered exciting ways to recognize the interest in this "ordinariness", so that the literacy of the kitchen may be as interesting as the "important" literacy of published history and literature. (Among many interesting chapters in Denny Taylor's book on family literacy, for example – which I recommend to you – is that in which she gives examples of the notes, left on the kitchen table, written between members of a family (Taylor 1983).) The ordinary and incidental kinds of writing and reading that mothers' undertake in the routines of the lives of their families became suddenly fascinating to the women in the Swansea project (described in Chapter 6). As their own ethnographers, they were undertaking a mini-research project on their own family literacy and in so doing, giving recognition to what they already knew – as well as continuing to think about what they still wished to learn.

By way of conclusion, I invite you to consider the signature – the conventional end to much paperwork, both mundane and ceremonial. There was a time when it was common to collect autographs in an autograph book. This is a different practice from getting celebrities to give their autograph – on a book they have written, on a cricket bat, on anything that the fan has to hand. The autograph book was something particular to girls at school; we got our friends to sign in it, usually at the end of term or when we all finally left school. (The practice of giving signatures on parting company continues today with the office leaving card or the practice of school-leavers writing messages and signatures on each others' shirts.) Messages and rhymes would go with the signature – "By hook or by crook I"ll be last in this book".

The signature in the autograph book on the next page is that of "mother". She has signed the book of her daughter (then aged 19), with a careful rhyme.

> May the one to whom this book belong
> Few trials have if any
> Her hours of sorrow be they few
> Her sunny moments many.

This, then, was the impersonal/personal signature of the (as usual) nameless "mother" with the personal/impersonal rhyme addressed, not to her daughter's name, but to "the one to whom this book belong".

The double meaning of signatures – personal, impersonal, formal, informal – is played out, too, in the way that they represent formal agreement to legal arrangements. This agreement cannot be accepted as binding until and unless the very personal mark of each party has been given to it. The signature, referred to in Chapter 5 as the single measure of literacy levels in the nineteenth century, is an intensely personal matter, used today for the most official events. David Vincent has pointed out that it is a special feature of a society with advanced writing

May the one to whom this book belong,

Few trials have if any,

Her hours of sorrow be they few

Her sunny moments many

mother
Dec 1915

Signing off

technologies (first typewriting, then electronic) that the artifice of the illegible signature has reached its summit. Until this century, the handwritten name was set down with the express intention that it could be read in full: "Only the gentry and the occasional lawyer drew attention to their learning by the elaboration of their writing; few adopted the twentieth century conceit of cultivated illegibility" (Vincent 1993: 21).

The signature on the marriage register provides the single trace we have of the literacy of our antecedents in the early nineteenth century. As historians have recognized, the ability to sign said little about anything else in the user's literacy life. To be able to write our own name is one of the oldest and deepest of literacy ambitions. To be able to write it illegibly is a relatively recent symbol of the fully literate citizen.

Most of this book has been about the past, not the future. That is because, as I said at the start, this was the approach I chose with which to look differently at the present. We live in a time when it is assumed that terrible things are happening to national standards of literacy. On a daily basis, complaints are made about the standard of spelling, reading, or writing among today's children, compared with previous generations. Someone must be at fault; progressive methods of teaching are one scapegoat, poor standards of literacy in the home are another. It has not been my intention to arrive at a conclusion either way, for, like Margaret Meek, I am doubtful that the complaint itself has any basis. I have certainly not set out to "prove" that mothers (or any other family members) do or do not cause children to fail in school, because that is not an issue that interests me. Rather, I have been exploring what mothers themselves might want literacy for. I have been seeking to tease out with you how we may put the two words "mothers" and "literacy" next to each other without it being assumed that we are only talking about children. And in doing so, I have been inviting you to play a little.

Notes

1. The Research and Practice in Adult Literacy (RaPAL) network was established in 1985. It is a national network of learners, teachers, managers and researchers in England, Scotland, Wales and Ireland who are engaged in adult literacy and basic education. Supported by membership subscription, it publishes a bulletin three times a year and aims to promote democratic practices in adult literacy work.

2. The reading of knitting patterns is not usually seen as a literacy activity in its own right; plenty of knitters read patterns without knitting, of course – if only to decide which pattern they like. Someone might do some research on this, perhaps. Mary Hamilton and David Barton have found people who read cookery books in bed at night for the fun of it – so why not knitting patterns? (Barton & Hamilton 1998). I have knitted too, but less skilfully than my mother or mother-in-law. My tension is tight; and for years I had the disappointment of making up a finished garment only to discover it was one size too small. When my children went to university, I knitted each of them a jumper. Choosing the thickest yarn and the fattest needles, I thought I could not fail. The jumpers were to be warm and large; and I became nervous in another direction: I thought they would end up knee-length. So once made up, it turned out that the sleeves were fine, but the body was three inches too short. The pattern brings it all back to me:

Using $6\frac{1}{2}$ mm needles cast on 47 (51, 53, 55, 57,61) sts.
Rib row 1: P.1 *k.1, p.1, rep. from * to end.
Rib row 2: K.1, *p.1, k.1, rep. from * to end.
Rep. these 2 rows for 3 in., ending rib row 2.
Change to 8 mm. needles.
Proceed in fisherman's rib as follows:
Row 1: (Right side) K.
Row 2: K.1 *p.1, k.1B., rep. from * to last 2 sts. p.1 k.1
These 2 rows form the patt.
Continue in patt. until back measures $13\frac{1}{2}$(14,14,14,14,14) in. from cast-on edge, ending wrong-side row. *(Length can be adjusted here)*
(my emphasis)

References

Adler, R. 1984. *A family of shopkeepers* (2nd edn). London: W.H. Allen.

Altick, R. 1983. *The English Common Reader: a social history of the mass reading public, 1800–1900*. Chicago: University of Chicago Press.

Armour, J. 1996. Teach the mother to reach the child? In *Lifelong literacies: papers from the conference*, S. Fitzpatrick & J. Mace (eds), 34–6, Manchester: Gatehouse Books.

Atwood, M. 1992. Significant moments in the life of my mother. In *Close company: Stories of mothers and daughters*, C. Park & C. Heaton (eds), 5–20. London: Virago.

Auerbach, E. 1989. Towards a social-contextual approach to family literacy. *Harvard Educational Review* **59**(2), 165–81.

Auerbach, E. 1994. Feeding the disease metaphor of illiteracy. *Fine Print* (Journal of the Victorian Adult Literacy and Basic Education Council, Australia) **16**(2), 11–18.

Ballard, B. & J. Clanchy 1988. Literacy in the university: an anthropological approach. In *Literacy by degrees*, G. Taylor (ed.), 8–23. London: Society for Research into Higher Education.

Barton, D. 1994a. Exploring family literacy. *RaPAL Bulletin* **24** (Summer), 2–5.

Barton, D. 1994b. *Literacy: an introduction to the ecology of written language*. Oxford: Blackwell.

Barton, D. & M. Hamilton 1998. *Local literacies: reading and writing in one community*. London: Routledge.

Barton, D. & R. Ivanic (eds) 1991. *Writing in the community*. Newbury Park: Sage.

Barton, D. & S. Padmore 1991. Roles, networks and values in everyday writing. In *Writing in the community*, D. Barton & R. Ivanic (eds), 58–78. Newbury Park: Sage.

Basic Skills Agency 1993. *Family literacy: read and write together – getting started*. London: Basic Skills Agency.

Beauman, N. 1983. *A very great profession: the woman's novel 1914–1939*. London: Virago.

Bird, V. & K. Pahl 1994. Parent literacy in a community setting. *RaPAL Bulletin* (Summer), **24**, 6–15.

Boland, E. 1996. *Object lessons: the life of the woman and the poet in our time.* London: Vintage.

Bourke, J. 1994. *Working-class cultures in Britain 1890–1960.* London: Routledge.

Bowlby, J. 1953. *Childcare and the growth of love.* Harmondsworth: Penguin.

Bown, L. 1991. *Preparing the future: women, literacy and development.* Chard/London: Action Aid.

Brooks, A., F. Fletcher & B. Lund 1982. *What the postman saw: a lighthearted look at old picture postcards and their messages.* Nottingham: Reflections of a Bygone Age.

Brooks, G., P. Gorman, J. Harman, D. Hutchison & A. Wilkin 1996. *Family literacy works: NFER's evaluation of the Basic Skills Agency's family literacy programmes.* London: Basic Skills Agency.

Brown, A. 1993. Adult illiteracy: still a crying shame. *Reader's Digest* (April), 137–43.

Campbell, B. 1991. *More than life itself: a handbook for tutors of adult literacy.* Melbourne: VALBEC.

Chlebowska, K. 1990. *Literacy for rural women in the Third World.* Paris: UNESCO.

Cohen, D. 1993. Private lives in public spaces: Marie Stopes, the Mothers' Clinics and the practice of contraception. *History Workshop Journal* **35**, 95–116.

Cook-Gumperz, J. 1986. *The social construction of literacy.* Cambridge: Cambridge University Press.

Dallimore, P. 1982. Shush – mum's writing. In *The republic of letters: working class writing and local publishing*, D. Morley & K. Worpole (eds), 89. London: Comedia.

David, M. 1989. Home-school relations. In *Mothers and education: inside out?*, M. David, R. Edwards, M. Hughes & J. Ribbens (eds), 31–59. London: Macmillan.

Davies, K. 1996. Capturing women's lives: a discussion of time and methodological issues. *Women's Studies International Forum* **19**(6), 579–88.

Davin, A. 1996. *Growing up poor: home, school and street in London 1870–1914.* London: Rivers Oram Press.

D'Cruze, S. 1995. Women and the family. In *Women's history: Britain, 1850–1914*, J. Purvis (ed.), 51–85. London: UCL Press.

Deem, R. 1986. *All work and no play? The sociology of women and leisure.* Milton Keynes: Open University Press.

East End Literacy Women's Group 1990. *I call it the curse: a book about periods.* Toronto: East End Literacy.

Edmond, L. 1996. *A matter of timing.* Auckland: Auckland University Press.

Elfyn, M. 1994. Writing is a bird in the hand. In *Our sisters' land: changing identities of women in Wales*, J. Aaron, T. Rees, S. Betts & M. Vincentelli (eds), 280–87. Cardiff: University of Wales Press.

Ericsson, B. (ed.) 1991. *Swedish Aspects on Literacy*, Stockholm: Skoloverstyrelsen (Swedish National Board of Education).

Fazackerley, A. 1984. Why I write poetry. In *Yes I like it: poems by new writers*, Gatehouse (eds), 51. Manchester: Gatehouse Books.

Fingeret, A. 1983. Social network: a new perspective on independence and adult illiterates. *Adult Education Quarterly* **33**(3), 133–46.

Firth, J. 1995. *A time to trust*. Stocksbridge: Stocksbridge Writers Group.

Fitzpatrick, S. & F. Mumin (eds) 1996. *Our experience: women from Somalia, Tanzania, Bangladesh and Pakistan write about their lives*. Manchester: Gatehouse Books.

Forster, M. 1995. *Hidden lives: a family memoir*. London: Penguin.

Frow, M. 1996. *Roots of the future: ethnic diversity in the making of Britain*. London: Commission for Racial Equality.

Giere, U. 1992. *Worlds of words: an international exhibition of literacy posters*. Stuttgart: UNESCO.

Gittins, D. 1982. *Fair sex: family size and structure 1900–1939*. London: Hutchinson.

Gonzales, Y. 1991. This story is about my mother. In *Parkdale Writes: New Writing from Parkdale Project Read*, 96–7.

Greenhalgh, L. & K. Worpole 1995. *Libraries in a world of cultural change*. London: UCL Press.

Hackney Reading Centre 1980. *Every birth it comes different*. London: Centerprise.

Hall, E. 1977. *Canary girls and stockpots*. Luton: WEA.

Hall, R. 1981. *Dear Dr. Stopes: sex in the 1920s*. Harmondsworth: Penguin.

Hall, R. 1984. *Just relations*. Harmondsworth: Penguin.

Hamilton, M. 1997. Keeping alive alternative visions. In *Alpha 97: basic education and institutional environments*, J.P. Hautecoeur (ed.), 131–50. Toronto: Culture Concepts.

Hamilton, M., D. Barton & R. Ivanic 1994. *Worlds of literacy*. Clevedon: Multilingual Matters.

Hannon, P. 1995. *Literacy, home and school: research and practice in teaching literacy with parents*. London: Falmer Press.

Hannon, P. 1997. Two decades of family literacy in the UK. Unpublished paper, Division of Education, Sheffield University.

Harrison, C. 1996. Family literacy: evaluation, ownership and ambiguity. *RSA Journal*, **CXLIV**, 5474, 25–9.

Heath, S.B. 1983. *Ways with words*. Cambridge: Cambridge University Press.

Holmes, K. 1995. *Spaces in her day: Australian women's diaries, 1920s–1930s*. NSW, Australia: Allen & Unwin.

Horowitz Murray, J. (ed.) 1984. *Story minded women and other lost voices from 19th century England*. London: Penguin.

Horsman, J. 1990. *Something in my mind besides the everyday: women and literacy*. Toronto: Women's Press.

Howard, U. 1991. Self, education and writing in nineteenth-century English communities. In *Writing in the community*, D. Barton & R. Ivanic (eds), 78–109. Newbury Park: Sage.

Institute of Practitioners in Advertising 1997. *It pays to advertise: learning from the 1996 IPA award winners* (Advertising effectiveness teaching video). London: IPA.

Ivanic, R. & M. Hamilton 1990. Literacy beyond school. In *Emerging partnerships*, D. Wray (ed.), 4–19. Clevedon: Multilingual Matters.

Josipovic, G. 1977. *The lessons of modernism and other essays*. London: Macmillan.

Kelly, T. & E. Kelly 1977. *Books for the people: an illustrated history of the public library*. London: Andre Deutsch.

Lawrence, J. & J. Mace 1992. *Remembering in groups: ideas from reminiscence and literacy work*. London: Oral History Society.

Levine, J. 1994. Illiteracy: women wear the chains. WFS Bulletin newsgroup, http://www.igc.org.

Liddington, J. & J. Norris 1978. *One hand tied behind us: the rise of the women's suffrage movement*. London: Virago.

Mace, J. 1979. *Working with words: literacy beyond school*. London: Writers and Readers.

Mace, J. 1983. Women talking: feminism and adult literacy work. *Frontiers: A Journal of Women's Studies* **VII**(1), 38–44.

Mace, J. 1987. Adult literacy: campaigns and movements. In *Time off to learn: paid educational leave and low paid workers*, J. Mace & M. Yarnit (eds), 79–94. London: Methuen.

Mace, J. 1992. *Talking about literacy: principles and practice of adult literacy education*. London: Routledge.

Mace, J. (ed.) 1995. *Literacy, language and community publishing: essays in adult education*. Clevedon: Multilingual Matters.

Mace, J. & M. Wolfe 1990. Identity, authorship and status: issues for Britain in International Literacy Year. *Adults Learning* **1**(10), 264–6.

Mace, J. & M. Wolfe 1995. That old story: illiterates and fiction. In *Living literacies: Papers from a conference on multiple literacies and lifelong learning*, F. Savitsky (ed.), 37–42. London: London Language and Literacy Unit.

Manguel, A. 1996. *A history of reading*. London: Flamingo.

McAleer, J. 1992. *Popular reading and publishing in Britain 1914–1950*. Oxford: Clarendon Press.

McCrindle, J. & S. Rowbotham 1977. *Dutiful daughters: women talk about their lives*. London: Pelican.

McLeod, D. 1993. Literacy drive puts accent on family. *Guardian*, 16 June 1993, 4.

Meek, M. 1991. *On being literate*. London: Bodley Head.

Minto, A. 1979. Let loose. *Write First Time* **4**(4), 7.

Morley, D. & K. Worpole 1982. *The republic of letters: working class writing and local publishing*. London: Comedia.

Morton, S. 1996. Family learning in West Glamorgan. In *Lifelong literacies: papers from the 1996 conference*, F. Fitzpatrick & J. Mace (eds), 39–44. Manchester: Gatehouse.

Moss, W. 1995. Controlling or empowering? Writing through a scribe in adult basic education. In *Literacy, language and community publishing: essays in adult education*, J. Mace (ed.), 145–71. Clevedon: Multilingual Matters.

Naughton, B. 1961. Maggie's first reader. In *The goalkeeper's revenge and other stories*, B. Naughton (ed.), 112–18. Harmondsworth: Puffin.

Nederkoorn, A. 1993. Martha. In *Women's lives, women's literacy: papers from the 1993 Women and literacy conference*, J. Mace (ed.), 31–2. London: Goldsmiths College University of London.

Nickse, R. 1990. Family literacy and community education: prospects for the nineties. *Journal of Community Education* **8**(2), 12–18.

Nurss, J. & S. Ketchum 1995. *Papers from the first international conference on women and literacy*. Georgia: Center for the Study of Adult Literacy, Georgia State University.

Olsen, T. 1980. *Silences*. London: Virago.

Olsen, T. (ed.) 1985. *Mother to daughter, daughter to mother, mothers on mothers: a reader and diary*. London: Virago.

Pahl, K. & V. Bird 1996. Family literacy in the UK: an overview from the National Literacy Trust. Unpublished conference paper.

Portelli, A. 1998. What makes oral history different. In *The oral history reader*, R. Perks & A. Thomson (eds), 63–75. London: Routledge.

Purvis, J. 1989. *Hard lessons: the lives and education of working-class women in 19th century England*. Cambridge: Polity Press.

Ramdas, L. 1990. Women and literacy: a quest for justice. *Convergence* **xxiii**(1), 27–43.

Rane-Szostak, D. & K.A. Herth 1995. Pleasure reading, other activities and loneliness in later life. *Journal of Adolescent and Adult Literacy* **39**(2), 100–108.

Rich, A. 1980. When we dead re-awaken: writing as re-vision. In *On lies, secrets and silence*, A. Rich (ed.), 33–51. London: Virago.

Roberts, E. 1984. *A woman's place: an oral history of working-class women 1890–1940*. Oxford: Basil Blackwell.

Robinson, J. 1992. Autobiographical memory. In *Aspects of memory, Vol. 1: The practical aspects*, M. Gruneberg & P. Morris (eds), 223–51. London: Routledge.

Rockhill, K. 1993. Gender, language and the politics of literacy. In *Cross-cultural approaches to literacy*, B. Street (ed.), 156–75. Cambridge: Cambridge University Press.

Salmon, P. 1992. Old age and storytelling. In *New Readings – contributions to an understanding of literacy*, K. Kimberley, M. Meek & J. Miller (eds), 216–23. London: A. & C. Black.

Savitsky, F. 1997. *Report on the London Language and Literacy Unit's first Family and Community Involvement in Literacy Conference*. London: London Language and Literacy Unit.

Scribner, S. 1984. Literacy in three metaphors. *American Journal of Education* **93**, 6–21.

Scribner, S. & M. Cole 1981. *The psychology of literacy*. Boston, Mass.: Harvard University Press.

Sheridan, D. 1993. Writing for . . . questions of representation/representativeness, authorship and audience. In *Ordinary people writing: the Lancaster and Sussex Writing Research Projects*, D. Barton, D. Bloome, D. Sheridan &

B. Street (eds), 17–23. Lancaster: Centre for Language in Social Life, Lancaster University.

Sheridan, D. 1996. *"Damned anecdotes and dangerous confabulations": Mass Observation as life history*. Mass Observation Archive Occasional Paper No. 7. Brighton: University of Sussex Library.

Stanton, E. 1986. Mum's career. In *The common thread: Writings by working class women*, J. Burnett, J. Cotterill, A. Kennerley, P. Nathan & J. Wilding (eds), 40–41. London: Mandarin.

Steedman, C. 1986. *Landscape for a good woman: a story of two lives*. London: Virago.

Steedman, C. 1992. *Past tenses: essays in writing, autobiography and history*. London: Rivers Oram Press.

Sticht, T. 1993. Workforce education, family literacy and economic development. In *Viewpoint 15: family literacy*, ALBSU (eds), 9–16. London: Adult Literacy and Basic Skills Unit.

Street, B. 1995. *Social literacies: critical approaches to literacy in development, ethnography and education*. New York: Longman.

Stromquist, N. 1992. Women and literacy: promises and constraints. *Annals of the American Academy of Political and Social Science* **520**, 54–65.

Sulter, M. 1987. A portrait of the artist as poor, black, and a woman. In *Glancing fires: an investigation into women's creativity*, L. Saunders (ed.), 148–61. London: The Women's Press.

Swansea Mothers' Writing Group 1997. *Portraits in time*. Swansea: Swansea Mothers' Writing Group.

Taylor, D. 1983. *Family literacy: young children learning to read and write*. Exeter, New Hampshire: Heinemann.

Thomson, A. 1995. Life histories, adult learning and identity. In *The uses of autobiography*, J. Swindells (ed.), 163–77. London: Taylor & Francis.

Urwin, C. 1982. Constructing motherhood: the persuasion of normal development. In *Language, gender and childhood*, C. Steedman, C. Urwin & V. Walkerdine (eds), 164–203. London: Routledge & Kegan Paul.

van Dijk, F. 1990. Women and illiteracy. In *Alpha 90: current research in literacy*, J.P. Hautecoeur (ed.), 209–18. Hamburg: UNESCO Institute for Education.

van Dijk, F. 1994. Gender-specific images in reading and writing. *RaPAL Bulletin*. (Spring), **23**, 1–9.

Vincent, D. 1993. *Literacy and popular culture: England 1750–1914*. Cambridge: Cambridge University Press.

Walker, A. 1995. *In search of our mothers' gardens: womanist prose*. London: The Women's Press.

Walkderine, V. & H. Lucey 1989. *Democracy in the kitchen: regulating mothers and socialising daughters*. London: Virago.

White, C. 1970. *Women's magazines 1693–1968*. London: Michael Joseph.

Wickert, R. 1993. Constructing adult literacy: mythologies and identities. In *Literacy in contexts: Australian perspectives and issues*, A. Luke & P. Gilbert (eds), 29–39. St. Leonards, NSW: Allen & Unwin.

Williams, R. 1984. Notes on English Prose 1780–1950. In *Writing in society*, R. Williams (ed.), 67–121. London: Verso.

Withnall, A. 1994. Literacy on the agenda: the origins of the adult literacy campaign in the United Kingdom. *Studies in the Education of Adults* **26**(1), 67–85.

Woolf, V. 1981. *A room of one's own*. London: Granada.

Woolf, V. 1990. Introductory letter to Margaret Llewellyn Davies. In *Life as we have known it: letters from Co-operative Women*, Llewellyn Davies, M. (ed.), xvii–xxxxi, London: Virago.

Yarmol-Franko, K. 1990. *Literacy, popular education and democracy: building the movement*. Proceedings from the 4th World Assembly on Adult Education. Toronto: International Council for Adult Education.

Zmroczek, C. 1994. The weekly wash. In *This working-day world: women's lives and culture(s) in Britain 1914–1945*, S. Oldfield (ed.), 7–18. London: Taylor & Francis.

Appendix 1

Mass Observation Directive No. 46, November 1995 Part 2: Mothers and literacy in the early 1900s[1]

Jane Mace of Goldsmiths' College, University of London, has asked for this subject to be included in the directive at this time. She will be analyzing your replies as part of her research. This is her summary of the research question she is asking:

Today's educational policies stress the importance of mothers in young children's literacy development. Illiterate mothers, it is suggested, raise illiterate children.

But is this true? A generation of women in the early years of this century had little if any schooling as children. As adults, many therefore had little or no literacy in English.[2] Yet, as a population of older people today can testify, many of the children of those women grew up not only able to read and write, but also positively to enjoy reading and writing in their adult lives. Maybe then, it didn't matter if a mother could not read and write in English? Or maybe it did, but the child learned from others? Or maybe mothers provided something else even though they had no skills in reading and writing themselves?

Please help us create a portrait of some of these mothers from your own experience. What we are looking for is anything you remember or anything you know about a woman who was a mother raising children between 1890 and 1930. You may need to talk to your own parents or grandparents to get this information. *You should not use real names.*

To begin with, please note down (if you know them) the dates of birth and death of the woman about whom you are writing. You can write about more than one woman if you wish. Then make a note of whether you are writing about her as:

a) her child
b) her grandchild, or
c) in some other relationship – please specify this.

Please try and offer your reflections in two parts. As always, the points below are guidelines, and although it would be useful if you could try to cover them all, you are welcome to add additional points wherever you feel they are important.

(1) Her childhood: say anything you know about where she grew up, with how many brothers and sisters, and in what circumstances. What reading or writing occurred in the household? Was English the first language of the home? If not, what was? Did she go to school at all? For how long?

(2) Her life as a mother: how many children did she have? What reasons, if any, might she have had to want to read and write? For example, did any of her children, or her husband, live away for any time? Was she involved in religious, political, or other groups? Write anything you know about her literacy. Did she ever, as far as you know, read anything? If so, what? What about writing? If she couldn't read or write, who did she rely on for different kinds of literacy? Did she sing, tell stories, or talk to her children? What was her health like?

(3) If you were her child or grandchild: your memories of her attitudes to *your* reading and writing. Did she comment on your early efforts to read and write? What kind of things did she say? What feelings do you think she had about her own literacy?

Notes

1. Part 1 of Directive No. 46 was on: images of where you live: cities, towns and villages.
2. My reasons for expressing the issue in this way, and the reactions to it, are discussed in Chapter 4. Directives, as Dorothy Sheridan puts it, "have a tradition of provocation" (conversation with author February 1998). The pleasure I had in working with her and with the Mass Observation Archive was the hospitality this offered me to invite writers to engage with the topic.

Appendix 2
Holy literacy

Fifteenth century Italian "masters" of painting depicted images of family literacy. The mother is the humble learner from the literate child, a child who is no mere consumer, but the producer of the text between them. Sandro Botticelli's painting of "Madonna and Child" (now in the Poldi Pezzoli Museum in Milan) shows a tender scene. The young mother, her eyelids lowered, and one hand resting on the open book, bends her head as if listening to the child who, seated on (or rather half-falling off) her lap, turns his head up towards her while laying his hand on hers. With her other hand she gently holds him.

Bernardo Luini's portrait of the Holy Family includes the father, Joseph. This time, it is he whose eyes are lowered; while Mary, standing in front of him, gazes at their son, standing proudly on a table. Again, one of her hands keeps him safe from falling; and again, the other touches a book: in fact, she is holding the book to her bosom with this hand, one thumb caught inside it as if to hold the page. It is as if she is interrupting her own reading to hold the naked baby from falling. But we know that this is not any book that she is holding: it is a holy scripture, for which her holy son holds the key, just as his eyes hold her gaze.

In Christian morality, literacy is something taught as precious, necessary and important. Like Botticelli, Luini shows the Holy Mother as the parent of a literate child. Paintings of the annunciation from the same period show the Angel Gabriel holding a scroll announcing her sacred destiny to the teenage Mary. The image suggests that the mother was literate, too. The message of paintings that depict her with the infant Jesus, however, show her as a mother not only listening to but also learning a new literacy from her holy son.

The historian Albert Manguel (1996) tells us that, until the fourteenth century, the Virgin Mary was depicted as innocent (or ignorant) of the written word. It was only a hundred years before these two paintings that she had first been allowed the possibility of literacy: "Traditionally, in Christian iconography, the book or scroll belonged to the male deity, to either God the Father or the triumphant Christ, the new Adam, in whom the word was made flesh" (Manguel 1996: 217).

The decision by the painter Simone Martini in 1333, in his painting of the Annunciation, to show the Virgin Mary holding a book was, it seems, a bold, and

Madonna and Child: Sandro Botticelli

even risky one. The painting, frequently reproduced (like Botticelli and Luini's) in postcard form, hangs in the Uffizi Gallery in Florence. Golden angels cluster at the apex of the central arch; a vase of lilies stands between the kneeling angel and the submissive, almost cowering figure of the Virgin. One hand grips the Virgin's cloak under her chin; her eyes gaze on the words, streaming out in letters of gold from the angel's lips; and in her left hand she holds a book, her thumb keeping the place on the page she has just been reading (like Bernardo Luini's Madonna, over a century later). What book did Martini intend this to be? Could it be a Book of Hours (likely to be the only book possessed by many wealthy homes of the time, and the one used by mothers and nurses to teach their children to read)? Could it be one of the Old Testament Books, in which Mary might have been reading (in a chapter of Isaiah) the prophecy of her own fate? Or could it (the option Manguel prefers) have been one of the Books of Wisdom? If it was, then this portrayal of Mary might be seen, he argues,

> as an effort to restore the intellectual power denied to the female godhead. The book Mary is holding in Martini's painting, whose text is hidden from us and whose title we can only guess, might suggest itself as the last utterance of the dethroned goddess, a goddess older than history, silenced by a society that has chosen to make its god in the image of a man. Suddenly, in this light, Martini's "Annunciation" becomes subversive. (Manguel 1996: 221)

Index